LIBRARY LIT. 15-
The Best of 1984

edited by

BILL KATZ

The Scarecrow Press, Inc.
Metuchen, N.J., & London
1985

ISBN 0-8108-1808-6

Library of Congress Catalog Card No. 78-154842

Copyright © 1985 by The Scarecrow Press, Inc.

Manufactured in the United States of America

CONTENTS

Introduction   v

PART I: LIBRARIES AND LIBRARIANS   1

Forging Coalitions for the Public Good (E. J. Josey)   3
The Modifiable Ergonomic Dimensions of the English Language
    (James C. Thompson)   10
Beyond the Appendix With Gun and Camera (Paul Barnett)   19
Think Globally--Act Locally (David H. Stam)   25
Reflections of a College Librarian: Looking for Life and
    Redemption This Side of ARL (William A. Moffett)   31
Myths, Misconceptions & Management (Michael E. O. Koenig
    & Herbert D. Safford)   48
Librarian, Scholar, or Author? The Librarian's New Dilemma
    (Frederick Isaac)   61
Myths and Realities: The Academic Viewpoint II (Gresham
    Riley)   71

PART II: COMMUNICATION AND EDUCATION   75

User Categories and User Convenience in Subject Cataloging
    (Francis Miksa)   76
Archivist's Perspective: Archivaphobia: Its Causes and
    Cures (Virginia C. Purdy)   93
The Proposed National Periodicals Center, 1973-1980: Study,
    Dissention and Retreat (Mary Biggs)   100
Must We Limit the Catalog? (Maurice J. Freedman)   120
The Developing Crisis in Information: A Librarian's Perspective
    (Thomas T. Surprenant & Jane Zande)   128
An Exploration Into the Social and Economic Effects of Informa-
    tion Technology (Donald Wray)   138
The Underside of Computer Literacy (Douglas Noble)   148
The Reference Librarian Who Teaches: The Confession of a
    Mother Hen (John C. Swan)   169
Minds Alive: What & Why Gifted Students Read for Pleasure
    (Susan I. Swanton)   179
Critical Decisions: Reflection on the Changing Role of a Chil-
    dren's Book Reviewer (Elaine Moss)   191
Refereeing and the Editorial Process: The AHR and Webb
    (Margaret F. Stieg)   198

PART III: THE SOCIAL PREROGATIVE 217

The Publishing Culture and Literary Culture (Ted Solotaroff) 219
Government Secrecy (Richard Schmidt & Cecile Shure) 227
Nuclear Holocaust and Public Policy (Joe Morehead) 246
The Threat to Library Circulation Records: A Case Study
   (Richard Rubin) 263
Spreading the Word: The Billion Dollar Christian Book Industry
   (Audrey Eaglen) 274
Our Commission, Our Omissions (Eric Moon) 280
Women, Power, and Libraries (Patricia Glass Schuman) 292
"Huckleberry Finn" and the Traditions of Blackface Minstrelsy
   (Frederick Woodard & Donnarae MacCann) 305
Selection and Censorship (Lester Asheim) 318
The "Adulteration" of Children's Books (Jo Carr) 326
School Book Club Expurgation Practices (Gayle Keresey) 336

Notes on Contributors 345

INTRODUCTION

This is the fifteenth year of naming the 30 best articles about libraries and related areas. As in past years the selection is the work of a jury of editors, teachers, and librarians. The articles appeared in numerous periodicals from about 1 October 1983 to 1 October 1984. They are chosen from a preliminary list of suggestions made primarily by the editor, but filled out by the jury and by individuals.

Librarians are invited to send citations for articles for next year's annual collection. These to the editor at: School of Library and Information Science, State University of New York at Albany, 135 Western Avenue, Albany, NY 12222. Please try to get the candidates to the editor no later than mid-September of 1985.

The need for this work seems by now fairly well-established. Its purpose is twofold. First and foremost it is to recognize superior writing, research, and opinion. Second, it is to help the reader separate out a few jewels from the mass of undifferentiated material which finds its way into librarianship and information science. A third justification might well be self-congratulations. If anything, librarians seem to be writing better and better about more and more useful, practical, and startling topics. This collection underlines that marvelous development. At the same time, the 30 articles are not limited to the work of librarians alone. Usually there is a fair representation of laypersons who write about libraries and related material. The increased interest of the general public, as well as the few specialists and intellectuals in libraries is equally encouraging.

To repeat part of the introduction from last year's volume, here are a few points about how the judges arrive at a decision. First, consideration is given to scope. The jury tries to cover topics of interest to all librarians, not simply those dedicated to research, or to getting through the day behind the circulation desk. Various types of library service are dutifully weighed, and selection is made of the best articles which do justice to those areas. Still, it is hardly a rule that all sections and divisions of the profession must be viewed in any one volume.

Style, or, if you will, the ability to express oneself clearly and with some wit and authority, is regarded favorably. Even the best research is lost when the author (or the editor) fails to offer up an exact and lucid report. This is equally the case of a librarian observing and writing about activities from the front lines of library service. At the same time judicious account is taken of someone who may not write like Henry James or Ann Tyler, but who has an important idea to express. No jury member insists that everyone write as a professional author, but there is no excuse for sloppiness either.

Here it seems worth repeating that librarians write no worse, possibly much better, than most; and the day is long gone when librarians need apologize for their journals. Anyone who scoffs at this conclusion need only take a cursory glance at an issue of an endorsed medical, legal, English, or undertaker's journal to see librarians owe no one an apology for their style.

Other matters which are deemed important range from the timeliness of the message to its appropriate place in the stream, or flood tide of writing on the subject. Then, too, an effort is made to strike a balance between sources of publication so that everything in here is not out of only two or three journals.

Finally, though, and this seems most important of all, the jury and the editor determine what is best by intuition, experience, and luck--to quote the introduction from the thirteenth collection. This may annoy those who long for a methodical approach, for a scientific method of selecting the best and the better, but anyone who has considered manuscripts will be glad to admit to the fault of less than objectivity, of working on hunches as well as reasoned criteria.

The end result of all this discussion and consideration is the collection at hand. Some may object it is too radical, too conservative, too weighted in favor of information science, too this or that. Well, none of us claims to be such an expert that mistakes are not made. At the same time, over the years a fair balance seems to be struck, flags put out in all areas of interest.

For those who may object to failure this year, you are urged, once again, to insure success by sending the editor your choice(s) of the best writing in 1984-85. Meanwhile, the jury thinks the present awards well-deserved and with some assurance recommend them to you, the reader.

The 1984 Jury

John Berry, editor of the Library Journal; Mary K. Chelton, coeditor of VOYA (Voice of Youth Advocates); Arthur Curley, Deputy Director of the Research Libraries of the New York Public Library and editor of Collection Building; Wm. R. Eshelman, President, Scarecrow Press; Pat Schuman, President, Neal-Schuman Publishers; and the undersigned.

--Bill Katz

Part I

LIBRARIES AND LIBRARIANS

FORGING COALITIONS FOR THE PUBLIC GOOD*

E. J. Josey

To be inaugurated as the 101st President of the American Library Association would be a moving experience for anyone. But there are reasons why this particular event has special significance for me, and I would like to mention four of them for the historical record. Firstly, I am the second librarian of African descent to be inaugurated as president in the 108-year history of the Association. Secondly, I am the first librarian from New York State to be inaugurated president in 24 years. Thirdly, I am the second librarian from the New York State Library to be elected to this post. And fourthly, I am reminded that it was exactly 20 years ago that black librarians were not allowed to hold membership in four state associations in this nation, and, because of this fact, I raised the issue in a resolution at the 1964 Annual Conference in St. Louis. But beyond the historical notations cited, I am deeply honored and humbled by your trust and confidence placed in me, and I promise to carry out any responsibilities to the best of my ability.

As we begin the 109th year of the Association, I am reminded that ALA is the oldest and largest library association in the world. Over the years, we have had disagreements, and some have called for secession or federation. Nevertheless, we have been able through dialogue and debate to solve our problems and work together for strengthening library service in our nation. Never before has there been a time for all members of our profession and our Association to come together in unity of purpose and spirit, so that we can speak with one voice in support of quality library services for the American people. If we are to overcome zero funding for libraries in the federal budget and if we are to obtain the proper recognition that should be given to libraries, it is more important than ever that those of us in ALA must band together in a powerful unifying force to remind this nation that libraries not only support the demands of an information age but they also ensure an informed citizenry, which is essential to a democratic republic.

We must not forget the words of Thomas Jefferson who said:

---
*Reprinted by permission of the author, this was his inaugural address as President of the American Library Association, June 27, 1984.

If a nation expects to be ignorant and free in a state of civilization, it expects what never was and never will be ... if we are to guard against ignorance and remain free, it is the responsibility of every American to be informed.

As a venerable organization, ALA has a distinguished history in supporting librarians and in supporting the strengthening of the delivery of library and information services to the American people. In spite of this enviable record, we cannot allow the Association to rest on its laurels. There is much to be done.

The American Library Association is not just a professional organization. It is the leading force in the field that is becoming the major industry in the world--the information industry. As that leading force, ALA needs a program that ties our organization and our activities to the most fundamental goals of the American people.

In the current period of stress and uncertainty for great numbers of the American people, it is desirable to reemphasize the unity of our goals with those of other leading organizations that are also concerned with the public interest, and to focus on building strong coalitions for the public good. While we continue to hone our own skills and improve the methods by which libraries provide information and recreational services, we need to develop new ways to explore the many common objectives that we share with other professionals and with community leaders.

General Concepts

Many will ask: What do we mean by "the public good"? The phrase is well known and often used, but, like other frequently used terms, its common acceptance may hide a failure to probe its meaning.

General use of the term as used today dates at least from Adam Smith's Wealth of Nations, but distortions of his theories permeate the contemporary business world and are influencing the outlook of many in library leadership. Smith supported the idea that public works were an essential element in the economy and that the state was obligated to provide financial support to those institutions that benefited the whole society and whose costs of service would prohibit sufficient profit accruing to private individuals or organizations to make their investment in such services worth their effort.

The "general welfare" phrase in the preamble to the U.S. Constitution best epitomizes for most of us the purpose of such activity in the public interest. The public good embraces the public sector human services without sacrificing them to or putting them in competition with armaments, which leads to an unnecessary guns or butter debate. Central to the public good concept is the idea of general social benefit rather than individual gain to those who provide the service, pointing clearly to libraries as a first example of a public good meriting support from public funds.

Libraries and Librarians 5

Why "the public good"

One reason why we need to assert that libraries (and, indeed, other cultural and educational institutions--which is why coalitions) constitute "a public good" is the growing frequency of talk about "alternative sources of funding" for libraries. Since I am one who champions the proposition that ALA should establish a Development Office, I would be the first to say that, clearly, it would be foolish to oppose or reject funding from any legitimate source, providing such funding does not come with strings that may undermine the impartiality expected of a publicly supported institution or that create different levels of service and/or access for different user groups or individuals. It is the word "alternative" that is offensive and misleading, because it suggests that such funds may or will replace public support, rather than complement or supplement it. We need to stress that the primary source of funding and the primary responsibility are both still public.

Another reason for asserting the "public good" theme is the rapid growth of information services provided by the private sector, and the apparent inclination in some circles, including the current administration in Washington, to believe that these services can replace services provided by public institutions, and without expense to the taxpayer.

Again, nobody would deny the utility of many of these services provided by the private sector, but are not available to all of the American people; their purpose is to yield a profit, and they are designed only for those who can pay for them. Nor do they have any obligation to provide access to all or any information; only that information which the suppliers deem profitable or potentially so. Only the preservation of public services, publicly supported, can assure that each individual has equal and ready access to information, whether provision of that information to that individual is economic (i.e., profitability, in private sector terms) or not.

The public good, in an even broader sense of the general welfare, is closely related to progress for libraries. So long as the general population is victimized, economic problems will grow, and, as a result, libraries will be inadequately supported. In a time of attack on the basic freedoms and elementary well-being of the most vulnerable sections of the population, professional groups must recognize their stake in the outcome of that attack and their responsibilities to support the freedoms and welfare of the majority of the population. ALA therefore needs to integrate its goals with the goals of greatest importance to the American people, i.e., the preservation of basic democratic liberties, the enlargement of equal opportunity for women and minorities, and the continuance of earlier national planning to raise the level of the educational and economic well-being of greater numbers of the population.

We need to foster the recognition among ALA members that the future of libraries is clearly linked to the welfare of the American people and to reaffirm the inseparable relationship between libraries and the traditional democratic liberties. Our internal organizational problems may be more effectively resolved as we turn to the larger society and join with others in assisting the citizenry to use information services towards the solution of the immediate social problems. There is, in fact, an obvious interconnection of public issues with library issues: the effort to force release of government-controlled information is one part of the fight for intellectual freedom; the reduced availability and increasing cost of government sources of information limit the librarian's ability to provide information. Librarians are in a special position to know of restrictions on government information and to alert the public to act to force a change in policy when needed. The "right to know" and the "right to read" cannot be separated in the long run.

Economic self-interest for libraries is the most obvious reason for joining with others to support the needs of the American people, and for combining that effort with public education on libraries' value, both in an economic sense and in a broader social context. There is need to combat the recent government outlook that "information is not a free good" by emphasing the substantial value of this information to those who cannot pay for it. One of our goals in this effort must be to reaffirm the public sector's responsibility to support such institutions as the public library and its sister agencies, and to combat the present moves to consider information to property of the private sector. We need to put the public sector back where it was in the national consciousness as the responsible agent for institutions of public interest. This is a public responsibility of which individual taxpayers should be more aware. All sectors of government have the obligation to support libraries, but it is a part of our job, as librarians, to educate the public to respond to that obligation.

We also must clarify the direct effect of economics on the character of our services. Low budgets and fees for services can have the same result as censorship in limiting public access to ideas. But there is also the long-range negative effect of the decisions made by the librarian when under economic pressures. When fees are charged for library services, the resulting assumption is that the services are not needed by the whole society and therefore do not deserve public support. And when "cost effectiveness" becomes our guide to which services will be offered--e.g., cutting branch libraries hours without consulting the community, or eliminating outreach services when seed-money funding is lost--we further undermine potential tax support.

Suggested Methods for Implementing the Theme

In adopting this theme of working for the public good through coalitions representing large segments of the American people, we are directly pursuing three of ALA's priorities: access to information, legislation and funding, and public awareness, and indirectly assisting in the improvement of intellectual freedom and personnel resources.

Libraries and Librarians

What are the programs and methods that can advance the theme goals as well as ALA's priorities? Some will be extensions of programs already under way, others will be breaking new ground in the following ways and with innovations developed across the ALA spectrum:

- Identify organizations locally and nationally to serve as bridges to proposed activities. (We have made some contacts nationally with business groups, but need to join together with labor organizations, women's organizations, national ethnic organizations, etc.)

- Work with national organizations, business, labor and our representatives in Congress on economic and educational issues, to strengthen the nation and remind the American people that libraries are a vital component and among the nation's most essential institutions.

- Find specific ways to integrate ALA's priorities with the general, political, and economic welfare of the country.

- Develop support for publicly funded institutions, revitalizing support for public libraries on a broader funding base.

- Reaffirm the need and right to federal support of libraries, but raise the consciousness of local communities also to their responsibility for better funding.

- Continue ALA's strong advocacy role in defense of intellectual freedom on behalf of librarians, boards of trustees, and library users.

- Use the political process to champion federal support of libraries.

- Anticipate issues rather than react to circumstances that affect libraries.

- Maintain and develop a vigorous national library awareness campaign through our Public Information Office.

- Develop or extend programs for Literacy and for outreach services.

- Work for full and accurate interpretation of "national security" based on the general welfare, with adequate attention to freedom of information and the library's responsibility to protect every patron's access to information.

- Develop ways to use technology for positive gains to the majority of the population and to those at lower economic levels, focusing on the need of the American work force to be better educated to deal with the continuing technological explosion.

Central Responsibilities in ALA

Within our Association, the following means are envisioned to achieve the goals suggested:

- Develop, with the assistance of ALA units, public awareness programs demonstrating the ways in which libraries contribute to the economic health of their communities, their states, and the nation.

- Strengthen the Office for Library Outreach Services to support more adequately programs for literacy and for other outreach services both locally and in concert with other organizations.

- Strengthen the ALA Washington Office and the legislative network to stimulate and support state and local activities directed to the legislative/political process.

- Strengthen ALA's leadership role in working with other organizations and coalitions, developing a significant role for the minority caucuses and other special ALA groups.

Women and Minorities

Every president of this Association comes from a certain kind of background and/or orientation. Most of you are aware that all of my adult life I have been concerned about human rights and civil rights --the plight of women, minorities, and the poor. Continuing my concern for these areas, I have received the approval of the Executive Board to establish a Commission on Pay Equity to help us overcome the pay inequities suffered by women librarians. Moreover, I also have established a Presidential Committee to examine library services to minorities as well as to suggest ways in which the Association might implement recommendations made by the National Commission on Library and Information Science Report on Library Services to Cultural Minorities.

1985 Presidential Program

I wish to take this opportunity to invite you to participate in the 1985 President's Program in Chicago. It will be an all-day conference within a conference format that will focus on the theme: "Forging Coalitions for the Public Good." I envision about two thousand or more ALA members participating with representatives from other national organizations. Those who participate will be exposed to ideas and information on a state effort in coalition building, which will begin very soon in Minnesota, as a result of the J. Morris Jones--World Book Encyclopedia Goal Award, that will be a model that other ALA chapters may wish to replicate. It is also planned that the President's coalition program will bring into reality a Commission on Public Support of Libraries.

The Commission is needed because public support for libraries has been waning, indeed has been under attack, in recent years. The Commission is critically needed because there is a growing belief that public services can be more economically and more efficiently provided by agencies from the private sector and not be a burden to the taxpayer. Only through publicly supported institutions can we guarantee that restrictions will not be placed on the availability of information or on the potential users, who may wish access to it. In the establishment of such a Commission, we are affirming our belief in a process that has made the system of American libraries among the strongest in the world, and the need to transmit that belief much more clearly and effectively to others than has apparently been the case in recent years. An adequately supported library system, we assert, is vital both for an informed society and for the preservation of our democratic freedoms.

Finally, as we begin our journey through the ALA 1984-85 year, with our plans, programs, and projects, as well as our hopes and dreams, let us approach our task with high spirits, anticipation, and lofty vision. We can do what we will and make of it what we can. It is our faith and trust in each other that will give us the strength and courage. Together we shall go forth incorporating our hearts and goals as one.

THE MODIFIABLE ERGONOMIC DIMENSIONS OF THE ENGLISH LANGUAGE*

James C. Thompson

> It's a paradise of tools, where instead of buying books, librarians press buttons. All you have to do is locate one stupid librarian who is interested in buying a book, and everyone can have it.
>
> Frederick A. Praeger
> President and Publisher
> Westview Press

Mr. Praeger, as reported in the Chronicle of Higher Education,[1] offered the above analysis of library operations not long ago at a meeting sponsored by the University of Chicago. If his statements were quoted accurately--and he has said they were, though sometimes "out of context"--he will be well advised to go armed into the next library he visits.

The explanation which suggested itself to me when I read his remarks might occur to any librarian faced with such an attitude: that the speaker knows nothing about libraries and how they are run. This would not be a surprise; for after a decade of purchasing from, corresponding with, and consulting for scholarly publishers, I am convinced that library operations are a complete mystery to them, and they have abandoned all hope of unraveling it.

Under normal circumstances, they accept the unfathomable workings of the library as they do the rotation of the earth--they know it affects them, but there's not much they can do about it. But a danger arises when publishers and librarians are at odds, as they are increasingly during these hard times. When libraries stop buying as many books, the obscurity of their methods provides an attractive opportunity to construct facile but erroneous explanations suggestive of conspiracy.

---

*Reprinted by permission of the author and publisher from American Libraries, 15:3 (March 1984) 138-141, Copyright © 1984 by the American Library Association.

Libraries and Librarians 11

The library tongue

After much consideration, however, I am forced to conclude that the fault lies more with librarians and the ways we talk and write about our work than with the publishers. No two libraries operate in quite the same way, and no two librarians use the same words to describe what they do, even within one library. It would be hard to get even a small group of librarians to agree on the usage of such common terms as serial, series, periodical, continuation, or analytic. Perhaps because such words are used inconsistently, library staffs often develop unique local vocabularies and come to rely on them until they can no longer refer to things any other way. Here are the names of some files I encountered in one library--and what they really turned out to be:

The Departed File: A slip for every book that ever departed from Technical Services, filed by year and then by call number. It proved that a missing book was someone else's problem.
The Source: A hard card for every book ever ordered, whether or not received, filed by decade and then by main entry (not to be confused with the completed-order file). It was filed first, was thus the only current file, and so became essential.
Harry's Slips: A slip for each book sent to the bindery, filed by call number. It helped Harry expose errors on the part of the bindery.
Bruce's Papers: Left by Bruce in ages past.
The Tub: The on-order file.
The Box: Slips to be matched with incoming OCLC cards.
Lucy's Looking: Someday, Lucy will solve these cataloging problems.
Give to J. A. Cabeen: This file could not be identified, so it was given to J. A. Cabeen.
Series Decisions: Every series title ever rejected as a subscription, with reasons for the decision. Used to suppress any subsequent interest in the material.

Seeding our clouds

Since the limitations of such terminology are more obvious in print than in conversation, library writing is comparatively free of it. But our literature has other means at hand by which to cloud an issue. One subspecies is based on the art of saying nothing at great length.

A common technique for avoiding content calls for filling the first half of the article with questions, and the latter with admonitions to answer them. This is found particularly in the literature of automation, and in the editorials of certain journals. Readers who expect to find information simply handed to them can avoid disappointment by steering clear of articles in which question marks and the word "must" appear prominently.

Sometimes a valid point is hidden in an overabundance of

words. For example, the authors of an otherwise excellent article could probably have found a more succinct way than this to suggest that research is important to the faculty:

> The potential for conducting research forms the next component of analysis. It is beneficial to reiterate that research is usually by far the pivotal criterion in evaluations of faculty or faculty-like personnel. Excellence in job performance being simply assumed, research competence continues to grow in importance, greatly influencing the possibilities for both institutional success and marketplace flexibility.[2]

A sufficiently stretched metaphor can stop readers dead in their tracks at the opening sentence, as with this comment on citation analysis:

> An area of science can be viewed as an Euclidean space with documents or authors located at the points.[3]

Librarianship is sometimes considered a soft science, akin to sociology or psychology. Perhaps that is why we imitate those disciplines in relying heavily on impressive, but essentially meaningless, pseudoscientific jargon. We seem to lack confidence in our professional status, as indicated by the number of articles we produce on that question--one that does not arise in the literatures of the more established professions. It is also evident in the amount of journal space devoted to issues of a suspiciously nonprofessional nature, such as a running debate in College & Research Libraries News on the best method of loading booktrucks.[4] Possibly tenure requirements contribute to the proliferation of unneeded treatises in uncountable and unaffordable journals; if so, library literature stands as a prima facie case against faculty status for librarians.

Overheard at ALA

But my aim is not to speculate on why library expression is so uncommunicative--merely to give a few illustrations of the havoc it can cause. Here are some quotations copied down during presentations at the most recent ALA Annual Conference:

modifiable ergonomic dimensions
extrinsic modification strategies
cognitive ergonomics
sophisticated search strategies
powerful retrieval capabilities
improved retrieval technologies
negative impacts
viable terminal operator
holistic information processing
uniform search protocols
differential experiences

an expand of cognition
locally relevant information processing
end-user access
classical ergonomic solution
information equalizers
a certain skewness of library outreach
information transition
proportionate system modifiability
conceptual structures

Libraries and Librarians

spatial conceptualizers
cognitive frameworks
transformable command structures
small-process rewards

intermediate motivators
adaptation decisions
systemic relationships
knowledge-intensive mass media

All of the above represent concepts that would be recognizable if described in plain English. For example, "modifiable ergonomic dimensions," a phrase destined to become notorious and which was cited within 48 hours, [5] was used in reference to an adjustable terminal.

If the catchwords of "information science" are insufficiently convincing, they can be fleshed out with those of some other field:

> Just as "yin" and "yang" do not form a dualism that splits the universe in two, the apparent "yin yang" aspects of Penn State's authority control system cannot be considered as two separate systems linked together. At the core of the "yin yang" facets of the universe is "Tao," the Way, which is the unifying principle of the universe that maintains it and gives it motion and order. In the same way, the Universal Entry Control (UEC) system forms the "Tao" of Penn State's catalog access system and activates the relationships of the bibliographic records according to the interaction between user search requests and the universal entries. [6]

Even the names with which we label our jobs seem intended to confuse rather than clarify. Recent journals contain at least seven different synonyms for Head of OCLC Cataloging and five for Book Selector, not to mention such intriguing occupational titles as Preparatory Studies Librarian, Multitype Coordinator, Assistant Dean of Instruction, Assistant Librarian/Technical Services/Generalist, and a diminutive Microform Librarian. Since this is how we solicit applications, we would have no right to balk at a resume beginning in this fashion:

RESUME OF APPLICANT

Dimension Modifier. Resourcefully wrought end-user access while functionably piloting information transition. Halved negative impacts of differential experiences and trebled viable terminal operators. Soundfully prompted an expand of cognition and avidly contrived adaptation decisions. Clarified and keynoted cognitive framework.

This may be more than a bad dream: all the verbs and adverbs in that paragraph are suggested in a handout entitled "Power VERBS and ADVERBS which are active and/or descriptive,"[7] distributed at the ALA placement center during the Annual Conference.

Abstract expressionism

Where then should we look for writing on librarianship that is lucid and concise, once we have exhausted the small core of great writers in the field (the De Gennaros, Gores, and Fasanas, for example)? Surely it is to the abstracts that we must look first. An abstract conveys the gist of the article; it lets the expert reader know whether the whole is worth reading, and gives the browser the main points without further exploration. Being brief, it would seem to be simple to compose; being important, it is presumably composed carefully.

Unfortunately, even in our more prominent professional journals, the abstracts often are fully as obfuscatory as the articles:

ABSTRACT

A methodology is developed and applied to a data collection consisting of questions in order to discern the nature of the cognitive need "to know": the information need.... Two experimental hypotheses guided this methodology for a "closed" problem situation: H_1 where the number of questions generated varies directly as the information need varies, and H_2 where the number of questions generated varies inversely as the data input varies. The results of the statistical analysis supported the indicated trend to decreasing questioning activity as the data input rose. The results of the linguistic analysis revealed a consistent question formulation pattern between the two "closed" problems. Thus it follows in theory that the nature of information need can be discerned indirectly through question generation and formulation. [8]

Which is to say: if they don't know, they'll ask. Thus overly elaborate language can disguise the truistic nature of the point being made, as in the following:

The application of Kantor's demand-adjusted shelf availability model to a medium-sized academic library is described. The model can be applied in a working library environment with relative ease. The data indicate that there are significant differences in shelf availability when the data are sorted, adjusted, and analyzed by last circulation date, acquisition date, and imprint date. There is also a significant difference between the results of data gathered during periods of low and high use. [9]

In other words, popular and recent books have been popular recently; books are used more when they're more in use. When the abstract contains the whole substance of the article, it is as reliable an indication of a problem as, in the previous example, when one must read the article to make sense of the abstract.

Libraries and Librarians 15

ALA has its own ways of contributing to the verbiage. A novice conferee faced with a program listing two thousand meetings will feel little sympathy for whoever named the Association for Library Service to Children, Priority Group II--Evaluation of Media: Toys, Games, and Realia Evaluation Committee; or the Resources and Technical Services Division, Serials Section, Ad Hoc Committee to Study the Feasibility of Creating Dynamic Lists of Core Serials.

It doesn't always help to abbreviate these unwieldy appellations; one industrious researcher has discovered that there are at least 37 legitimate library initialisms made up from the letters A, C, R, and L. [10] This is not amusing to one university library director whose president won't let him drop out of CRL (Center for Research Libraries) because he has it confused with ARL (Association of Research Libraries). "It's worth $10,000 a year," this director has been heard to say, "not to have to point out the president's mistake to him."

Tools for bibliographic befuddlement

In addition to those already cited, there are other genera of doubletalk that can profitably be used to reduce comprehension:

- Euphemisms help keep the skeletons in the closet and are much favored in references to processing backlogs. My library had backlogs known as "on location," "the N.P.'s," and the ominous "B-52 books" until the catalogers, with commendable courage, collected them all into one sequence called "the backlog" and proceeded to catalog the books in it.

- Obsolete terms are passed down from one library generation to the next, the original meanings lost in history. "P slip" has become a shibboleth for detecting pre-OCLC catalogers, "s.n.m." appears widely in serials authority files, but few remember its etymology (it does not stand for "series not made"). Some of our, "N.P.'s" were also "s.s.o.'s," but opinion varies as to the meaning of that.

- Implications are conveyed by loaded terms such as "authority control," the very name of which implies a stern correctness and a right to exist. It hints at masochism; seen in that light, "interactive authority control" becomes vaguely perverse, while "fully automated interactive authority control" takes on a whole new aura.

- Code words look like common English terms but have different meanings. This is not like the use of technical terms in other professions. When the doctor refers to a hemostat, or the lawyer to a subpoena duces tecum, these are understood to be meant for a select group. But library designations which are second nature to librarians may be composed of words deceptively familiar to others--terms like "blanket order," "main entry," or "shelflist." The professor who wants a new book and is told "we could firm-order that as a do-not-duplicate under our approval profile, but if it's a continuation it should come on standing order" is liable to give up on the library as well as the book.

Biblish

All these categories together constitute what H. H. Neville has termed "Biblish," the language of librarians.[11] But has it always been so? The journals of fifty or a hundred years ago are, if anything, more readable now than today's publications. The professional vocabulary before the age of automation was comparatively stable: the 1943 A.L.A. Glossary of Library Terms,[12] begun in 1926, was still in print in 1973 (and not superseded until 1983). But it does contain some entries which would give pause to a modern holistic information processor, such as "Gouge Index," "Divinity Calf," "American Russia," "Fatface," and "V Slip" (a competitor of the "P Slip," which is also included, though with a dubious etymology).

Of course, for all the confusion it can cause, Biblish does have its good side. It enables members of a group to converse effectively without inviting continual interruption from curious onlookers, an advantage it shares with the rhyming slang of the Cockney underworld. In the past, a library or one of its departments could safeguard its autonomy by suggesting, through cryptic descriptions, that any intrusion would risk interference with a complex operation better left to itself.

But library administrators and their bosses are no longer so easily put off, nor can they afford to be in a time when every dollar counts and every dollar is counted. They are increasingly concerned with how their departments function, and reluctant to accept, without question, decisions of major and prolonged impact on the library as a whole. This is especially true in technical services, at once the most costly and most easily examined area of the library.

When procedures supplant goals

There is a tendency within complex organizations to lose sight of the goals for which operational procedures have been created. When people can attain their goals only through an effort of many years, procedures established to promote such goals take on a life of their own. A shorthand vocabulary springs up, which simplified daily activities but distracts people from their original objectives. (Whereas "backlog" implies a problem, for example, "on location" is neutral, with a suggestion of propriety.)

In time, the organization ceases to think about its aims, since the various interested parties have no common language with which to discuss and reconsider them. Routines become habits, and habits traditions. These traditions are reflected in the language by which they are passed on, and the language in turn perpetuates the traditions. And that is where the danger lies.

Still and all, library writing and speaking is no worse than that of other professions, and better than some (such as data processing). And the confusion the language sometimes causes can lead to fascinating and delightful encounters with those vast portions of the world which are not libraries.

A few years ago, at the annual conference of the Maryland Library Association, the exhibitors and their customers were intrigued to find that the first and largest exhibit was one displaying Sanyo brand vibrators and massagers. As librarians entered the hall, attractive young people of the opposite sex would lure them into the booth, remove their shoes, and massage their feet. This was pleasant but mysterious; the other vendors whispered about it throughout the conference until finally someone noticed the slogan on the exhibit banner.

SANYO IMPROVES YOUR CIRCULATION

Presumably Sanyo had noticed the codeword "circulation" in an index to conventions and assumed that the "M" in "MLA" stood for "Medical." The Sanyo people were obviously as puzzled by our presence as we by theirs. But how much drearier such a conference would be if there were nothing to do but listen to the presentation of papers.

References

1. Karen J. Winkler. "Publishers vs. Librarians: Economic Woes Pit Former Allies Against One Another." Chronicle of Higher Education. May 25, 1983, p. 29, 31.
2. Ed Neroda and Lana Bodewin, "Institutional Analysis for Professional Development." Journal of Academic Librarianship. 9:158. July 1983.
3. Peter Lenk. "Mappings of Fields Based on Nominations." Journal of the American Society for Information Science, 34:115, March 1983.
4. Anthony J. Amodeo, "Helpful Hints for Moving or Shifting Collections." College & Research Libraries News, 44:82-83, March 1983; response by Brian Alley, 44:182, June 1983; response by Alexandra Mason, 44:232-33, July/August 1983.
5. Cited by Richard W. Boss in his presentation at the LITA/ISAS program. Los Angeles, June 25, 1983.
6. "Dual-Faceted Authority Control System" (University Park, Pa.: Pennsylvania State University Libraries [n.d.]).
7. It credits "U.W. School of Librarianship Course L593--Ruth Hamilton--Career Development for Librarians; Winter Quarter, 1981."

8. Esther E. Horne, "Question Generation and Formulation: An Indication of Information Need," Journal of the American Society for Information Science, 34:5, January 1983.
9. Philip Schwarz, "Demand-Adjusted Shelf Availability Parameters: A Second Look," College & Research Libraries, 44:210, July 1983.
10. Lynne Lysiak, communication with author.
11. "Computers and the Language of Bibliographic Descriptions," Information Processing & Management, 17:137, 1981.
12. A. L. A. Glossary of Library Terms, prepared by Elizabeth H. Thompson (Chicago: American Library Association, 1943).

BEYOND THE APPENDIX

WITH GUN AND CAMERA*

Paul Barnett

What indexes mean to me

As a freelance editor, a compiler of multi-author reference works, and a writer of non-fiction books, virtually every day I am led to speculate in one direction or another on the role and art of the indexer. As a writer I have to rely fairly heavily on indexes to other people's books, since clearly I can't hope to read all my reference sources from cover to cover. And in my guises of indexer and compiler of reference books I have to go through all the so familiar thought processes; what is the best way of indexing a particular book so that the index will be of the greatest possible use to the reader? The question is not really quite that simple: it's rather, "What is the best way of indexing this book so that the index will be of the greatest possible use to the reader, bearing in mind that the designer has left only pages 639 and 640 for the index, and the publisher's production department insists that it can't be set in anything smaller than 14 on 15? And they need the index by tomorrow and won't pay more than £30."

All told, the depth of my interest in indexes is necessarily quite great. I rely on the ones I compile myself for an important, if not major, part of my income; I rely on those compiled by others to give me more rapid access to information than would otherwise be possible, thus enabling me to do more work each day.

Sometimes, I rely on other people's indexes to provide me with innocent merriment at the end of a hard day's work editing the manuscript of The World Guide to Concrete, or something of that ilk. Recently, for instance, I came across these subheadings in the index entry on Colin Wilson in his "preliminary autobiography", Voyage to a Beginning (published by C. and A. Woolf in 1969):

  becomes the confidant of his landlady's daughter, 110
  her spare-time occupation, 110
  and her unattractive practice in bed, 110

*Reprinted by permission of the author and publisher from The Indexer, 13:4 (October 1983) 232-235.

Those raising their brows and turning to page 110 will find the following:

> The daughter soon made me her confidant, explaining that her husband had left her and that she supplemented her National Assistance with a little street-walking. I did not in the least object to the street-walking, but I found it tiresome to discover in my bedroom unmistakeable signs that it had been used to receive her male friends. The girl herself seemed to have a curious preference for eating fish-paste sandwiches in bed....

Index as selling-point

I am convinced that indexes sell books. I know that they affect my own book purchases. I cannot offhand recall a single book that I've rushed out to buy because of the high quality of its index, but I do know that, often, the converse process has taken place: I've put books back on the shop's shelves because their indexes have been so manifestly useless, and bought others instead. I know there are plenty of other people who do the same--about 50%, or even more, of my book-buying friends. If, say, 10% of the book-buying public behave in this way, then there is a fairly colossal number of book-sales at stake. If a publisher gets an extra 10% of sales on an £8.95 book that would have sold 5000 copies without an index, then for the investment of perhaps an extra couple of hundred pounds in procuring a good rather than a bad index, he can increase his turnover on that project by just under £3000. When you remember too that he's more likely to get an American deal, you can see that he is getting excellent value for money by providing an index to the book.

Computers that are to come

But I have the feeling that the index as we know it won't be around for much longer than the next few decades. I think it's quite likely that nonfiction will no longer be preserved in book form. I'm aware that ever since I entered publishing people have been saying that the day of the printed book is done; also that, should the nonfiction book disappear, with it will go a large slice of my own income. Nevertheless, I think we have to face the unpleasant facts.

What will replace the printed nonfiction book? Easy: the computer/word-processor that will inevitably come into being within the next few decades, the device which I shall call the "world-computer."

A few years ago someone at ASTRA (the Association in Scotland to Research into Astronautics, the former Scottish wing of the British Interplanetary Society) calculated that, if all the knowledge gained by the maximum possible number of intelligent civilizations

Libraries and Librarians

in the Universe were to be stored in one computer, that computer would be no larger than about the size of our Moon.

By comparison, of course, the size of the computer theoretically needed to store all human knowledge is relatively small. To give you some idea of how small it could be, think of the human brain. Thoughts come about because two precise points in the brain are linked: the linkage--the electric current running between two cells--is, in essence, the thought.

Because there are so many cells in the brain, the number of possible linkages between cells is enormous: so much so, that it's substantially greater than the number of subatomic particles in the Universe. It is awesome to think that any one of us is capable of having more ideas than there are subatomic particles in the Universe.

Since, essentially, ideas constitute knowledge, and since there must be fewer items of knowledge than there are elementary particles in the Universe, it would seem that in theory all the knowledge in the Universe could be stored inside a fleshy gray computer called the brain. In terms of size, computers still have some way to go--but in the course of time they'll get there.

Even if they don't, a computer the size of the Moon may seem large to our limited imaginations, but in fact isn't. As with so many of the mind-boggling engineering projects envisaged by the futurologists, the building of a computer the size of our moon is quite within the scope of our current technological ability. It would take a long time and cost a great deal, but we could do it.

We may indeed construct a comparatively small computer which can act as the repository of all human knowledge. Over a rather longer timescale, every human being on this planet should be granted constant access to this computer: no longer will it be necessary to obtain a biography of Winston Churchill, for example, because all you'll have to do is punch into your domestic terminal the words "Winston Churchill," and up will come reams of information containing everything ever known about Churchill, without any repetitions.

The art of indexing will then have to change, because undoubtedly the "world computer" will have an index. But computers aren't really interested in abstracts like alphabetical order--in fact, the storage of large quantities of data in alphabetical order would be counter-productive, in that the computer would spend 99 or more per cent of its time hunting related items that happen to be at opposite ends of the alphabet--aardvarks and zoo animals, for example. The "world-computer" is more likely to store things in thematic order, so that if you request from it all the information about zoo animals it will go to a single place in its data file and churn out everything on the subject, including all known about aardvarks.

You may think that the age of the "world-computer" lies long in the future, but the same sort of a thing, on a smaller scale, is

just around the corner. Most homes, if not every home, will have
a little humming beasty in the corner to which they can turn for information
on virtually everything. And these domestic computers will
be "indexed" not in alphabetical but in thematic order.

Already we have the current edition of the Encyclopaedia
Britannica, whose editors have seen fit to include an additional
volume, the Propaedia, as a thematic index to the whole work.

To place things in thematic order, the indexer has to be omniscient:
only one such can hope to spot all the natural cross-references
between superficially disparate subjects. This poses a
hard problem, but the solution is easier than it might seem: all
that is needed is another computer. Each time a linkage between
two subjects turns up, one of the "people's indexers" can plug in the
necessary datum, which is processed by the control computer and
added to the "world computer's" data store.

A place for indexers

This doesn't sound as if there's much of a future for the humble
indexer: all we can hope to be is a sort of glorified computer operator--not
even a computer programmer. But the hardware is only as
good as the software with which it is supplied. Because the "world-computer"
will be such a complicated gadget, the people supplying
the software--who will be, in today's terms, both authors and indexers--will
have an important job to do. Once the "world-computer"
gets a misapprehension into its "head," it will be hard to remove it;
every safeguard will have to be taken to ensure that misapprehensions
don't get there in the first place. The indexer/data supplier will
therefore have the most important job of being both censor and interpreter.
He will also have the exciting task of rooting out misapprehensions
that the "world-computer" has gained as a result of
the human race itself having misunderstood something. For example,
were the human race still to subscribe to purely Newtonian mechanics,
the job of inserting the qualification of Newtonian mechanics known as
Relativity would be extremely subtle. The unfortunate indexer, in
such a case, must have an omniscient overview of the entire contents
of the "world-computer's" data bank in order to be able to "guess"
every single area in which modification will be required.

Is the time of the traditional indexer drawing to a close?
Will we all be, in the harsh light of the bright new technological
dawn, nothing more than computer operators? I think not. There
is a kind of satisfaction to be gleaned from the compilation of an
index which will ensure that, for at least the next few decades, the
art will not die. It may sound optimistic, but I can even envisage
our descendants compiling indexes just for the fun of it.

Tachyons and tardyons

Perhaps the most exciting job of the future indexer will be born from the field of tachyon physics. To explain tachyons: most people suppose that nothing can travel faster than the speed of light. This is false. On a minor point, by "speed of light" we in fact mean "the velocity of light in free space" since a bullet can travel through your hand faster than the average ray of light can. But there is a more major flaw in the cliché. What Albert Einstein said, and subsequent theorists have confirmed, is that nothing can travel at the speed of light.

This may seem an artificial distinction. If nothing can travel at the speed of light then we cannot accelerate a spaceship up to faster than the speed of light. Perhaps this is so (although quantum physics would seem to suggest that there ought to be, as it were, a way of tunnelling through the light barrier); however, the equations of Relativity in no way proscribe the existence of faster-than-light particles. There may be particles in the Universe that have always been travelling faster than light. These particles are called tachyons; the rest of us time-servers being composed of mere tardyons.

Tachyons, if they exist (and a certain amount of experimental evidence suggests that indeed they do), have some odd properties. The most mind-boggling is that while tardyons require the input of energy to make them go faster, tachyons require the input of energy in order to go more slowly. Their equivalent of staying perfectly still is to travel at infinite velocity. A single tachyon in a state of rest is therefore everywhere in the Universe at once.

But the property of tachyons which concerns the indexer is this: in order to conform to the equations of Relativity tachyons have to travel through time in the opposite "direction" to the one we tardyons take. This is difficult to accept, but after all, it's little more than a matter of convention that we think about the "flow" of time going from the past through the present to the future.

Old Moore's indexing

How do tachyons affect the indexer? The fact of their existence conjures up an exciting indexing possibility. This is that every indexer can look forward to the day when we can hope to index books, or computer data banks, before they've actually been written!

Tachyons are rather hard things for us in the tardyonic Universe to catch. It's unlikely, therefore, that anyone in the future will be able to send us back verbatim versions of books written in AD 2500: just as you don't get much of a picture on the television when someone switches a hoover on, there'll just be too much "noise" to be able to receive the definitive version of a book from our descendants. But, making the assumption that tachyons exist, there is every possibility that our descendants will be able to send back to us the body of any forthcoming advance of human knowledge.

I am quite serious in suggesting that, a good long way in the future, there will be a role for the indexer in the practice of picking up stray signals from times which are yet to come. There's every possibility that, certainly at first, those signals won't be transmitted deliberately--converting information into tachyons isn't much fun-- but, at least according to the theory, every incident in the entire history of the Universe transmits/will transmit/has transmitted a record of its occurrence. Two records, rather: one whose shock waves travel out in the "future" direction and another with shock waves moving towards the past. It is conceivable that at some time we will be able to devise a receiver capable of picking up the second of those sets of shock waves.

The information we garner will almost certainly be bitty--at least in the early days of the art. For exactly that reason the indexer will be important. A book with half its pages missing can yet, assuming there's a good index intact, still be pieced together. The content of the missing pages can be worked out by using the content of the surviving pages in tandem with the information derived from the index. Hints of future knowledge picked up by our hypothetical tachyon receiver will be served in the same way. As indexers, we must face the fact that ourselves or our spiritual descendants will have to take on the task of piecing together fragments of information gathered from the future. Here we have a paradox: as soon as we start doing this, future generations will have the memory that we're able to do it, and so will start consciously transmitting information back to us. At that point, time will cease to have any real meaning: the knowledge of all future ages will be ours, <u>now</u>.

This sort of time-hopping extravaganza may seem far-fetched; it's hard to reconcile such grand phrases as "the knowledge of all future ages" with sitting with our card indexes thumbing gloomily through to record yet another mention of asparagus. But the reconciliation will have to be made--<u>if</u> tachyons not only exist but also can be picked up by previous ages. We may not like the picture--it may offend all our logical sensibilities--but that may be the way the Universe works. You can't argue with Nature.

Should we be happy to carry on in the same old way, satisfied that nothing will radically change? I think it would be foolish. If anything can be certain in this uncertain existence, it is that life a few decades from now will be totally alien to anything we can now imagine. We can cheerfully forget such phenomena as the indexing word-processor--a short-term gadget, useful only for as long as the traditional index is useful. Unrecognizably different will be the gadgets used by our children or our children's children, and the main reason for the difference will be that not only the means of data storage but also the data themselves will be different--and, on top of all that, the desires of the "consumer" will be different. The indexer of tomorrow faces a hard task.

We live in interesting times, as the old Chinese curse has it.

Abridged version of the address given to the Society of Indexers, Bristol, 10 July 1983.

THINK GLOBALLY - ACT LOCALLY:
COLLECTION DEVELOPMENT AND RESOURCE SHARING*

David H. Stam

Some of you may be familiar with the music of a somewhat offbeat rock group called The Police, and specifically their song called "Too Much Information." The most qualified teenagers I know are unable to decode all of the words, but for the uninitiated, it goes something like this with a fair amount of repetition:

> Too much information
> Running through my brain
> Too much information
> Driving me insane
>
> Seen the whole world six times over
> Seen the passage....
>
> Overkill, overkill, over my dead body,
> Over me, over you, over everybody
>
> Too much information
> Running through my brain
> Too much information
> Driving me insane
>
> Stop.... [1]

That song may seem an odd point of departure for a discussion of resource sharing, but it does, as far as I can judge, illustrate one of the two major concerns of resource sharing: the sheer quantity of information with which we have to cope. The other, quality, might best be seen in "The Sixth Sally" of Stanislaw Lem's Fables for the Cybernetic Age called The Cyberiad.[2] In that story, Lem's two hero-constructors venture into the wastelands of extra-galactic space to find an insatiable robot named Pugg whose Faustian dream was to know everything. Pugg was rusting out his mechanical life collecting "precious facts, priceless knowledge, and in general all information

---
*Reprinted by permission of the author and publisher from Collection Building, 5 (Spring 1983) 18-21.

of value." When Pugg encounters the invaders he holds them captive until they promise to construct a machine, with a printout tape which would select out of all the possibilities of jostling atoms only that information which has meaning.

The story suffers in my summary, but what Pugg eventually gets from this Metainformationator is a wonderful litany of golden fleece awards. The constructors manage to escape while "poor Pugg, crushed beneath that avalanche of facts, learns no end of things about rickshaws, rents and roaches, and about his own fate, which has been related here, for that too is included in some section of the tape--as are the histories, accounts and prophecies of all things in creation, up until the day the stars burn out; and there is no hope for him, since this is the harsh sentence the constructors passed upon him for his pirately assault--unless of course the tape runs out, for lack of paper." But before that happens Pugg realizes that "all this information, entirely true and meaningful in every particular, was absolutely useless, producing such an ungodly confusion that his head ached terribly and his legs trembled."

That may be a good description of how research librarians often feel in facing what's now known as The Glut, but few of us are able to take refuge or comfort in the other extreme, the library of Walden Two:

> As to a library, we pride ourselves on having the best books, if not the most. Have you ever spent much time in a large college library? What trash the librarian has saved up in order to report a million volumes in the college catalogue! Bound pamphlets, old journals, ancient junk that even the shoddiest secondhand bookstore would clear from its shelves--all saved on the flimsy pretext that some day someone will want to study the "history of a field." Here we have the heart of a great library--not much to please the scholar or specialist, perhaps, but enough to interest the intelligent reader for life. Two or three thousand volumes will do it. [3]

The novel does refer elsewhere to an old barn where all the weeded books are kept for the insatiably curious, but obviously there are few in Walden Two. Skinner's hero gives, to the best of my knowledge, a unique fictional accolade to the collection development librarian, based solely on good choices.

There are of course more serious arguments for selectivity in collection development policies, such as Margit Kraft's landmark article in the Library Quarterly in 1967 and the more recent work sponsored by the Rockefeller Foundation on Coping with the Biomedical Literature. But I use these more dramatic literary examples to illustrate one of the illusions associated with cooperative collection development, namely the notion that with adequate distribution of responsibilities we can reintroduce the notion of complete coverage of all material. Even in a wide sharing environment such a goal remains chimerical and is in any case not a desirable objective--one of the elements of sharing has to be the expertise needed for the right filtration devices or the quality control on what goes into our collections.

In considering collection development in a resource sharing environment, we have to ask at the outset whether that environment in fact exists. We do of course hear a good deal of lip service to the ideals of cooperation, often tinged with a sense of desperation at our inability to keep up even with our past performance or to meet the local demands placed on us. But we also hear considerable argument against the notion, including charges of a communistic conspiracy to defraud publishers of their captive markets and accusations that we are selling out on individual responsibilities which we ought to fight harder to honor without jumping on some cooperative band wagon. Apropos of costs, it is often argued that cooperation won't save money, that access to shared materials may be as expensive as purchasing them, that prices will rise as orders decline, and that it will be even more expensive, if not impossible, to fill gaps if sharing agreements fail.

In terms of service, some argue that "conventional resource sharing is cumbersome, unreliable, and frustrating" (Downes) and a disservice to users who want material at hand as soon as they need it. Others contend that cooperative agreements create inevitable hardships for larger institutions which must always place the interests of their own constituents above those of outsiders. Nor can those large institutions rely on the agreements made by other institutions where resources may be reallocated as priorities and programs change. Others fear that the distribution of collection responsibilities will lead to the decline of the collection and quality of all participating libraries.

As a believer, I don't intend to comment on these doubts, except to note that among the many cogent arguments remains an ostrich-like case against change and for business as usual. Unfortunately, in collection development matters, business as usual no longer works for any of us. Over the past three years, the Collection Management and Development Committee of the Research Libraries Group has attempted to face these problems with the clear purpose of assuring adequate coverage of the research materials needed within the membership in particular, and for scholarship in general. Although our membership, especially in the early days, represented a small fraction of the research libraries of the nation, we did hope to form the basis of a shared national collection development plan, identifying areas of strength and neglect, and to see what we could do about them.

From the beginning we made certain assumptions which have been tested along the way. One assumption was the voluntary nature of our association--that there would be no central authority reducing the autonomy of individual members, but that their own enlightened self-interest would be adequate for participation. We also assumed

that a prime requirement for the national scheme we envisioned was
an effective means of communication of the intentions, decisions, and
alterations in policy which members might make. We believed that
the failure of the Farmington Plan was largely due to the lack of such
communication. For the most part we put aside or left to others
the questions of access, sharing of resources, and delivery systems
on the assumption that there could be no access without coverage.
We also took seriously the term collection management in our name,
especially in seeing a close relationship between collection building
and collection maintenance or preservation.

The RLG Conspectus

Our first order of business and our most difficult task was and is to
assess what the current collection development policies and practices
of the participants are. Building on much of the work of this Committee, we developed a device now known as the RLG conspectus.
The conspectus is intended to provide a composite picture of collection
strengths and current collecting intensities by Library of Congress
subject fields, using a numerical range of designators from zero
(out of scope for that collection) to five (a comprehensive collection).
Literally hundreds of selection officers in individual libraries have
been involved in describing collection strengths and collection policies
on worksheets used to submit the raw data to RLG central staff. The
Library of Congress has participated in this work from the beginning
and more recently five non-RLG members of ARL have been testing
selected subject areas of the conspectus with a view to adoption of
this methodology of collection analysis by other members of ARL.
Concurrently, we have been pursuing the development work for putting
the conspectus online as a special database, thus answering our original desideratum for an efficient communication device to indicate
changes in policy throughout the network.

I won't dwell on the various problems we have encountered
in the development of this tool, the recurrent concern for the problem
of excessive subjectivity, the arguments over language codes, the
detail or lack of detail in L. C. subject breakdowns, the need for
uniformity of approach among diverse bibliographers, the peculiar
problems presented by area studies. We do believe that the most
critical stage in conspectus building is in very careful review of the
comparative data after it is first tabulated. Reasonable assessments
can sometimes look quite different when compared to other known
collections. We have a great deal more work to do in that respect,
though we have put together a remarkable amount of raw data about
our collections and collecting policies.

While our original purpose in developing the conspectus was
for communication and for the assignment of primary collection responsibilities (known as PCRs), we were somewhat surprised to find
that our work also yielded a number of by-products. It has and will
be useful in identifying regional as well as national strengths. It
has already indicated a number of fields uncovered by RLG librarians;

although these may be covered in non-member libraries it has been helpful for us to know of these weaknesses.

For the public service librarians the conspectus is already useful in referring readers to strong collections elsewhere and for general questions of interlibrary loan sources. For members who had no formal collection development policy the conspectus has in effect created one, without all the agony that many of us experienced. In a few cases the conspectus analysis has pointed out funding possibilities for specific areas of weaknesses in our collections. To many of us it has been an important training device in introducing collection evaluation issues to many staff. The most important advantage, it seems to me, for staff at all levels, is that in getting to know something about other collections, our staffs have also learned more about their own. I don't want to underestimate the problems and the uncertainties involved, or the need for more quantitative measures to confirm or change the subjective judgments that we have made. All in all the work of this Committee has been a very positive experience from which I hope many will eventually benefit.

That brings me to my final point and at last to the title I've chosen for this article. Despite the alleged aloofness and elitism of large research libraries, you must all realize, no matter what the nature of your own institution, that all libraries are linked in a great chain of access and that what each has and does will have importance for the whole universe of libraries and their users.

Research libraries are dependent on a whole range of libraries to provide services which large libraries can't provide well or which they couldn't afford to pick up if the smaller libraries didn't exist. In turn, the libraries of Walden Two can rely on us as the overgrown barns which even the apostles of selectivity recognize as a necessity. What I want to emphasize is that resource sharing does not remove in any way the obligation for any institution to fulfill its local mission.

In Rene Dubos' last book, Celebrations of Life, [4] there is a lengthy section from which I've taken my title: Think Globally but Act Locally. His story behind that phrase is that in lecturing at universities on environmental matters he often met faculty and students who were concerned, if not outraged, about environmental pollution, oil spills, atomic waste disposal etc., but left their own dormitories, cafeterias, and campuses a mess, and their social relationships in disorder. I find the analogy to libraries apt. Resource sharing is a necessity and it will continue to grow. But it has to grow from a strong local base, one which defines the individual institution's mission clearly and carries it out well.

I want to end with a brief passage from the final section of the Dubos book, appropriately called "Optimism Despite it All," and as you read it you can substitute library terms for the human ones he uses:

This is not the best of times, but it is nevertheless a time for celebration because, even though we realize our insignificance as part of the cosmos and as individual members of the human family, we know that each one of us can develop a persona which is unique, yet remains part of the cosmic and human order of things. Human beings have been and remain uniquely creative because they are able to integrate the pessimism of intelligence with the optimism of Will.

Properly translated that represents the challenge of resource sharing.

References

1. The Police. "Too Much Information," from Ghost in the Machine. (Hollywood, Calif.: A & M Records, 1981) (A&M SP 3730).

2. Stanislaw Lem. The Cyberiad: Fables for the Cybernetic Age. (New York: Avon Books, 1980), pp. 119-134. First English edition, 1974.

3. B. F. Skinner. Walden Two. (New York: Macmillan, 1948), p. 121.

4. Rene Dubos. Celebrations of Life. (New York: McGraw-Hill, 1981), Sections 3 and 6, p. 251.

REFLECTIONS OF A COLLEGE LIBRARIAN:

LOOKING FOR LIFE AND REDEMPTION

THIS SIDE OF ARL*

William A. Moffett

I have been asked to speak on myths and realities: the college perspective. It doesn't sound like the kind of subject that lends itself to oratory, does it? I regret that. Just for a change, it would be interesting to have a library conference talk that would rouse us. Along with all our bland earnestness at library gatherings, I'd like a good peroration occasionally, wouldn't you? A stirring exhortation! Something memorable!

But there are perils in that. I should have learned that in the little high school I attended in the bayou country of southern Mississippi. That was back in the days when there were frequent student assemblies, and it was an accepted thing to bring in the local ministers and other public figures of the village to give us inspirational talks. I recall that we made it pretty tough for the speakers. You might say that we defied them to inspire us. We were bored. We were inattentive. We dozed. We worked math problems. I'll never forget one desperate clergyman who apparently decided we would remember his message. At the climactic moment, he drew from his vest pocket a wooden object and blew what was indisputably the loudest duck call ever heard in that room. As we sat there stunned, transfixed, he rendered his words of wisdom. And his talk was remembered. For years we laughed about that crazy preacher and his duck call. None of us, regrettably, harbored the slightest recollection of what it was he had so earnestly wished to leave indelibly printed on our young minds.

And it is true that a few years ago in an address to the plenary session of the ACRL at an ALA meeting in Chicago, I determined that a crucial part of my talk was written on a tombstone. So I lugged the darn thing all the way up to the podium, and for years I have been encountering people at these conferences who come up to me and say: "Hey, weren't you the guy with the tombstone?" And I say, "Yep!" And then they usually say, "Um, hmm." Do I ask

───────────────
*Reprinted by permission of the author and publisher from College & Research Libraries, 45:5 (September 1984) 338-349; copyright ©1984 by the American Library Association.

them if they remember the point I was trying to make? Oh, no! I know better. Being memorable has its perils.

Bearing that in mind, I want to talk a bit about the decline of the status of the college library in ALA and ACRL. I want to talk some about the crises of higher education and the special dilemma it holds for colleges. And I want to talk about the implications of both for college librarians.

The "college perspective"? There are in fact lots of college perspectives, but nothing that could be said to represent all colleges, or even colleges generally, for there are so many and they are so varied in size, type, and purpose. That variety constantly undermines the effectiveness of the College Libraries Section--a section which in terms of clout is, I'm afraid one of the weakest in ACRL. The only thing we seem to agree on is that if we abolished the section today, someone would try to resurrect it tomorrow. There has to be a college libraries section; it is the oldest--indeed, ACRL itself grew out of the College Library Section of ALA.

But if one looks at the membership list to see who's on it and what libraries they work in, one soon discovers a range from small institutions such as the College of the Desert in Twentynine Palms, California (one of my favorite place-names), with fewer than 50,000 volumes, to Wesleyan in Connecticut, which is fast approaching the million mark. There are lots of colleges in between. They are private; they are state-supported. They are church-affiliated; they are nonsectarian. Some think of themselves as traditional liberal arts colleges; others, following the lead of the community colleges-- which, of course, have their own section--are heavily committed to individualized, consumer-oriented education. Some are part of urban university complexes; others stand alone in the vastness of the prairie. They just don't hang together neatly as a group. About the only thing they have in common is that when you compare them with the top hundred or so universities in ARL (and the next phalanx of large institutions whose librarians apparently yearn to be in that select group), the purely undergraduate colleges--let's face it--are small.

Much of what I want to say has to do with the implications of that last statement. What are the effects--real and perceived-- of being part of a small academic institution in America?

Who Are the "Colleges"?

For the purposes of this address we have to agree on some useful generalization that will serve as the idea of what is meant by the term college. In the absence of a conventional definition that embraces the variety of institutions I have noted, I had thought that we could use a definition that emerged from the statistical delimiters of a recent survey--indeed, one of the first fairly comprehensive studies of college libraries to appear in our literature in many years.[1] In his report, Dennis Reynolds focused on the approximately three hundred academic libraries listed in The American Library Directory supporting institutions in which the highest degree granted was the baccalaureate, where the enrollment was between 500 and 2,000 students, and whose shelves contained between 65,000 and 250,000 volumes. For our purposes, however, those delimiters are not entirely suitable, for they exclude a number of well-established, mostly undergraduate institutions in which a lot of us work. (Indeed, I should observe that it does exclude my own institution, for example, because we have about 2,750 undergraduates, counting those in the Conservatory, many of whom take double degrees in the College of Arts and Sciences, and our library has around 900,000 volumes--if one counts all those thousands of books too brittle to use.) Perhaps it would be better to think in terms of mostly undergraduate institutions with less than 4,000 students and with libraries of no more than one million volumes, while remembering that there are many institutions well below those limits.

I should also say at the outset that a key frame of reference for me--but not an exclusive one--is the concept of the liberal arts college: that undergraduate institution which offers an education both sequential and cumulative, theoretical yet practical, specific and interrelated; which seeks to nourish the mind without neglecting the interests of the whole person. Put differently, I have in mind the kind of institution that accepts the assertion advanced by one of Oberlin's most articulate sons, Robert Maynard Hutchins, who insisted that the aim of higher education should be to produce men and women of goodness and wisdom.[2] In short, I mean those institutions deliberately attempting to serve as a bit of leaven in the lump of Western civilization.[3]

Back to myths and realities. It is a fact that through the nineteenth century, when the traditional liberal arts colleges were still ascendant, the term college simply meant "academic." The word was used indiscriminately for all institutions of higher learning well into this century, including those now largish institutions whose constituents would be somewhat offended if one misspoke and called them colleges today. With the rise of the modern university in the early part of this century, and the flowering--if that's the right word--of the multiversity after World War II, things were different. The term college had acquired a more restricted meaning; it now referred to a subset of higher education, the most obvious characteristic of which was that its individual members were comparatively small and insignificant.

Decline of the Status of the
College Library in ALA and ACRL

That development was reflected, of course, in the history of our own professional associations. When the American Library Association was founded, its first president was an academic librarian--a college librarian, if you will--Justin Winsor of Harvard. Yet almost from the first there was grumbling from the academics about the association's orientation toward the public sector, and that dissatisfaction--which expressed itself most pointedly by the threat of holding separate meetings such as the very one we're having in Seattle--led to the formation of the College Library Section in 1890, not officially recognized by ALA until 1900.

Perhaps I could digress here to remind you that only a fifth of ALA presidents have been academic librarians. For a time it appeared to have been ordained that a college librarian was to be made president at thirty-year intervals. Thus, William Isaac Fletcher of Amherst so served in 1891-92; and exactly three decades later, it was the turn of one of my esteemed predecessors at Oberlin, Azariah Root; and in another thirty years it was the librarian of Mt. Holyoke, Flora Belle Ludington.

But the thirty-year cycle has been broken. Indeed, as the mystical year of 1981-82 approached, and passed, it seemed hard to imagine ALA ever again electing a college librarian to its presidency. For that matter, fifteen years have passed since ALA has had a president who was indisputably an academic librarian, if you reckon Russell Shank as having come from the Smithsonian. (It is probably significant that during the past fifteen years seven ALA presidents have come from the field of library education.)

To return to my narrative, it is fair to say that throughout the early years academic librarians' loyalties in ALA turned to the College Library Section, which itself went through several changes. First of all, its name was changed to the College and Reference Libraries Section in recognition of the affinity with the reference specialists of the major public libraries. Subsequently it was called an association instead of section and elevated to divisional standing. In the reorganization of 1938, it set up five distinct subdivisions: one for junior colleges (eventually to be called community colleges), one for reference librarians in the large public libraries, one for librarians of teacher-training institutions, and, formally splitting the universities from the colleges for the first time, one for each of those categories. Actually, only a few years earlier some of the directors of the large institutions had taken the first steps that were to lead to the formation of the Association of Research Libraries-- and that, as nothing before, marked a refinement of what was meant by college. Fifty-three percent of the libraries represented among the original membership of the College Library Section became charter members of the new ARL fraternity. [4]

In 1939 when the new associational journal (C&RL) appeared, the R no longer stood for reference but for research. As A. F. Kuhlman explained in the first issue, three of the association's sections were for "colleges," and "as for the other two [sections], in the strict sense of the word, 'university' stands for research."[5]

Eventually the association, too, changed its name to the Association of College and Research Libraries, thus reenforcing the sense that college and university libraries were two quite different kinds of enterprises. Indeed, the college library had plainly fallen to a very secondary status in the profession, and as the modern university came increasingly to represent American higher education, the college librarian's role in the association was predictably much reduced. In a way that diminution of status is symbolized, no doubt inadvertently, by the very arrangement of the theme addresses at this conference: leading off with the university perspective and letting the college librarian tag along at the end, like a caboose.

The Crisis in Higher Education

Occasionally at this conference we've heard some allusions to the present crisis in higher education. Actually, it has always been possible to describe American higher education in any decade as being in a state of crisis. That's the way educational pundits talk. But as one gloomy Carnegie report after another has described what the future seems to hold in store for us, crisis does not seem an inappropriate word.[6]

In part, I suppose, it represents the legacy of a loss of confidence in all our institutions that young people have felt beginning with the trauma of Vietnam and the troubles of the sixties. Doubtless, part of it is economic: the contracted jobs market, the overall decline in growth that became acutely felt in the seventies and continues, in higher education, at least, today. In part it must reflect a dissatisfaction with the alienation, depersonalization, and shallowness that is commonplace in our colleges and universities, as well as throughout our society.

Sometimes the very reading of the various reports of anguish and alarm emanating from academia conjures up for me a frightful phantasmagoria, a circus of the macabre:

In the center of the arena lumber those ponderous, overgrown educational behemoths, fattened on government grants, showing a growing appetite for research contracts with multinational corporations, recognizable by their massive institutional services, their global ambitions, and their blinkered faculty attendants (themselves preoccupied with personal research and individual aggrandizement, innocent of a shared purpose, who mill about, disheartened, while teams of bureaucratic mahouts try vainly to gain control of the massive beasts) and hectored all the while by people with sharp-pointed sticks marked GOVERNMENT REGULATIONS, RETRENCHMENT, COLLECTIVE BARGAINING, COST EFFECTIVENESS, and COMMERCIALIZED ATHLETICS. For all their size, there is about these Gargantuas a look of sameness and conformity that is curiously disquieting.
From seemingly everywhere throngs of community colleges--looking for all the world like fast-food vendors--hawk their wares through the assembled spectators. They already account for more than 50 percent of the postsecondary students in the country, but still hustle in order to expand their markets.

Here and there someone has set up a stand to tout the latest faddish panacea. COMPETENCY-BASED EDUCATION reads one old banner; LIFE-LONG LEARNING proclaims another. Neither is attracting great enthusiasm.
Passing over a variety of other institutional creatures on the floor of the arena, one is conscious of some frightened figures huddled in clusters around the periphery, eyeing one another somewhat suspiciously. They're the four-year colleges. They've just been reminded by the public address system for the umpteenth time that the pool of available freshmen is still shrinking and there will not be nearly enough to go around. Some of them are not going to survive! Frantically a few attempt unconvincingly to disguise themselves as universities by expanding their course offerings. Others start following the community college vendors into the crowd. Some are nervously studying their mission statements, and here and there you see one scanning the yellow pages in search of a good public relations firm to help polish its image. From time to time you find one slumped in disbelief, paralyzed by uncertainty. An air of anxiety and sadness hangs over the whole scene.

It's not a pretty picture. Is it myth or reality?

Well, the plain truth is that there are serious challenges all of us face in higher education, and the conventional wisdom is that smaller institutions are in trouble. [7]

Special Implications for Colleges

With fewer students coming from the secondary schools, colleges have been preoccupied with survival strategies. But if you cut back your curricula and scale down your programs, your institution risks making itself less attractive to your traditional clientele. If you try to maintain your student enrollment by lowering admissions standards, or by endeavoring to attract new students by changing the mission of the college, you can lose in another way. There are many other factors that exacerbate the enrollment plight of the small private colleges. For example, because the education of secondary school teachers and guidance counselors has passed almost entirely to large public universities in every state, there is decreasing awareness in the schools of what it is that smaller, and often private, institutions have to offer, creating yet another twist to the colleges' admissions problem.

In any event, it seems the future of the smaller institutions may be in doubt, if not in actual jeopardy. That's an eventuality the large institutions apparently do not face. There one may fret about the effects on individuals of retrenchment and budget reallocations-- and even the loss here and there of a program or a department, including some of those superfluous schools of library science. One may, of course, become rightly anxious about the quality and direction of the overall educational program. But the question of the long-term survival of the university does not hang like a pall over the campus.

Being small in American academia means living with that terminal question.

Being small in American academia means being ineligible for many research grants, being nosed aside from the trough of many federal and state subsidies. [8]

Being small means limited resources for capital improvements; it means being hard-pressed to buy the instruments essential for first-class instruction in analytic chemistry.

Being small in academia means having difficulty attracting and sustaining the ablest teachers and librarians and providing adequate opportunities for personal development for both faculty and staff throughout their careers. As someone reminded me recently, even those colleges that succeed in creating stimulating environments in which college students may grow and develop for four years of post-adolescence may not be able to provide the most suitable places for adults to grow and flourish for forty years after attaining adulthood.

Being small in academia often means a lack of social and cultural diversity. Many colleges were established in little towns that are now off the beaten track. For residents of some such locations, one might not be able to find a decent Chinese restaurant within an hour's drive! Sad to say, some people dwell in towns in which the aroma of a freshly baked bagel has never brought joy to the human nostril!

But underlying it all, being small in American academia means having to endure the nagging sense of being in the minors. In our country size confers authority, prestige, legitimacy: the big time! the major leagues! the super bowl!

Nothing illustrates this so well perhaps as the appearance not long ago of something called The Gourman Report (Los Angeles: National Education Standards, 1983), a two-volume work purporting to be a guide to the quality of undergraduate and graduate education in the United States and abroad. You may have seen an article about it in the February 15, 1984, issue of the Chronicle of Higher Education. For that matter you may have seen something in your local newspaper because it triggered wide reaction by educators, ranging from skepticism to outrage.

Aside from a highly suspect system of consecutively ranking about a thousand undergraduate institutions, for example, it characterized more than 80 percent of overall academic programs in the country as being no better than "adequate" or "marginal," and of the 16 percent that were "acceptable plus" or better, it reckoned only 3.5 percent as "strong." Four-year liberal arts colleges invariably fell within the merely "adequate" or "marginal" categories, including the country's best--and private colleges generally ranked poorer than publicly supported ones.

The reason is not hard to discover, although Gourman is rather vague about his methods. All his indicators are utterly and consistently skewed by one crucial factor: size.

The Gourman Report has been labeled a fraud, and no one I know takes it seriously. Loren Pope, director of the College Placement Bureau, is quoted as calling it a "phony thing" and asserting that "anyone who would rank big institutions like Michigan [which ranked very high] over institutions like Swarthmore, Reed, and Carleton Colleges for undergraduate programs simply has no idea what he is doing. For undergraduates, the big universities are a gyp."[9]

The Gourman Report is interesting, however, because what it asserts in print--and ostensibly on the basis of objectivity--is what many Americans apparently assume: bigger means better. It underscores just one more handicap the colleges face in their struggle for survival, and one the colleges can do nothing about.

The Bias Against "Small" in Academic Librarianship

Academic librarianship is by no means immune to this bias. Indeed, one can argue that the effect is both pervasive and pernicious.

The final discontinuation of funds for Title II-A, the federal government's assistance to college libraries, comes to mind as the most obvious expression of a belief that the well-being of smaller academic libraries is unimportant.

Of much greater consequence, however, are the effects of the bias on the assumptions and practices of the members of the library community. For example, our library schools, as has been pointed out,[10] have made little effort to prepare their graduates for reference work and collection development in college, as opposed to university, libraries, where the function is different in direct proportion to size and mission, a point on which the speakers in our second theme session concurred.

Our library literature, dominated by editors and writers associated with the concerns of large institutions, has very little to say about college libraries, a discovery Bill Miller and Stephen Rockwood made when they began to put together their book on college librarianship a few years ago.[11]

Moreover, assistance to the profession by library agencies-- such as the management internships sponsored by the Council on Library Resources--almost invariably tilts to the very large institutions. We cannot even justify such a tilt by calling it a "trickle down" approach, since no one seriously thinks that the benefits to university libraries from such programs ever do trickle down to the colleges; there's certainly no evidence that they do.

Furthermore, a single anecdote may suggest how the bias in favor of size can operate within ACRL's executive office. One of the early and continuing advantages of ARL to its member-directors has been the sharing of basic comparative management data in a timely fashion. For the non-ARL libraries, the cumulated HEGIS statistics --in the days when they appeared at all--tended to be out-of-date and misleading. The ACRL subsequently undertook to collect and distribute data on behalf of the non-ARL members, but not for all dues-paying institutions. Where was the cutoff point drawn? Why, at the line separating institutions that grant doctorates and the rest of us who do not. College library administrators, whose need for up-to-date, accurate, comparable figures is no less pressing, have always had to write back and forth to one another, rely on state cumulations when they existed, or join in small data-sharing cooperatives, such as those voluntarily and unofficially organized by Dennis Ribbens of Lawrence and Arthur Monke of Bowdoin.

Professionalism

The triumph of professionalism in academic librarianship reinforces the bias. It is possible to construct a continuum of our ACRL membership at one end of which there are those academic librarians who tend to see themselves as professional librarians employed in academia; and at the other, those who tend to regard themselves as academics working in libraries. That is, professional specialists, on the one hand, whose first loyalties are to the values of the guild; and on the other, generalists whose professional skills are clearly subordinate to the educational function to which they are committed. By such a continuum, might we not be describing the difference--or at least the different tendency--that characterizes university and college librarians?

One can easily overstate the case, but it seems incontrovertible that in the large academic library, specialization and professionalism can lead individuals to think of the library and librarianship as ends in themselves. In smaller institutions it is less likely that librarians will lose sight of the fact that our mission is really the promotion of learning, not libraries.

The other day I came across an old article by Jerrold Orne (written, I think, to explain why participatory management would not work) in which he described the irresistible process, driven by automation, which was transforming librarians into specialists (especially directors and departmental heads), [12] a trend we do see in research libraries. But I found myself contrasting this trend with the actual experience of the college librarian who is the very epitome of the generalist. As Charles Maurer recently demonstrated, the successful head of the smaller academic library still has to be able "to do everything, and to do it at the same time."[13]

In such a library--even with pressing decisions to be made about the judicious application of computer technology (decisions that were not commonplace in 1951)--the essential qualities needed by the librarian in a college environment are even now those that Louis Round Wilson enumerated thirty-three years ago as traits desirable in the director of a research library: high intelligence, fine personality, wide educational interests, an understanding of how the library can contribute to the advancement of educational programs, imagination, sound common sense, intellectual drive, experienced and capable administrative ability, capacity for dynamic leadership, scholarship, an understanding of the spirit and purpose of research, a broad, humanistic outlook on books and all that enriches life.[14]   There's not a word in Round's list about specialization; not a line that smacks of narrow professionalism!

Compare that list with the hallmarks of professional success recognized in this association: credentials; expertise within fairly circumscribed fields of technical specialization; visibility on committees and councils; authorship of arcane publications; membership on prestigious boards; strings of consultantships--all of which we readily associate with career advancement in the large institutions, and much less frequently with advancement in the small.

Visibility on ALA and ACRL committees requires--among other things--assured funding for repeated travel to national professional meetings, something most small college librarians simply don't have or may not think is a leading priority.   Indeed, it is unclear whether the reason we don't see much of the college librarians at ALA meetings is due to their lack of funds, or because college librarians find gratification in their work and are not driven to seek fulfillment in so-called professional growth.[15]

Be that as it may, size of library (and the professionalism and specialization associated with it) does determine the conventional definition for accomplishment in this business.   Take a look at a recent issue of C&RL, for example, where you will find this assertion confirmed in a study describing the profile of the "successful" librarian: the probability is high, it says, that he or she works in a large academic library, and more than likely an ARL library at that.[16]

Being small in academia--it may be inferred--means being unsuccessful.

The pernicious effects of the bias I have described operate within the very precincts of the smaller institutions themselves. Evan Farber pointed this out a decade ago in "College Librarians and the University-Librarian Syndrome," a paper in which he discussed the pattern of attitudes that may ultimately cause college faculty, administrators, and even college librarians themselves to think of their own libraries in terms of university libraries--and then to imitate university practices, attitudes, and objectives, often with very detrimental results.[17]   For faculty and librarians essentially serving undergraduates, the model of library services driven by research (the model articulated by Paul Olum in the second of our theme sessions[18] and the model with which college faculty and librarians become familiar during their own graduate school experiences) is an unreliable guide. It is the operation of that syndrome, Farber argued, which largely explains why college faculty display a lack of confidence in their own librarians as colleagues, why they often neglect the importance of insuring that their students are taught how to use the library intelligently and independently, and why administrators are often more concerned about whether the library's budget is well managed than whether their students are deriving much benefit from it.

Being small in academia, then, does not mean you escape the larger institutional mind-set even when you're miles from the beast.

Reform and Renewal

As a result of such inherent difficulties, can there be any surprise that the smaller college library often fails to attract and retain the most appropriate personnel? Is there any wonder that the prospect of life in the minors can foster a set of self-fulfilling, low expectations? I rediscovered this reality during the past year while serving as a consultant to some midwestern colleges searching for head librarians. The opportunities for challenging and highly gratifying career advancement were clearly there; the number of good applicants was abysmally low. Why? It was as if smaller institutions had simply ceased to be attractive.

If colleges are going to survive, if they're going to prosper, I believe that they're going to have to be able to recruit good people for their libraries who understand the difference between the function of the research library and the purpose of the teaching library. One of my personal hopes is that the Great Lakes College Association (and perhaps other college consortia) can be persuaded to offer internships in college library administration, much like those for prospective managers of university libraries offered by the Council on Library Resources--and more recently the residencies developed by the University of Michigan.[19] By doing so we may be able to compensate for the lack of a recognizable career ladder for college library directors and perhaps counter some of that bias which discourages good people from seriously considering careers in smaller institutions.

That is important because the well-being of our colleges is important. It is so, first of all, because of the contribution to American life they have been making all along. Let me cite but a single statistic, one whose significance may not be well understood. If one ranks all colleges and universities by the percentage of their baccalaureate graduates who go on to obtain Ph.D.'s, one finds that seven of the top eleven are independent liberal arts colleges.[20]

Such institutions have been making a contribution to American life and letters out of proportion to their size.

But we need not belabor that point. The well-being of colleges may be even more important for what they may yet become.

For with all the talk of the disintegration of American higher education, and the stultification for undergraduates, especially, in large institutions, it is interesting to find so many thoughtful writers turning once again to the smaller institutions as a possible source of reform and renewal for postsecondary education generally. The liberal arts colleges, the argument runs, are less scarred by the student unrest of the late sixties, less dependent on government, less compromised by research contracts with the private sector, less fragmented, less captive of the false gods of professionalism, more responsive to leadership, more open to innovation, better able to confront ethical questions. The classic conservative exponent of this hope was undoubtedly Russell Kirk, but one finds it, too, in the work of Alain Touraine, in some of the later work of David Riesman, and in the recommendations of the Carnegie Foundation--with its emphasis on the importance of colleges with a sense of mission, an identity, a separate and discernible character.[21]

And one finds a particularly useful expression of it in Warren Martin's book A College of Character. Martin defines the essence of character as "disciplined, evident, enduring commitment to principles, usually to goals and purposes seen as moral or ethical, and expressed institutionally." And it is this kind of institution, he argues, not the multiversity, not the miniversity, not the university, that is best able to set the mark for the kind of leadership necessary for fundamental educational reform.[22]

It is not just an ideal or an abstraction. There are colleges of character, and they do serve as models of reform. I commend to you Thomas Cottle's loving evocation of one such place, a Quaker college where a commitment to interactive teaching and to the examined life--not quantifiable education--provides the power that infuses its campus. At Earlham, he wrote in his book College--Reward and Betrayal, devotion to students means helping young people to become more flexible in classes, less hostile toward imaginative experiences; it means postponing consulting jobs and delaying research at times in order to leave one's door open, to talk, to comment often and in depth on student papers; to return in the autumn or in a summer preterm session with new plans, recharged enthusiasm, and endless temerity.

Nor is the chemistry that makes Earlham effective confined to the teaching faculty. It includes, Cottle writes, the "kindness of a librarian" whose concern for students convinces him that a library must be a place for students not only to do research--which he teaches them how to do--but also to browse and nap and dream. "The man whose task it is to oversee this genuinely spiritual center is a part of the lives of students."[23]

Libraries and Librarians 43

For those of us in this room who are familiar with that particular librarian's efforts to foster close collaboration between teachers and librarians, it was especially interesting to hear Gresham Riley's appreciative statements about the role of the academic librarian in the small college. [24] We know how he came by that understanding, for Evan Farber's work at Earlham has been a source of inspiration to many others throughout the country, and not merely in small institutions, either, as many of you can doubtless attest.

Apotheosis

Is there life this side of ARL? There certainly is at Earlham. And elsewhere. Hear this testimony from the librarian of a small college located near the very center of this country; it is from a letter I received within the past few weeks.

> Why do I like being a college librarian? Most importantly, I am aware that my being here has made a real difference for the college. I can see the good things that have happened because of my leadership. I know that they probably would not have taken place if I hadn't had the chance to invest my talents here and in the way I have. Moreover, I know that I am directing the library, not just presiding over it. In short, I have a genuine and a realistic sense of accomplishment.
>
> I have had an opportunity to construct a library building that is the envy of my peers who have seen it. In the process I had a chance to work with, and to become the friend of, one of the most exciting client-oriented architects at work today. My position here is not so remotely managerial that I do not get to put a substantial share of my effort into collection building; although I have a full-time acquisitions librarian I hold that--after providing strong leadership and able management--collection building is the library director's primary responsibility, one upon which all else hangs.
>
> Our library staff is big enough to do its job, but small enough for me to know every member personally and usually to have some conversation with each person every day. We have been able to recruit and to retain the ablest library staff I have ever encountered; there is not one weak link in the whole chain; and I will pit them person-for-person against any library staff in the country for ability, commitment, enthusiasm, and energy. I have only to travel sixty miles down the road to the University to see a library staffed by crabby, burned-out librarians, laboring on such a tiny part of the mountain as to have little concept of the whole. They stand in contrast to the eager, highly motivated people who staff our college library and seem to have one hell of a good time doing it.
>
> While my job has been demanding, it has not been so absolutely time-consuming that I have been unable to remain

active as a working scholar in my academic specialty. Last summer and fall I was able to contribute chapters for two collective volumes as well as continue work on a major book. My spouse and I have a busy social life with a circle of faculty colleagues who are intellectually stimulating and thoroughly cosmopolitan.

Nor has my role been confined within the walls of the library. I have served on several faculty/student committees--of which my long time favorite has been Art Acquisitions, the policy-making body for the College's permanent art collection.

Finally, in purely material terms, I think the financial rewards of my position have been competitive with those I would have received in a large research library. Probably they have been even greater, if one adjusts my generous salary against the higher cost of living in a major university location.

"I have friends who are executives in ARL libraries," the letter concludes. "I am not envious of them."

For this librarian, life in the academic minor leagues, one sees, is both more and less than what it's cracked up to be.

Making One's Career Count

I said that I did not have a ringing peroration with which to conclude, and I do not. But since I already have a reputation for bringing you messages engraved on stone, at least you won't be startled if in closing I do that again. This time, at least, I don't have the stone with me. It sits--or at least it did when I saw it many years ago--on the other side of this continent, as part of a monument on the battery overlooking the harbor of Charleston, South Carolina. It is, as I recall, an unremarkable monument, but somehow its words have stayed with me over the decades. They say: Count Them Happy Who for Their Faith and Courage Have Endured a Great Fight.

In our time America's colleges are quietly engaged in a great, a momentous struggle. Far more than their own survival is at stake. It is their mission to produce women and men of goodness and wisdom. The nation, the world, needs them.

Liberal arts colleges may no longer prevail, but they do endure. In not all of them will their librarians attain the full potential of the role I have described here in an admittedly idealized way. Certainly, that potential is not often enough understood by their own faculty and administrative colleagues, and sometimes not by librarians themselves. For those who do understand, and especially those who bear their part of the struggle in those purposeful "colleges of character," there is a special satisfaction that comes in knowing that the investment of their time, their personal talents, their energies, and their professional skills counts for something.

And so they soldier on. The least that their colleagues in the profession at large can do is to give them some understanding and cheer them on!

This paper was presented at the ACRL Third National Conference, April 4-7, 1984, Seattle, Washington. The author would like to acknowledge with gratitude the comments and suggestions of many colleagues, especially Edwin Bronner (Haverford), Evan Farber (Earlham), Michael Freeman (Wooster), Charles Maurer (Denison), Christopher McKee (Grinnell), Mahlon Peterson (St. Lawrence), Herbert Safford (Muskingum), and Bill Miller (Michigan State).

References and Notes

1. Dennis Reynolds, "A Survey of Libraries in American Four-year Colleges," in College Librarianship, eds. William Miller and D. Stephen Rockwood (Metuchen, N.J.: Scarecrow, 1981), p. 7-29. For other useful discussions of the types of colleges and their roles, see Algo D. Henderson and Jean Glidden Henderson, Higher Education in America (San Francisco: Jossey-Bass, 1979), p. 28-39; David G. Winter, David G. McClelland, and Abigail T. Stewart, A New Case for the Liberal Arts: Assessing Institutional Goals and Student Development (San Francisco: Jossey-Bass, 1981), p. 151-57.
2. Robert Maynard Hutchins, The Higher Learning in America (New Haven: Yale Univ. Pr., 1936).
3. To borrow a phrase from Russell Kirk, Decadence and Renewal in Higher Learning: An Episodic History of the American University and College since 1953 (South Bend, Ind.: Gateway Editions, 1978), p. xvii.
4. One of the most convenient short accounts of association development is that by the late W. Carl Jackson, "The National Organizations--ALA, ARL, ACRL: Meeting Academic and Research Librarians' Needs?" in Academic Librarianship: Yesterday, Today and Tomorrow, ed. Robert Stueart (New York: Neal-Schuman, 1982), p. 207-30.
5. Introduction to the initial issue, College & Research Libraries 1:10 (Dec. 1939).
6. Sidney Hook, Paul Kurtz, Miro Todorovich, eds. The Idea of a Modern University (Buffalo, N.Y.: Prometheus Books, 1974); Alain Touraine, The Academic System in American Society, Carnegie Commission on Higher Education series (New York: McGraw-Hill, 1974); The Carnegie Foundation for the Advancement of Teaching. More than Survival: Prospects for Higher Learning: An Episodic History of the American University and College since 1953 (South Bend, Ind.: Gateway Editions, 1978); Kenneth H. Ashworth, American Higher Education in Decline (College Station: Texas A & M Univ. Pr., 1979); The Carnegie Council on Policy Studies in Higher Education, Three Thousand Futures: The Next Twenty Years for Higher Education (San Francisco: Jossey-Bass, 1980); Ernest A. Lyndon, "Reexamining the Role of the University: A Crisis of Purpose,"

Change 15:18-23, 53 (Oct. 1983); George B. Weathersby, "Our Fading State Colleges: Have They Lost Their Vitality and Mission?" Change 16:18-23, 49 (Jan./Feb. 1984); Sherman Jones, "Difficult Times for Private Black Colleges," Change 16:24-31 (Mar. 1984); Dorrit Cowan, "The Expanding Conflict: Society's Demands/Academic Independence," Change 16:34ff. (Apr. 1984). Perhaps the most recent comprehensive review was volume 35 of the Proceedings of the Academy of Political Science, published as The Crisis in Higher Education, ed. by Joseph Froomkin (New York: Academy of Political Science, 1983).
7. David W. Breneman, "The Coming Enrollment Crisis: Focusing on the Figures," Change 15:14-19 (Mar. 1983); Stephen P. Dresch, "College Enrollment," in The Crisis in Higher Education, p. 108-18.
8. For example, despite general increases in the budget of the National Science Foundation, that agency has apparently written off liberal arts colleges and other institutions lacking a graduate program. The Department of Education refuses to fund foreign-language programs except in the large universities. The revolving door of personnel appointments between the universities and these government agencies, moreover, seems likely to reinforce the attention being given to the interests of the former. Insofar as large also means public, the bias is reflected on the federal level in the recent cuts in financial aid to students, which are especially injurious to private education. At the same time, on the state level public institutions are becoming much more aggressive, and successful, in going after foundation support once regarded as the special source of help for institutions lacking state revenues. There is a special irony here. Being small and first-class in academia usually requires efficient and prudent fiscal management. State-supported higher education, while almost invariably more expensive and less efficient (running perhaps 40 percent higher in costs per student), reacts to budget cuts not necessarily by belt-tightening and greater efficiencies, but by raiding the revenue sources of the private institutions.
9. Beverly T. Watkins, "New Edition of a Guide to College's Quality Gets a Mixed Response," Chronicle of Higher Education (Feb. 15, 1984), p. 12-13; Susan Goldberg, "Michigan Colleges Rankle at Rankings: Educators Criticize Guidebook, Author," Detroit Free Press (Mar. 5, 1984).
10. Evan Farber, "College Librarians and the University-Librarian Syndrome," in The Academic Library: Essays in Honor of Guy R. Lyle, eds. Evan Farber and Ruth Walling (Metuchen, N.J.: Scarecrow, 1974), p. 20.
11. Miller and Rockwood, College Librarianship, p. 1.
12. Jerrold Orne, "Future Academic Library Administration--Whither and Whether," in The Academic Library, p. 82-95.
13. Charles Maurer, "Close Encounters of Diverse Kinds," in Miller and Rockwood, p. 97-105.
14. Louis Round Wilson, "What Type Research Librarian?" in Reader in the Academic Library, ed. Michael M. Reynolds (Washington: Microcard Editions, 1971), p. 219-22.

15. The more crucial problem for the staff on the smaller academic library is not the lack of travel funds so much as it is the lack of enough professionals to constitute the critical mass necessary for healthy dialogue and mutual in-house support on a daily basis.
16. John N. Olsgaard, "Characteristics of 'Success' among Academic Librarians," College & Research Libraries 45:5-13 (Jan. 1984).
17. Farber, "College Librarians and the University-Librarian Syndrome," in The Academic Library, p. 12-23.
18. The theme paper of Paul Olum can be found on p. 362-66 of this issue of C&RL.
19. Richard M. Dougherty and Wendy P. Lougee, "Research Library Residencies: A New Model for Professional Development," Library Journal 198:1322-24 (July 1983).
20. In an unpublished study of the baccalaureate origins of doctorate recipients, Carol Fuller determined that the top twenty-four most productive institutions for 1960-80, in order of rate of productivity, are: California Institute of Technology, MIT, Reed College, Swarthmore, University of Chicago, Haverford, Oberlin, Amherst, Pomona, Carleton, Wabash, Rice, Princeton, Case Western Reserve, Grinnell, Cooper Union, Harvard, Wooster, Wesleyan, Davidson, Hamilton, Wheaton (Ill.), Williams, and Bowdoin. A comprehensive study of the overall performance of private institutions is summarized in Alfred E. Hall, "Starting at the Beginning: The Baccalaureate Origins of Doctorate Recipients, 1920-1980," Change 16:40-43 (Apr. 1984).
21. Kirk, Decadence and Renewal, p. 293-301; Touraine, The Academic System, p. 261-62; Gerald Grand and David Riesman, The Perpetual Dream: Reform and Experiment in the American College (Chicago: Univ. of Chicago Pr., 1978); Carnegie Foundation, More Than Survival, p. 6-7.
22. Warren Bryan Martin, A College of Character (San Francisco; Jossey-Bass, 1982) p. 177-97.
23. Thomas J. Cottle, College: Reward and Betrayal (Chicago: Univ. of Chicago Pr., 1977), p. 64-84.
24. The theme paper of Gresham Riley can be found on p. 367-69 of this issue of C&RL, and at the end of Part I of this volume.

MYTHS, MISCONCEPTIONS & MANAGEMENT*

Michael E. D. Koenig & Herbert D. Safford

In ACADEMIC librarianship, concern about the provision of suitably skilled and competent persons to assume managerial positions is voiced with increasing frequency. The problem is generally perceived as the result of the inability of our profession to attract sufficient numbers of first class people, coupled with the inadequate professional training of those who do enter librarianship.[1-3] While both recruitment and professional training for librarianship need improvement, there is an even more fundamental problem within our profession that, we submit, is the principal but largely unrecognized cause of the malaise.

The problem: stratification

That problem is professional stratification, specifically vertical stratification--the difficulties our field place in the way of horizontal mobility. Part of the reason we don't recognize the problem is that we are not accustomed to problems of vertical stratification. We are accustomed to thinking of and perceiving problems of horizontal stratification--the inability to move up in the organization, typically because of racial or sexual discrimination. Such problems certainly exist in libraries, but there is also a concomitant lack of horizontal mobility. This problem is particularly acute in academic libraries. To put it very bluntly, if one aspires to a senior position in a large academic library, one had best move into a large academic library environment very early in one's career. There are exceptions to this precept, but they are rare.

This mindset of the profession runs counter to generally recognized principles of good management. The naval analogy used below, because of its clarity, is one that is frequently used in a management context. It is in that broad context that it is intended. Typically, the conventional management thinking goes, the best way to become the C.O. (Commanding Officer) of a battleship, is to have been C.O. of a cruiser, and the best route to that command is to have been C.O. of a destroyer.

*Reprinted by permission of the authors and publisher from Library Journal, 109 (October 15, 1984) 1897-1902. Published by R. R. Bowker Co. (a Xerox company). Copyright © 1984 by Xerox Corporation.

The reasons for preferring to select the C.O. of a cruiser rather than the department head on a battleship as the next C.O. of a battleship are logical and persuasive. First, the C.O. of a cruiser has had decision making and managerial experience of a kind that has not been available to the department head aboard the battleship. Second, the quality of the performance of the C.O. of the cruiser is verifiable, at least to a greater degree than that of the department head, who may have had support from above as well as below. Third, and perhaps most important, is that people of the quality one wants for C.O. of a battleship, in general, will not have come up through the ranks in battleships. They will have taken command positions, first on a destroyer and then on a cruiser. They will have done so partly because they realize that that is the preferred route for advancement, but far more important will have been their perception that route is where the action is. Aggressive, confident, competent young professionals will seek to maximize the frog-to-pond ratio. They will seek duty stations where they can get the most responsibility the quickest, and those duty stations are generally the small command, not the large one.

Type of library mythology

In librarianship however, we have developed a mythology that runs counter to the battleship, cruiser, destroyer analog. We have developed a perception in our field that academic research librarianship, public librarianship, industrial research librarianship, etc. are distinct career paths to which one must make a commitment early in one's career. We have, in short, vertically stratified the profession and thereby we have made horizontal mobility extremely difficult.

This vertical stratification is particularly acute in academic research libraries. Directors of large academic libraries in contrast to directors of large public libraries, for example, are much less likely to have had previous directorial experience as directors at smaller institutions. They are far more likely to have come up through the ranks within the same sort of institution which they direct. [4]

Foreclosed opportunity

Our mythology, the belief that career paths must be pursued in one type of library because of its special unique quality, is doing a great disservice to the profession, and the academic library community in particular. Positions are filled from a pool of applicants that is much smaller than the number of qualified candidates available, and many highly qualified and competent individual librarians find that important career opportunities are foreclosed to them.

The central thesis of this paper is that the more aggressive, competent young professionals in the library field have tended, particularly in recent years, to choose destroyers where they will see more action and assume more responsibility sooner.

In addition to the principle of maximization of the frog-to-pond ratio, there have been in the last decade and a half two other major factors driving the pattern of job selection.

The best look elsewhere

The first factor is simply the very pragmatic question of job opportunities. In the last dozen years, the proportion of library school graduates opting for special library and nontraditional jobs has doubled (from 15 percent to 30 percent) while the public and school library proportion have stayed relatively unchanged. Academic job placement, on the other hand, has fallen from 34 percent to 22 percent.[5] The increase in special library placement is widely acknowledged in the library community, but it seems to be little recognized that this proportionate growth has come principally at the expense of academic libraries, not at the expense of public and school libraries. Job opportunities in academic libraries have been very much constricted in recent years, and students are probably a great deal more perceptive about job opportunities than they are generally thought to be.[6] It is not unreasonable to assume that it is the sharper students who are the more perceptive and have taken themselves elsewhere.

Where the action is

The second factor is that the special library/nontraditional sector of library employment (including the information industry) is where the action is, and this has been so for a decade and a half. This phenomenon is largely the consequence of the electronic revolution, "the information controllability explosion."

This effect, described in more detail elsewhere,[7] arose because of the sequence of development of electronic data processing technology. The library and information retrieval applications of data and information processing are very storage dependent. That is, library applications typically do not require sophisticated number crunching capabilities, but they do require extensive and relatively inexpensive storage capacity. However, cost-effective processing capabilities were available well before there were cost-effective storage capabilities.

Special libraries, in contrast to academic libraries, had appropriate applications such as chemical substructure searching, that utilized the number crunching capabilities, required relatively modest storage capabilities, and were also of prime importance to the parent organization.

For many similar reasons, automation was applicable to creating databases for print products in abstracting and indexing organizations well before it was applicable to manipulating them as databases in a library environment. As a consequence, data processing was justifiably and economically applicable to special libraries and "nontraditional" functions well before it was to other library sectors. This comment is in no way intended to denigrate the competence of any sector of librarianship. The application of data processing to librarianship for the most part proceeded in a very logical and predictable fashion, with the automation of a function occurring first in that sector in which it was most justifiable and cost effective. The automation of monograph related library functions, for example, was therefore pioneered by academic libraries and the consortia they founded, the automation of circulation by public and academic libraries, and the automation of serials functions by industrial research libraries, abstracting and indexing organizations, and serials agents.

The consequence has been that special libraries, particularly those supporting research intensive industries, and nontraditional sectors, have presented far more attractive job opportunities for the aggressive young professional than have academic research libraries. It is no accident that almost all of the early users of commercial online searching were special libraries, principally those serving pharmaceutical and chemical companies.

How are jobs selected?

The thesis relating job selection to the frog-to-pond ratio is certainly not one that can be easily demonstrated in any definitive sense. Any serious attempt would require an expenditure of resources out of proportion to the benefits to be achieved. There is, however, some evidence that lends considerable support.

The change in the marketplace and the changing distribution of jobs is clearly demonstrable.[8] More than simply the proportion by type of job has been changing however. A decade and a half ago, the proportion of placements by type of library was relatively constant from one library school to another. That is no longer true. Now the schools that are perceived to be "the better library schools" (the perception of "better" is based on Herbert White's attitudinal survey of library school education[9]) produce a disproportionately large number of placements in special libraries and nontraditional jobs.

This phenomenon is discussed at greater length elsewhere,[5] but two points should be noted. First, the phenomenon is a very marked one, and it is statistically highly significant. Second, the phenomenon does not appear to be a function of location. It persists when analyzed by geographic region, or when limited to library schools in urban areas.

One can conjecture as to the cause of this change. Perhaps, for example, electronic information technology was introduced into the curricula of the "better" library schools earlier, so their graduates were better prepared for jobs in the areas where those competencies were more in demand.

There is another plausible explanation. There is, at least, some link between the perceived quality of a school and the quality of its graduates, and that the phenomenon simply reflects the job selection of the more aggressive and more capable students. (Lest the authors be thought to be self-serving, they suggest that the correlation between the perceived quality of a library school and quality of its students is primarily a function of self-selection by the prospective student, and less a function of the quality of the educational experience.)

In reality, the phenomenon is probably a function of several considerations. It is highly likely however that an adaptive market mechanism of job selection on the part of students is a major component. If so, then the data above provide evidence in support of the hypothesis that the more able students have taken themselves to "where the action is, " in special library and nontraditional jobs.

Dimensions and causes

Even if one remains dubious about that hypothesis, the fact remains that the number of young professionals entering academic libraries has tumbled dramatically in the last decade, from over 1, 100 per year in the sixties to half that (556) in 1982.[8] This is not surprising given such factors as the economic pressures upon universities, and the transfer of some functions to bibliographic utilities. The number of managerial jobs to be filled has not decreased however. The result, even with no diminution of quality, is that there has been a halving of the candidates to jobs ratio. This reduces by half the number of new potential managers even though there is no diminution in the number of managerial jobs to be filled.

As an aside, it is interesting to note that in eschewing sex discrimination we should have tapped a large, previously "unavailable" pool of candidates for top jobs. There should be no dearth of qualified candidates for senior positions. The fact that there is still a strong perception that there is a dearth[1] of such candidates strengthens the argument that the best candidates, both female and male, have selected jobs elsewhere.

Providing people for the next generation of leadership in academic libraries is a major problem in any case. The phenomenon of the more able people increasingly taking positions elsewhere is not the cause of the problem, but it has amplified it to major proportions. It is not surprising that a recent survey revealed that 19 percent of academic research library searches for middle and senior level positions had to be reopened.[2] Vertical stratification is the cause of the problem. It developed because the profession, particularly in academic and research libraries, strongly held to its belief in two misconceptions: inappropriate specialization and collegial management.

Inappropriate specialization

The first misconception is the error of inappropriate specialization. In the library field, we act as if public librarianship were almost a different career from, for example, academic research librarianship, or industrial research librarianship. There are differences, of course, but hardly the sort that should prevent individuals from moving from one venue to another. If we were to attempt to design a business school curriculum based upon our attitude toward career paths, instead of having functional majors such as marketing, or finance, or quantitative methods, we would have industry majors such as foodstuffs or transportation. In fact we are so parochial in our views, that we would probably narrow things even further and have majors within industry, for example, by type of transportation (rail, air, etc.).

In terms of modern management thinking, the management of services in the provision of information, much less libraries in particular, is a rather narrow focus of specialization. It is certainly unnecessary to erect vertical stratifications to divide the field still further, yet that is exactly what we have done.

The collegial fallacy

The field's second misconception concerns the nature of management in the context of the academic research library. We have been guilty of using a false analogy for academic research library management. The false analogy is "collegial;" This analogy with the members of the professorial or teaching faculty is inimical to defining the nature of directorship, it is beside the point, irrelevant, to what the director may be or should be.

A good case can be made for the view that managers and directors are not like other teaching academics, nor even very much like the librarians they manage. Library directors are more closely analogous to the "heads" of almost anything on campus: the computer center, the physical plant, etc. They are certainly more nearly analogous to Deans, Provosts, and Vice Presidents for Academic Affairs, those academics who might be called "meta-managers."

They handle large budgets, hire and occasionally fire staff, monitor and increase production and output in a way utterly foreign to the classroom. They have universal responsibility to the academic community rather than a parochial one. They function on a decision-making level in such areas as space needs and allocation, personnel, resources, buildings, technology, and the like; all more administrative than collegial.

This kind and level of competence which defines directoral adequacy by stipulating the nature of the director's tasks, is largely irrelevant to the kind of competence sought in teaching posts, despite the integral involvement of the library in the curricular processes of the institution.

An even more striking analog is that of the doctor who moves from being a skilled surgeon to being a hospital administrator. There are some things about being a skilled surgeon which help that surgeon to be a good hospital administrator (native intelligence, calm during crises, etc.) but probably not very many. Indeed, many a surgeon can be heard bemoaning the day he or she moved from manual dexterity to administrative complexity.

Certainly it should be agreed that administering a hospital is both different from being a doctor and to some extent, dependent upon having been a doctor. Indeed, keeping one's identity with the profession of medicine with the point of view of the practicing doctor is both wise and constructive. Hospital administrators should know as much as possible about surgery, but they are no longer merely surgeons. They should identify with the profession of medicine, but they are no longer doctors in a sense derivative from their previous duties.

The hospital administrator is, qualitatively, in a new job, and success or failure will be dependent upon his or her performance as an administrator rather than as a surgeon.

In the same way, administrating a library is much easier and better done if one knows the library from a librarian's point of view. Library administration is, despite this, a quite different thing from any particular practice within the library. The consequences of this vertical stratification are of three kinds: institutional, individual, and professional.

Institutional consequences

We are crippling academic research libraries, institutionally, by so narrowly delimiting the field from which they recruit managerial personnel. This affects the quality of management and leadership in those institutions and that, in turn, affects the quality of the professional life of all those employed by those institutions. We hear the poorly articulated response to this problem at meetings, and read it in the literature. This effect is not limited to academic research libraries, but the pinch is felt more strongly there.

Individual consequences

We are crippling individual librarians by limiting the range of their career opportunities. In effect we are saying, "If you choose destroyers early in your career, you'll have to stay in destroyers, or get out of the service." Obviously, this is not conducive to good morale. A classic complaint about special librarianship, particularly in industry, is that while a librarian's initial career velocity is rapid, when a senior job in the organization is achieved, one stays there, with a feeling of stagnation. A lowering of the barriers to horizontal mobility would ameliorate this situation.

The other result of vertical stratification is to force good people out of the field. Industrial research librarians, instead of moving into academic research library jobs, are commonly forced to leave librarianship, to go either to the information industry, or to general administrative jobs if they wish to be promoted within their organization. We hear little about this problem because the people affected often leave the field and take their concerns with them. From the point of view of the profession however, it may be a more serious problem than the institutional one, for it means the loss of some of our ablest people. Similar, but perhaps not quite so pronounced, comments could be made about public librarianship.

Professional consequences

In terms of the total profession, vertical stratification limits our ability to communicate. This, in turn, limits our ability to efficiently take advantage of and build upon what is developed in our field. This topic deserves a paper in its own right.

An anecdote will illustrate the problem: In his presentation at a Library Information and Technology Association conference on serials automation in 1980, an academic research librarian, to his misfortune, described the online serials system with which he had been associated as one of only two such systems (the "only" other system he mentioned was also at an academic institution) in the country.

Literally dozens of librarians in the audience had been involved with the development of online serials systems at industrial research libraries, serials agencies, and abstracting and indexing organizations. Many of those systems were substantially more sophisticated than the one being described.

Although those librarians responded with surprising charity, the speaker still left the podium very red faced. The presentation proved that there had been much unnecessary reinvention of the wheel at the speaker's institution, a very different point from the one he thought he would be making.

Bringing change

The first step toward ameliorating the problems caused by vertical stratification is to be aware of them.

Librarians, particularly those who work and manage in academic research libraries, will have to revise their attitudes toward stratification, and their perception of their field and work as very special.

In short, those who hire for academic research libraries should not only be willing to consider hiring managerial level personnel from outside the academic research library ranks, they should recruit them. There are some examples. New York University chose a library director because of demonstrated competence in library administration at a public library. Rutgers (via Cornell) chose a librarian with demonstrated managerial competence in the book trade. Purdue chose a librarian because of demonstrated competence in research library administration in an industrial research library. None of these institutions seems to have suffered thereby.

Recruitment from public and college "librarianship" is probably relatively straightforward in terms of salary comparability. The realities of academic research library salary structures in relation to special library (particularly in industrial research libraries) and information industry salary structures imposes some economic constraints.

Special library and industry salaries are sufficiently attractive that a librarian can only afford to make the shift from industry if the shift is to relatively senior levels in an academic research library. This difference in salary structure supports, in part, the argument that academic research librarians are underpaid (which is probably the case). Therefore, one logical step is to improve middle management academic salaries so that such jobs are more attractive.

The salary scale differential is, to large degree, an irreducible function of a different notion of the measure of management scope. Special libraries (industrial research libraries) are perceived as small in comparison to academic research libraries because they are much smaller in terms of staff, books on the shelf, serials subscribed to, etc. In terms of dollars spent and resources expended, however, they are often surprisingly large.

A recent article[5] pointed out that a pharmaceutical company such as Pfizer may run an information system, that while much smaller in staff, is larger than an ARL library such as that at MIT in terms of resources expended in support of research.

To academic library eyes, then, special library experience may, in relative terms, seem to be mid-level experience. In truth, if it is seen in terms of the management and deployment of resources, special library experience ranks with the senior levels in all librarianship.

This explains much of the apparent difference in salary structures, but it also implies that in assessing external candidates, academic research librarians will have to rethink their implicit view of managerial equivalency.

Furthermore, those academic research library managers should anticipate horizontal moves at rather higher levels than they might have liked. It may, ideally, be more desirable to bring people horizontally into academic research libraries at middle management levels, with some time for seasoning and observation before promotion to senior levels, but the difference in salary structure may not make that feasible in many cases. Academic libraries therefore have to prepare themselves to bring in new blood at senior levels.

Shedding the collegial fallacy

Academic librarians should shed their collegial misconceptions concerning the function of management. Management positions are not and should not be collegial. This, in turn, implies that those positions should not be afforded tenure. It is precisely those senior positions, with their attendant qualification, for which tenure is most defensible in the eyes of the faculty.

This has serious implications for the whole notion of tenure for academic librarians. This also implies that the selection procedure for senior academic library positions should not be collegial. Just as the selection of a dean of a library school is probably too important to be left to the recommendation of the professors, the selection of a university library director is probably too important to be left to the recommendation of the librarians. In both cases, a universitywide search committee with heavy managerial representation would seem to be most appropriate.

Another corollary is that the notion of academic research libraries educating their own future managers, as expressed in a recent article, [1] is indefensible. That notion is analogous to having the future C.O.'s of battleships educated aboard battleships. The objection is not that the battleships could not do a good job of education. The problem is that such a process excludes so many other potential C.O.'s including many of the best candidates. Similarly, the notion of developing programs at the master's level to specialize in academic research librarianship simply reinforces the very stratification that we should be dismantling.

Needed: managerial skills

A much greater emphasis on management skills in the MLS curriculum is needed. It is here that the attitudes of academic research librarians are particularly distressing. In a recent survey, directors of academic research libraries ranked management skills only 15th out of some 19 attributes they desired in new professional academic librarians.[10, 11] Even more distressing, it was still ranked only 15th of 19 when they were asked to identify what attributes academic librarians should have after five years on the job, when presumably at least some should have begun to assume managerial responsibility.

Such an attitude on the part of management is, in itself, enough to convince able and ambitious young professionals that they ought to go elsewhere.

To be fair, it should be added that another recent survey conducted in academic research libraries[2] concerning the recruitment of personnel for middle and upper level positions revealed a much greater concern for "managerial ability experience." Such managerial experience was the quality to which importance was most frequently attached in recruitment, and by an even wider margin, it was the quality most often found wanting in applicants.

There is a striking inconsistency between those two surveys. The respondents to the first survey (directors) attached almost no significance to managerial training or skills for entry level hirees, nor for persons with five years experience. The respondents to the second survey (directors, associate directors, and personnel administrators), on the other hand, attached the greatest importance to managerial ability and experience when recruiting for middle and upper level positions.

The obvious implication is that what comes out of the faucet depends upon what goes into the pipeline. What is not valued at input is not likely to be available at output. To provide candidates with suitable management ability and experience, we need to put more appropriate candidates into the pipeline, by recruiting the C.O.'s of cruisers, and by providing more management training as a part of the MLS program.

Needed: programs for top managers

Senior-level programs in academic library management are needed. Ideally they would be programs to which a library could send a senior level person after that person had made a horizontal move into an academic position. The model for such a program would be the sort of summer programs that first rate business schools run for senior executives. The salient characteristics of such programs are intensity, relatively short duration, and that the expense is borne by the institution, not the individual.

An organization such as the Council on Library Resources could have major impact by using the power of the purse strings to establish an admission system which would allow libraries to send in-house up-from-the-ranks candidates, only in some proportion to the number of candidates they sent who had been recruited from sources external to academic library ranks. The creative use of the carrot has been successful in breaking down horizontal stratification. We should try using that same carrot to break down vertical stratification.

It should be added that such programs need not be the exclusive province of the library school and the school of management or administration. The involvement of the academic research library community, the battleships as it were, would be extremely beneficial. The programs would not be unrelated to CLR's present program, but at a higher level, and oriented toward the infusion of new blood.

Libraries and Librarians

Wide open for recruits

Of course there are other major problems in our field relating to recruitment and education that also bear on the problem of producing an adequate stream of good future managers. Clearly vertical stratification and overspecialization make the field unattractive in terms of recruitment. The more wide open the field the more attractive it becomes in terms of recruitment in general. The more wide open the field the more attractive it is, in particular, to the aggressive and able persons who have the potential to be good dynamic managers. Anything we do that increases stratification or premature specialization simply exacerbates our recruitment problem.

Removing the causes

In short, our field has a major problem with unwarranted and counter productive vertical stratification. That stratification creates problems in staffing, in management, in morale, in recruitment, and in the expeditious development of the field. The greatest disutility is found in the academic research library where vertical stratification is most strongly practiced.

The solution to vertical stratification, just as for horizontal stratification, is to do away with the discrimination and narrow thinking it reflects. This requires an awareness of the problem, and it requires changes in the attitudes and the practices of librarianship. In addition, curricular changes at the MLS level are needed to emphasize managerial skills.

Finally, intensive, senior-level management skills programs, initiated with support from the Council on Library Resources, could, with creative use of the power of the purse strings, be a major force in removing the vertical stratification plaguing the library field.

References

1. Battin, Patricia, "Developing University and Research Library Professionals: A Director's Perspective," American Libraries, January 1983, p. 22-25.
2. Mayeski, John K. & Marilyn J. Sharrow, "Recruitment of Academic Library Managers: A Survey," Journal of Academic Librarianship, July 1982, p. 151-55.
3. McClure, Charles R., "Library Managers: Can They Manage? Will They Lead?" LJ, November 15, 1980, p. 2388-91.
4. Karr, Robert D., "Becoming a Library Director," LJ, February 15, 1983, p. 343-346.
5. Koenig, Michael E. D., "Education for Special Librarianship," Special Libraries, April 1983, p. 182-196.
6. White, Herbert S. "Education of Information Professionals" in Careers in Information, Jane F. Spivak, ed., Knowledge Industry Pubs, 1982, p. 135-156.

7. Koenig, Michael E. D. "The Information Controllability Explosion," LJ, November 1, p. 2052-54.
8. White, Herbert S., "Perceptions by Educators and Administrators of the Ranking of Library School Programs," College and Research Libraries, May 1981, p. 191-202.
9. Learmont, Carol L. & Stephen J. Van Houten, "Placements and Salaries 1981: Still Holding," LJ, October 1, 1982, p. 1821-27.
10. Association of Research Libraries, Education for the Research Library Professional, Minutes of the Ninety-Seventh Meeting, October 15-16, 1980, Arlington, Va. (Washington D.C., The Association, 1981), p. 28-35.
11. Marchant, Maurice & Nathan M. Smith, "The Research Library Director's View of Library Education," College and Research Libraries, November 1982, p. 437-444.

LIBRARIAN, SCHOLAR, OR AUTHOR?

THE LIBRARIAN'S NEW DILEMMA*

Frederick Isaac

Librarianship in the past 15 years has simultaneously faced old nemeses and found itself confronted by new challenges. Such perennial issues as budgeting and censorship have been joined, more insistently with every passing year, by the sets of problems created by computers. This development by itself would be adequate for us to ponder, as we will struggle with it for the predictable future. The other major issue of the 1970s, has been the question of our status within the academic community. Are librarians to be considered a professional group within the university setting, with special skills which deserve recognition? Or will librarians continue to be treated as secondary personnel on campus, subject to a different set of rules and circumstances from both teaching faculty and other members of the campus body.

In most of the instances where this question has been answered, the response has been positive. More promising still, the changed economics of the 1980s, while serious, have not yet eroded librarians' gains of academic rank and status, improved benefits, and more equitable pay scales. Even so, the continuation of difficulties has raised a different specter: the challenge of librarians' responsibilities as members of the scholarly fellowship. In particular the increased number of advanced degrees among librarians has been known since the mid-1970s. Additionally, the pressure on all librarians to contribute to the profession through the development, achievement, and publication of significant research has become more pressing than at any time in the past. These trends, both separately and in combination, and their relation to librarians' traditional role as providers of a service, constitute a three-part challenge to academic librarianship in the foreseeable future. As they are indivisible, they form a three-headed problem. Cerberus, the three-headed dog who guarded the ancient gates to Hell, is a legitimate comparison to our task.

*Reprinted by permission of the author and publisher from The Journal of Academic Librarianship, 9:4 (September 1983) 216-220; copyright © 1983 by the Journal of Academic Librarianship. All rights reserved.

To find the path which will best serve in the future, it is vital that librarians understand first precisely what the three concepts are. Second, we need to appreciate the place each of them has in the present situation. Finally, we have to begin to consider the role each of them can play in advancing the profession, and the possible ramifications various decisions might have. This essay is not intended as an exhaustive survey of our state, or as an argument in favor of one decision or another. Instead, it is an overview, containing suggestions for present and future analysis. Because the literature is not extensive and the condition recent, librarians cannot rely on the past for solutions. On the other hand, we must not act as if the gains already achieved are secure and inviolable.

Research and Publication in Librarianship

The earliest relevant work on the problem of research and publication by librarians may be Masse Bloomfield's article in College and Research Libraries.[1] While its statistical compilations are now more than 15 years old, and its stated purpose was to note the research done by members of the profession and correlate that to educational level, the results are striking enough to suggest major differences. Bloomfield's work confirmed the assumption that increased status (administrative positions) and the holding of earned degrees beyond the M.L.S. (primarily the Library Science doctorate) were reflected in the publication credits of librarians.

During the late 1960s, several articles, primarily in College and Research Libraries, discussed the primary issue of the time--gaining faculty status. In every case the authors saw the development as positive for the profession. They warned, though, that its attainment would require library directors and staff members to judge their performance on criteria similar to that employed by teaching faculty. On the other side of the question, it was generally agreed that adjustments in technique and measures used in evaluation should constitute an alternative to those used by teaching colleagues. A set of equivalent standards, never clearly specified or enumerated, was advocated instead. Lewis C. Branscomb's collection of these articles shows the development of this "parallel" evaluation concept, and clarifies the point that no discussion of the question-beyond that point was held at that time.[2]

Virgil Massman's book on faculty status, while it does not discuss at length the question of library research in its relationship to the added stature of the profession, does urge it strongly.[3] Librarians, he says pointedly, "have not even made a substantial beginning toward finding answers to the critical questions of how and why people use books, and what influence books exert on the reader." Elsewhere, Massman indicates the amount of publishing contributed by librarians and faculty members in a survey. Even the most cursory inspection of his charts finds less involvement by librarians of a decade ago than that of teachers.[4]

The achievement of the desired position as members of the faculty over the past decade has increased the need of librarians to employ their skills both in the library and in the wider academic context. The number of articles devoted to advice on increased interactions with the other faculty, and especially toward increased research, has grown substantially in the past few years. Notably, however, the articles have been neither consistent over time nor balanced through the literature. Three journals are the source of nearly all substantive information in this vital area since 1976: College and Research Libraries[5]; the Journal of Academic Librarianship[6]; and the Journal of Education for Librarianship.[7] It appears that no major articles have appeared in the other important academic voices of the profession: RQ; Library Trends; or Library Quarterly. [8]

While it would be unreasonable to characterize all of this publication, it is true that a sizable portion of it affirms the authors' commitment to the necessity for and value of research by librarians at the college and university level. The most negative response was by John Campbell, in a Wilson Library Bulletin article entitled "Overdue." Campbell expressed a sense of frustration at changes in the profession, and dismay at what he saw as undue emphasis on activities not devoted to service[9]. The preponderance of other negative comments falls into two major categories: the problem of research as it relates to the internal working of the library; and a venting of frustration at those who seem oblivious to the needs the writers see for continued examination of our work.

Among those articles which favor increased research by librarians, though, not all attitudes are positive. David Kaser, in his summation of the history of library publication, noted that "a very small segment of the profession at any given moment is the fountainhead of a very large share of the writing in the field.[10] Robert Steuart, commenting on the effects of library publishing, stated that "only a few articles ... by librarians have had an impact on nonlibrarians."[11] This, then, leads to the second question: Assuming the benefit of research, ought librarians to restrict it to their own discipline?

Publishing in Other Disciplines

Rush G. Miller, in the same issue of College and Research Libraries as Kaser's and Steuart's articles, verified the growing number of earned doctorates in librarianship.[12] His essay serves much the same purpose as Bloomfield's work a decade earlier by making us aware of our changed situation. And while Miller does not attempt to answer the question of his title, "Intrusion or Transfusion," his concern is obvious. He clearly wishes to awaken the profession to the need for continued education, both doctorates in librarianship and advanced degrees in other subject disciplines. Without additional study no absolute numbers are available, but it appears that since Miller's article the trend has gained strength. Holders of advanced degrees continue to enter the profession, while working librarians increasingly return to school, part- or full-time, for additional training in the subjects of their choice. Advertisements in the Chronicle of Higher Education now routinely ask for linguistic competence as well as training in a field of specialization, especially (but not solely) where the position demands unique bibliographic skills.

With this process already under way, it is notable that only in 1981 did the situation appear directly in the journal literature. In one instance Priscilla Heahigan and her colleagues at Purdue University gave a summary of their work in establishing a specific set of criteria for judging the value of research and publication; this appeared late in the year.[13] As revised in 1978 the Purdue policy on promotion and tenure (which involved the retention of staff as well) states that library-related publication will receive preferential treatment over articles in future evaluations of staff members. Only months before, M. Kathy Cook published her study of Southern Illinois University at Carbondale faculty.[14] This work suggests that librarians (those at Carbondale, at least) have substantial support from teachers in their search for equality, but that this approval is by no means overwhelming; pockets of resistance still continue.

In addition to these elements the 1981 American Library Association Conference in San Francisco gave even greater currency to the question of education and research. At the RTSD Collection Development meeting the half-dozen speakers first presented their impressions of skills needed and assumptions they felt the audience (bibliographers, collection development specialists, and acquisitions librarians) must make in the coming years.[15] The lengthy floor discussion which followed the talks, though, revolved mostly on the question of obtaining credentials (should I get a Ph.D.?) and on the demonstration of competency in areas visible and acceptable to faculty. This expression of concern (mixed at times with resentment) reflects the widespread willingness of academic librarians to meet the standards of the rest of academia. It also brings forth a worry that, by not advancing into the realms of nonlibrary scholarship, librarians risk at some point relinquishing at least a portion of their hard-won gains, psychological if not actual.

In this connection research and publication take on different tones. Geahigan and her coauthors note that the "clarification" of the policy originated when an applicant for a library job "stated that she would only publish in English Literature."[16] With such a possibility increasingly likely in the future, it seems at least reasonable to ask if we ought to refuse those who seek such rewards the satisfaction of their success. At worst, librarians may find themselves haunted, when teachers and administrators suggest that librarian's skills as scholars do not meet their criteria of academic competence. In addition, is anyone willing to say that the high level of talent now entering librarianship will continue without our acknowledgement of all significant achievements by librarians?

Those Who Don't Want to Publish

The third group in the library profession is composed of those who either find little interest in publishing, or remain satisfied with fulfilling the historic mission of service. Their major concerns have not been adequately heard, for obvious reasons. When librarians of this persuasion do express their fears, the matter grows more substantial and more difficult to deal with. John Campbell's essay, already cited, speaks of librarians being "hidden away" and "service ... moved to the back burner." "I'm here in the library," he says, "for the students and faculty of the college."[17] Several participants in a Journal of Academic Librarianship symposium, "The Role of the Academic Librarian," expressed interest and worry over the effects of research on the performance of our traditional, service-oriented jobs.[18]

Additional concerns refer to the effects of library research on the internal functioning of the institution, particularly if it results in the granting of "research leave time" during normal working hours. Cook's research notes that 8 percent of her respondents "indicated that librarians should not conduct research" and "13 percent ... indicated that no time should be given to librarians for research use." [19] At the California Library Association's California State University and College Librarians' section meeting in December 1981, one of the participants raised other essential questions: What, for example, are the morale problems of nonresearch librarians, doing the work temporarily relinquished by those given leave? What staffing adjustments must be made to accommodate the time and work alterations? What sorts of compromises will be required to properly evaluate and compensate those whose decision not to pursue research results in their receiving an increased workload, unwanted responsibilities, and possibly additional time on the job?[20]

Added to all of these concerns of librarians who do not choose to advance through research channels, Kellam and Barker's study of libraries in the late 1960s sheds still another light on the question. Their survey suggested that, far from pushing in only one direction, directors advocated a large number of activities for staff members. Ten of these received approval from 70 percent of the respondents, and three of these were unanimously supported: "Writing and Publication"; "Campus Committee and Similar Assignments"; and "Professional Service on Local, State and National Basis." "Research," with no designation of publication, was encouraged by 97 percent of the survey.[21] Notable too is that neither the publication nor the research categories are specified as library-oriented. While the intervening years have probably altered the percentages, the support for involvement in research may not be as simply decided or as clear-cut as some of its advocates now maintain.

Avoiding a Caste System

These, then, are the three divisions into which Academic librarianship is being segmented on the question of research. One sees the call by Massman and the others for investigation of these problems as paramount, and wants to focus all possible effort into library-oriented examinations as the major aim of the profession. Another branch wishes to be free of such limits and to work in fields beyond our immediate discipline's bounds, even if, as in Purdue's policy, it is "interpreted broadly."[22] The third portion, as constituted and understood here, is satisfied with our conventional role; even so, it asks whether, in light of the presence of the others and their direction, its members should be considered in light of their increased contribution. The conflicts among these bodies of opinion may well turn them into factions in the coming years. If librarians are not wary, the groups interested in research could attempt to exclude the third, creating a sort of caste system. Similarly, the current discussion of criteria for faculty-library relations, education, and research, will likely intensify, to our dismay and the possible long-term destruction of our recently acquired status.

Role of Professional Education.

Even if librarians do not descend to internecine warfare, a great deal of discussion needs to take place. A host of determinations must be made in the space of the next few years. The role of professional education should be examined to determine whether--and if so, to what extent--library schools dissuade their students from pursuing advanced research, and further education in subject disciplines. This will lead to problems related to library-user interactions (especially with faculty) and librarians' competency as on-the-job researchers and analysts of abstruse data. On another level the continuing segmentation of the profession should be scrutinized. (We have already effectively withdrawn information science from library science; might the functions of administration be presently growing distant from the more directly book-related functions we perform?) In short, are we reaching a level where the profession is developing fissures among its parts and roles? In a related area, despite the large number of journals in the field, the continued narrowing of their content is evidence of the widening gap among practictioners. Finally, the practice of encouraging research and allowing working time for it should undergo inspection in light of the current situation. Given the restricted availability of money and staff, are we properly utilizing all of the possible options?

The inquiry carries into all three "classes" of librarians defined here. Those interested in library study should be asked to defend their work, both for the institutional value and for the profession at large. To assume that a particular study is valuable simply because it is related to the library may not be wise. Librarians cannot stop investigating themselves, and should do it more, but must also remain wary and rigorous as they proceed, responsible both to themselves and their standards, and to the general high academic level they aspire to attain. There may be, for example, too many "gee, look what we found" studies still receiving praise in library

Libraries and Librarians 67

circles. Prestige should be neither automatic nor easy to obtain, but should be available to those who deserve it.

Relationship With Other Academic Realms.

On the second side of the question, librarians no longer consider their discipline either superior or inferior to other academic realms. Librarians need the wider relationships and recognition that can come only from challenging the professionals in departmental subjects in their own spheres. Those present at the RTSD meeting cited earlier clearly felt a need to provide their institutional colleagues with credentials that command respect. The growing number of librarians with further background testifies to the broadening of our responsibilities. [23]

To be thought of as full members of the academic community, librarians should be open to all avenues of serious research. One study on this path might attempt to discover whether nonteachers (librarians especially) who attempt to publish in subject-scholarly journals are published; or are they overlooked because they lack the recognized affiliation, the proper departmental letterhead, or the name of a friend of the editor which would ensure quick consideration? Last, James Wyatt, in the JAL symposium, notes that not all faculty members are constantly immersed in their work as scholars. [24] If this is so, much academic publishing may not be beyond reach. If librarians can help to raise the level of a discipline's discourse, or can change its direction by submitting their own work, they should be encouraged to do so.

Performance Within the Library.

The clichéd argument in defense of those librarians who do not perform outside their narrow area is that "after all, this is what we are paid to do." In fact this response does not respond to the problems raised here. The question for the future is the relationship of the variety of roles librarians must perform. Hiding behind the simplest definition of the work will not help us. On the other hand, the question must be asked by all of us whether librarians can afford to do without those who care more about the book, the catalogs, and the public than outside options. Are we willing to downgrade such people because they express no interest in the wider areas of publication or the problems of the investigator, but who wish instead to perform the library's every-day tasks? What will be the ramifications of inserting a third level into the already controversial gap between professionals and nonprofessionals, support staff, library assistants, etc. who already do many of the institution's chores? What are the internal politics we might expect as the dichotomy grows? Friendships, working groups, rivalries and competition will be constantly growing and shifting as librarians involve themselves in on-the-job research projects. How much thought has yet been given to this aspect of the library as a social organization? Additional work should clarify the effects of increased part-time staff (or decreased available full-time personnel), interdepartmental workers, and intrusions caused by the researchers themselves as they hunt for their data within the library.

Conclusion

This ongoing specialization has created a new relationship between librarians and the rest of the academic community. To continue to enhance service, librarians clearly will need more and better research into all aspects of the profession. Moreover, teaching colleagues will expect us to study our tools and methods and improve them, to serve their own needs. If the conferring of faculty status on librarians is significant, it means most of all that we are at last seen increasingly as equals, and not merely the servants of the university community.

While agreeing with Paula Watson and all of the others who have advocated continued and increased library research, we cannot retreat into a corner and isolate ourselves. Watson's call for "clear and reasonable criteria ... in all areas ... of academic excellence" should not result in a narrowing of our vision.[25] Placing librarians apart from others denies, first of all, the interrelationship of all knowledge, which is the very premise of the university. Also, if librarians are unable to use the tools we give to our colleagues in our own work, our practical skills become suspect. Third, as mentioned above, the development of a scholarly group of librarians is already in progress, and is in fact a long-sought goal of the profession. If librarians refuse to allow coworkers the benefits of their special tools and resources, we do our cause no good, while encouraging them can only enhance librarians' status.

While we urge the advancement of the profession in all scholarly ways and by all avenues, librarians must not forget that the underlying reason for all research we do is to help our clients, universities, and the world. Better performance of these immediate, assigned tasks is the hoped-for result of all of our efforts. To deny recognition to those who perform this work so that others can follow other roads is at least questionable in a political sense. At worst, it demeans the work itself.

The conflict between and among the three groups, their interrelations, and the increasing complexity of their needs are only beginning to be felt. The library field is growing ever more sophisticated, as computers and cataloging, administration and acquisitions all develop in slightly different ways. Librarians face difficult times in many areas, internal, institutional, and societal. As the major collectors, organizers, and purveyors of information, we need to develop all of our resources and study all portions of the academic world. To propound solutions for any part of the problems faced, without understanding the intent, immediate results, and long-term implications of our actions can only lead to more serious situations than we can now envision.

References

1. Masse Bloomfield, "The Writing Habits of Librarians," College and Research Libraries, 27 (March 1966): 109-119.
2. Lewis C. Branscomb, ed., The Case for Faculty Status for Librarians (Chicago: American Library Association: ACRL Monograph #33, 1970).
3. Virgil Massman, Faculty Status for Librarians (Metuchen, NJ: Scarecrow, 1972).
4. Ibid., p. 62, 140-141.
5. With 12 usable citations, College and Research Libraries is by far the most fruitful journal for information in the area.
6. Journal of Academic Librarianship's four articles include two symposia: "The Three Faces of Eve: or the Identity of Academic Librarianship," edited by H. William Axford with 10 participants, 2 (January 1977): 276-285; and "The Role of the Academic Librarian," edited by Beverly J. Toy with 8 participants, 3 (July 1978): 128-138. The discussions are extremely thought-provoking.
7. The five citations here are deceptive. Four of them are derived from talks given at the AALS conference of January 1979. See Journal of Education for Librarianship, 20 (Fall 1979): 114-148.
8. If there exists a serious lack in the situation to date, it is here. These journals appear to have underestimated the problem thus far.
9. John Campbell, "Overdue: Publish or Perish; Library Style," Wilson Library Bulletin, 52 (November 1977): 250.
10. David Kaser, "A Century of Academic Librarianship as Reflected in its Literature," College and Research Libraries 37 (March 1976): 125.
11. Robert D. Steuart, "Writing the Journal Article," College and Research Libraries, 153 (March 1976): 37.
12. Rush G. Miller, "The Influx of Ph.D.s into Librarianship: Intrusion or Transfusion," College and Research Libraries, 37 (March 1976): 158-165.
13. Priscilla Geahigan, Harriet Nelson, Stewart Saunders, and Lawrence Woods, "Acceptability of Non Library/Information Science Publications in the Promotion and Tenure of Academic Librarians," College and Research Libraries, 42 (November 1981): 571-575.
14. M. Kathy Cook, "Rank, Status and Contribution of Academic Librarians as Perceived by the Teaching Faculty at Southern Illinois University, Carbondale," College and Research Libraries, 42 (May 1981): 214-223.
15. American Library Association Conference Program, San Francisco, June, 1981, p. 142 and Author's notes.
16. Geahigan, "Acceptability," p. 571.
17. Campbell, "Overdue," p. 250.

18. Most notable of these are Willis Bridegam, "A Research Requirement for Librarians," and Thomas M. Schmid, "Shoemaker, Stick...." in Toy, Journal of Academic Librarianship, 4 (July 1978): 135-137.
19. Cook, "Rank, Status and Contribution," p. 218.
20. California Library Association Conference Program, San Francisco, December 1981, p. 33 and Author's notes.
21. W. Porter Kellam and Dale L. Barker, "Opportunities and Activities of University Librarians for Full Participation in the Educational enterprise," in Branscomb, The Case for Faculty Status for Librarians, p. 61.
22. Geahigan, "Acceptability," p. 573.
23. Geahigan, "Acceptability," p. 572. Ironically, Geahigan cites proponents of a strong statement favoring library-related publication, who commented on the "inappropriate" nature of outside research in the tenure of teaching faculty. The example of Alchemy and Arthurian Legend may be designed to discourage further discussion. In fact, it raises again the question of crossing academic disciplines (Historians of Science, for example). The give-and-take of other academics is growing, and there is a question whether, by limiting our scope, we may not do ourselves a disservice.
24. James F. Wyatt, "Defining 'Academic' Librarianship," in Toy, Journal of Academic Librarianship, 4 (July 1978): 133.
25. Paula deSimone Watson, "Publication Activity among Academic Librarians," College and Research Libraries, 38 (September 1977): 375.

MYTHS AND REALITIES: THE ACADEMIC VIEWPOINT II*

Gresham Riley

The word myth is clouded in ambiguity. On the one hand, myth can mean a false belief or a belief that, if not false, has no determinable basis in fact. An example would be the belief that it is possible for one of the superpowers to be the winner in a nuclear war. On the other hand, myth can mean a story or fable that, although lacking factual or historical accuracy, nevertheless contains profound insights about the human condition or that of a people or a culture. Myth, in this sense, brings to mind Prometheus, Icarus, or the Garden of Eden. In this paper, I shall use myth as "false belief" and suggest seven such myths.

The first two myths have to be discussed together because they are mirror images of each other.

Myth #1: The library is the heart of a college, with classrooms and laboratories serving (to extend our anatomical image) as the brain.

Myth #2: The classroom and the laboratory are the center of the educational process, with the library functioning in a secondary support role.

Clearly, these two myths are contradictory and would cancel each other if they were not held by different groups: librarians and academic faculty. What are the realities?

Reality #1: The library is not the heart of a college for many faculty members. Teaching faculty do not view professional librarians as equal partners in the teaching-learning process, but view them as they do residence hall directors, counselors in the career center, or athletic coaches. As scholars, most academic faculty are not predisposed to recognize and to acknowledge a legitimate educational role for the library and for librarians. Faculty members often need to be brought to this recognition and acknowledgment through education. Further, they are more likely to be influenced

---

*Reprinted by permission of the author and publisher from College & Research Libraries, 45:5 (September 1984) 367-369; copyright © 1984 by the American Library Association.

by local conditions (in particular, the attitude of key college or university administrators toward the role of the library) than by their prior experience or their role as scholars. Finally, many faculty members consider bibliographic instruction as an "add-on" to the basic course work, they consider mastery of the library to be an easy task, and they believe extensive use of the library to be appropriate for only the brightest students. For the majority, the library should serve as a study hall.

Clearly, the library is not the heart of a college if one takes seriously the beliefs and practices of many faculty members. Moreover, the transmission of information, the trial and error of experimentation, and the give and take of ideas in seminar discussions are all made possible by the classroom and the laboratory. They have to be placed at the heart of the college even if they must share this central spot with other functions.

Reality #2: It has been argued that the principal objectives of an undergraduate liberal arts and science education are the following:

- Preparation for responsible citizenship in a democratic, pluralistic, and technological society.
- Understanding of and appreciation for the actual and the possible relationships between and among disciplines--in short, the gaining of interdisciplinary insight.
- Development of the ability to think critically and analytically about normative issues.
- Acquisition of skills related to lifelong learning.

Because our formal education in the classroom and the laboratory represents only a small amount of time in the average life span, this last objective (skills related to lifelong learning) is especially important if we are to avoid intellectual and creative stagnation. What are these skills? Among them, certainly, are the following:

- The ability to identify a problem or issue worthy of investigation.
- Knowledge of relevant sources of information that might solve the problem or clarify the issue.
- Possession of criteria that allow one to know when a problem has or has not been solved or when an issue has or has not been clarified.

I believe that the library and the professional librarian have a major and equal role to play in meeting at least one of the objectives of a liberal arts and science education. The obvious basis for this belief is that the mastery of library search strategies is central to those skills that make lifelong learning possible. Consequently, no matter what other functions and other people might be found at the center of the educational process, the library and librarians have a legitimate claim on that space.

If the acquisition of lifelong learning skills is one of the primary objectives of higher education and if the library and librarians can play a vital role in the development of these skills, then we can expose three additional myths.

Myth #3: Extensive use of the library is for only the brightest students; for the rest, it is merely a study hall.

Reality #3: The reality is that we have failed our students if they graduate without possessing those skills that will allow them to continue to learn once their formal schooling is over. Life expectancy in the United States is seventy-three years. For most of our graduates, this means fifty-two years during which their minds can continue to be challenged and expanded. Consequently, every student must become familiar with the library as a learning laboratory that can be used throughout life.

Myth #4: Bibliographic instruction is an "add-on" to the disciplinary content of a course.

Reality #4: The reality is that knowledge of how to frame a question for investigation and of how to identify and locate relevant resources for answering the question--in short, knowledge about how to solve problems--is as central to academic disciplines as their factual content. Course-centered bibliographic instruction, as a joint effort by both library and instructional faculty, can result in the acquisition by the student of skills in learning how to learn. As such, bibliographic instruction is integrally related to the primary content of every course.

Myth #5: The teaching faculty in the various academic disciplines are the only educators.

Reality #5: The mistaken assumption upon which our fifth myth is based is that the classroom exhausts the educational universe. This myth is deeply rooted in the erroneous belief that "education" and "schooling" are the same. Education involves any experience or activity that yields instructive insights about nature, men and women, society, or about the processes by which such insights are gained. Education, in this sense, is virtually coextensive with life. Schooling, on the other hand, involves the orderly transmission and evaluation of formal bodies of knowledge, skills, and values. As such, schooling requires some degree of structure, regimen, and discipline--thus, the formal curricula that we have in our colleges and universities.

Once the distinction between education and schooling is acknowledged, it is easy to see that the classroom does not exhaust the educational universe. Furthermore, it becomes clear that librarians are educators no less than are biologists, political scientists, and philosophers. This conclusion is underscored by the fact (which has been demonstrated in the discussion of the previous myth) that bibliographic instruction is integrally related to the primary content of every academic course. Librarians are, indeed, equal partners in the teaching-learning process. This brings us to our final two myths.

Myth #6: Learning how to use an academic library is an easy task.

Reality #6: The reality is that learning how to learn is as complex as learning philosophy or chemistry. It should come as no surprise, then, that course-centered bibliographic instruction, if done properly, will be gradated and differentiated. This is to say that specialized bibliographic instruction is needed at different points in a student's educational career. For example, certain resources and certain search strategies are appropriate for general reference work in a freshman composition course; others for an introductory biology course; yet others for an advanced course in genetics; others in a student's major field of study; others for a particular course in a discipline; and still others in interdisciplinary subject areas such as urban studies or women's studies.

Mastery of the library will not result from a tour during student orientation, from viewing a slide-tape production in the learning resources center, or from taking an adjunct course. The issue is simply more serious and more complex than suggested by such responses.

Myth #7: The library is a well-defined place on campus.

Reality #7: The reality is that an academic library is less a place than an array of functions and services to be found in many locations. If bibliographic instruction is course-centered (as I believe it should be), then faculty members and professional librarians will be working together for the purpose of determining how best to intergrate bibliographic instruction with the other objectives of the course. This means that librarians will be called upon by faculty not only to plan courses but also to evaluate the bibliographies that students use for their research papers. As a result, the library is wherever courses are.

Furthermore, as card catalogs are taken out of boxes and placed in computers, and as lending networks are created through ever-more-sophisticated programs, library search activities will spread across the campus, and the library will become all those places from which documents can be drawn. Even now, but more so in the future, academic libraries will be less substance or a place than function or an activity.

Myths, in the sense of stories that convey profound insights about the human condition, are to be cherished, preserved, and transmitted. Myths, in the sense of false beliefs, are to be exposed. For too long, myths have prevented academic libraries from fulfilling their educational mission within our colleges and universities. The time has come for these myths to be broken.

Part II

COMMUNICATION AND EDUCATION

USER CATEGORIES AND USER CONVENIENCE IN SUBJECT CATALOGING*

Francis Miksa

Introduction[1]

One of the most pervasive beliefs of American subject catalogers is that the subject heading element of the dictionary catalog should be constructed on the principle of user convenience. In its narrowest sense, this means that individual subject headings should be chosen on the basis of what terms are commonly used by patrons in their subject searching. Charles A. Cutter had this in mind in his discussion of equally useful compound subject names: "When there is any decided usage (i.e., custom of the public to designate the subjects by one of the names rather than by the others) let it be followed.[2] In a broader sense the idea of user convenience means that all aspects of subject heading work--choices concerning specificity, term syntax, synonyms, etc.--should reflect the way users approach the catalog. David J. Haykin, the first chief of the Subject Cataloging Division of the Library of Congress, expressed this more comprehensive view in 1951 when he concluded that, "the reader is the focus in all cataloging principles and practice."[3]

The chief difficulty with these conceptions, and one which has led some to doubt the idea of user convenience, is their vagueness in referring to users. It is not enough to say that the subject heading system should be convenient to users. One must also be able to identify in some meaningful way who the users are that are to be served and what constitutes their "convenience." Paul S. Dunkin, among others, questioned whether this could be done:

> Is there such a creature as "the user"; or are there (as with costs) many users each with his individual habits?....Even if we find "the user," can we safely build our practice to fit him--or shall we keep on making studies to find out if "the user" (just as you and I) changes habits and ways of thinking from time to time?[4]

---

*Reprinted by permission of the author and publisher from The Reference Librarian No. 9 (Fall/Winter 1983) 113-132; copyright © 1984 by The Haworth Press, Inc. All rights reserved.

Dunkin's questions to the contrary, subject catalogers have not been remiss in identifying users and what is necessary for making the subject catalog convenient for them. They have done so in terms of user categories--identifying users in terms of recognizable groups. The makeup of these user categories has changed significantly over the years, however, and aspects of user categories, especially those more recently identified, raise questions as to whether they are a meaningful way to conceptualize patrons at all.

The purpose of this paper is to summarize and offer critical observations about the kinds of user categories to which subject catalogers have resorted over the years. It is assumed that the usefulness of this task is not limited to what it says for subject catalogers alone, but extends as well to other kinds of library professionals-- in the case here to reference librarians--insofar as they too tend to justify their work on the basis of user categories and their characteristics.[5]

Cutter and User Convenience[6]

Charles A. Cutter, who is generally thought of as the father of the dictionary catalog and the first to state the idea of user convenience, divided the library's public into three general kinds of "inquirers":

1. those who want something quickly;
2. those who want to make a thorough study of some specific subject; and
3. those who want to study fully some general class of subjects.[7]

He concluded that the first group was the "loudest and largest" of the three. While this group was most dependent on a catalog and was, in fact, the reason for the popularity of the "ordinary dictionary catalogue," its members were essentially "desultory" in their approach to books, subject searching, and the use of the library in general. They were impatient, wanting an answer for their book search as quickly as possible, regardless of what that yielded. They were also generally undisciplined in their searching and, in fact, "averse to mental effort," often uncomprehending of the fact that useful information might be found under synonymous terms or that topics were by definition part of a structured universe of subjects. What they most often searched for were books that were listed under captions for general categories of literature--as if to say, "I want a philosophical work" or "I want a fiction work" or "I want a religious work." In Cutter's opinion, they did not care "about the particular subject of the book so much as whether it be well written and interesting."[8]

The other two groups of inquirers were set apart from the first by two essential factors. First, to varying degrees they approached subject searching with an awareness of classificatory subject relationships. Second, to varying degrees they understood that subject searching was tantamount to disciplined investigation that required patience, effort, and the realization that not all their needs could be met by any catalog. These two categories differed essentially only in the breadth of their searching strategy. The second group tended to focus on specific subjects, aware of the need, for example, to find the various works on those subjects and compare them critically as to their worth, but not always insistent on searching for such topics in terms of their larger classificatory relationships. In contrast, the third group tended to approach any subject search in terms of a strong sense of classificatory structure, beginning broadly and working downward to the more specific elements of the whole.

Some of the foregoing characteristics of Cutter's user categories might well be familiar to the modern cataloger or reference librarian. For example, in the course of meeting the public, what librarian has not encountered at least occasionally the aimless user whose appreciation of the library's attempts to organize its resources for subject access are almost nil; or in contrast, the patron who approaches a subject area in such a structured way that any variation from that structure appears as a hindrance.

What will not be generally apparent among moderns, however, is the fact that Cutter's user categories and characteristics actually arose from a highly structured and uniform sense of the universe of subjects and from a well-developed psychology of the public. Both of these factors came from his exposure to the tenets of the philosophical school called Scottish common sense realism commonly taught at most American institutions of higher education before the Civil War. Cutter did not approach the universe of subjects represented in the subject heading system as a conglomerate of separate specialized fields each with their own unique logics and structures, but rather as a unified whole. Furthermore, he subdivided that unitary universe of knowledge into classes and subclasses not only by intrinsic logical relationships within cohesive subject areas, but even more so by a categorical approach to subjects themselves. In his system, specificity or the degree of narrowness in any particular subject was a function of the relative degree of concreteness or abstraction that the subject term represented. Thus, great specificity meant greater concreteness whereas great breadth referred to greater abstractness. On this basis, the subject relationships between all subjects could be determined with some facility. And because they could be so determined, both the subject catalogers and the user (once having learned the idea of degrees of concreteness) could predict entry patterns and citation order in the system with consistency and ease.

User categories were also not distinct and mutually exclusive for Cutter, but actually elements of a single continuum of use. Desultory and advanced readers were differentiated not in some absolute way but rather only in terms of the respective development of the same set of mental powers that all readers had. In short, there was no essential difference between the basic mental structure and thinking processes of any of the three categories of inquirers. Their minds functioned in the same way. The only difference was in the way the minds of the different categories of users had been educated (i.e., cultivated) and, therefore, how much of their natural mental potential for knowledge acquisition was brought to the subject searching process. Desultory readers, because of their lack of mental conditioning, tended to search only for the simplest of subjects-- those that were most concrete (i.e., works about individual subjects represented especially as persons or places)--whereas advanced readers went well beyond such simple or specific subjects either by searching under equivalent meanings or by searching subjects of greater generality (i.e., of less concreteness). In either case advanced readers developed search strategies that depended on their varying knowledge of the unitary universe of knowledge of which all subjects occupied categorical positions. The essential point to be noted was that any desultory reader could through mental exercise and self improvement move into the other categories in a natural way. The groups were not in effect separated by some insurmountable and necessary barrier.

Cutter's sense of unity in the world of subjects and among users had a striking effect on his approach to the subject element of the dictionary catalog. The most important result was that it allowed Cutter to justify the specific entry structure of his dictionary subject catalog. Specific entry, which required entry of a work under the single most concrete subject treated in the work--especially persons and places--was necessary because the largest class of users (desultory readers) would be most helped by that approach. At the same time, advanced readers were also served by his catalog because the various specific entries had been tied together with an infrastructure of cross-references that referred from subjects of greater generality to concrete and, therefore, more specific subjects and by subarranging the works under specific entries by terms of greater generality that would indicate to advanced readers the broader topics to which the specific or concrete topics were related.

Cutter's sense of unity also allowed him to justify particular subject heading decisions related to user convenience. For example, in the common absence of any indications of which one of several equivalent compound subject names in a book was to be chosen as the heading he regularly chose the one that began with terms of greater rather than lesser concreteness because it was more likely to be looked up by the largest class of inquirers. At the same time, advanced inquirers, those of the second and third types, would be provided with great predictability in subject searching. Given a subject search of any coordinated set of subjects, one need only look under the more concrete subject in the coordination to see if it were in the catalog. If it were not found, one might then look under the less concrete topic to see if there were some more general works that upon close examination included the more concrete qualification in their texts. It was this kind of predictability that was the basis of Cutter's remarks that his specific entry system provided "facility of reference."[9] He meant that because the system always had a most specific or concrete beginning point for entry, all categories of inquirers could depend upon it in a predictable way.

User Categories: Shifting Ideas at the Turn of the Century[10]

Cutter introduced the foregoing ideas about users and subject headings during the mid-1870s and did not thereafter alter them in any significant way. In fact, there is a distinct sense that when he wrote them they were already outdated because the Scottish thinking upon which they were based was already a century old and fast being replaced by such newer currents of thought as idealism and pragmatism. Thus, when the fourth and posthumous edition of his Rules were published in 1904, it is not surprising that a new generation of subject catalogers, while just as concerned about user convenience as Cutter had been, was expressing that concern in a way significantly different than Cutter had expressed it in the subject heading section of his Rules.

Several different aspects of this newer point of view are important to note. First, the unitary universe of subjects and subject relationships that had been fundamental to Cutter's approach to subject access was already beginning to disintegrate into the more familiar twentieth century panoply of subjects as a vast array of widely divergent fields each of which has a distinct and unique classification structure. No better example of this change can be found than in the construction of the Library of Congress Classification between 1898 and 1910, where the scheme was developed as a series of relatively separate topical areas united superficially only by a vague overall organizational structure and by such mechanical internal arrangement features as alphabetical, chronological and geographical subdivision patterns. Second, the notion of scholarly endeavor itself was changing at an accelerated pace. In Cutter's scheme of things a scholar referred to a person whose mental cultivation was sufficiently advanced that he or she pursued subject knowledge with an understanding of the uniform classificatory structure of the singular universe of subjects and their relationships. By the first decade of the twentieth century, however, a scholar was already coming to mean one who had become familiar with or who was in the process of learning a special segment of the universe of subjects. In other words, a scholar (and the idea of scholarliness) was becoming defined not simply by how a person knew what he knew, but more importantly by what he knew in terms of a specialized subject area.[11] Third, the organization of professional library interests had become sufficiently advanced that the library movement itself began to be self-differentiated into the more specialized library interests and tasks. This, in turn, provided a basis for two essentially new approaches to user categories that, when combined with the idea of special areas of knowledge and the notion of specialist scholars, had a profound effect on how user categories and, therefore, user convenience were viewed. Those approaches were library differentiation by size and library differentiation by type.

Library Differentiation by Size[12]

The first decisive break in the cohesiveness of the expanding American professional library community after its beginnings in 1876 occurred as librarians began to differentiate their tasks and needs in terms of the relative sizes of their libraries. Specifically, librarians from small, often rural or small town libraries and mid-western in location, found themselves at odds with librarians from larger, principally urban, public libraries, often located in the East. The conflict between these segments of the professional library community was expressed in such ways as the rise of competing organizations both within and outside the ALA, the growth and role of the ALA Council, the concern of the ALA Publishing Board especially between 1895 and 1915 to publish practical works for librarians of small libraries and, ultimately, the move of ALA headquarters in 1909 to the Midwest.[13]

Subject catalogers expressed this same conflict in a period of public debate during the first decade of the twentieth century by focusing their attention on the differences between subject catalogs made for large libraries and those made for small libraries. It should be noted that the fact that such a debate took place at all was due to the advent of readily available subject heading copy, first after 1895 in the form of the ALA List of Subject Headings, and, second, after 1901 in the form of subject headings included on the printed cards of the Library of Congress. Prior to those innovations, subject catalogers either had to devise their own subject headings or copy the subject headings found in exemplary printed catalogs. Because both methods were difficult, however, they tended to discourage subject catalog construction. In contrast, the appearance of readily available subject heading copy brought the reality of subject catalogs within the reach of every library.

The use of lists and copy for card catalogs brought about two unique difficulties of their own. First, their availability began the long tradition of list-oriented subject cataloging in which the idea of making subject headings that adequately expressed subject specialization in particular instances became subservient to subject heading choices more or less confined to those headings already devised by the authorities who supplied the headings. Second, and more important for the discussion here, subject heading lists, with their extensive subheadings, and subject heading copy found on catalog cards promoted a new sense of what a subject heading was. Prior to this time a subject heading was considered the lead term above a columnar listing of works in a printed dictionary catalog (i.e., it was a subject term at the "head" of each such list or file). Any particular listing might also be subarranged by still other terms placed among the entries below the heading but those terms were not technically a part of the heading. Their separation from the heading was emphasized by the use of different type faces for each. In contrast, card catalogs required that a heading and its subarrangement terms be listed together as a string-of-terms on the top of a unit card entry. This format change encouraged subject catalogers to identify the entire string-of-terms found together on the top of any one card as a subject heading rather than only the conventionally named initial term found in the string. And identification of entire strings-of-terms as subject headings in turn raised questions of complexity in syntax that had not previously been encountered. In fact, questions of complexity constituted the chief issue that highlighted the public discussion of the differences between subject catalogs made respectively for large or for small libraries.

"Small libraries" was the common term used to identify a cohesive group of institutions that included smaller and medium-sized public libraries, and branches of large urban libraries, and libraries or departments of libraries that served children. Large libraries included the main headquarters of urban libraries and academic libraries of all kinds. A moment's reflection will show that the difference between these groups was not actually the physical size of the libraries involved nor even in many respects the sizes of their collections, although collection size was important. Rather, the chief difference was in the kinds of clientele they served. It was concluded that large libraries principally served what had come to be known by the turn of the century as scholars and students, those patrons who used books and searched for subjects in a serious and disciplined manner. These users had the skills necessary for using such subject access tools as complex dictionary subject catalogs, subject bibliographies, and classified catalogs; in short, bibliographical tools that were generally sophisticated in their structure and that arranged subjects with some regard to their classificatory relationships. In contrast, small libraries primarily served that much more extensive population of readers whose bibliographical skills and intellectual motivation were thought to be much less developed and, in many cases almost nonexistent. The former were characterized as above-average, the latter as average readers.

The similarity between these two categories of users and Cutter's categories of users is striking. Cutter had also envisioned a range of users that at either extreme appeared to include the same characteristics as those listed here. But this is as far as the similarity goes. The user groups representing extremes in Cutter's portrayal of the public, while differing in their abilities in somewhat the same way, retained an important likeness. They all functioned with the same mental processes, their differences owing only to the lack of the development of mental potential among average or desultory readers. Here, the two groups were essentially different. The notion of advanced or above-average readers which implied the kind of subject specialization already described as having occurred by the turn of the century suggested that scholars and students were different from average readers not simply because of their intellectual skills, but also because of their specialist training. In practical terms this meant that the two kinds of users were different in kind as well as in degree and that there was a necessary and significant gap between them. Furthermore where Cutter's approach to users led him to conclude that the same subject system might structurally serve the entire range of users, here for the first time one finds the conclusion that libraries of either type and, therefore, library users were different to such a degree that the subject catalogs that served each group must also be different in some significant way. Incorporating that difference in subject heading systems constructed for the two kinds of libraries--large and small--was the essential question addressed during the first decade public debate on subject cataloging.

Subject catalogs made for large libraries with their primarily more sophisticated and specialist scholar and student users required headings of greater specificity. This meant that headings were needed that more nearly matched the topical scopes of the increasingly "minute" (i.e., more specific) subjects of a growing volume of publications then beginning to be issued by an active and expanding scholarly press. These catalogs also required the use of greater numbers of subdivision devices in order to control the length of individual subject heading files. And, most importantly, because subject heading workers remained committed to the idea that headings must represent a serious attempt to use conventional subject names, they had to resort to still other devices that controlled the normal scattering that the use of conventional subject names promoted.

The most important effort to fulfill these needs occurred in the initial development of the subject heading system of the Library of Congress between 1898 and 1910. J. C. M. Hanson, the chief architect of the system, was aware from the beginning that the Library of Congress system needed large numbers of complex headings to meet its needs. He also incorporated significant incursions of classificatory sequencing in the architecture of the system, some of it by the outright choice of undivided class entry terms, some of it by the outright choice of divided class entry strings-of-terms, and much of it by the use of manipulated heading syntax, especially through inversion. As a result, the Library of Congress subject heading system that Hanson created was not a pure dictionary subject catalog of the kind that Cutter had designed but rather a hybrid catalog of a distinctly unique cast. Its classificatory features were especially striking because the various classificatory sequences chosen for inclusion in the subject catalog reflected and were often based on the Library's classification scheme then being developed. In other words, choosing one or another subject area collocation pattern in the subject heading system functioned as a shadow of the classification scheme, sometimes following it closely, sometimes purposefully providing its opposite, but in each case bound to the same kind of field-by-field special subject structure that characterized the shelf scheme. Hanson's justification for the results of these measures was not to deny their classificatory basis (in this case, a strong bent towards alphabetico-classed structure), but rather to claim its necessity in light of the fact that the Library of Congress' chief clientele then and presumably in the future consisted of scholars and students who needed that kind of subject catalog structure.

In contrast to the foregoing, advocates of subject catalogs for small libraries loudly called for subject catalog simplification that would more readily serve the needs of average readers. They faced a formidable task, however. On the one hand, the chief source of such headings, the ALA List, the second 1898 edition of which had been reprinted several times, had no ongoing organization like the

Library of Congress to keep it current. The task was also formidable because the basis for simplicity that matched the needs of users was not known.

Some direction toward solving the latter problem was suggested by Theresa Hitchler who noted in her 1905 Cataloging for Small Libraries that choices in subject heading terminology for average users in small libraries should be based on observations of what such users ask for and how their minds work.[14] Thereafter, in the attempt to solve the problem of an updated list to be compiled, the first editor of the new edition, Esther Crawford, took up Hitchler's challenge of identifying just what that terminology should be. Through a series of articles in the Library Journal, Crawford requested catalogers of small libraries to send their observations to her about appropriate choices for a great number of individual subject terms.[15] Unfortunately, her findings were inconclusive and she was able to make few such determinations with any finality.

A new edition of the list was eventually completed by Mary Josephine Briggs, Crawford's successor on the project. But Briggs' resolutions of the problem of terminology and syntax choices had a significant effect on how the notion of user convenience was to develop in the succeeding decades. First, Briggs concluded that consistency in subject heading terminology was neither obtainable nor necessary because average users themselves were fundamentally unpredictable in the way they used subject terminology. Second, where evidence gathered by Crawford indicated any particular patterns or choices, she followed it. As a practical solution for the much larger number of instances in which no evidence was forthcoming, however, she simply followed Library of Congress choices and patterns. This not only had the effect of incorporating into the ALA List much of the classificatory structure of the Library of Congress subject heading system but labeling the result as acceptable for small libraries and their average users. Third, she suggested in almost an offhanded way what eventually would become a significantly new approach to categorizing users--that is, that grouping users by type of library was a more adequate way to deal with how subject catalog choices should be made.[16]

Library Differentiation by Type

The differentiation of libraries by the types they represent, like differentiation by size, also began late in the last century. But its basic nomenclature--academic libraries, public libraries, school libraries, and special libraries--did not become fully standardized until after the First World War. This typology is important in the development of subject cataloging in two ways. First, at about the same time that the above nomenclature became widely accepted, subject cataloging (along with the entire field of librarianship) entered an era of significant self examination and reflection that ultimately led to the identification of library science as an explicit field of study. Accompanying that intellectual shift in perspective was a significant

Communication and Education

number of works that, in the course of attempting to explain various elements of the field in a more rigorous fashion than previous writings, adopted the new nomenclature. This was no less exemplified than in subject cataloging, for example, in both the first edition in 1930 of Margaret Mann's classic work, Introduction to Cataloging and the Classification of Books and the 1933 explanation of subject heading work provided by Minnie Earl Sears in the third edition of her List of Subject Headings for Small Libraries. These works were striking in their attempts to provide some kind of rational explanation of the subject cataloging process in the context of types of libraries. They were especially important because little of importance had been written on the topic since the first decade of the century, a period during which subject cataloging had had to face such new problems as the increasing size of catalogs and the first calls by library administrators for catalogers to assume greater responsibility for cataloging costs. Their subsequent adoption in the field as basic works helped to ensure that the categorization of users by type of library and the application of those categories to subject cataloging were also adopted.

The second reason why the appearance of a new type of library nomenclature was important in the development of subject cataloging was that, following Briggs' comments in the third edition of the ALA List, it provided a more convenient, seemingly more logical, and obviously more refined approach to users and their convenience in subject heading work than categorizations by size had provided. In this approach, the clientele of a particular type of library was viewed as having unique characteristics that set it apart from the clienteles of other types of libraries. Thus, if one could identify the most salient features of the subject searching characteristics of the users of a particular type of library, it then seemed reasonable to assume that subject headings could be tailored to the needs of that kind of user. For example, following this reasoning, it seemed logical to assume that because the children who searched for subjects in children's or school libraries approached their task with relatively simplistic ideas, the subject headings in children's libraries must necessarily be "simple" rather than complex. Likewise, because patrons of special libraries more often than not used specialized terminology in their subject searching, that same specialized terminology must necessarily be incorporated into the subject heading vocabulary of the catalogs used by them. Only in this way could subject catalogs for either type of library clientele be made user convenient.

The Failure of User Categories Based on Types of Libraries[18]

The concept that user convenience was oriented to the user categories associated with types of libraries flourished for approximately three decades to the 1950s and in some respects still continues, particularly in efforts to provide special subject heading lists or thesauri for particular kinds of special libraries and collections. Ultimately it too, like user categorization by size of library, failed to provide an adequate basis for determining user convenience in subject heading work.

There are three probable reasons for that failure. First, although categorizing users by type of library seemed like a logical way to speak of highly distinctive types of libraries such as special libraries associated with well-defined special fields of inquiry, the logic behind it broke down for other types of libraries that were not associated with special subject fields. Thus, Margaret Mann in 1930 and, following her, Julia Pettee in 1946, after having put forward elaborate schemes of types of libraries, found little that could distinguish, say, public libraries from academic libraries except general differences between scholarly users and average users of the kind that had been current decades earlier. With that limited basis upon which to devise specific procedures, Mann for one could do little more than suggest that subject headings in public library catalogs be kept relatively simple in formulation and length. She suggested this both as an aid to generally unsophisticated public library users and as a way to keep file length under individual headings from becoming too small. Likewise, a close examination of Elva S. Smith's arguments in favor of simple headings for children's and school libraries will show that the notion of simple headings, based as it was on the analogy of simplicity in the subject searching habits of children, was actually a very indistinct concept.[19]

The second reason why differentiation of users by type of library failed to provide an adequate basis for making subject catalogs user convenient was that after more than two decades of user studies, themselves based for the most part on types of libraries, no extensive objective evidence was ever uncovered to support the basic equation that users can be adequately characterized by the types of libraries they frequent. If anything was concluded by the mid-1950s, in fact (besides, that is, the frustration of inconclusiveness), it was a reformulation of user categorization similar to that found at the beginning of the century. Studies appeared to show that there were actually only two essentially distinct kinds of users--specialists and general users--and that these appear in all kinds of libraries in varying proportions.

There were differences between the reformulation of the 1950s and the user categories proposed in the earlier period, of course. For one thing, the two categories of users were no longer tied to library size. For another, the subject heading system in the dictionary catalog had by the 1950s become indelibly associated with general users, this despite arguments proposed by Julia Pettee that suggested how a dictionary subject catalog made for general users should and could be made to differ from that constructed for scholars and specialists. This association of the dictionary subject catalog primarily with general users was aided in no small part by the identification of adequate subject access tools for specialized libraries with the spate of new methods that appeared after the late 1940s. The most notable advances of the latter kind were faceted classification schemes and coordinate indexing systems. The identification of the dictionary subject catalog with general users was also aided by an even deeper chasm that had appeared between general and specialist users in attempts to characterize them. Some indication of this increasingly radical separation may be found in Pettee's analysis in 1946. There, Pettee described the academic scholar with attributes very much like those found in descriptions of specialists who used special libraries. Further, she pictured the academic scholar as existing in an almost rarefied intellectual atmosphere while searching for subject information. This in turn contrasted sharply with Pettee's description of the general user as for the most part intellectually inept and frivolous, needful mainly of "casual" information. Finally, Pettee's subsequent characterization of the dictionary subject catalog made for scholars and specialists as little more than a starting point for research which was actually of little help in finding very discrete bits of information that scholars and specialists needed, and her characterization of the dictionary subject catalog made for general users as a kaleidoscope of temporary encyclopedic references, replete with a great deal of redundant entry, and ever changing to meet new popular subject demands, provided little assurance that the dictionary catalog subject heading system could ever be much more than a very imprecise subject access tool. In short, the dictionary subject catalog was useful mainly for the imprecise subject searching needs of general users.[20]

The third reason why differentiation of users by type of library failed to provide an adequate basis for making the dictionary subject catalog user convenient resided in the increasing importance and dominance of subject heading lists and copy, especially that which was supplied by the Library of Congress. This ensured that problems associated with Library of Congress headings and with its questionable approach to user convenience became the problems of all libraries that depended on its subject cataloging products.[21]

By 1940 Library of Congress subject headings had become much more complex than J. C. M. Hanson had, perhaps, ever imagined possible. Subject heading syntax variation and inconsistency had increased to a noticeable degree so that a variety of syntax patterns--brief headings, extended but straightforward phrase headings, inverted and other forms of phrase headings, and strings-of-term headings involving subdivisions--all competed as legitimate subject heading forms. Furthermore, the way headings were used to specify the subjects of books had also come to vary greatly, particularly as the use of multiple entry terms, none of which by themselves matched the scopes of the books to which they were assigned, increased in frequency.

When David J. Haykin became the first chief of the library's newly created Subject Cataloging Division in 1941, he immediately took measures to reverse the deteriorating situation; and it was due in no small part to his efforts that striking changes were made. Among the latter were a more strict adherence to the use of conventional subject names rather than resorting too easily to subdivided headings, the employment of greater numbers of subject specialists in order to deal more adequately with a rising number of special subjects, an increase in the annual number of new subject headings, better provisions for the dissemination of subject heading additions and changes to the general cataloging community, and, finally, publication of the first reasonably useful and extensive description of subject heading practice written since Cutter's Rules--Haykin's Subject Headings, a Practical Guide.

One might reasonably assume that by means of such measures the goals of user convenience might have had some chance of being met. Certainly, this goal seems to have been squarely on Haykin's mind. User convenience, which he spoke of in his manual as the idea of "the reader as the focus," was in Haykin's opinion the most fundamental principle of subject heading work. Furthermore, Haykin provided even greater forcefulness to the concept by going well beyond user categorization based on the simplistic notion of broad types of libraries. In place of that earlier approach, he called for the more precise identification of the actual social groups that a library served and for making the dominant group or groups thus identified the basis for user convenience. In short, subject headings should be made with the actual group (or groups) of users that a library served in mind, regardless of the library's particular type. That user identification being accomplished, all subject heading decisions--those related to the degree of the specificity needed, those related to syntax, etc.--should be made carefully on a case-by-case basis in order to make the catalog as user convenient as possible.

Haykin's goal of making subject catalogs user convenient in terms of the distinct social groups that libraries served was not only an admirable goal but also served in many respects to bring subject cataloging back full circle to ideas that had been expressed nearly fifty years earlier. Hitchler, Crawford, and others had suggested that user convenience required that subject catalogers attempt to find out how users actually think in the subject searching process. Haykin's concept of the reader as the focus also stressed the same objective. With Haykin's thorough appeal to the idea, however, one also comes face to face with its contradictory nature. First, Haykin freely admitted that solid evidence for reader's habits in subject searching even in terms of groups was not really available. What was available were librarians' casual opinions about how users searched for subjects. But opinions of that kind constituted little more than the inconclusive kind of evidence that Crawford had discovered so many years earlier. Second, in the absence of any solid evidence of what users do in fact do in subject searching, regardless of whether they do so individually or in terms of groups, the actual decisions that have been based on such appeals (of which Haykin as well as those who have succeeded him at the Library have made in abundance) also have little objective basis. In fact, one may reasonably conclude that decisions made on that basis serve as much to rationalize past practice, as for any other need. Last, despite the glowing and enthusiastic way Haykin spoke of the necessity of providing for user convenience, he seems not to have been aware of the logical contradiction between that goal and still another goal that he strongly promoted and which has come to occupy an increasingly powerful role in the broader subject cataloging community since his time. The latter goal is the necessity to achieve subject access economically by means of centralized and cooperative cataloging--in this case through the use of Library of Congress subject headings in the forms of both its standardized list of headings and its subject cataloging copy. User convenience based on the dominant group or groups served by a particular library implied that the subject heading needs of each local library will vary significantly from those of other libraries and from those of the Library of Congress itself, at least to the extent that they vary from the dominant groups they serve. Thus, unless the local library serves users that match or nearly match those that are served by the Library of Congress, user convenience will not be served.

Observations

Appeals to user categories of the kind discussed here continue to be made and, in fact, are not confined to subject catalogers. They have been used, for example, in discussions of reference work and of bibliographical instruction as a way of showing how those two kinds of activities differ among different types of users. User categories of this kind appear to this author as a legacy of questionable worth, however, especially when they are used as a way to approach information retrieval patterns among users.

One aspect of such categorization that seems questionable is the conclusion expressed more than once over several decades that there are two kinds of users--specialists and general users--and that these groups are so distinct that they require essentially different kinds of subject access tools and, for that matter, different kinds of a wide variety of library service activities designed to help them find information. The questionable nature of this conclusion lies not so much in the concept of specialists as in the general user category. Most descriptions of the general user category express little more than the idea that general users are the opposite of specialists. They are, in effect, non-specialists. But characterizing general users as non-specialists makes the group into a moot category because that characterization says nothing about how general users actually do search for information. Even when attempts have been made to describe this category in a more positive way, however, the results have been equally dissatisfying because little more has been concluded of general users than a general disparagement of their intellectual abilities. On the basis of some descriptions of general users, in fact, one may reasonably wonder whether general users have mental processes that function at all. All of this leads to the question of whether there is any such real category as the general user. Furthermore, even if the existence of such a category could be demonstrated, it seems doubtful if it would provide anything in the way of a predictive basis upon which to construct information access tools and services.

The foregoing observation about the general user category is actually only an element of a second and far greater problem associated with user categorization. That problem is the questionable nature of devising user categories on the basis of social factors that are only accidentally related to the main concern of information access--that is, how the mental activities of users function in the information seeking process. What, for example, does the size or type of library that a user frequents really say about how users actually search for subjects, or use reference tools, or perform any of a variety of tasks associated with their library activity? It is entirely possible, of course, that in some particular instances, a correlation might be observed. To turn the observation around, however, and use it as a way to characterize the users of all libraries of any one size or type is not only supercilious but has a debilitating aspect as well because it easily leads to the specter of treating users in a presumptive fashion in which one simply assumes that the unfounded assumptions about the user category in question are true of the actual patrons who walk through the library door.

A far better approach to the matter of determining how to base decisions for making information retrieval tools or service that are user convenient is to observe, study and categorize use, not users. One reason for this seems obvious. Library patrons regularly display differing patterns of use depending on the information searching situation in which they find themselves. Specialists, for example, do not always search as specialists, and even when they do they may proceed in strikingly different patterns of information seeking behaviour depending on their information needs. Likewise, so-called general users often search as specialists in many particular instances, although their specialties may not in fact be those formally identified as special fields of literature or activity. This same line of reasoning may be applied to the whole range of users that are commonly placed in presumptive user categories.

A second reason for proceeding in this fashion is that it places users in a common arena based on their common intellectual habits rather than separating them into diverse categories based on what at best are only secondary social attributes. It is this view of users, in fact, that is so striking about Cutter's approach to the public in the last century. Cutter did not first separate users by some social distinction such as the size or type of library they frequented and then characterize the use in each of those categories. Instead, he began with a single public, divided its use patterns into a single continuum of behavior, and then observed that behavior in libraries. For him, all users' minds functioned in the same way, although not with the same efficiency or result. On that basis, Cutter was then able to design and rationalize a common system of subject access for all.

Cutter's use descriptions were based on an early hypothetical view of how the human mind functions, of course, and the applicability of that view would be a questionable starting point for the same effort today. But his approach does point out an important issue. If librarians begin with the idea that because users differ in social characteristics, their mental processes also differ in some absolute way, then they have logically excluded the possibility that the same information access tools may be made convenient to each group. That appears to be what has caused the opinion that the dictionary subject catalog is an imprecise tool useful only for general users rather than also for specialists. If, on the other hand, users are viewed as having common mental processes, there is then some possibility that such tools (and services as well) might be designed with an eye to being useful for the entire range of users in a useful and predictable fashion.

References

1. The substance of this paper is taken from Francis Miksa, The Subject in the Dictionary Catalog from Cutter to the Present (Chicago: ALA, 1983) where the topic of user considerations is discussed in much greater detail but is scattered throughout a much longer text as a subsidiary theme. The documentation of the topic in that work is repeated here only sparingly.
2. Charles A. Cutter, Rules for a Dictionary Catalog, 4th ed (Washington, D.C.: U.S. Government Printing Office, 1904), p. 74.
3. David J. Haykin, Subject Headings, a Practical Guide (Washington, D.C.: U.S. Government Printing Office, 1951), p. 7.
4. Paul S. Dunkin, "Cataloging and the CCS: 1957-1966," Library Resources and Technical Services 11 (Summer 1967): 286.
5. The term "dictionary subject catalog" is used in place of the more awkward statement, "the subject element of the dictionary catalog." It is preferred to "subject headings," which does not convey the idea of a catalog system, and to "subject heading system," which does not identify the kind of catalog in which the system is found. There is no such separate thing as the dictionary subject catalog, of course.
6. The Subject in the Dictionary Catalog, pp. 37-44, 58-61, 72-86, and 126-43.
7. Charles A. Cutter, "Library Catalogues," Public Libraries in the United States of America, their History, Condition and Management; Special Report, Part I (Washington: U.S. Government Printing Office, 1876), p. 541.
8. Ibid., p. 530.
9. Cutter, Rules for a Dictionary Catalog, 4th ed. p. 79.
10. The Subject in the Dictionary Catalog, pp. 158-77, 204-211.
11. For the role of specialists, see Alexandra Oleson and John Voss (eds.), The Organization of Knowledge in Modern America, 1860-1920 (Baltimore: Johns Hopkins University Press, 1979), especially chapters by John Higham, Edward Shils, and John Y. Cole.
12. The Subject in the Dictionary Catalog, pp. 178-79, 236-53.
13. Wayne Wiegand, The Politics of an Emerging Profession: the American Library Association, 1876-1917 (Forthcoming).
14. Theresa Hitchler, Cataloging for Small Libraries, A.L.A. Publishing Board, Library Handbook, no. 2 (Boston: A.L.A. Publishing Board, 1905), p. 8.

15. Esther Crawford, "A. L. A. Subject Headings," Library Journal 32 (October 1907): 435-36; (November 1907): 500-1; (December 1907): 560-61.
16. Mary J. Briggs, "The A. L. A. List of Subject Headings," Bulletin of the A. L. A. 6 (July 1912): 227-31.
17. The Subject in the Dictionary Catalog, pp. 256-73.
18. Ibid., pp. 284-91, 295-304.
19. Ibid., pp. 258-63; Elva S. Smith, Subject Headings for Children's Books in Public Libraries and in Libraries in Elementary and Junior High Schools.... (Chicago: ALA, 1933)
20. Julia Pettee, Subject Headings: The History and Theory of the Alphabetical Subject Approach to Books (New York: H. W. Wilson Co., 1946), chs. 5-6.
21. The Subject in the Dictionary Catalog, pp. 304-8, 332-40, 364-82.

ARCHIVAPHOBIA: ITS
CAUSES AND CURE*

Virginia C. Purdy

When archivists attend scholarly meetings, they are often astounded to discover among their colleagues in the historical profession advanced cases of archivaphobia in almost epidemic proportions. This malady is easily diagnosed. As its name suggests, the major symptom is a morbid fear of archives. Persons who wade joyously into manuscript collections and spend hours--nay, days and years--deciphering crabbed handwritings of the past for usable tidbits of information about the lives and times of eminent Americans become trembling wrecks at the prospect of undertaking research in archives, particularly in federal archives.

Archivaphobia is also marked by outbursts of bellicose hostility, not only toward government records but toward archivists. Researchers exhibiting this kind of reaction challenge the veracity of the archivist who tries to extoll the treasures in the National Archives. "You tell us," they protest, "about these wonders, but you hide them from us where we cannot possibly find them, among 'Letters Sent and Received,' or 'Records of the Administrator' of this and that." This interaction leaves the researcher feverish and irritated, and the archivist--usually a gentle soul--in a state of deep depression.

Since most of the cases that I have observed at first hand have been among scholars in women's history, the discussion below will deal largely with causes and cures of the affliction in that field. Archivaphobia, however, is widespread, and cases could be cited in almost any area of American history.

Now what are the causes of this phobia? First, the sheer volume of records is intimidating. The thought of 700 linear feet of records in the Records of the Women's Bureau brings initially a feeling of euphoria--all that marvelous data about women! But this is quickly followed by a throwing up of the hands: "How can we cope with so much?" The reverse is the problem of the General

---
*Reprinted by permission of the author and publisher from Prologue, Summer 1983, pp. 115-119.

Records of the Treasury, some 3,000 feet of records in which perhaps 50 items may be related to women's history. "How can we find the scattered items in such a large mass?" Less than 5 percent of the records created by the federal government find their way into archives heaven. The other 95 percent are cast into outer darkness and consigned to the shredder because they are not considered to be of permanent value. So the problem of volume could be worse. In any event, let us agree that the quantity of records is awe-inspiring.

Another cause of archivaphobia evinces the symptomatic wail from the patient, "Why isn't there a card catalog, a subject index?" On hearing this, the archivist blanches at the thought of the sheer volume of materials involved. There is one body of records that has been indexed by computer: the Papers of the Continental and Confederation Congresses, 433 linear feet. In this five-volume index there are, for the edification of the historian of American women, listed under the term "women" a grand total of 29 entries. That tells us a couple of things: either the infant republic was a very masculine world, or indexing the content of records is not the best way to locate or identify certain subjects in the records. This index also illustrates the impracticality of this approach. At least three people, and at the peak of activity, eight, worked full-time for about six years to produce this index. Taxpayers are not enthusiastic about spending that kind of money routinely; the PCC project was possible only with support from private foundation.

The third and most devastating cause of archivaphobia is the arrangement of the records. The basic principle of archival arrangement is that records are filed under the name of the agency that created them, and thereunder according to the administrative structure of the agency. Archivists make every effort to keep the records in the order that the creating agency kept and used them. The researcher's reactions on discovering this fact are excruciating pain accompanied by melancholia. Cries of anguish are directed as usual toward the archivist: "What good are the records when they are arranged that way? What can you do with them except write a history of the agency, and, for example, how many histories are needed of the Bureau of Agricultural Economics? Why don't you organize the records by subject so that reasonable people can find things in them?"

The problem of arrangement is the toughest one for researchers. There are several reasons for the present system. Archives are preserved for a number of different classes of users. First of those is the government itself. An agency does not surrender its records to the archivist of the United States as long as they are in daily use within the agency itself. After they have been retired to the archives, however, the agency can be confident that, if it needs to refer to the records, it will find them in the order in which they were maintained by the agency. Next, the records are valuable to private citizens as evidence in defending legal claims. Land titles, veterans' benefits, citizenship proof, patents--these are but a few of the areas in which the records of the federal government can be important to the average American in a court of law. Leaving the records in the order in which they were originally set up facilitates this use. Finally, the records are used by scholars, genealogists, journalists, and history buffs. Even for these researchers, the original order is the safest arrangement that has been found. Rearrangement of records by subject to suit the needs of the researcher in black history might disorganize materials sought by the diplomatic historian. Nor would the subjects of traditional history necessarily be the ones that interest students of women's history.

One reason it seemed a good idea to index the Papers of the Continental and Confederation Congresses was that these records are not in their original order. In the nineteenth century, someone in the State Department, trying to be helpful, tried to put them in rough subject order. The result is a colossal mess. Transmittal letters are separated from what was transmitted. Copies of letters in one place duplicate orginals in another, and no one knows who made the copies, or why, or who received the copies, or which are the record copies kept by the sender. Sometimes this kind of information about a letter can tell the researcher almost as much as the contents of the letter.

For example, in the Papers of the Continental and Confederation Congresses, one item that contains information about women is "Papers and Affidavits Relating to the Plunderings, Burnings, and Ravages Committed by the British, 1775-85." Among these are depositions of women who were raped or otherwise ill-used by the enemy during the Revolutionary War. The depositions, however, are all that is there. Related papers that would tell us exactly why the depositions were made and whether they were the basis of claims are not with them. Whether the women collected damages from anyone we cannot tell from the volume of depositions. Documentation answering our questions may exist elsewhere in the PCC or in other pre-Federal records, but these depositions have been wrenched out of context, leaving us only an incomplete story.

Thus, archives are not arranged by subject, and they are not indexed, as a rule, or catalogued. How then do we find our way into them? How do we discover what they hold that will aid our research? In other words, it is time to consider prescriptions and treatments for the cure of archivaphobia.

First, we must be convinced that there are similarities between archives and personal papers. Personal papers and archives are both created in the process of the normal activity of the creator. The papers of Eleanor Roosevelt are the files that she accumulated for her own use as she pursued her many interests throughout her long life. The records of the Federal Trade Commission are the files accumulated during the course of carrying out the agency's legal responsibilities. Neither was established for the convenience of future researchers.

Accordingly, the basic principle for research in archives is the same one that yields results from research in manuscript collecttions. Where do we look for letters written by a particular woman? Perhaps in her own papers, if she used a typewriter and kept carbons, or if she had a secretary, or if some conscientious collector has gathered up all her autograph letters signed. But more likely, we turn to the papers of her family and friends and associates, people who corresponded with her. These are also the people who might have written to each other about her activities. Therefore we have to know a good deal about a person before we can begin research in original manuscripts. What were her interests? With whom would she have corresponded on each of her interests? Where are the papers of those correspondents? At what dates would such correspondence have taken place? Armed with this information from secondary sources or from the subject's own papers, we go to the papers of the correspondents, ask to see those of the appropriate date or writer, and we may find a gold mine.

Exactly the same type of reasoning yields results in dealing with archives. What were the subject's interests? Would she have dealt with the federal government in pursuit of those interests? What part of the federal government was concerned with her field at the time she was active?

An intern from a Washington-area university was searching for documents about Sara Winnemucca, the Piute Indian leader who became the spokesman for the Indians of the Pacific Northwest. The agency primarily responsible for Indian relations during Winnemucca's lifetime was the Bureau of Indian Affairs. Sure enough, in the records of the BIA, the researcher found a fine packet of letters about her, with the special bonus that they were written by Elizabeth Peabody and Mrs. Horace Mann.

Broadening our thinking to include records of governments other than the U.S. federal government, we might consider where we might be likely to find records dealing with Dorothea Lynde Dix. She lobbied for the establishment of better institutions for the care of the insane in many states, especially in Massachusetts and New Jersey, as well as in the U.S. Congress. She was superintendent of army nurses during the Civil War. There should be records relating to her work in the appropriate state archives, in the records of the two houses of Congress, and in the records of the office of the Surgeon General in the National Archives. Her part in getting the British government to establish the Scottish Lunacy Commission should have created records in the British Public Record Office. There may even be some Dix records in the Public Archives of Canada or of Nova Scotia because of her efforts to supply life boats and rescue equipment for the shipwrecked on Sable Island. She may hold some kind of record for the number of public archives having records about her.

Once the researcher has adjusted to the thought processes required to approach archival materials, the next step in the cure of archivaphobia is a good dose of finding aids. Archivists spend a great deal of their time producing finding aids and making them available in libraries across the land so that researchers can learn about the holdings of the archives. Most major libraries have in their collections a copy of the Guide to the Archives of the United States. In it the researcher will find a brief description of all the records of the federal government deemed permanent or of enduring value. The records of a single government agency constitute a record group to which a record group number is assigned. The researcher must use the thought processes described above to decide which agency or agencies may have dealt with the subject of research and turn to the description of the records in the record group for that agency. In addition, there is an index to the text of the Guide (not to the records). For a more detailed description of a record group, the researcher must ask for another type of finding aid, the preliminary inventory or the inventory of the record group.

A record group is not unlike a collection of personal papers, and the register for those papers corresponds to the record group inventory. Each entry in an inventory describes a series of records, telling the researcher the type, quantity, arrangement, dates, and something about the subject matter of the records, as well as whether or not there are indexes.

Suppose we were making a study of the relationship of farm women to community and women's organizations. We would expect to find records on this subject among the records of the Department of Agriculture. On reading the descriptions of the activities of the various agencies in the USDA, we would learn that the Bureau of Agricultural Economics, Record Group 83, had a Division of Farm Population and Rural Life, and, using the inventory, we would find in the Bureau's General Correspondence that one subject noted is "farm women." Another series, called the "Manuscript File," contains studies of rural life, including such topics as: church organizations, "Farm Community Life in Wisconsin, " and "The Leisure Year of the Farmer and his Wife." In the inventory of the Records of the Office of the Secretary of Agriculture, Record Group 16, subject headings for the general correspondence series, 1906-56, include such entries as "Farm Women's Bureau, " "General Federation of Women's Clubs, " "Women's War Relief Association, 1917" and others that might yield research materials on our subject.

Another kind of finding aid is the subject guide and, in the National Archives, its smaller cousin, the reference information paper. There are book length guides to records about the Civil War, the Confederate States of America, Africa, American Indians, and Alaska, as well as to records useful for genealogical research. In preparation are guides to some records about black Americans, American women, and Hispanic peoples of the southwestern United States. Each guide and, on a smaller scale, each reference information paper, describes pertinent records in every record group that contains any appreciable amount of material about its designated subject, giving the researcher some idea of what he or she might find and what will not be found. Guides, unlike most inventories, are

indexed. Good guides are very useful, but they take a great deal of
time to prepare, and most archives have a hard enough time just
keeping up with the task of getting out inventories and keeping them
up to date. There are, therefore, not a great number of guides for
the records in either the National Archives or other repositories.
However, guides on one subject can be used to search for records
on other subjects. We have already noted that records in the Bureau
of Indian Affairs yield records about compassionate New England
women who were interested in Indian affairs. A study by the Women's
Bureau of working conditions for women employed in the meat packing
industry can be used to research meatpacking methods in the 1920s.

In a word, finding aids are excellent medicine for archivaphobia. The patient, however, must learn to revel in the sometimes
dry and colorless language in which they are written. The archivist's
unembellished description does not mean that he or she lacks interest
in the records being described. Rather, the archivist is merely following a basic tenet of the archival profession: to describe the
records, not to interpret them.

A third treatment for archivaphobia is for the patient to learn
the best ways to tap the vast amount of information in the heads of
friendly, accommodating archivists. Whether the researcher is
writing to the archivist for information or visiting the archives, it
always pays to tell the complete story, including the subject of research and the ways in which the particular records being sought
will fit into that research. The archivist will often mention other
records whose existence was totally unknown to the researcher and
among which may be found the most exciting items to prove the researcher's hypothesis. Many researchers seem reluctant to announce
their topics above a whisper for fear that someone will snatch it
away and write the definitive treatment, completely destroying their
precious project. This may occasionally happen, but not because of
garrulous or unscrupulous archivists. Archivists are responsible
and honorable. The more they know about a researcher's concerns,
the more help they can provide.

The researcher should be as specific as possible. A request
for "everything in the archives about Italian women in Illinois between
1850 and 1967" will bring a very short response. But if the inquirer
knows that Italian women were involved in a strike of candy-makers
in Chicago in 1919, good results will come from asking for information about records dealing with that incident. Better results yet can
be obtained if the request is for the case file on the subject in the
Records of the U.S. Conciliation Service, Record Group 280. The
archivist will reply stating the kind and quantity of material available,
the cost of reproduction if it is a small quantity, and whether or
not the records have been microfilmed. At the same time, the
archivist may cite other records of related interest.

For a researcher considering a visit to the National Archives
(or one of the regional archives branches or presidential libraries
that make up the National Archives and Reference Service)--or any

other archives--an exploratory letter may save travel costs or time lost after arrival.

Assuming that these prescriptions are taken as directed, a cure for archivaphobia is assured. Lest one frustrating experience should cause a relapse, it is important for the patient to know a little more about what is likely to be found and not likely to be found in the records of the federal government. Some time ago, a paper based on records in the Children's Bureau astonished me with its rich detail--colorful descriptions of the plight of isolated mothers appealing for aid to an impersonal government agency regarding their most intimate concerns, and an account of the warm response of Julia Lathrop, director, 1912-21. I had not encountered much of this kind of material in my experience with those records. The author's response to my question about how she found the letters quoted was, "Well, I had to go through a lot of junk, too."

This points up two things about federal records, about which a researcher should be forwarned. First, it is unusual to find in a federal employee's official correspondence a great deal of information about the writer himself or herself. Josephine Roche was chairman of the Executive Committee of the National Youth Administration from 1935 to 1943, but beyond a brief biographical sketch, the records tell us absolutely nothing about Roche except that she was present and presiding at meetings of the Executive Committee. Julia Lathrop's warm personal style in the correspondence of the early years of the Children's Bureau was unusual. After her retirement, the agency became larger and less personal.

Second, a researcher may indeed have to go through a lot of irrelevant and uninteresting material to find the great report or document that makes it all worthwhile. Archives are not kept selectively. "Letters Sent and Received" between two dates means just that--all of the letters. But any research requires patient digging. The archeologist may sift sand for days before finding a single fragment of a Grecian urn. However, nothing is more thrilling than finding the documents that no one else has troubled to search for, but which may divert the stream of history--even a little.

The prescription for archivaphobia is not quite as simple as, "take two finding aids and call the archivist in the morning." But the researcher who is cured should not be surprised to develop "archivaphilia"--the love of archives--and that is an incurable condition.

THE PROPOSED NATIONAL PERIODICALS CENTER, 1973-1980:

STUDY, DISSENSION, and RETREAT*

Mary Biggs

Introduction

The National Periodicals Center proposal was important in itself as an attempt to ease some of the most severe pressures on research libraries--and, to lesser and varying degrees, on all libraries. In this paper, it is also presented as a case study illustrating obstacles which librarians may face when they attempt to unite behind an issue and effect federal action.

Perhaps the overriding problem, from which most others stemmed, was the profession's lack of unified national leadership. The Library of Congress (LC) maintains the country's largest collection and generates bibliographic data for the use of all libraries, but it is not truly a national library and does not always behave like one. Absorbed with its internal functions, and sensitive to the wishes of Congress, LC has not taken the lead in fighting at the national level for the resolution of library and bibliographic problems. The stands taken by other major national organizations--notably the National Commission on Libraries and Information Science (NCLIS) and the American Library Association (ALA)--were weakened by conflicts among the several sectors of librarianship. Adding to this obstacle was the aggressive opposition of publishers and, particularly, information entrepreneurs to plans for interlibrary cooperation--which they see as posing a direct threat to their survival. Somewhere in all of this were the concerns of library users and, in the case of school, academic, and most special libraries, of administrators of the parent institutions, who may sometimes have received mixed signals.[1] Though these groups did not enter the fray directly, librarians were strongly influenced by their real and anticipated reactions.

Finally, despite their role as collectors and disseminators of information, librarians sometimes exhibited a lack of sufficient knowledge regarding funding sources, legislative processes, and significant

---

*Reprinted by permission of the author and publisher from Resource Sharing and Information Networks, 1:(3/4) (Spring/Summer 1984) 1-22; copyright © 1984 by The Haworth Press, Inc. All rights reserved.

pending issues. [2] As a result, then, of interpersonal, interinstitutional, and inter-industry frictions, of an inadequate knowledge base, and perhaps a characteristic bureaucratic reactions, librarians tended to generate paper instead of actions around the NPC concept.

It now seems unlikely that the Center will ever be established in anything like its originally envisioned form--or indeed in any form which will substantially relieve the pressures on libraries.

Precedents for a National Lending Center

In 1899 Ernest C. Richardson, librarian at Princeton, recommended the establishment of a national lending library in order to avoid needless duplication of materials, assure complete coverage of all important materials, and thus encourage scientific research. Several decades later, citing the same and additional reasons, American librarians agitated for a diminished goal of a national lending library for periodicals only, having abandoned the concept of a more comprehensive center as desirable, but impossible to realize. However, since Richardson's day, successful models had been developed which stood as proofs of the feasibility of his idea and served to deepen the frustration of NPC advocates.

These included the National Library of Medicine (NLM) and its associated Regional Medical Library Network, so widely regarded as adequate to serve the nation's medical research needs that medicine was the only subject area routinely excluded from plans for a "comprehensive" periodical collection; Chicago's Center for Research Libraries (CRL); and the British Library Lending Division (BLLD). The latter two, both single-institution dedicated collections, were frequently cited as models for a national periodicals center.

Center for Research Libraries (CRL)

Established in 1949 by ten midwestern universities with the assistance of foundation grants, CRL was designed to be a repository of research esoterica, some purchased, some donated by member libraries eager to save space. [3] Among its characteristic acquisitions were entire archives on microform and all publications of the Soviet Academy of Science. [4] Borrowing privileges were extended only to member libraries, which by the end of 1981 numbered 185. However, the Center has been plagued by space constraints, alleviated since the opening of a new facility in the summer of 1982, inadequate bibliographic access tools, and the persistent problem of institutions' economic naivete when calculating the benefits of membership. Fussler has pointed out, the benefit to an institution is not the simple quotient of membership fee divided by number of items borrowed. Much more significant are the accumulated values of items not acquired because of their sure availability through CRL, processing not performed, space not consumed, maintenance not required, and increased user convenience. [5] A similar failure in judgment surfaced in the opposition to an NPC.

Not surprisingly, given its central location, existing collection, and well-developed operating procedures, CRL has for years been suggested as the nucleus around which a national lending library might be built. [6]

British Library Lending Division (BLLD)

The government-funded British Library Lending Division, founded in 1961 as the National Lending Library for Science and Technology and merged, twelve years later, with the newly-formed British Library, [7] was established with an opposite purpose: to provide British industry with access to the most heavily used periodicals in science and technology. It has since grown to cover all subject fields, to include monographs and less heavily used materials, and to provide service to libraries throughout England and abroad. It is widely considered the most useful and efficient dedicated collection in the world --tangible evidence that centralized sharing can work.

Supporters of the NPC concept urged a wedding of the two initial purposes of CRL and BLLD. Both heavily used and little used periodicals, they said, should be provided.

Studies and Proposed Legislation

General Assumptions

Proponents of a national periodicals center were not entirely in agreement on the exact sort of center needed or the functions it should perform. However, they agreed generally on the following goals: an NPC should provide faster, cheaper, more fully reliable access to periodical literature in such a way as to facilitate the more rational allocation of local library funds and to lighten the load on heavy net lenders. Periodicals in all languages, on all subjects except medicine, and of all degrees of use, should be collected. This comprehensive collecting should move forward from a set starting date, and back files should be acquired as opportunity might permit. (The NPC, like CRL, would presumably receive some back files as gifts.) Center operations should be flexible enough to exploit new technology as it became available and cost effective. A highly efficient and accurate computerized bibliographic finding tool should be developed. Full, systematic compliance with copyright regulations would be necessary. Substantial federal funding would probably be required in practice, though not in theory. Membership fees had not been sufficient in the case of the private CRL, and to set transaction fees high enough to recover costs would effectively exclude all but the richer libraries from access.

Goals often mentioned, but less often agreed upon, included a full-scale preservation program (interestingly, listed first in H.R. 5192, under the proposed NPC's functions[8]--cf. page 107); the opening of access to all types and sizes of libraries; collaborative ventures with publishers to facilitate the development of technologically sophisticated "alternative" publishing and the sale of publishers' reprints, back files, etc. If the last sounded like a placating bone tossed to the private sector, it may well have been. The number of current titles which planners usually envisioned the NPC collecting was 45,000 (perhaps more if the number of serial titles were to continue to grow), very close to the British Library Lending Division's volume of subscriptions in the mid-seventies and enough, hypothetically, to satisfy nearly all current-title interlibrary loan requests.[9] A figure of 36,000 was frequently advanced as an appropriate startup number of subscriptions.[10]

An early reason set forth for centralized sharing was the need to reduce local acquisition rates. Publishers' opposition to such a maneuver was predictable. Surprisingly, given the space, money, and management pressures bearing on libraries in the seventies, at least one library researcher/educator[11] and one administrator of a large public library system[12] agreed that sharing should not be used to limit buying or reduce collection levels.

Stevens's Feasibility Study (1973)

Conducted and written for the Association of Research Libraries (ARL) by library educator Rolland E. Stevens, this study's report provided a survey of interlibrary loan deficiencies and argued in favor of developing a system which would be centrally planned and coordinated but would offer "highly decentralized" lending services. Stevens asserted that such a program was most appropriate for the United States because existing libraries already held as many resources as were needed, "probably because [they] have enjoyed relatively liberal acquisition budgets for the past two decades, and have made strong efforts to ensure that at least one copy of every current publication of potential research value is acquired in some library. [13] Unlike James Wood of Chemical Abstracts--whose research had uncovered a serious gap in United States holdings of chemistry periodicals[14]--Stevens did not attempt to confirm this impression, nor did he analyze CRL-BLLD borrowing statistics,[15] nor did he speculate on what might happen if library budget growth rates lagged behind inflation rates--a trend already evident in the early 1970s.

Stevens's system would be anchored by three types of centers, to be developed in already established libraries. Federal funds would be required to get the system under way and, on a continuing basis, as a source of compensation to those libraries serving as lending centers.[16] Many parts of this report were highly vulnerable, and some of its suggestions surely impossible or, at least, badly worded (for example, a back-up center should "acquire everything published in the world" in certain subject areas[17]).

Palmour's Access to Periodical Resources (1974)

Funded by the National Science Foundation, published by (again) ARL, and bearing the name of Vernon E. Palmour as senior author, this study considered several possible national periodical lending systems, including a "regional resource network" similar to the one recommended by Stevens. After weighing benefits and costs of each, the authors decided in favor of a single BLLD-like national center.[18] After various methods of funding were discussed at some length, the authors appeared to prefer federal funding because of its relative stability and potential volume, though at least "nominal" borrowing fees were also seen as necessary.[19] This report was more thorough and apparently better received by ARL than was its predecessor. It formed the basis for subsequent studies (a fact criticized by the influential 1979 Little report), and ARL's post-1974 position dovetailed with its recommendations.

The NCLIS "Green Book" (1977)

Composed by the NCLIS Task Force on a National Periodicals System under the guidance of Vernon E. Palmour, this report outlined the familiar dimensions of the "periodicals crisis,"[20] discussed new technology, described existing sharing networks and services,[21] and proposed a three-level "hourglass"-shaped national system. This would consist of present systems at "level 1" for meeting "routine needs for periodicals," a National Periodicals Center at "level 2" (the narrow midsection of the "hourglass"), and, at "level 3," existing national libraries and other "unique collections" to back up the other two levels.[22] After considering other alternatives, the Task Force unsurprisingly selected NCLIS as the most suitable body to handle "overall coordination" of the system.[23] The amount of space needed for the warehouse-style NPC building was estimated at 200,000 square feet at a cost of $6.5 million in federal funds.[24] Annual operating costs were estimated at $3.5 million for the first year (1978), reaching nearly $8 million by the fifth year (1982). The largest portion of these expenses was to be federally subsidized, but by the fifth year, transaction fees would cover approximately 40 percent of costs.[25]

CLR "Technical Development Plan" for the NPC: The "Burgundy Book" (1978)

At the request of the Library of Congress, the Council on Library Resources (CLR) prepared the Burgundy Book after LC was invited by NCLIS to head any future periodicals center. Accordingly, the Council declined to explore alternatives and simply proceeded to draw up a minutely detailed blueprint for an NPC. Thirty-six thousand current titles was the figure mandated for a start-up subscription list. It was predicted that this might eventually grow to over 60,000 current titles plus appropriate deceased titles. A national-level "two-tier structure" would be created to govern the center and its associated programs.[26] One hundred thirty thousand square feet was thought by the CLR group to be adequate for the NPC building, and construction costs were estimated at $5 to 6.5 million. Again, the entire initial cost would be covered by the federal government, as would all operating expenditures for three years, after which time transaction fees would absorb much of the expense. Showing less optimism, or more realism, than the NCLIS Task Force, CLR pegged first-year operating costs at $3,750,000.[27] Rather than assuming that the NPC would start at once to serve all libraries, the report writers recommended a carefully organized and justified four-phase system of graduated access.[28]

The Burgundy Book represented a highly ambitious attempt to address every detail of NPC operations; indeed, it seemed at times to be absurdly detailed. In any case, the report was doomed by its stipulation that the center would take part in preservation and even sales of some materials (functions which were not accepted by a clear majority of librarians) and, more importantly, by its proposal for the creation of a strong national governing body.[29] Librarians' consternation over the latter proposal may have been at least partially the product of the report's relative vagueness on this point (for once, the Burgundy Book neglected details). Who, librarians asked, would appoint members? How much authority, if any, would the governing body have over existing local, state, and regional agencies? Might it divert public funding from other library programs? And who were the actual sponsors of the NPC anyway? CLR? ARL? NCLIS? CRL? All were strong NPC advocates. Where, if anywhere, did the ALA fit in?[30] An apparent pro-NPC consensus was shattered, and controversy swirled around the Burgundy Book.

In March 1979, at Kansas City, participants in the Midwest Regional Conference on the NPC declared the painstakingly prepared report "invalidated ... as a blueprint for NPC,"[31] and the NCLIS Advisory Board finally refused to endorse it. Before mid-1979, the Burgundy Book had become "basically a piece of history."[32]

H.R. 5192: Title IID of the Higher Education Act of 1965 (1979)

On September 6, 1979, a proposal for an NPC was appended to the Higher Education Act as Title IID, introduced into the House of Representatives, and passed "before most librarians knew it was in the hopper."[33] At the time of H.R. 5192's House debut, an NCLIS drafting team composed of diverse "stakeholders" was at work hammering out a generally acceptable bill. The team was taken by surprise and fur began to fly. Team members and other interested parties became embroiled in an argument over whom to blame for covertly pushing the proposal into Congress. The American Association of Universities was rumored to be the culprit, as were the CLR and the ARL.[34] It seemed possible that this speculation might be a smokescreen to cover NCLIS's embarrassment at having been taken unaware. On September 14, nine of the Commission's fifteen members assembled in a hastily called meeting and unanimously approved Title IID. This approval did not present an ideological conflict as the amendment was almost identical to a draft drawn up earlier by an NCLIS task force.[35]

Essentially, H.R. 5192 authorized creation of a center "to serve as a national periodical resource by contributing to the preservation of periodical materials and by providing access to a comprehensive collection of periodical literature to public and private libraries throughout the United States."[36] Not to be considered "an agency or establishment of the United States Government," a nonprofit corporation would be created to establish the document delivery system and NPC would be the linchpin. Some of the more interesting provisions of the proposal gave the corporation authority "to enter into cooperative agreements with the Library of Congress, the National Library of Medicine, the National Agricultural Library," and other institutions, and to "coordinate the training of librarians and other users in the use of the Corporation's services."[37] (This latter project, listed last as if by afterthought, seemed potentially more ambitious and complex than establishment of the NPC itself!) A corporation board of fifteen members, fourteen to be selected by the President from a broad range of interested sectors, would be established.[38]

Even had Title IID soared as easily through the Senate as it did through the House, the NPC was still made highly vulnerable by a "trigger mechanism" included to insure that all other parts of Title II would be funded at least at the level of fiscal 1979 before NPC funds could be appropriated.[39] Whether the trigger would be sprung became an academic question. The proposal was stalled in the Senate--largely, it seemed, because of still another NCLIS-commissioned study.

Arthur D. Little Report (1979)

In October, less than one month after the House passed Title IID, the Arthur D. Little research organization published a report to the NCLIS. Noting that the Burgundy Book had simply built on the Green Book, and that indeed all previous studies focused only on the past and present, Little researchers declared them basically invalid in an age of technological revolution. The report's findings were summed up in this statement: "the time for ... a centralized National Periodical Center has come--and it also appears to have gone."[40] Looking primarily at those supporting arguments which emphasized the need for cost-effective and rapid service--and giving very little attention to the more significant issues of periodical coverage, duplication, and rational allocation of library funds--the report identified three possible alternatives: "System A" would let matters take their course unimpeded and unaided; "System B" would create an NPC; and "System C," a "subsidized switching network plus a dedicated back-up collection."[41] After evaluation, future projections, and the concession of many advantages to "System B," the Little researchers seemed to show some preference for the

"System A" laissez-faire approach, but finally advocated abandoning B and making further comparative studies of A and C. [42]

Senator Claiborne Pell, chairman of the Senate Subcommittee on Education, Arts, and Humanities, which was then considering H. R. 5192, apparently received a copy of the Little report [43] and soon began asking questions which suggested its influence.

Of possible relevance and considerable interest, was the subtly shifted position of University of Pennsylvania library director Richard De Gennaro, who very likely read the report as soon as, or even before, [44] it was published. In a much quoted and reprinted 1975 article, De Gennaro had declared: "Technology will help in time and in very significant ways, but we should not allow its promise and glamor to keep us from coming to grips with the immediate and critical problems of exponential growth. The solution to these problems lies in the adoption of more realistic acquisitions policies and the development of more effective means of resource sharing, not only through computerized networks but also through the creation of new and improved national resource centers." [45] In the same article, he was sharply critical of existing interlibrary loan networks. On November 15, 1979, a second and in some respects contradictory De Gennaro article appeared. Quoting at length from Research Libraries and Technology, Herman Fussler's 1973 report to the Sloan Foundation, De Gennaro went on to declare it invalidated by recent technological developments and by much improved hierarchical ILL networks. [46] He offered no proof for either assertion, and other expert testimony, as well as the daily experience of most librarians, suggested that, improved or not, ILL was still beset with problems. However, De Gennaro remained an NPC advocate because he considered the Center not "System B," but as one element of "System C."

Indeed, many observers, including the System C-endorsing NCLIS, seemed confused about which alternative was actually addressed by Title IID. [47] Although it focused exclusively on the NPC, Section 243 did state that the NPC Corporation "shall seek to establish a national system to provide ... document delivery from a comprehensive collection of periodical literature" (my emphasis). [48] Apparently such language was considered sufficiently vague to puzzle and/or satisfy most factions within academic librarianship. Although the NPC proposal in H. R. 5192 definitely conformed to "System B," it did not, by any means, rule out the development of a "System C."

H. R. 5192

The Senate Subcommittee shared the librarians' puzzlement. After reading studies and hearing testimony, Pell listed for NCLIS three issues which he considered still unresolved: "1) the degree to which the operation of the center takes advantage of already existing resources, including existing commercial document delivery services, or the degree to which the proposed center would be a subsidized activity competing with them; 2) the degree to which the National Periodicals Center would draw on a single centralized collection, or the degree to which it would draw on existing distributed resources; 3) the costs projected over a five- to ten-year period, including measures of cost-effectiveness of alternate approaches and justification for the subsidy concerned."[49] Satisfactory answers to these questions were not forthcoming. Subcommittee member Jacob Javits, professing a "great fear we are compromising the sources of American excellence should we establish such a system,"[50] proposed a compromise measure which was passed on February 28, 1980. A Presidentially-appointed corporation (significantly renamed the National Periodicals System Corporation) was to "assess the feasibility and advisability of a national system and, if feasible and advisable, design such a system to provide reliable and timely document delivery from a comprehensive collection of periodical literature." The deadline for submitting the "design" to Congress was set at December 31, 1981, but it would not be implemented until approved by further Congressional action. To fund this assessment, the compromise measure called for a three-year appropriation at $750,000 per year--again subject to the "trigger mechanism" guaranteeing priority funding at 1979 levels for other Title II programs.[51] A relieved Pell declared this "a good approach and a proper Senatorial one."[52] House conferees later approved the Senate's revision.[53]

As of this writing (October 1982), no further action has been reported.

Opposition to the NPC

The Promise of New Technology

As we have seen, an argument raised frequently both within and without the library community and given added authority by the Little report, was that new technology would soon render the Center obsolete. In the first place, critics said, increasingly inexpensive computer applications had made possible online bibliographic search services and rich databases, thus improving the efficiency of conventional ILL and promising more improvement in the future. Better communications systems were expected also to have an enormous impact in the near future.[54] In the second place, the Little researchers and other observers predicted, publishing processes would be revolutionized in the coming decade: "Almost all important [periodical] publications will [eventually] be photocomposed out of computerized data bases"[55] and, by 1990, "many journal publications will have for all practical purposes ceased to exist except as demand publications, available in whole-copy or partial-copy form."[56] Users would "browse" not on shelves, but electronically via terminals, video disks, and so forth.[57] All of this, the Little report concluded, made it "clear that the NCP has a very limited future as long as it remains a paper- or microform-based organization."[58] In rejecting "System B," the researchers assumed that there would be no way of adapting an established NPC to take advantage of new technology and incorporate new formats into its collection. Yet this did not seem a necessary assumption.

In any case, none of these observations was new. F. W. Lancaster and others had predicted, in many publications, an increasingly "paperless" society.[59] On the other hand, Herbert S. White,[60] who had studied the journal publishing industry for several years, and Don R. Swanson,[61] a specialist in computer applications, seemed skeptical of the apocalyptic tone of these predictions.

Opposition Within the Library Community

Another source of opposition to the NPC was the public library sector. Although the NPC proposal was tacked rather hurriedly and awkwardly onto the Higher Education Act, its presence there was not inappropriate--as some public librarians were quick to point out. Research libraries, most of which are attached to universities, would undoubtedly benefit most from an NPC--followed by smaller academic libraries and by special libraries.

Interlibrary loan use studies had shown that academic and special libraries requested substantially higher proportions of serial materials than did public libraries.[62] Perhaps impolitically, the NCLIS National Periodicals System Committee, which was named in 1978, reflected this imbalance of interests: it was topheavy with representatives from academia. Of its fourteen members, six were from academic libraries (including one from a community college); the remaining eight were drawn from a variety of sectors, including two persons from the publishing industry; only one was a public librarian.[63]

In 1973, Fussler had predicted the political unacceptability of the oft-proposed concept of federally funded "national centers of excellence" based on existing collections. To fund the nation's greatest libraries at still higher levels, and out of the national treasury, would be seen, he argued, as helping the rich to get richer and the poor, by contrast, poorer. Improved ILL accessibility to these grand collections would not, he believed, suffice to stem opposition. It was his view that a generally accessible national center could bypass the worst political briar patches.[64] Perhaps this was true: Ralph F. McCoy, who was Interim Executive Director of ARL and deeply involved in the NPC debate and lobbying, wrote rather cheerfully in 1980 that the dissension within the library profession was par for the course and not insurmountable.[65]

However, the huge public library sector (which in many localities during the seventies was starved almost to death) was unenthusiastic at best. Donald J. Sager, then director of the hard-pressed Chicago Public Library System and a spokesman for the Public Library Association (PLA, a division of ALA) published a September 1979 article in American Libraries (an ALA publication) assailing the

NPC on several counts. His essential argument was that public libraries simply did not need the Center. He explained that a "study" of ILL at the Chicago Public, conducted over a one-year period, had revealed only 190 patron requests for periodicals not in the library's holdings--and very little interest of any kind in back files.[66] The impact of these findings was diminished by Sager's failure to describe the design and methodology of his study. More disturbing, however, were his anti-"elitist" underpinnings. Several times in his two-page article, Sager referred slightingly to the "scholarly elite." After noting that "the most public libraries are concerned with satisfying the everyday needs of the average layperson--a noble enough purpose and one which most libraries find difficult to achieve these days," he declared: "The NPC proposal, designed to improve service to a scholarly elite, appears almost frivolous, and reveals a serious confusion of priorities which is tragic for American libraries."[67] This denigration of the needs of scholars betrayed an ignorance (or unconcern) about how knowledge advances that was surprising in a librarian. It was likely, of course, that Sager feared federal money to be used for an NPC would be diverted from programs more directly affecting public libraries.

By February 1980, Sager appeared to be in a state of confusion. At the ALA midwinter conference, he said that PLA had not yet taken a stand, but would probably "go along to support the others." He reiterated, however, this time speaking explicitly for PLA, that the NPC would not benefit public libraries. Yet he emphasized that if the Center were established, it should be structured to serve public libraries.[68]

A second major source of opposition within the library profession came from the regional ILL networks, especially the Pacific Northwest Bibliographic Center (PNBC), based at the University of Washington. Many NPC advocates, including Richard De Gennaro and the NCLIS Task Force on a National Periodicals System, stressed the importance of maintaining present ILL systems. And many people, from all sectors, who had withheld full approval expressed concern about the role and strength of these systems were an NPC to be created.[69] Their concerns were based on the assumptions that networks were essential to provide access to strong existing collections and to hold the NPC's request load to a manageable level.

In its Burgundy Book, CLR took the aggressive--and politically injudicious--stand that, while "It is not the intent of the NPC to disrupt any effective local document delivery or ILL service ... it is conceivable ... that the NPC would become so effective in responding to requests that the continuation of an existing ILL network might properly be questioned. Thus, the rationale for that network's existence could no longer seem to be valid." In the meantime, CLR cautioned, networks with "slow, laborious response times and mechanisms" should try to improve.[70] This very likely alarmed the networks and contributed to the disfavor into which the Burgundy Book fell. Networks are, after all, providers not only of services, but also of jobs and personal power bases.

Communication and Education   111

William DeJohn, director of the PNBC, vacillated on the NPC
issue, but finally seemed to oppose the Center. At the March 1979
Arlington meeting, DeJohn stated that his and other ILL systems
viewed NPC not as a threat but "as a source of relief and an answer
to some of the very frustrating problems that exist in filling requests
from a non-dedicated library collection." PNBC, he said, had only
an 80-85 percent fill rate. He urged that networks be brought immediately into the NPC planning process,[71] which suggested that
NCLIS blundered politically by neglecting, or seeming to neglect, that
sector. That summer, DeJohn told Library Journal that the NPC
"seemed to be a necessity," but in December, he announced that
PNBC's Board of Directors had decided to oppose the concept of
centralized resource sharing in general and Title IID in particular.
[72] However, not all network representatives agreed. Alice Wilcox
of Minnesota's MINITEX, which had often been cited by observers
(including DeJohn) as one of the most successful ILL systems, took
issue with DeJohn at the Arlington meeting: "MINITEX is a myth....
It's not as good as has been said.... It was an ad hoc solution ...
developed because of the void.... It's imperfect, slow and costly,
and should not be considered as an ideal."[73]

Other, more specific, criticisms from within the library
community focused on: (1) the presumed completeness of existing
library resources and resultant lack of need for central and/or
dedicated collections[74]; (2) fear of federal government domination
of the Center and increased interference in other library-related
matters; (3) fear of Center control by research library grants, a
concern probably stimulated by ARL's support and leadership; (4)
the unwise exclusion from the planning process of key associations,
ranging from the National Library of Medicine to ALA and its various
suborganizations[75]; (5) the frequent citation of the British Library
Lending Division as a model, or proof of feasibility, despite the
significant differences between the United States and Britain geograph-
ically, in copyright law, in mail service, and in richness of library
resources and size and diversity of library communities[76]; and (6)
the difficulty of achieving anything like a consensus, or even a persuasive degree of support, for the NPC.[77] The decision of the
Senate Subcommittee was obviously affected by the conflicting testimony of interested parties.

In his November 1979 article, which represented a partial
retreat from his earlier[78] enthusiastic support of centralized resource sharing, De Gennaro wrote: "I am becoming increasingly
pessimistic about the ability of the library community to come to a
consensus on any major program and line up the political support
needed to get it through Congress."[79]

Opposition from the Publishing and Information Industries

Reflecting on the split between librarians and the publishing and information industries over the NPC, Milo Nelson observed: "The irreconcilable difference ... had to do with positions held by individ-

uals accustomed to viewing the dispersion of information as a profit-making activity and persons trained to think of the sharing of information as a public service."[80] The ARL's McCoy, while playing down tensions within the library profession, declared (exactly one year after the publication of Nelson's editorial): "The serious and seemingly irreconcilable differences over the NPC are ... between the library community and the information industry."[81]

Publishers' primary concerns appeared to center on retaining their copyright protection and on the possibility of libraries' cutting their subscription lists if they gained access to a periodicals center. The first fear seemed baseless, since very study and proposal--including H. R. 5192--provided for full compliance with copyright regulations. Indeed, the efficiency of a centralized system of payment (partially achieved now through the Copyright Clearance Center) was sometimes cited by both librarians and publishers as an advantage of the NPC. The publisher-weighted national study group which prepared a significant report on scholarly publishing endorsed the NPC partly because it would insure full compliance with the law.[82]

The conventional response to publishers' fear of lost subscriptions was that while periodical expenditures might decline, with the more esoteric titles most vulnerable to cancellation, overall materials expenditures would surely remain the same, which would be a boon for book publishers. Furthermore, several studies (most notably the first one reported by White in Library Quarterly[83]), as well as reports from England, showed that increased sharing did not seem to affect libraries' subscription rates.[84] Publishers, and librarians such as Donald Sager,[85] abetted by studies like that of the Little corporation,[86] were not mollified by such examples. A major advantage of a dedicated national periodicals collection was that it would permit more rational funding allocations than had ever been possible before. Since this would offer an unprecedented opportunity, no one could know what its effects on collection building would be. NPC supporters placed themselves in a strange position when they argued, on the one hand, that a Center would have no impact on subscription decisions, and on the other, that it would facilitate making more sensible decisions.

A second White Library Quarterly article appeared in July 1980 and provided publishers with fresh documentation for their position on the NPC. While he had previously found no indication that libraries tended to cancel subscriptions based on ILL availability, in this study (conducted 1978-79), White discovered that 8.1 percent of libraries cancelling scholarly journals based their decision at least partially on the ILL factor. Titles known to be available for loan were more likely to be dispensed with. While 8.1 percent is not a huge proportion, White thought it significant because, as late as 1976, he had been unable to discern even a trace of ILL influence. Sensing the beginning of a trend, he wrote: "It is likely that this process, once begun, will accelerate." At the same time, he noted that the root cause of cancellations was internal economic pressures, and with or without ILL, some cancellations would occur.[87]

It may be that no library actions could have appeased publishers since many of them, like many libraries, claimed to be fighting for their very survival. Diminished library budgets and resource sharing could be expected to take the heaviest toll of those journals already most unstable: scholarly publications dependent on the academic library market.[88]

At Arlington, in March 1979, Carol Risher of the Association of American Publishers (AAP), declared that publishers would support the NPC provided it conformed to various copyright practices and there were "substantial publisher participation" in its governance.[89] That October, Risher again affirmed AAP's conditional support, but seemed to attach a new stipulation: that no publisher be forced to participate--that is, to have its products housed in the Center.[90] As the Little researchers pointed out in their report published that same month, voluntary participation would render the NPC collection "a Swiss cheese instead of a solid block."[91] By the time of the February ALA meeting, further "erosion" seemed to have occurred in the AAP's support,[92] and its Senate testimony was mixed.

Fussler had suggested that those journals which had such a "marginal existence" that they would be driven out of business by a Center might need to "adopt alternative methods of publication and distribution,"[93] and White noted that most publishers, despite their financial predicaments, had never been eager to explore such alternatives as microform publishing and on-demand publication.[94] It was suggested also that the NPC might cooperate with publishers to exploit new technology.[95]

As McCoy observed, perhaps the most intransigent opposition group was the Information Industry Association (IIA). This industry comprises suppliers of microform, tear-sheet services, reprints, computer software, indexes and abstracts, and related products. Its representatives gave negative testimony before Pell's Subcommittee; a key argument was that the private sector already provided sufficient information services. Indeed, Allan Wittman of John Wiley believed that this sector constituted a "de facto national periodicals center." [96] Librarians responded by noting the steep fees charged, lack of coordination and unevenness of coverage.[97]

As usual, some of the strongest, most sensible responses to the representatives of private enterprise could be drawn from the statements of De Gennaro and Fussler. Incensed by Wiley's Allan Wittman, De Gennaro told publishers, essentially, to withdraw from the debate: "Libraries need NPC. I don't think publishers need it. What publishers are in effect asking us to do is carry on as usual ... with our purchasing power cut in half."[98] Six years earlier, Fussler had put it this way: "...publishers simply cannot expect libraries to provide access in a traditional way to an unlimited number of traditionally generated publications at steadily increasing prices."[99]

Richard Dougherty, an editor and academic librarian, pointed out that in the final analysis, librarians must make their own decisions and press for legislation by themselves if need be: "The voices of opposition will not be muted. The library community should not be alarmed nor let its attention be diverted; opposition from the information sector is inevitable."[100]

In Summary

NPC study, planning, and debate--from 1973 through 1980--were fraught with politically unwise statements and choices, vague definitions, conflicting designs, venturings forth with incomplete information, and failures to meet vulnerable challenges logically and effectively. It was distressing and embarrassing that the piles of printed studies devoted to an NPC, together with the most expert witnesses the library community could produce, were not able to resolve to Pell's satisfaction the questions he put to the NCLIS (see page 109). But it was even more disturbing that Trezza of the NCLIS, and the sixty other organization leaders who assembled at the 1980 ALA midwinter conference to discuss the NPC, decided that despite years of study, there were as yet no agreed-upon answers to those questions. This admission laid bare the difficulty of effecting Congressional action without a recognized, decisive national leadership.

In the case of the National Periodicals Center proposal, the American library community revealed itself to be a collection of clashing Indians without any chief.

References

1. For example, some university press directors opposed the NPC proposal in their appearances before Congress, while university library directors favored it.
2. See, for example: "NPC, Dept. of Ed, Title 44: Old Games Take New Twists," American Libraries 10, no. 10 (November 1979), p. 574.
3. Richard De Gennaro, "Austerity, Technology, and Resource Sharing: Research Libraries Face the Future," Library Journal 100, no. 10 (May 15, 1975), p. 920.
4. Herman H. Fussler, Research Libraries and Technology: A Report to the Sloan Foundation (Chicago: University of Chicago Press, 1973), p. 39.
5. De Gennaro, "Austerity, Technology," p. 920; Fussler, Research Libraries, pp. 40-43.
6. For example: De Gennaro, "Austerity, Technology," p. 922; "National Journal Lending Library," American Libraries 4, no. 1 (January 1973), p. 10; Noel Savage, "A National Periodicals Center: The Debate in Arlington," Library Journal 104, no. 10 (May 15, 1979), p. 1110.
7. A. G. Myatt, "National Lending Library for Science and Technology (British Library Lending Division)," in Encyclopedia of Li-

brary and Information Science, vol. 19 (New York: Marcel Dekker, 1976), p. 92.
8. United States. House of Representatives. 96th Congress. 1st Session. H. R. 5192. Title IID: Higher Education Act of 1965 [proposed amendment], p. 25.
9. Alphonse F. Trezza, "Toward a National Periodicals System," Special Libraries 68, no. 1 (January 1977), pp. 10-11.
10. For example, see: "National Periodicals Center Backed at Kansas City Meeting," Library Journal 104, no. 11 (June 1, 1979), p. 1201.
11. Rolland E. Stevens, A Feasibility Study of Centralized and Regionalized Interlibrary Loan Centers (Washington, D.C.: Association of Research Libraries, 1973), p. 35, 41.
12. Donald J. Sager, "A National Periodicals Center: Too Limited a Goal," American Libraries 10, no. 8 (September 1979), p. 465.
13. Stevens, A Feasibility Study, p. 30.
14. Reported in: Vernon E. Palmour, Marcia C. Bellassai, and Lucy M. Gray, Access to Periodical Resources: A National Plan (Washington, D.C.: Association of Research Libraries, 1974), p. 29. Wood identified 16,361 serials important to the fields of chemistry and chemical engineering and then surveyed 325 specialized American libraries. Complete runs of only 10,810 titles were available in those libraries; no single state held more than 6,000; and only 5,000 were available in the average region.
15. At the 1979 Arlington debate, H. William Axford pointed out that the Center for Research Libraries in Chicago was the British Library Lending Division's biggest single customer--and 40 percent of CRL's requests were for items published in the United States: "Thus we have the truly ironic situation wherein the wealthiest nation in the world is dependent to some extent on one that is nearly bankrupt for rapid access to certain types of scholarly information" (quoted in: Savage, "A National Periodicals Center," p. 1110).
16. Stevens, A Feasibility Study, pp. 2-3.
17. Ibid., p. 44.
18. Palmour, Bellassai, and Gray. Access to Periodical Resources, p. 53.
19. Ibid., pp. 155-61.
20. National Commission on Libraries and Information Science, Task Force on a National Periodicals System, Effective Access to the Periodical Literature: A National Program (Washington, D.C., [1977]), pp. 5-7.
21. Ibid., pp. 24-32.
22. Ibid., pp. 38-45.
23. Ibid., p. 63
24. Ibid., p. 72.
25. Ibid., p. 80.
26. Council on Library Resources, Inc., A National Periodicals Center: Technical Development Plan (Washington, D.C.: Council on Library Resources, Inc., 1978), p. xi.
27. Ibid., pp. xii-xiv.

28. Ibid., pp. 28-30.
29. Ibid., pp. 131-36.
30. Robert Wedgeworth, "Implementation: The Hidden Question of WHCLIS," American Libraries 10, no. 9 (October 1979), p. 545.
31. "National Periodicals Center Backed at Kansas City Meeting," p. 1202.
32. Savage, "A National Periodicals Center," p. 1115.
33. "NPC, Dept. of Ed, Title 44," p. 574.
34. John Berry, "National Periodicals Center Challenged," Library Journal 105, no. 6 (March 15, 1980), p. 658.
35. "House Gives Initial Boost to Periodicals Center," American Libraries 10, no. 9 (October 1979): 509.
36. H.R. 5192, pp. 25-26.
37. Ibid., p. 27.
38. Ibid., p. 28.
39. Berry, "National Periodicals Center Challenged," p. 659.
40. Arthur D. Little, Inc., A Comparative Evaluation of Alternative Systems for the Provision of Effective Access to Periodical Literature: A Report to the National Commission on Libraries and Information Science (Washington, D.C.: National Commission on Libraries and Information Science, 1979), p. 6.
41. Ibid., pp. 3-5.
42. Ibid., pp. 7-12, IV 50-56, V 8-21.
43. Berry, "National Periodicals Center Challenged," p. 659.
44. That copies of the report were circulated to interested parties prior to final publication was suggested by a sentence in Sager's September 1979 article which seemed to echo (though without attribution) the language of the report. Sager wrote: "This leads me to wonder if the NPC is an idea whose time has come, and gone" (Sager, "A National Periodicals Center," p. 466).
45. De Gennaro, "Austerity, Technology," pp. 918-19.
46. Richard De Gennaro, "Research Libraries Enter the Information Age," Library Journal 104, no. 20 (November 15, 1979): 2405-10.
47. Berry, "National Periodicals Center Challenged," p. 658.
48. H.R. 5192, p. 26.
49. Berry, "National Periodicals Center Challenged," p. 659.
50. "National Periodicals Center 'A Buzz Saw' to Senate Group," American Libraries 11, no. 4 (April 1980), p. 185.
51. James D. Lockwood, "Inside Washington: National Periodicals Center," College and Research Libraries News 41, no. 4 (April 1980): 92.
52. "National Periodicals Center 'A Buzz Saw'," p. 185.
53. "Washington Conferees Agree on Periodical System," American Libraries 11, no. 8 (September 1980): 464-65.
54. For example, see: De Gennaro, "Research Libraries Enter," pp. 2407-8; Arthur D. Little, Inc., A Comparative Evaluation, p. 7, V-21; and Ron Diener, quoted in: Savage, "A National Periodicals Center," p. 1115.
55. Arthur D. Little, Inc., A Comparative Evaluation, p. V-5.
56. Ibid., p. V-6.

57. Ibid., p. V-11.
58. Ibid., p. V-13.
59. For example, see: F. W. Lancaster, Toward Paperless Information Systems (New York: Academic Press, 1978); and F. W. Lancaster and Linda C. Smith, "Science, Scholarship, and the Communication of Knowledge," Library Trends 27, no. 3 (Winter 1979): 367-88.
60. Herbert S. White, "Publishers, Libraries, and Costs of Journal Subscriptions," Library Quarterly 46, no. 4 (October 1976), p. 376.
61. Don R. Swanson, [review], Library Quarterly 51, no. 3 (July 1981): 316-19.
62. For example: Stevens, A Feasibility Study, p. 1, 26.
63. "National Periodicals System: Committee Named by NCLIS," Library Journal 103, no. 9 (May 1, 1978), p. 917.
64. This and other advantages of centralized over decentralized sharing were identified succinctly by Fussler in 1973 (Research Libraries, pp. 36-38).
65. Ralph E. McCoy, "NPC Debate: Normal Process" [letter], Library Journal 105, no. 10 (May 15, 1980): 1112.
66. Sager, "A National Periodicals Center," p. 465.
67. Ibid.
68. Berry, "National Periodicals Center Challenged," p. 659.
69. For example, see: Sager, "A National Periodicals Center," p. 466; and Berry, "National Periodicals Center Challenged," p. 659. A useful summary of loan networks and service as 1977--about two years before this time--can be found in the Green Book (NCLIS, Effective Access, pp. 24-32).
70. Council on Library Resources, Inc., A National Periodicals Center, p. 22.
71. Savage, "A National Periodicals Center," p. 1110.
72. "PNBC Declares Opposition to NPC Legislation," Library Journal 104, no. 22 (December 15, 1979): 2605-6.
73. Savage, "A National Periodicals Center," pp. 1110-11.
74. For example, see: Ibid., p. 1111; Stevens, A Feasibility Study, p. 2, 30; and David A. Kronick, "Preventing Library Wastelands: A Personal Statement," Library Journal 105, no. 4 (February 15, 1980): 483-87.
75. For example, see: Savage, "A National Periodicals Center," p. 1115; and Wedgeworth, "Implementation," pp. 545-46.
76. Trezza, "Toward a National," p. 7; Rolland E. Stevens, "Commentary: Other Answers to ILL Problems" [letter], American Libraries 10, no. 10 (November 1979): 582. The advantages of the BLLD would have over any central United States lending library were well stated by Fussler in 1973 (Research Libraries, p. 38); however, he did not see these advantages as constituting a sufficient argument against an NPC.
77. For example, see: Savage, "A National Periodicals Center," p. 1114; Wedgeworth, "Implementation," p. 546; Milo Nelson, "The Month in Review: Some Uneasy Friends Reach an Agreement of Sorts," Wilson Library Bulletin 53, no. 8 (April 1979), p. 554; and "NCLIS Forces $ $ 'Review,' WHCOLIS, and NPC Criticism," Library Journal 104, no. 13 (July 1979), p. 1399.

78. De Gennaro, "Austerity, Technology."
79. De Gennaro, "Research Libraries Enter," p. 2407. For the record: those library organizations which registered clear support for the NPC included NCLIS; ARL: the delegation to the 1979 White House Conference on Library and Information Services (White House Conference on Library and Information Services 1979; Resolutions [Washington, D.C.: White House Conference on Library and Information Services, 1980], p. 30); the Special Libraries Association ("SLA Backs Periodicals Center," Library Journal 104, no. 15 [September 1, 1979]: 1609); the Medical Library Association ("NPC Draft Proposal Endorsed by MLA, " Library Journal 104, no. 17 [October 1, 1979]: 2022); ALA (Savage, "A National Periodicals Center," p. 1115); and the Library of Congress.
80. Milo Nelson, "Letter from New York/Editorial," Wilson Library Bulletin 53, no. (May 1979): 612.
81. McCoy, "NPC Debate."
82. Scholarly Communication: The Report of the National Enquiry (Baltimore: Johns Hopkins University Press, 1979), p. 19.
83. White, "Publishers, Libraries."
84. Council on Library Resources, Inc., A National Periodicals Center, p. 33; Savage, "A National Periodicals Center," p. 1113; Scholarly Communication, p. 19; Berry, "National Periodicals Center Challenged," p. 660.
85. Sager, "A National Periodicals Center," p. 465.
86. Arthur D. Little, Inc., A Comparative Evaluation, p. V-14.
87. Herbert S. White, "Factors in the Decision by Individuals and Libraries to Place or Cancel Subscriptions to Scholarly and Research Journals," Library Quarterly 50, no. 3 (July 1980), pp. 305-6.
88. Herman H. Fussler, "Current Research Library Trends," in Reflections on the Future of Research Libraries: Two Essays, by Herman H. Fussler and Harrison Bryan (Victoria, Australia: Monash University, 1978), p. 16; White, "Publishers, Libraries," pp. 363-64.
89. Savage, "A National Periodicals Center," p. 1112.
90. Judith Brody Saks, "House Unite Releases Bill for National Periodicals Center," Publishers Weekly 216, no. 15 (October 8, 1979): 22-23.
91. Arthur D. Little, Inc., A Comparative Evaluation, p. V-14.
92. Berry, "National Periodicals Center Challenged," p. 660.
93. Fussler, Research Libraries, p. 39.
94. White, "Publishers, Libraries," p. 374.
95. For example, see: Scholarly Communication, p. 14.
96. Savage, "A National Periodicals Center," p. 1109.
97. Ibid., p. 1110; NCLIS, Effective Access, p. 30; Jerry B. Post, "Information Industry Reps Challenge Federal Role," American Libraries 9, no. 10 (November 1978): 573. An inconsistency lurked here. Information industry spokespeople had long defended their profits derived from reprinting and selling uncopyrighted government information gathered and reported at public expense (for example: Carlos A. Cuadra, "The Role of the Private

Sector in the Development and Improvement of Library and Information Services," Library Quarterly 50, no. 1 [January 1980]: 94-111).
98. Quoted in: Savage, "A National Periodicals Center," p. 1112.
99. Fussler, "Current Research Library Trends," p. 16.
100. Richard M. Dougherty, "Editorial: A National Periodical Center," Journal of Academic Librarianship 5, no. 2 (May 1979): 59.

MUST WE LIMIT THE CATALOG?*

Maurice J. Freedman

The four people generally acknowledged as the greatest thinkers in cataloging, at least in the Anglo-American tradition, either imperfectly, implicitly, or explicitly had the same thing to say about the functions of the catalog. Rereading and study of their writings as part of a recent academic exercise convinced me that any current cataloging discussion must occur either in the framework of the cataloging ideology developed by the "holy four" or prove the deficiencies of that ideology before proposing some alternative to it.

The "holy four"

The "holy four" have shaped our thoughts, to the extent that we think at all about catalogs, their function, and their organization. First on the list is Antonio Panizzi, the Italian anarchist lawyer who immigrated to Great Britain, and who was also the country's greatest librarian. Charles Coffin Jewett, a second cataloging immortal, was Librarian of the Smithsonian Institution and a tinkerer with a failed technology. Fred Kilgour will be the first to admit that Jewett's ideas served as a model for the OCLC network. The third member of the quartet, Charles Ammi Cutter, was probably the greatest librarian this country has produced, and the only accepted cataloging theorist who had any perception that there are public libraries. The only living member of the esteemed foursome is Seymour Lubetzky, a Polish-Jewish immigrant to the United States, and certainly the best thinker of this century on the functions of the catalog. Lubetzky's analysis provides a definition of what is necessary for a catalog, and a point of departure for this discussion.

Functions of the catalog

Two conditions that pertain to most published materials have tended

*Reprinted by permission of the author and publisher from Library Journal, 109 (February 15, 1984) 322-324. Published by R. R. Bowker Co. (a Xerox company). Copyright © 1984 by Xerox Corporation.

Communication and Education

to guarantee a livelihood for catalogers. First, any given publication is a representation of a work. In other words, the publication may be one of several editions or translation of a given work. These different representations or publications each bear a title as the means by which they are identified, but there is no guarantee that these titles are identical--even though they are carried on editions or translations of one singly identified work. The first condition, simply stated, is that a work may be represented by publications with different titles. All the titles identifying editions and translations of Hamlet illustrate the variability of titles of publications.

The second condition--and another traditional guarantor of employment for catalogers--is the peculiar human condition whereby a given author is identified in nonidentical ways. Either the author or the publisher, or for that matter anyone else connected with the publication or citation process, may choose to identify the person or body responsible for the creation of one or more works in more than one way. The multiple pseudonyms of John Creasey and such seemingly minor variants as Chester B. Himes, author of If He Hollers Let Him Go and Chester Himes, author of Cotton Comes to Harlem illustrate the variability of individual identification.

Since there are various ways by which a given work is represented and by which a given author is identified, it has been the traditional job of the cataloger to demonstrate the relatedness of a given work's various representations. In traditional catalogs under the uniform bracketed title [Hamlet] all of the editions and translations of the work Hamlet are entered. It was also the cataloger's job to demonstrate that the various names by which a given author has been known or identified are all the names of the same person. The techniques for accomplishing this identification of an author's various names have been twofold, depending on which catalog rules, whose interpretation of them, and/or whose catalog department prevails. One method is to identify a person by a single form of his or her name and refer to that name from all of the other forms by which the person has been known.

Old hands at cataloging know that this was why readers of Harold Robbins were forced to look under Rubin, and devotees of Victoria Holt and Jean Plaidy were (are they still?) directed to Margaret Hibbert (apparently a name never used professionally by Ms. Hibbert). The other means of identifying a person who has been known by a variety of names has been to relate all of them to each other by the device of the "see also" reference. Hence there developed entries such as: "Donald Westlake see also Richard Stark and Tucker Coe"; "Richard Stark see also Donald Westlake and Tucker Coe"; and "Tucker Coe see also Donald Westlake and Richard Stark." It should be obvious why, in manually created catalogs, the single name identification to which all other identifiers were referred was chosen as the rule.

Noting this variability we see that the library catalog, unlike finding tools such as Books in Print, had to meet specific demands.

These demands went beyond informing the user whether a given publication is held by the library, or whether a given publication could be found under the form of the author's name as used in the publication when it was issued.

What has been demanded of Anglo-American catalogs, and required by the "holy four" in the rules and the catalogs they constructed, was that all of an author's works be presented to the user, and that all of a work's editions and translations be presented to the user as representations of that given work. These demands for comprehensiveness, or in another way, these conditions of bibliographic control make the library catalog a tool that transcends simple finding lists, inventory lists, Books in Print (BIP), most dealer catalogs, and all trade bibliography which all take as their primary, if not always their sole focus, the listing or presenting of publications. It is not fair for us to criticize BIP for having Lord Byron's works entered under several unrelated names. We do say, however, that the library catalog is deficient if it does not tell us one way or another that The Melancholy Dane is yet another edition of the work that is usually identified as Hamlet.

As a devotee of Donald Westlake, I would be cheated of the joys of his writings as Tucker Coe and Richard Stark if the catalog did not properly discharge its function of informing the user of all of a given author's works regardless of the names under which they appeared.

Technology and function

The clear necessity for the library catalog to perform those traditional functions is established, and those functions follow from normal and continuing bibliographic phenomena. The question then, is what becomes of such essential catalog functions with the advent of closed catalogs, computers, minicomputers, microcomputers, and in view of the utterances of recent cataloging gurus who tell us of "revolutions" in cataloging. Even less recent gurus tell us that the minicat has replaced the classical catalog. What about all the other yeasayers wearing the blue blazers of circulation control salespeople and consultants? What has become of the traditional and basic functions of the library catalog in this changed environment?

The degraded catalog?

Whether the catalog is a single-entry union catalog or a PAC (the much touted public access catalog that allegedly exists) makes no difference. If the catalog is going to present all of an author's works, someone is going to have to tell that catalog (whether it is in card form or little pixels glowing on a technicolor CRT screen) that Coe, Stark, and Westlake are indeed the same person, that The Melancholy Dane is another edition of Hamlet. If the "revolution" means that these basic catalog functions are now unnecessary, then

Communication and Education

I, for one, take my place with the forces of reaction and announce that the catalog has been degraded in fundamental functional ways.

This is not simply a Luddite response. I started working with computers when a CPU with 32,000 bytes of memory was considered a powerful beast and required a refrigerated room the size of a pool hall, a full-time trained attendant, and dropped ceilings and raised floors to ensure the proper functioning of all of the cables and refrigeration. I work with computers to this day, believe in their usefulness, and am in no way anti-computer. I am only against the unfortunately exaggerated claims made on their behalf.

Making the connections

The catalog's assembly functions with regard to all the works of an author and all the representations of any work still require, and in principle will always require, the research to accomplish the connections. The computer will not eliminate that work, but it can facilitate it. When our new gurus tell us that the online PAC (let's call these gurus the "PAC-people") does other stuff like use our fingerprints to call up entries, or array before us one or 25 citations which all have as the same root "westl," I say thank you and congratulations. These advances are important, but I must ask two questions: 1) Have we looked at what we left behind?; 2) Why are the PAC-people depriving us of access to some of the works by that person variously identified as Coe and Stark than don't show up in the "westl" array?

Boolean or key word searching and all of the analytical and combining capabilities of the computer are fine. They complement the catalog's traditional functions, but they do not replace them. A finding list whether in print or online is still simply a finding list and not a catalog.

Computer possibilities

The computer can be a godsend once the cataloger's work has been completed. Instead of that traditional cataloger's system of references to establish links between all the forms of an author's name, the online computer can display or present all of an author's works under any of the variant names by which that author was ever identified or by which any user queries the catalog.

The linear nature of the old static forms of the catalog practically precludes the gathering of all appropriate data under each and every occurrence of a name. The size of a catalog on cards, COM, or any other static display medium, makes it practically impossible to display all of Creasey's works under each of the names he wrote. The online catalog, assuming that the cataloger has done the research and appropriately related these forms of his name, can assemble and display all of his works under each of them on demand. Only with the cataloger's help can computer technology provide us with this major advance.

The answer counts

In a similar way, but equally or even more demanding of the cataloger and the computer, a query either by the title of a given publication or by the work must ultimately be capable of assembling for display all of a work's editions, translations, and the like under any of the individual titles or identifiers. If the user only wants to know about one particular representation there is no problem, but frequently there is benefit in knowing about other editions and translations even though they were not part of the original search. As Lubetzky has asserted, it is what the user obtains as a result, not how that user started the search that is our concern. We must know which questions the catalog user asks, but our overriding and most expensive concern as library professionals, regardless of the catalog medium, must be with the answer that the catalog provides.

I enjoyed Donald Westlake's first few books so much I became insatiable for his work. I did not know that he wrote as "Tucker Coe" or "Richard Stark." When I looked up his works, the catalog informed me of these other names and the works associated with them. As far as I know, few, if any, of the online PAC catalogs are capable of relating the various works of an author writing under more than one name; and none of them can do it, under any circumstances, if the links are not first established by the cataloger. The same goes for a work's representations or variant titles.

More than books

The traditional catalog since the catalogs of Cutter and Poole has not included access to an author's articles or other works shorter than the normal book. Today's computer memory size, speed, and online storage capacity make it practical to have computer access to all of an author's works and their representations. It has been financially impossible, however, to have catalogers authenticate and link the names employed by the authors of articles in serial and other article-bearing publications such as signed articles in encyclopedias. This limitation on the catalog is due to the lack of cataloger firepower.

Access to nonbook publications, or to serial publications and other sources of articles have traditionally been excluded from library catalogs. As with authors and titles, catalogs must not discriminate among the media forms and formats that the publication of a work may take. The filmstrip-cassette kit of Where the Wild Things Are is another edition of Sendak's book by the same title. Limiting the catalog to books alone, as libraries have traditionally done, has separated books from the other information-bearing media, and has violated the essential and traditional assembling functions of the catalog. It is also true that such comprehensiveness is not possible in the local catalog, whether it is an online PAC or an old-fashioned one.

In short, the integrated all works catalog is not possible if we require that it offer universal coverage, comprehensive inclusion of articles, chapters, and shorter than book-length publications as well as book-length works.

Subject access

Traditionally, the catalog has been required to gather and present every item on a given subject. The control problems are similar, if not identical, to those related to authors known by several names. Subject concepts have been expressed in several ways, for example: "Psychology of Children," "Psychology, Child," "Children, Psychology of." In the traditional library catalog, regardless of the variety of ways a concept can be expressed, everything held by the library on a given topic is presented to the user directly or via supplementary references. Despite a running battle over the selection of terms to represent a given topic (the LC way or the reality of the rest of the culture, to oversimplify), there is agreement that regardless of the term selected, the library catalog--unlike SDC, Lockheed, BRS, keyword, etc., databases--must present everything on the topic to the user under a single heading or set of explicit, connected, and related headings through "see" and "see also" references. The user of the library catalog should not be confronted with separate files of publications under "butterfly," "butterflies," and "lepidoptera." In even some of the best library catalogs, the user may be directed to look under different, but linked by "see also" terms to find everything on a topic. The linking, albeit clumsy, does ensure that the catalog displays all the library's holdings on a given topic. The PAC-people's catalogs hold the greatest potential for improving subject aid to library users. Libraries (in large part because of their slavish adherence to LC) have been stuck with a subject terminology and structure which frequently causes disservice to the user. Such "end-arounds" as title keyword, Boolean, and other searches using textual and fixed-field information found in the catalog record can improve the user's success at finding works on all kind of topics from "hospices" to "punk rock." Even if all of the library's works are not found in the individual search, access is usually better than that achieved by direct subject heading searches under the LC accepted forms for such current topics.

Being able to search a catalog through the use of word or name fragments and to combine given words or data elements on an interactive basis is clearly an advancement and will yield information to catalog users that traditional catalogs or traditional cataloging practice will not. Libraries must take advantage of these enhancements. The library system for which I work does this kind of subject searching for the users of its member libraries.

Must catalogs be limited?

From an ideological, professional, and traditional standpoint, there can be no retreat from the demand that a catalog present to the user the complete works of an author, all of the various editions and representations of a work, and all of the library's holdings on a given subject or topic.

We must treat users better regarding nonbook media. When someone searches our catalog for the poems of Dylan Thomas, recordings of that poetry ought to be presented along with the books. This long-standing unwillingness to integrate nonprint with print formats in library catalogs is neither technically nor professionally defensible, despite our print origins and the prejudices they created. Nonprint formats are being cataloged and they are finite, unlike the infinitely expanding universe of journal articles.

From the standpoint of practicality, in terms of cataloging resources--the funds to pay for it--there are obvious limitations on the ability to integrate serial and monograph data in local and even network catalogs. Technology notwithstanding, such an integrated catalog is not practically possible for a library of any significant size. The technical problems are probably as difficult to solve as the problems of controlling and searching such an awesome catalog.

The "unlimited" catalog

It is not necessary to put new limitations on the library catalog. The traditional card catalog satisfies the requirements of the great thinkers in library cataloging, at least it has until now, warts, blemishes and all. Certainly the great "improvements" and the "revolution" claimed by the PAC-people with the advent of online catalogs ought to be able to accomplish what the failed technology did.

We can welcome the improvements that come with the online "catalog," but they should not be made at the sacrifice of the essential and traditional features of Anglo-American bibliographic control. We must not accept, for example, limitations like those in one of the new online "catalogs" in which no more than six subject headings can be assigned to a given work. We must not shape or limit our catalogs to fit current technological fashions.

I hesitate to call the PAC's "catalogs" because, in addition to other defects, many (even most) do not rigorously control or link the variations present in basic, normal bibliographic representations of works. Indeed, they put limits on the number of data elements that can be assigned to a work. It is an Orwellian redefinition of the term "catalog" when you simply put a holdings list online and call it a Public Access Catalog. It is not a catalog just because we call it a catalog.

We must not give up almost 250 years of Anglo-American

cataloging service for technological sizzle. We must not limit the catalog. We must exploit the new technology to enhance its proper performance of its essential, historic, and traditional functions: the provision of full access to and control over the library's materials.

THE DEVELOPING CRISIS IN INFORMATION:

A LIBRARIAN'S PERSPECTIVE*

Thomas T. Surprenant and Jane Zande

Introduction

The remainder of this decade will see increased attention to the problems created by the transition into the electronic information age by the industrial nations and attempts by the developing nations to move rapidly through, or jump over, industrialization. Nowhere are the conflicts more apparent than in the changes to the electronic grid which carries information worldwide through telecommunications, and in control over what is allowed onto the grid in the form of information. Since librarians from all nations have a considerable interest in the transmission, storage, and use of information it is important to become aware of the issues that will affect the very nature of our profession in the coming years.

There are three separate yet interdependent issues that have the potential to inhibit the flow of information in the near term, and to effect substantive modifications in the long run. They are Radiofrequency Allocation, the New World Information Order (NWIO), and Transborder Data Flow (TDF). It is the intention of the authors to examine each of the three issues and to suggest ways by which librarians from all nations can help to resolve the problems that threaten the very nature of information itself. This article is not to be considered the definitive statement on the three topics as they relate to librarianship. Rather, it is an attempt to outline the problems, alert the international library community and, hopefully provide a basis for discussion and action.

Background

We are living in a world that thrives on the access, distribution and use of information. Each nation's economic, political, and social environment is affected by the kind and amount of information that is produced and received. Telecommunications, supported by the develop-

*Reprinted by permission of the authors from IFLA Journal, 9:3 (1983) 222-229.

ment of the silicon chip, allow for unparalleled opportunity for information exchange among nations. Our world is becoming smaller and Marshall McLuhan's notion of the "global village" is being fulfilled.[1] But this sophisticated technology has also created a tremendous potential for problems. There has been a restructuring of the electronic grid over which information flows, creating technological and political problems for the nations of the world. There has also been a rethinking of the nature, use and flow of information on the grid. Alvin Toffler has called this the "info-sphere" and it is here that a series of major conflicts and transformations will take place.[2]

As all nations in our global village increase their production, distribution and consumption of information the role of the library must rapidly evolve into one that will play an important part in the new electronic information environment. Librarians have, traditionally, reacted to changes in the info-sphere by defending their position here, compromising there and adapting when necessary. However, the need to cease being reactive and to become proactive is increasing. Radical changes are taking place in the info-sphere and librarians must present proposals that will insure their continued place in the information environment. It is necessary to act on an international basis and to become acquainted in subject areas dictated by the shift into the information society.

The Radiofrequency Spectrum and the ITU

The radiofrequency, or electromagnetic, spectrum is a worldwide resource which cannot be expanded or extended, although it can be enhanced through more sophisticated telecommunications technologies. It is an extremely fragile environment and as such must be managed efficiently and effectively. Any misuse of the spectrum results in radiofrequency interference (RFI) which can inhibit electronic transmissions or even prevent them from reaching their destination.

The International Telecommunications Union (ITU), an agency of the United Nations, regulates and controls the use of the spectrum through a series of voluntary treaties and agreements. The ITU also has the responsibility to allocate radiofrequencies for various tasks (i.e. shortwave radio transmissions) including the use of satellites for telecommunications. Membership in the ITU is presently 155 nations with two-thirds of the membership Third World or developing nations.[3] Thus, those who have the least developed telecommunications systems but the greatest needs make up the majority of the membership.

A major reconsideration of the allocation of frequencies takes place every twenty years at an international ITU sponsored conference. The last World Allocation Radio Conference (WARC) was held in 1979. Called WARC79, it set a table of frequency allocations until 1999 and produced the operational agreements necessary for efficient and interference free use of the electromagnetic spectrum. These agreements were reached through the work of committees and subcommittees and culminated with recommendations voted by the assembled members. Nations that disagreed with the specific allocations added what are called footnotes or reservations which set their operations apart from the overall treaty. In essence, they are declarations of intent, objections, or practices concerning a particular portion of the spectrum. Thus, even though a majority voted to accept the general table of allocations, any country that disagreed could add a footnote and ignore the stipulations of the treaty. Unfortunately, the more reservations, the greater the danger of RF interference and disputes with other nations.

Prior to this conference, the United States and other developed countries relied on the use of consensus to achieve their goals. This procedure operated efficiently due to the technical sophistication of the developed countries and relatively little involvement of the Third World. However, increasing technical capability, the demand on use of the spectrum, and the realization of the importance of information by the Third World have altered the rules of the game. As a majority, the Third World nations are increasingly able to influence and shape international communications policies. Where consensus was once the accepted norm, voting is now required on all issues. The developing countries have taken a highly political stance. They now recognize that the spectrum is an environmental resource of limited capacity, and are pressing for a reserved place for future use. Otherwise, there is real fear that all of the places in a particular portion of the spectrum will be taken up before Third World countries develop the technical capability to utilize them. One particular concern is the allocation of the geostationary satellite or fixed satellite service (FSS).[4] While relatively few satellites are now in orbit, larger numbers could eventually create crowding and interference problems, thus limiting the number of satellites that could be placed in orbit. There are demands to assure access to satellites by all countries by reserving specific slots for every country. From the purely political standpoint, telecommunications could be used as a "tool for development" and are a key resource to increase information capacity and power.[5] Third World countries are also pressing for a transfer of technology that would allow them to control the flow of information. Technology transfer includes both the hardware and associated technology to maintain a sophisticated telecommunications network, and the knowledge and skills necessary to produce the software. In other words, the Third World is seeking to influence both their means of communication as well as their messages.

The 984 page document, of WARC79, that set forth the regulations, resolutions, and recommendations for worldwide radio communications is a highly technical document. It does not represent the political aspects of WARC79 which revolved around spectrum reallocation, equitable access, and technology transfer.[6] The following trends can be identified as a result of the politicalization of the radio frequency allocation procedure.

1. Developing or Third World countries now form a majority in

the ITU.
2. Basic differences exist over the principles that should govern allocation and use of the spectrum, especially where satellites are concerned.
3. Third World countries are increasingly able to influence and shape communications policies in international forums--voting has replaced consensus.
4. A shift towards non-technical factors (political and cultural interests and values) is occurring.
5. There is a growing disparity between nations in their ability to use the spectrum which is leading to disagreements over specific portions of the spectrum.
6. Regional and domestic policies are beginning to predominate. [7]

Libraries in the developed nations will eventually be affected by the political disputes over satellites and frequency allocations. This is especially true for those libraries that are beginning to incorporate use of various sophisticated information and telecommunications technologies. Cable Television (CATV) is a good example. Much of what CATV has to offer comes via satellite. Libraries are just now beginning to realize the potential use of one and two way CATV for information activities. The promise of being able to communicate as well as transfer information over long distances will be threatened if continued pressure for satellite channels results in either decreased or no access for these activities.

Controlling Information Worldwide

Two acronyms identify the attempt by many nations of the world to control and regulate the flow of information. They are NIIO (New International Information Order) and NWIO (New World Information Order). Both of these terms means the same thing, an

> ... international exchange of information in which nations, which develop their cultural system in an autonomous way and with complete sovereign control of resources, fully and effectively participate as independent members of the international community. [8]

Unesco has been interested in information flow since its establishment. The earliest documentation of the United Nations incorporates the goal of global "free flow of information."[9] During the 1960's, it took on new meaning as the Third World began to charge developed countries with "media imperialism." In 1972 the debate began in earnest. The 17th General Conference of Unesco considered for the first time what became, in 1978, the Mass Media Declaration. Though it was never formally adopted, its basic tenets involved the responsibilities of nations to regulate information moving in and out of their own countries. This conference also passed an additional resolution calling for a declaration of guiding principles on the use of satellite broadcasting, including provision for prior consent by receiving countries. This resolution passed in the General Assembly in 1973. The 19th conference resulted in the implicit agreement by the United States that an imbalance in information did, in fact, exist coupled with a pledge of assistance to Third World countries in the development of communications capabilities. This conference also laid the groundwork for the MacBride Report that was issued at the 21st General Conference in 1980.

The overall motto of the NWIO, the "free and balanced flow of information"[10] is reflected in the MacBride Report.[11] This report attempts to take a comprehensive look at the problems of information worldwide and makes recommendations for change. It is clearly stated that the report is the result of negotiation and is not a scholarly analysis; in other words, the MacBride Report is a political document prepared by a panel of experts for a large international audience.[12] Yet, despite its political nature, the report does address the "totality of communication problems in modern society" [13] worldwide. There is no doubt that it deals with issues that have been ignored or glossed over in the past. A full discussion of all of the issues would take a book, but what one gets from reading it is a sense of the many problems that have to be overcome if we are to progress fully into the age of information. A few of the key issues in the report are: censorship, information or communication imperialism, ownership of the means of communication, transborder data flow, gatekeeping of information, advertising, effects of communications on weak or developing countries, international code of ethics for journalists, and increasing information and communication access to those currently deprived of the right.[14] The common thread running through the entire report, and indeed, throughout the NWIO is that of "...elimination of 'cultural imperialism' and 'information dependency' and the fostering of communications technology transfer and the balanced flow of information between 'have' and 'have not' nations.[15]

Response by the developed countries has been less than positive and has tended to focus solely on the issues related to control of the mass media. While the concept of freedom of the press is an important cultural value for many countries, as well as an important element in the transition to the information society, it should not be allowed to obfuscate other important elements of the report. It is critical to read the entire text of the MacBride Report in order to begin to understand the basic problems associated with the NWIO and the post-industrial society.

Transborder Data Flow

A major example of concern other than mass media is transborder data flow (TDF) in the NWIO. Cees J. Hamelink has argued that the international news is only a small part (10%) of total worldwide information flow. The word "informatics" is used to describe the other 90%. Informatics consists of the infrastructure and management techniques employed to transmit, use, apply, and integrate information. Included is data transmitted by computer to computer as well as all data transmitted via the traditional telecommunications networks that are essentially computer-based information sources. He also goes on to point out that informatics is the third-largest industry in the world and is controlled by a few Western transnational corporations. [16]

Not only is TDF a problem for the Third World, it is also a growing problem for the developed countries. A number of nations, including the FRG, France, Luxembourg, Denmark, Norway, Sweden, Austria, Canada, Australia, Japan and Brazil have enacted data protection and privacy legislation that restricts and controls the flow of data out of their countries. [17] Similar legislation is under consideration in at least a dozen other countries. For the most part, the reason given for such legislation is to protect the privacy of citizens. However, the debate over TDF reveals that there are at least four additional reasons for concern. The first is American domination of the computer and service industries. This dominance has retarded the development of competing industries in other countries and has made them dependent on the United States for equipment, software, and the related services necessary to operate it. This problem is lessening as other nations strive to develop their own silicon chip and computer industries but it is still a major factor. The second reason is the use of TDF by transnational corporations and the implications for national sovereignty. It is feared that decisions about how to run a particular industry can easily be made outside of the country. The net effect could be actions that work directly against the best interests of that country and threaten its sovereignty. The third reason is the coming of what has been termed the "vulnerable society." This is a concept of national vulnerability to the hostile actions of other nations or terrorist groups in the selective destruction or withholding of vital computer-based information. The fourth concern is the impact of increased TDF on international, national, and local affairs. The sophistication of the electronic technology and the volume and quality of information create fear that established decision-making structures will be disrupted. [18] Thus, the underlying reasons for control of TDF are primarily economic and political.

What Librarians Can Do

The issues described here cannot be treated as purely theoretical problems by the international library community; all librarians must act personally, politically and professionally. These are issues that affect the very heart of our profession and their resolution, or lack thereof, will have profound results on how we conduct our business in the new information order.

There are many things that librarians can do personally. We must try to understand the issues, implications and effects of the NWIO, TDF and the WARC. This can only be accomplished by reading and talking to subject experts. The end of this article lists some recommended readings. While not exhaustive, they will assist in developing and expanding an understanding of the issues. Librarians must also be willing to accept the legitimacy of the arguments of others. Everyone involved in the debate over the future of telecommunications has cultural, political and religious underpinnings for his or her rationale. We are in a situation where cultures come into direct confrontation and we must be able to deal with the ambiguity created when these differing value systems clash. Everyone must realize that information is not free nor is it without value laden content. Objectivity and unbiased information is a perceptual construct as well as a true reality. And, the wrong information at the wrong time and place does have the potential for damage to individuals and cultures. Thus, we must become aware of the implications of the phrase "free and balanced flow of information". A thorough examination of our commitment to "free flow" versus the need for data protection and privacy must be addressed by all information professionals. Those in the developed countries should consider the effects of the massive onslaught of information over the electronic grid on the less developed nations of the world. How to control this problem to everyone's satisfaction is easy to address in general but solutions are not as easy. Honest dialogue is necessary to further identify the commonalities and agree on them before going to areas of disagreement. Librarians, with their expertise in the collection, processing, storage, access and use of information can make significant contributions towards these ends.

In the political sphere there are a number of things that librarians can do. A program is necessary to achieve the goals of international librarianship. Part of the political action program should be positions and recommendations for action on the following items. Active support should be given to the UN, ITU and Unesco. The international forums are important arenas for considerations that affect everyone.

Every country must contribute funds for the maintenance of these agencies and try to sustain an active association with them. Librarians must urge their governments for continuous support of these organizations. This is especially true when conflicts arise over disagreement with the stated political aims of the country in which the individual librarian resides. The most important political stance, outside of unqualified support of the international organizational structure, is the push for technology transfer. Librarians in the developed countries should urge their governments to increase and expand the transfer of technology to Third World or developing countries. Programs must be developed and/or maintained for the transfer of the latest electronic technologies as well as the training of personnel to initiate, control and service the telecommunications systems. Only when every country has control over the content as well as the method of transmission can we truly begin a dialogue on the electronic information grid.

Librarians in the developing countries have the responsibility to help sort out the myriad of possible applications of the telecom-

Communication and Education

munications technologies in light of their cultural and economic needs. There should not be a blind acceptance of the "technological fix" of a particular approach without a thorough understanding of the impact of the technology on the culture of the recipient nation. A particular technology should not be accepted if it results in the destruction or impairment of major societal and cultural norms and values. Alternatives abound and librarians must be able to provide information about them.

A specific goal of all librarians should be to support satellite allocations for each country. As we move further into the information age the identification of specific orbital slots for every nation could begin a more constructive dialogue on other issues. The developed countries must share a vital and limited world resource. They must assist others in planning and implementing satellite telecommunications systems that bypass many intermediate, and obsolete, technologies.

There should also be a regionalization of the ITU. This will promote agreements on telecommunications that affect neighbors and encourage resource sharing. In a region where no developed nation is a member there should be a consultative relationship with at least one developed nation. The most important act of resource sharing would be to launch and make available communications satellites for each new region of the ITU. This would give everyone the opportunity to have firsthand experience with satellite communications and create a network to maintain dialogue on common interests.

These political actions are challenging for all and will test our sincerity towards each other. They are controversial and conflict with the current policies of many. But a start must be made and information professionals must be in the forefront of such political activities.

Professionally, librarians have a number of responsibilities. First and foremost is to support national and international library organizations. IFLA is set up to coordinate activities worldwide and can act as the vehicle for coordinated action. Each librarian must have a knowledge of IFLA and be willing to cooperate in activities that will benefit all. A specific network should exchange information on telecommunications policies at both the national and international levels. All librarians must collect divergent opinions on the structure and use of the new telecommunications technologies. These collections have to be made available to public policy planners and have to be well advertised to insure recognition of their existence. All major libraries should subscribe to, and make available, information from Third World sponsored press agencies in order to balance off the natural biases of the major international news agencies. Finally, librarians throughout the world must sponsor debates, forums and presentations on the NWIO, TDF and WARC to inform citizens and the community of the tremendous issues that we face.

Our global village is beginning to take shape as the effects of the electronic grid become more prevalent. At this stage, information and communications problems abound, making it difficult for us to act like neighbors. This decade will be marked as a major transition point into the info-society. Librarians throughout the world must play an active part in the continuous process of drawing everyone closer together.

Recommended Reading

Beebe, George. The Media Crisis. Miami: World Press Freedom Committee, 1980.
Codding, George A. The International Telecommunications Union: An Experiment in International Cooperation. New York: Arno Press, 1972.
Hamelink, Cees, ed. Communication in the Eighties: A Reader on the MacBride Report. Rome: IDoc International, 1980.
International Commission for the Study of Communication Problems, Unesco. Many Voices, One World: Communications and Society Today and Tomorrow. New York: Unipub, 1980.
Power, Philip and Elie Abel. "Third World vs. the Media." Magazine Section, New York Times. September 21, 1980.
United States Congress. Office of Technology Assessment. Radio Frequency Use and Management. Washington: Office of Technology Assessment, 1982.

References

1. McLuhan, Marshall. Understanding Media. New York: McGraw-Hill, 1964.
2. Toffler, Alvin. The Third Wave. New York: Morrow, 1980, pp. 48-49.
3. United States Congress. Office of Technology Assessment. Radiofrequency Use and Management: Impacts From the World Administrative Radio Conference of 1979--Summary. Washington: GPO, 1982, p. 8.
4. Ibid., p. 5.
5. Ibid., p. 73.
6. Honig, David E. "Lessons for the 1979 WARC." Journal of Communication 30 (Spring 1980), p. 54.
7. United States Congress...p. 107.
8. Beebe, George. The Media Crisis. Miami: World Press Freedom Committee, 1980, pp. 4-7.
9. "Universal Declaration of Human Rights, 1948." In Sohn, Louis, ed. Basic Documents of the United Nations. Brooklyn: Foundation Press, 1956, pp. 132-135.
10. Krauthammer, Charles. "Brave News World." New Republic (March 14, 1981), p. 21.
11. International Commission for the Study of Communication Problems, Unesco. Many Voices, One World: Communications and Society Today and Tomorrow. New York: Unipub, 1980.

12. Hamelink, Cees, ed. Communications in the Eighties: A Reader on the MacBride Report. Rome: IDoc International, 1980, p. 18.
13. Kusom Singh and Bertram Gross. "McBride: The Report and the Response." Journal of Communication 31 (Autumn 1981), p. 107.
14. Ibid., pp. 108-111.
15. Clippinger, John H. "Hidden Agenda." Journal of Communication. 29 (Winter 1979), p. 198.
16. Hamelink, Cees J. "Informatics: Third World Call For New Order." Journal of Communication 29 (Summer, 1979), pp. 146-148.
17. Blumenthal, Michael. "Transborder Data Flow and the New Protectionism--A Comprehensive National Communications and Information Policy." Vital Speeches of the Day 47 (July 1981), pp. 550-554.
18. Jacobson, Robert E. "The Hidden Agenda: What Kind of Order." Journal of Communication 29 (Summer 1979), pp. 150-153.

AN EXPLORATION INTO THE SOCIAL AND

ECONOMIC EFFECTS OF INFORMATION TECHNOLOGY*

Donald Wray

Whenever I find myself confronted with the type of form that one has to fill in when passing through immigration control, or registering at a hotel or applying for a credit card I can usually remember my name and address without too much difficulty but I am becoming increasingly troubled when it comes to filling in the box headed "occupation". A few years ago I would have put in "telecommunications" or "telecommunicator" and would have felt confident that I knew what that meant even if the person reading the form did not--that is, if anyone does actually read these forms. But, during the course of last year--the year of Information Technology, IT82--it was borne upon me that telecommunications was but a sub-set of something much bigger and grander, namely Information Technology (IT). So should I say that I am an "information technologist"?

So here we have, straight away--albeit on a trivial level--one of the social effects of information technology. We all know that it means the amalgam of telecommunications, data processing, office machinery and perhaps broadcasting as well. The mircrochip comes into it somewhere, as does software. But the concept is still extremely vague and the words "Information Technology" do not convey the meaning that was intended. It is rather disturbing to find oneself a member of a profession when one does not quite understand its title.

If I reverted to the old-hat occupation description of "telecommunications" even that is not quite so clear in my mind as it was three or four years ago. In the past the job of a telecommunicator was to provide a channel of communication between any two people anywhere in the world virtually on demand. Telecommunicators were proud of the fact that they had created the world's most complex and expensive machine utilizing the highest of high technology--satellites, submarine cables, optical fibers and the rest. They could embark upon great projects, such as the laying of a transatlantic submarine cable, in which they would go weeks without sleep; smoking, drinking

---

*Reprinted by permission of the author and publisher from Aslib Proceedings, 35:10 (October 1983) p. 379-388.

and fretting themselves to an early grave and thoroughly enjoying themselves in the process. But if, at the end of all this and having provided a transmission medium between continents of almost perfect performance, it could still happen that someone at one end, speaking only Chinese, would try to talk to someone at the other end, speaking only Swedish so that communication was impossible. But that was not the fault of the telecommunicator. He had done his job; he had provided the channel, the conduit. He was interested in the medium, not the conveyance of the message.

That attitude is changing. Admittedly, we do not yet have a means of automatic translation between spoken languages, except at the most simple and formalized levels. In communications between machines, however, there is an immense amount of work going on to give the network the power to translate between one computer language and another and to translate the form of the message (which may, for instance, be one firm's internal document for ordering components) into a format which is instantly understood by the recipient. The telecommunicator is now appreciating that he must go beyond the mere provision of a channel; his job is to assist in communicating between man and man, man and machine, machine and machine.

Information technology and society

I would now like to explore with you the effects of information technology on society. I have used the word "explore" because, like so many explorations, our work in British Telecom (BT) has been spasmodic, has occasionally changed direction and has come across unexpected discoveries along the route. We discovered--although this was not unexpected--that the effects of a technology can be most clearly demonstrated when both the society and the technology are relatively simple. The effects become more obscure--and it becomes more difficult to distinguish between cause and effect--as both society and technology become more sophisticated. I will conclude with some recent developments which could have a profound effect on your particular interests.

The supreme world authority on telecommunications is the International Telecommunications Union (the ITU), which has been in existence for over 60 years. For the greater part of its existence its object has been to develop technical and operational standards so that national telecommunications systems can be interconnected in order to provide a global service. In this respect it has proved to be one of the most successful of all international organizations. More recently it has turned its attention to assisting developing countries in building up their telecommunications infrastructures; it has done this by seconding technical experts, providing training programs, producing technical handbooks and so on. Now this program can only succeed if the developing countries are themselves convinced that a telecommunications service will be to their benefit when compared with all the other demands upon their limited resources. So the ITU mounted a series of studies on the effects that a simple basic telephone service had on some developing societies.

Most developing countries are characterised by poor physical communications, a significant dependence on agriculture, a wealth of crafts and government-sponsored manufacturing industries. There is often the familiar drift from the countryside to the towns with all the administrative problems and squalor that it brings in its wake. This was the environment of a study carried out jointly by the Massachusetts Institute of Technology and Cairo University into almost 150 villages in Egypt which showed that the introduction of a basic telephone service produced some very significant economic benefits.

A "benefit" was taken to mean the monetary advantage to the correspondents after the cost of the telephone call had been subtracted; it took into account what the cost would have been had they used an alternative means of communication, such as travel; the time saving, measured by the number of working hours saved; the value of losses avoided due to the use of the telephone in emergencies; and the more efficient use of capital and capital equipment. The benefit of using a telephone was found to be a factor of:

      85:1 in service organizations
      69:1 in the trade sector
    126:1 in the capital equipment sector
and 78:1 in the artisan sector.

These studies help the administration of such countries to appreciate what they lose by not having a telephone service. There is also a likelihood--although it is very difficult to monitor--that the availability of a telecommunications service reduces the drift from country to city by easing communications and by reducing the feeling of isolation felt by the rural inhabitants.

One might be forgiven for thinking, seeing the rapid growth in the world telephone system, that the economic benefits of telecommunications are rapidly bringing relief to the Third World. But when one realizes that 90 percent of the world's telephones are concentrated in 15 per cent of the world's nations--and these are certainly not the developing nations--one appreciates there is a long way to go.

Telecommunications needs in industry

It is a comparatively simple matter to measure the effects of introducing a telecommunications service, or, indeed, any service, when it did not exist before and when other parts of the country can be used as a control. It becomes much more difficult when the service already exists and one has to determine the effects of extensions of or improvements to the service.

The next phase of this exploration was triggered off by some activities in the EEC. For the last four years or so the Commission, and particularly the division headed by Vicomte Davignon, has strenuously attempted to improve Europe's information technology activities

Communication and Education 141

both as a means of improving interworking between the EEC's constituent nations and to build up European export potential in IT. A European MP asked the fundamental question: were telecommunications and information technology all that important? Should not the Commission be devoting its energies to other matters such as nuclear power, fishing, aerospace or whatever?

BT started its attempt to answer this question by establishing when the major European nations changed from being manufacturing economies to service economies. We defined the service sector as comprising the wholesale and retail trade; restaurants and hotels; transport, storage and communications; real estate transactions; and finance, insurance and business services. We found that with the exception of Ireland and Greece (which have had a large agricultural sector and have only recently established manufacturing sectors) the proportion of GDP in Community countries arising from the service sector has been steadily increasing over the last 20 years whilst the manufacturing sector has been diminishing. The cross-over point is usually when each claims about 35 per cent of the GDP. This occurred in Germany in 1975, in Luxemburg in 1971, in France in 1969 and prior to 1960 in Belgium, Denmark, Italy, the Netherlands and the UK. The proportion of employment in the service sector has been steadily increasing even more rapidly.

TABLE 1. Change in proportion of GDP and employment in manufacturing and service sectors in last 10 years.

Country	Change in proportion of GDP Manufacturing %	Service %	Change in proportion of employment Manufacturing %	Service %
Belgium	- 7	+ 5	- 10	+ 9
Denmark	- 3	+ 4	- 6	+ 7
France	- 3	+ 6	- 3	+ 11
Germany	- 4	+ 4	- 5	+ 9
Ireland	- 4	- 4	- 0	+ 6
Italy	+ 1	+ 3	6	+ 12
Netherlands	- 4	+ 6	- 8	+ 9
UK	- 5	+ 4	- 6	+ 9

Table 1 indicates that the rising contribution to employment in the service sector has been, for the most part, even greater than the increasing proportion of the GDP. This is largely because most service sector activities are labor intensive and the productivity improvement in the service sector has been much less than in manufacturing. If we translate these proportions into absolutes, we find that during the last 20 years the number of people employed in the UK in the manufacturing industries has decreased by 1.5 million but the number of people in the service sector has increased by 3.3 million. And in times of recession the service sector is much more stable than the manufacturing.

The next step in this phase of our exploration was to take some examples from the manufacturing and service industries and assess their reliance on telecommunications. The factor we used was the price they paid for their telecommunications services as a proportion of the value of their output. The current figures for the UK are shown in Table 2.

TABLE 2. Telecommunications input ratio in UK industry

Sector	Telecom Input Industry Output %
Mining and quarrying	0.7
Construction	0.8
Gas, electricity, water	0.9
Manufacturing	1.3
Services (ex. distribution)	1.8
Distribution	2.7

Summarizing these figures very broadly, the telecommunications input per unit of output is about 40 per cent higher in services (excluding distribution) than in manufacturing; and distribution services make twice as much use of telecommunications than do the manufacturing industries.

So we had demonstrated that there was a relationship between telecommunications and the growth areas of the economy; but we had not separated cause from effect. However, several lines of speculation arose from the observation--made almost in passing--that improvements in productivity in the manufacturing sector were significantly greater than those in the service sector. It could be that much of this arose from an increasing use of information technology internally in the production process. If one imagined the history of a manufactured item it would commence with a rough design which would be re-drawn with precision as a blue-print which would be used for the subsidiary design of specialized tools and for ordering materials; and all of these activities consist of handling of information, as does the receipt and acknowledgement of orders, the instructions to the dispatch department and the subsequent invoicing and payment. And the production process itself was being automated by computer-aided design, computer-controlled machine tools and robots, even computer-controlled stores and warehouses. So to study the relationship between the economy and information technology merely in terms of communication between companies and the outside world was to ignore the internal revolution that was already occurring in the mid-1970s. As often occurs in explorations, the intrepid explorers had reached an interesting lake but they had not discovered the source of the river.

Social effects of information technology

The fact that manufacturing productivity improvements were appreciably greater than those in the service sector led to a concentration in much of the Western world on improving productivity in the service sector. From that sprang the new industry we are experiencing today, with its word processors, electronic offices and electronic mail systems. And that in turn generates the fearful question: that if the service sectors are now employing more people than manufacturing, will the productivity improvements springing from information technology result in even more unemployment that did the automation of the physical production processes?

Just as the widespread arrival of the computer in the 1960s created the impression that 'anything can be done by software'--an impression which was rapidly followed by disillusionment as the practitioners found out the hard way just how difficult and expensive software could be--so did the arrival of information technology in the 1970s create the impression, particularly in the minds of journalists and politicians, that we would soon be living in Wired Cities. In these Wired Cities we would work at home, shop from home, carry out banking transactions from home, confer with our colleagues and access our files from home terminals and increase our range of correspondents and our span of management control. And in so doing we would be saving that valuable commodity, energy, by not indulging in unnecessary travel. There were some who held the contrary view; they said that shopping, working in offices, going to the library, and attending business meetings were all social activities which Man, a highly sociable animal, would not willingly forego. And that if people attempted to work at home they would be distracted by domestic noises and crises. Work and leisure were two distinct activities and human psychology demanded they should be carried out in different locations. What has happened in practice? Let us look at one example of the forecast IT revolutions--teleconferencing.

Teleconferencing

At present there is little enthusiasm amongst businessmen for substituting teleconferencing for travel. There are signs, however, that teleconferencing is beginning to be used in situations where a need for communication exists but where face-to-face meetings are impracticable. The US National Aeronautics and Space Administration (NASA) and also one major US airline have set up extensive networks for crisis management. In Japan, video conferencing systems are being used for frequent and urgent communications between scattered sites of large companies. Here in the UK, BT has been offering its Confravision service for a decade; utilization has remained low but large companies are beginning to use it when briefing regional representatives at the beginning of a big sales campaign and we use it in BT quite extensively for internal conferences. The University of Wisconsin has brought educational courses to communities and individuals who would not otherwise have had access to them; and teleconferencing has been used for state hearings in Alaska, where people are scattered and travel is difficult. And in Phoenix, Arizona, the entire course of criminal proceedings have been conducted in which police interview witnesses, attorneys advise and consult their clients and the actual trial has taken place without the police leaving their stations, the attorneys leaving their chambers and the suspects leaving their cells.

So far, there has been little evidence for the de-centralization of organizations which the more enthusiastic proponents for teleconferencing had hoped it might promote. There are, however, indications of changes in social behavior when compared with face-to-face discussions. Teleconferences are much briefer than face-to-face meetings and are more directed to the task in hand rather than to personal exchanges. Participants are less inclined to seek personal approval so disagreements and aggressive behavior occur more frequently. The role of the chairman becomes reinforced if he can physically control access to the microphones and cameras.

IT and the economy

In the late 1970s BT once more found itself subjected to a limitation on its capital investment and so resumed its exploration into the relationship between information technology and the economy. Our objective was to demonstrate that a modern society will become so dependent on IT that to restrict investment in the national infrastructure--the telecommunications network--would be to hamper the nation's potential for profitable growth. Admittedly there was an element of parochial special pleading in this exercise but as it turned out, the study produced results which could be of considerable benefit to individual companies.

BT commissioned two consultancy organizations, Communications Studies and Planning International and Logica to explore the potential impacts of new IT services on the economy. Eight case studies were carried out in companies which fell into four industry sectors: distributive trades, professional services, banking and finance, and manufacturing.

In each case study an attempt was made to quantify in monetary terms the benefits arising from using IT instead of other forms of communication, e.g., the use of remote terminals to enter order or payment information instead of mail or paper-based alternatives. On the whole the benefits from this aspect were fairly small. An-

Communication and Education

other study was into the use of IT to reduce costs, eliminate waste or avoid losses; an example of this category was the optimization of stock holdings between different locations. Our consultants also looked at the potential for increasing sales by improving service to customers and the savings resulting from faster decision-taking in such activities as catalog preparation, planning cycles and the placing of investment funds. The companies which allowed themselves to be scrutinized in this way included a mail order company, an electrical retail company, an estate agent, an architect's office, a financial services company, a commercial bank, an engineering manufacturing company and a glass manufacturer.

The benefits to all these organizations was assessed in terms of a benefit/cost ratio and they ranged from 0.65:1 to 130:1 with a weighted average of 6:1. However, some of the benefits have to be regarded with some care. For instance, if the firms attribute benefits from increased sales, and if the market is not particularly elastic, then it is only a matter of time before their competitors adopt the same technology and recover their market share. If this debatable benefit is omitted from the evaluation, the overall net benefit/cost ratio falls to about 4:1.

This figure was borne out, in a slightly different context by Paul A. Strassmann, Vice President of the Xerox Corporation, who presented a paper to the IT '82 Conference in December of last year on the subject of "Information technology and organizations" in which he examined the effect of IT on companies such as his own. In one case study he considered the cost of producing various documents using conventional office equipment and compared this with the cost when using the full panoply of electronic networks and sophisticated terminals. The improvement in cost per page ranged from 2:1 to 4:1 according to its complexity. He also showed how preparing a document for printing in the conventional manner--starting with the author's script, then going through typing, checking, the insertion of graphics, making the printing plate, printing, collating, and so on --could involve anything from 25 to 35 job steps which could be reduced to six by exploiting an electronic delivery system.

Returning to BT's studies, we attempted to assess the effects of IT on the residential sector as well as on business operations. We examined in some depth the effects on over 250 households located in some London suburbs and in a more rural environment in Cheshire. We looked at the possibilities of working from home and from using transactional service such as teleshopping and telebanking. The social and economic consequences became almost inextricably intertwined in this sort of study because many people think of shopping as a social activity and we aroused the worries, mentioned earlier, that working from home would disrupt well-established attitudes, habits and the household routine. Nonetheless there was sufficient evidence to show that benefit/cost factors could range from 0.6 to 1.1 and we came to the very tentative conclusion that by 1995 about 4% of households would have people working from home and about 20% would be using electronic transactional services.

It is an even more tentative step to extrapolate from these
business and residential studies to a macro-economic aggregation to
the UK economy as a whole. By far the biggest impact would be on
business productivity; on the residential side, working from home,
telebanking and teleshopping would probably take off slowly but could
be quite significant by the end of the century. The manufacturers of
communications equipment would benefit by the expanding market as
would the providers of network services. A possible picture of the
total benefits arising from new services (i.e., not including the expansion of the telephone and other current systems) would be as
shown in Table 3.

TABLE 3. UK economy wide benefits

Benefits	1985	1990	1995	2000
Users	£m	£m	£m	£m
Business Productivity Gains	1000	4500	9600	23000
Residential Benefits	10	70	450	900
Output				
Equipment Manufacture	400	1100	2200	3900
Network Services	40	180	380	729

There are some negative aspects which should not be ignored.
For instance, an increasing proportion of IT equipment consists of
microelectronics components, many of which are imported. If the
present tendency continues into the future, the net imports could
amount to £85m in 1990 and as much as £700m in AD 2000.

Cable television

Finally, let me turn to a subject that has been exhaustively discussed
during the past year: cable television. This is not the occasion to
debate whether the technology should use coaxial cable or optical
fiber, or how large the franchise areas should be or whether or not
there should be a British content quota, (whatever that might mean)
or whether there will be a visual phone service. I would like to
concentrate on just two aspects: the role of the cable operator; and
one of the services that might be introduced: and I am bringing them
together because they could have a significant impact on your profession.

Those of you who studied Lord Hunt's inquiry into cable will
remember that he distinguished between four participants: the cable

provider; the cable operator, that is the person or organization who acquires program material and sells it to subscribers in the local cable area; the program provider, who distributes, probably nationally, channels of feature films, sports, educational material, or whatever; and the program producer, that is the organization having the studios and similar production facilities. One could look at the roles of the cable operator and the program provider in that the former is the retailer of services to the public and the latter is the wholesaler. Lord Hunt placed great emphasis on the role of the cable operator because it is he who assesses what his subscribers will want, it is he who buys in the appropriate programs, it is he who is responsible for his product maintaining acceptable standards of decency and impartiality; and it is therefore he who should apply for the franchise to operate in any particular area. His franchise CATV period will be for 12 years in the first instance but this can then be extended or re-allocated at subsequent 8 year intervals.

Now one of the services which BT's research laboratories are working on and which could be offered over a cable system is that of a video library. It would consist of a jukebox of video discs which subscribers could call up and have played over to them almost on demand. There are all sorts of technical and operational problems which have to be tackled but they can all be solved in time. At first, the choice available to the consumer will be limited by the number of discs that can be accommodated in the local video library, perhaps a few hundred. But it is not too fanciful to imagine that local networks will be interconnected by national networks enabling the more popular discs to be stored locally and the more recondite discs housed in a few national libraries; indeed, an arrangement broadly similar to the present library system, except that the information would be passed direct to the home electronically instead of by the physical transport of books.

When that day comes one can question whether there is a need for the cable operator at all. Why should one be in the hands of a middle man who selects a range of programs or information from which one makes a sub-selection when one can make one's own selection from the complete universe of recorded material? Will there be any need to renew franchises after the first 12-year period if the cable provider can deal direct with an association such as your own to offer the public almost unlimited choice upon demand?

I expect you can see now why I entitled my talk an "exploration" into the social and economic effects of information technology. That exploration is still in progress and we have not yet reached the goal. We do not know whether we will discover Eldorado or some uninhabitable desert. Some say it is better to travel hopefully than to arrive; it is certainly more comfortable--and probably cheaper-- if we travel electronically and not by jeep, canoe or camel.

THE UNDERSIDE OF COMPUTER LITERACY*

Douglas Noble

We are witnessing the installation of an enormous computer education infrastructure in this country. Each day offers new assertions of the urgent need to bring "Computer Literacy" (CL) to the masses of students, teachers, grandmothers, and businessmen ready to participate in the new computerized society. The coffers, federal and corporate, are opening wide as an urgent need for high skill in a high-technology world assumes central importance. As the computer insinuates itself further and further into our jobs and our lives, the need for some form of Computer Literacy for everyone comes to be accepted as reasonable, even reassuring.

Not surprisingly, computer education has become very big business. Although its focus has recently shifted from the child to the adult, CL educators are in fact advancing on many fronts, from management and parent workshops to teacher's colleges to computer camps. The number of computers in American schools is growing at the rate of 56 percent per year, with 90,000 microcomputers already in place. Atari, Apple, IBM, and Radio Shack all are pouring money and free computers into teachers' colleges, school districts, and universities across the country. One observer notes that "securing shares of the education marketplace may be critical in determining which computer manufacturers will still be in business several years from now." And it has been predicted that by 1986 training directed at the neophyte will be a $3 billion market. CL, the attempt to introduce the masses to computers, has become one of the nation's fastest growing businesses.

CL is a mass movement in education. Computer clubs and workshops, technical and vocational programs, graduate courses in computer science and engineering, constitute an understandable response to the new technology. Computer Literacy education, however, is more difficult to understand. CL does not propose to make engineers, programmers, and technicians out of everyone. Indeed, the focus is precisely the opposite: to provide the masses with some minimal introduction to computers so that we all may be "comfortable" with the new technology. There is considerable debate about

---

*Reprinted by permission of the author and publisher from Raritan, Spring 1984, pp. 37-64.

what CL courses should contain: the history of computers? the social impact of computers? hardware basics? flowcharts and logic? programming and software evaluation? But the common goal of all CL advocates is to "give as many people as possible the sense of belonging in a computer-rich society."* This sense of belonging is the main attraction of CL.

This is the first time in this century, if not in history, that a mass educational movement has followed so closely on the heels of a technological innovation. Seventy-five years ago automobile schools (most of them short-lived and out for a quick buck) sprang up overnight to train mechanics and drivers for the new horseless carriage. Radio, television, and telephone all generated thousands of clubs and technical schools, but there was no thought of reaching everyone, as with CL. None of these inventions, despite their promise for transforming society, triggered any such mass educational campaign as we are seeing with the computer. Nor were these inventions compared to the invention of print; competence with automobiles or television, however interpreted, was never equated with functional literacy, as Computer Literacy so often is. Nor did it seem urgent that everyone feel comfortable overnight.

The public interest in CL is essentially defensive; the oil lubricating the movement seems to be the fear of the uninitiated that they will be left behind by the "Computer Revolution." CL advocates, designating themselves as pioneers in a wave of enlightenment akin to the spread of print in the fifteenth century, feed this anxiety with warnings that "the ability to use and understand computers will [soon] be equivalent to understanding the printed word," and that "those who are not computer literate will be at as much a disadvantage in society as someone who cannot read is today." Failure to learn to use computers, we are told again and again, will leave one functionally illiterate, devoid of the skills needed to survive in a computerized world.

Such talk has caught on. "I'm an intelligent person," admits my mother, echoing the thoughts of millions, "but I feel dumb. I feel like an immigrant in my own country." Her solution? Take a computer course. This is the antidote, Jane Pauley of the "Today" show delights in telling us, for "computerphobia," a disease striking the vitals of (among others) uninitiated managers fearing replacement by others more "literate" than themselves. The computer is here to stay, everyone seems to be saying, so we have no choice about whether to get on board; our only choice is whether we will be eager or resigned as we do so.

___

*The quotations in this paper represent a selection from the inexhaustible rhetoric generated by computer enthusiasts in the past few years, much of which has been preserved in a single volume edited by Robert J. Seidel, entitled Computer Literacy: Issues and Directions for 1985, Academic Press, 1982. Similar sentiments may be found in countless journal, magazine, and newspaper articles.

Defensive self-preservation is the purpose of job-seeking kids, of their well-intentioned parents, of phobic executives, or grandmothers like my own mother, for whom learning about computers is as alarmingly demanding as going to the moon. It is also the motive of school administrators, who are heard saying that "nobody came to me to ask if a computer revolution should take place, but it's here and my students must be prepared for it."

It is taken as a given that everyone must be educated in computers, and, indeed, any suggestion that we allow segments of the population to be denied this knowledge sounds heretical in a democratic society. The powerful mythology of equality of opportunity, and the omnipresence of the computer itself, provide the most convincing justification for the necessity of CL.

The computer is here, everywhere, and we all must be helped to understand and use it. How can anyone argue with that? When a sense of urgency about our national priorities is added, the inappropriateness of debate seems clearer still:

> A computer literate work force is necessary to maintain our national defense and to improve our national productivity.

> A computer literate populace is as necessary to an information society as raw materials and energy are to an industrial society.

> Due to the decline in national productivity, the increase in foreign trade competition, and national defense and safety needs, computers have emerged as the major force ameliorating these conditions. Consequently, the shortage of computer specialists and knowledge-workers has raised the problem of computer literacy to the level of a national crisis.

But what particular decline in productivity? Which "knowledge-workers"? What shortage of computer specialists? What "problem" of computer literacy? Never mind. We are asked not to question even specious arguments when the Japanese are whipping us, and our own high technology (the answer to all our economic problems) is supposedly being stunted by American computer illiteracy. Although the authors of such statements systematically confuse minimal computer literacy with high technical skill, and although their appeals to productivity, national defense, and safety are characteristically vague, still they manage to make the crisis seem real enough to stifle debate.

Equally unexamined is the basic assumption about the importance of CL to the individual, namely, that computers are everywhere and so it is in everyone's interest to understand them. As well as indiscriminately confusing the future with the present (Are computers everywhere now? Is the Information Society here yet?), this assumption in its simplicity begs most of the important questions of fact and value. Where are computers used? What are they used to do? What do people need to know in order to use them? Does the computer enhance anyone's life? Whose? Does it hurt anyone's life? Whose? Who decides when and where computers will be used?

The alleged benefits of CL in meeting the needs of the American public can be grouped into four principal categories, each representing one role in the daily life of the individual--the individual as consumer, as student, as worker, and as citizen.

1. "The opportunities available to those who become educated consumers ... will be ... great" and therefore "federal emphasis should be on the production of a population able to cope rather than merely exist in an information society." CL will afford us the "survival" and "coping" skills we will need in the homecomputer revolution, which promises totally to transform our domesticity, our leisure, our shopping, and banking.

2. "To function effectively as students, our nation's youth needs to know how to use and program computers," since "computers contribute to the intellectual growth of human beings," and "computer literacy maximizes our problem-solving abilities." One benefit of CL, then, is its enhancement of learning by showing students how to participate in the computer-induced "revolution in learning" now beginning in the nation's schools.

3. "To function effectively as scientists, engineers, managers and teachers, the professionals of today ... need to learn how to use computers to enhance their specialized skills." Everyone will need to "emerge from school with the knowledge and skills that let them begin to work productively in the information sector" as more and more jobs are redefined as "hi-tech occupations that will require high-order skills." In a word, CL will help us get or keep a job, and may indeed determine whether we are employable at all.

4. "Some understanding of computer programming is necessary for the exercise of the rights and responsibilities of citizenship," for in order "to function effectively as citizens ... we will need to know how the computer impinges on and enhances our everyday lives." CL will create an informed citizenry which will determine the shape of the new technology and prevent abuse. It will also ensure equality of opportunity by making the technology accessible to all. CL will empower us by putting ultimate control of computer technology in our hands.

These advantages, then, are what CL has to offer, according to its proponents. Leaving to others an examination of the questionable relevance of CL to national defense and international competition, let us examine in turn the home, the school, the job site, and the political arena, to see if the reality corresponds to the promise.

● ● ●

Time's "Man of the Year" for 1982 was a machine, the computer, which is supposedly transforming the home into an "electronic cottage" and our daily lives into a sequence of interactions with microcircuitry. Estimates for the number of personal computers in use in the U.S. by the end of the century range as high as 80 million. (By comparison, there are now 83 million American homes with TV sets.) Already we are being bombarded by computerized telephones, autos, washer/dryers, watches, games, and toys. Outside the home we see computers in supermarkets, banks, airports, and libraries. Tiny chips of silicon are helping people find mates, protect their houses, record their favorite music. Computer buffs are transforming their houses into "smart homes," even as the first personalized robots come waddling off the assembly lines.

Meanwhile we are continually told how much we ourselves need a home computer to manage the bills, store the recipes, and edit the correspondence (although four out of five home computers are used exclusively for games). The future of the home computer promises to be truly revolutionary, once TV, computer, and telephone are linked together and become "videotex," with which we'll be able to shop, bank, and read the newspaper without ever leaving the screen. With such powerful telecommunications, more and more office jobs will be done at home, computer networks will provide community, and home entertainment systems will fill our leisure hours. Such are the predictions, for better or worse.

A number of observers have begun to warn of the dangers of videotex to individual security; they warn as well of the total marketization of the home. "With personal computers and two-way TV we'll create a wealth of personal information and scarcely notice it leaving the house. The TV will know what X-rated movies we watch." Our banking, shopping, and viewing habits will all become part of some data bank. "There will be tremendous incentive to record this information for market research or sale."

Even today the threat posed by the computer to home and family has become a growing concern of psychiatrists and marriage counselors. They are witnessing the "social disease" of the "computer widow" whose spouse spends all his free time in front of the computer, and they worry about the impact of the computer on children for whom playing with electronic machines takes the place of playing, or even just being, with other kids. "Bit by bit [sic] computers are changing the way people relate" and "hardly anybody is looking at the impact on family life." Specifically, CL educators are not looking. In fact, they are proceeding at an accelerated rate to "prepare" the public for the wondrous transformation of the home in a computer-rich world.

What is most evident, yet rarely noted, in all of this, aside from the fact that it's all happening without public knowledge or consent, is that one doesn't have to know very much in order to reap

Communication and Education

the benefits. Computerized telephones, watches, and dryers require no computer understanding by the user. However much the market, bank, garage, or airline relies on computers, still the consumer, even the wise consumer, needs to know nothing about computers in order to function or cope. Even where our direct interaction with a computer terminal is required, as in a library or using a bank "moneymatic" or home computers for budgets or games, what one needs to know about computers is minimal.

It might be argued that the consumer needs to know how to shop for computer products and how to fix or maintain all the computerized paraphernalia which one has become dependent upon. In fact, however, one doesn't need to understand the bewildering variety of competing computer products in order to make intelligent purchases. All one needs is a friend who is somewhat knowledgeable about computers, just as one may consult a mechanically inclined acquaintance when buying a used car. Even without such a friend, one can usually pick up enough information from the sales people at the computer store or take a look at <u>Consumer Reports</u> to make an intelligent decision.

The same may be said for fixing or maintaining one's computer or computerized gadgets once they are purchased. If they break, one need only bring them to the shop for servicing, just as most people now do with TVs and Cars. Although it is unquestionably an advantage to be able to fix one's car, or washer, or typewriter, those who depend upon the mechanic or serviceman are not failing to cope or function in a world of cars and typewriters. So it is and will be in the world of computers. In fact, considering the relatively few parts in a personal computer, repair might very quickly become possible for many consumers. The high technology of the computer is the microprocessor itself, which is simply replaced if a problem arises. To repair the rest of the computer requires electrical or electronic know-how, not computer literacy.

Those of us who have grown up around cars, televisions, and telephones are sufficiently literate in their use. No one ever trained us, as children or adults, to manage everyday technologies. We simply learned about them as we grew up with them, just as children who are interested now learn a great deal about computers from hanging around computer stores or their friends' houses.

The analogy will be clearer as computers become more and more "user friendly." Just as the automobile became accessible to millions once the electric starter and (later) the automatic transmission were added, so the personal computer will enter 80 million homes when its use requires only pressing a few buttons. (The new "Lisa" computer, at the moment an expensive business-oriented device, ushers in the age of friendly computing with its remarkable simplicity, which reduces instructional time from forty hours to forty minutes.) As advanced user friendliness reaches the average computer consumer (and there is no doubt that it soon will), what will happen to the urgency of CL? Will we continue to be told that we need CL to cope, function, or survive in the world of computers? Even today, such a claim makes astonishingly little sense. One just does not have to know very much to be a consumer in a computerized world, and one will need to know still less in the future.

Uncritical acceptance is the order of the day in the nation's schools, too. School districts are buying up microcomputers and commercially available software as if these would solve all of their considerable difficulties. Thousands of these shiny new symbols of high technology are being put in place by administrators eager to impress their school boards, enhance their school's image, or ease the pressures from affluent parents who already own home computers. Some of these administrators are themselves reluctant boarders of the technology bandwagon; others are among its prime movers. Eager or resigned, however, no one wants his or her school left behind. So the computers pour in and the NEA calls for "a massive infusion of funds to help schools close the 'computer gap' between students' and teachers' need to gain literacy in the new technology" and the schools' dwindling financial resources.

Impoverishment is but one of the problems for school districts anxious to bring computer literacy to their students. Some of the more cautious CL advocates have begun to warn against rushing too quickly into high tech. Although none suggests that CL is unnecessary, they worry that many administrators are making unwise purchases because they have not sufficiently defined their "instructional objectives"; the result too often is a roomful of unused hardware and inappropriate software. Teachers, too, are often unprepared to work with the computers. Often a single teacher becomes the resident expert, and some math or science teachers are coaxed into offering computer classes, learning as they go. The shortage of qualified computer teachers is in fact a primary complaint of CL enthusiasts, which is why their focus has shifted more and more to teachers' colleges and in-service workshops.

Doubts about the quality of commercial software and the reliability of some of the hardware have also begun to be heard. Most packaged learning materials now available are considered educationally unsound ("90 percent garbage" is the phrase often used), and free trial periods are seldom offered to the teacher who wants to know exactly what he or she is buying. Hardware servicing is often said to be erratic as well. None of these obstacles, however, seems to be deterring school districts from buying, even though the steadily decreasing price of computers suggests that they might do well to go slowly.

What is all the rush? Behind it is a belief in the power of the computer to transform education: "Just as education was reshaped five centuries ago by the printing press, education is going to be reshaped by computers." Never mind how much CL educators really know about the influence of printing on education 500 years ago; the historical allusion, the unexamined assumption buried within the term computer <u>literacy</u> itself, serves CL proponents by suggest-

Communication and Education

ing the totality of the computer transformation of the school. This transformation envisions the use of computers both as powerful instructional aids and as instruments for creative problem-solving. The potential value of such uses seems limitless to enthusiasts; let us examine some of the grounds for their enthusiasm.

The oldest, and lowliest, form of computer-aided instruction is drill-and-practice, in which the computer simply takes the place of a workbook, adding video-induced motivation and sound or graphic reinforcement for correct answers. The computer really does very little "teaching" of concepts, apart from providing printed text which might just as well be in a book. The big draw of this unsophisticated use is its ability to attract the attention of otherwise unmotivated students. The staying power of such motivation is very doubtful, although the student gains some "keyboard familiarity" and "enhancement of self-image."

A newer form of computer-aided instruction uses computers to teach in ways otherwise impossible, as in the use of sophisticated simulations of the circulatory system, number patterns, election returns, or conflicting physical forces. An example in game format is "lunar landing," which asks the student to make decisions simultaneously affecting fuel consumption, velocity, thrust, and distance from the moon's surface. Advocates of this sort of use claim that it gives students radically new opportunities to learn about complex relationships in a variety of subject areas. But such use is extremely rare; what "courseware" exists has been developed in a few schools blessed with high levels of commitment, funding, and personnel. And it proposes an arena of experimentation and risk which is scarcely feasible for the typical school district. Existing courseware, therefore, has not found a wide market, and it is relatively untested. Yet the dream of teaching a variety of subjects in a totally new way is selling a lot of computers in school districts where the dream may never be realized.

Computer-aided instruction, then, is either too sophisticated to be more than a wish, or too simple to justify much excitement. There are some interesting things going on in computer-assisted instruction; but they are far from becoming a "revolution in education," and there seems little reason for CL educators to be alarming students or their parents about such remote eventualities. Computers are used in another way in the schools, however, as the locus for creative problem-solving and new ways of thinking. "Children-friendly" programming languages such as Logo have encouraged many educators to believe that computers can lead children to more expansive ways of thinking and solving problems. Many teachers, myself included, are thrilled to observe young children programming computers to draw sophisticated shapes or "converse" intelligently, and it becomes seductively easy to believe that the key to intelligent cognitive behavior, and even to the "problem" of motivation, lies buried in the act of programming a computer.

Unfortunately, such enthusiasm is premature. "There is little objective evaluation data confirming the contention that computer programming enhances intellectual functioning or problem-solving." Despite the fact that "computer programming is often used explicitly to teach problem-solving ... current research has only begun to scratch the surface in exploring whether what students learn about problem-solving by programming computers has any carryover into non-computer situations." "The general picture from research on problem-solving and thinking is that the conditions under which transfer occurs from one domain to another are subtle and limited; ... one is more impressed by the extent to which transfer doesn't occur."

It appears, despite our intuitions, that we really know very little about the cognitive processes involved in programming, and still less about the transfer of these processes to other areas of intellectual activity. What about the motivational possibilities? Don't computers turn kids on to sustained, self-directed, eager learning? All of the evidence available is anecdotal; my own experience is that the flashy computers attract all kids for a short time but that only the ten percent or so who are truly interested stay involved past a month or two. It seems that the only thing learned from a century of research on motivation, namely that it is linked to interest, holds true with computers too, despite all the current excitement, my own, as teacher and programmer, included. The Learning Revolution in this form is barely off the ground. What is more, the very act of programming computers might itself become obsolete in the wake of ever "friendlier" computers, and "writing computer code will ... become redundant, [as] the ability to write programs [becomes] as relevant as the ability of an airline pilot to fly a kite." What is a curriculum planner to do?

A seldom addressed danger in this premature enthusiasm about the Learning Revolution is the widening of the gap between rich and poor school districts. While the NEA places "some hope for solution" in the $425 million American Defense Education Act recently passed by the House, and while Apple's Steven Jobs wants to put one free computer in each of the nation's 80,000 schools, these measures will not make computers as accessible to poor students as to wealthy ones. Some call for state intervention in computer distribution and funding to prevent a have/have-not society. Unequal access to computers has become a real concern to many CL enthusiasts, who argue that the solution is to provide more computers to poor schools and more training to their teachers. So long, however, as they also push for similar increments for affluent schools, there is no solution at all, since rich schools have access to alternative funding unavailable to poor ones.

No one seems ready to argue that rich districts be forced to wait while the have-nots catch up; waiting is not in the CL scenario. A better solution, unfortunately, is fast becoming untenable. If, as I am suggesting, CL is not very important (and if, as we shall see later, computer jobs--both in skill and in numbers--are greatly overrated), it could be argued that access to computers in schools is not very important, and that the exacerbation of inequality caused by computers is exaggerated. Reality supports this argument, but unfortunately we live in a world of appearances which function as reality. Consequently, we are seeing the invention ex nihilo, of a "need" for computer access, in the form of high school graduation requirements, college prerequisites, teaching qualification, and hiring practices. Overnight, the "need" for CL has begun to be manufactured, and survival, in education and employment, has become linked to computer access in school; the "inequality gap" and the "computer gap" have become one, and the answer to both is: more computers, more literacy. At this point the exaggerated claims about the revolution in education leave the realm of wishful thinking and start to become dangerous.

• • •

The hole card of the CL movement is jobs. Above all, CL educators invoke job preparation to explain the urgency of their enterprise. In fact, personal experience shows that some teachers are annoyed by any suggestion that they delay their students' preparation for the new jobs long enough to find out what these jobs will be. Most educators' knee-jerk acceptance of the mythology surrounding the "high technology workforce," and their astonishing ignorance of the real impact of computers on jobs in 1984, testify to the defensiveness underlying the computer education movement.

The basic supposition of the CL movement is that high-tech jobs require high-tech skills. Early in this century, the introduction of machinery into unskilled jobs automatically made these jobs "semiskilled"; just so, we are told, the introduction of computers will transform many jobs into "knowledge work" or "mind work." Somehow, mere interaction with a computer will transform the skills required and radically raise the level of intellect needed. Since computers are in fact being introduced into a vast number of jobs, it seems to follow that future employment will demand high levels of intellect and computer understanding. This is the prevailing view, and it sells CL to millions of people.

The currency of this view rests on a failure to examine how computers are used in various sorts of jobs. True, computers are being introduced into millions of jobs; but it hardly follows that the skills required for these jobs therefore become intellectually more demanding or stimulating. In fact, the contrary is more often the case: the jobs become deskilled, less creative, more highly controlled, and mindless.

It is important to realize, first, that many jobs are simply eliminated by the introduction of computers, and, second, that a large part of the service sector of the future will remain unaffected by computers. Examples of the former include craftspersons, machinists, textile cutters, compositors, auto workers, printers, telephone repairers, filing and billing clerks, and keypunchers. Regarding the latter, one observer notes that "the major demand for workers in the next decade will not be for computer scientists and engineers but for janitors, nurses' aides, sales clerks, cashiers, nurses, fast-food preparers, secretaries, truck drivers and kitchen helpers." Only seven percent of new jobs will be in high-tech areas, and the rest will not involve computers at all. And the computer assembly jobs themselves, upon which the entire industry depends, are rapidly being moved to places like Hong Kong and Taiwan, where labor is cheaper.

The surviving jobs that will be transformed by computers fall into four categories: 1) jobs that involve computers but require no interaction between the computer and the worker; 2) jobs that involve minimal interaction between computer and worker; 3) the "computer occupations" themselves, which require some level of computer knowledge; 4) the professions that require the use of computers as a tool.

The real estate agent reading a printout of listings, the supermarket checker using a scanner, the airline baggage handler using a computerized conveyor system, the retail clerk, the bank teller: these are some of the people whose jobs involve computers. In fact, the presence of the computer in such occupations is what leads to the idea that computers are everywhere. Yet what do these millions of workers need to understand about computers? The truth is that this sort of computer impact will be the most typical; yet in each case the degree of skill demanded by the job is reduced, not increased, by the presence of the computer (even though one supermarket manager suggested to me that passing groceries over a scanner requires more skill than running a cash register). Furthermore, any knowledge about the computer itself is quite irrelevant to the actual performance of the job.

Jobs which do require minimal interaction with a computer include those in computer-assisted manufacturing, drafting, machining, word processing, and data retrieval. Such jobs are significantly transformed, and some form of retraining is required. However, the retraining is far less than often imagined, rarely lasting more than a few weeks, and it usually is restricted to learning to operate specific instruments, something seldom included in a computer literacy curriculum. Here, too, it is arguable that the new skills demand far less intellectual participation by the worker than those which they replace. One need only compare a word processor to a secretary who used to run the office, or an N/C machine operator to a skilled machinist. Such jobs will represent a very high proportion of the computer-related work of the future.

Some argue that the office worker and industrial worker of the future "will soon have access to managerial information--and, hence, the ability to engage in tough and interesting problem solving along with her [sic] supervisor" and that "the new technologies [will] blur the invidious distinctions between the secretary and the boss and between the blue- and white-collar worker, [thereby providing] tremendous opportunities to those office and factory workers who are prepared by ... education to accept increased responsibilities." It is difficult to comprehend such observations, which represent a remarkable distortion of political realities. The evidence is uncontestable that computers give industrial and office management new and tighter forms of control and supervision, and that the push for greater efficiency and productivity reduces the worker's opportunity for skilled, knowledgeable participation in his or her own work. Nevertheless, the mythology that computers enhance all jobs they touch, transforming them into "mind jobs" filled with new responsibility, persists to feed the fears of those who hope for help from CL. For the vast majority of future workers, whether their jobs will be touched by computers or not, Computer Literacy education is a waste of time.

The last two categories are jobs in the "computer occupations" themselves, such as systems analysts, programmers, and operators, and the professionals involved in sophisticated computer use, such as scientists, business managers, and engineers. These categories constitute a relatively small fraction of the total employment picture of the next decade. The computer occupations, for example, are projected to increase in number by only one million in the next decade (totalling two million by 1990). This number is small when contrasted to the three million jobs predicted to be lost to computers by 1990, or when set against the millions of people who will be seeking employment in these valued occupations.

What about the businessmen, engineers, teachers, and scientists who will be using computer technology in sophisticated professional ways? To argue that teachers will need to be capable of sophisticated computer use would beg the very question we are discussing; if computer education is largely unnecessary, then teaching does not require sophisticated computer knowledge. Second, most independent businessmen and corporate managers who will be using computers will chiefly rely on prepackaged technical services or increasingly user-friendly computer systems (such as Lisa). The computer skills and knowledge they need will, like those of so many other workers, be far less awesome than computerphobics have been led to fear.

More importantly, those jobs that will continue to demand high levels of computer knowledge and understanding--in engineering, scientific research, statistics, finance, and specialized areas of medicine--constitute an extremely small part of the whole spectrum of jobs. These are the true mind workers of the future, but it seems certain that they will remain few in number despite fantasies of a workforce filled with engineers, scientists, and statisticians. There is virtually no room at the top of the labor market pyramid, given existing social relations of work in America, and high technology will almost certainly be used to preserve existing relations of power, status, and income rather than disturb them. The relative distribution of mind work, sophisticated, intellectually stimulating, and potent, will undoubtedly remain at or below present levels for the next few decades, if the masters of high technology continue to remake our world as they have begun to.

What does this brief survey of tomorrow's jobs tell us about the need for CL? First, many jobs will involve no computers at all. Second, the majority of jobs will involve only indirect use of computers or, at most, a level of computer use requiring a week or two of practical instruction. In all such jobs a prior introduction to computers such as CL is quite unnecessary, since no prior computer knowledge is required. Third, since, according to one CL educator, "for many years to come people will be able to acquire needed levels of computer-oriented skills on the job or in higher education programs," CL is even unnecessary in the training of those who will eventually become sophisticated computer workers. Fourth, the number and quality of jobs in the computer field itself is greatly overstated, and thus these jobs cannot be used to justify universal CL. Fifth, the number of knowledge workers, in any significant sense, will remain small despite the spread of CL. On all accounts, even from this admittedly cursory view of the future, CL makes no sense as job preparation. The hole card turns out to be the joker.

Nevertheless, the joke may be on us. We saw earlier how new educational requirements, however groundless, are rapidly making the need for CL a fact of life for today's students. Similarly, new hiring practices will most likely render CL necessary for employment. Just as good spelling is now required to fill out an application for a janitor's job and a high school diploma is needed to become a nurse's aide, and a college diploma is necessary for just about everything else, so tomorrow CL will be a requisite for many jobs that actually require no computer knowledge. With such credential barriers in place, CL will have created its own necessity, and employability will depend in part upon a parcel of useless knowledge about computers. Mythology will become the new reality. In the words of Atari's chief scientist, used originally in a different although not entirely unrelated context, "The best way to predict the future is to invent it." CL might turn up an ace whatever is in the deck.

Many teachers will argue that however few real knowledge-work jobs there may be, they want their students to have them. This competitive spirit (which parents share) feeds the momentum of CL: everyone wants his or her kid to become an engineer or a programmer, and an introduction to computers seems the best place to start. It is next to impossible to convince a particular parent or teacher that this does not make sense. A larger view, however, would unravel the twin mythology supporting this attitude. The idea that, no matter how few good jobs there are, there is still one out there for my child, depends upon a lingering hope that there will be enough for all; it assumes also that everyone gets an equal chance, and that success or failure depends solely on individual competence and preparation. There is nothing, even in the rhetoric of CL, to encourage a hope for equal opportunity in the world of high technology; all the evidence points in the opposite direction. Similarly, there is little reason to expect an abundance of decent jobs in the new workforce, despite the rhetoric. Some of us should begin to ask why.

Many will be squeezed out by the computer revolution. The

disenfranchised segments of the population, those who are already out of the running for jobs because of discrimination and inequality, will undoubtedly be pushed still further from access to jobs in the world of high technology. In a society where perhaps 25 percent of the population is functionally illiterate, in the original sense of that term, such people will be doubly condemned for being computer illiterate as well. The invented necessity of CL, in the form of credential barriers to employment, will serve to blame the victim in a new, insidious way: those who don't know computers will be firmly locked out of a workforce barely open to them now. Considerable lip service is being paid to these people, just as there is considerable discussion these days about the millions of people being replaced by automation. In all the talk, however, the only solution ever discussed is education or retraining: Let these unfortunate people learn computers so they can become knowledge workers. As we have begun to see, this is really no solution at all. CL, as job preparation, is in fact an obstacle to possible futures which might include these people. Perhaps the fundamental attitude behind CL, and the high-technology movement in general, is best expressed in the words of one of its popularizers: "The real measure of a revolution is not its casualty count, but its effects on the survivors."

● ● ●

We have seen that CL has very little to do with whether we will survive--as consumers, students, or workers--in the new world of high technology. There remains, however, one last justification for CL which we have not yet examined. It is frequently argued that the public needs to become informed about the new technology if, as citizens in a democracy, we are to be able to determine how computers will shape our lives. Public empowerment is an oft-stated goal of CL advocates, and it certainly appears reasonable that some understanding of the new technology is needed for controlling it. So long as computers remain a mystery to the majority of citizens, it is argued, the public will be an easy prey to vested interests, large scale abuse, and runaway technology. Society will be shaped by the designs of the few, and the masses will suffer the consequences, unless they are educated into computer literacy.

The irony of this argument is that we are already surrounded by computers and high technology without ever having been asked if we wanted to be. There has been virtually no public debate about whether the American people want the computerized information society we are now being forced to enter. The truth is that our society is already shaped primarily by the designs of the few and the momentum of technology, and it makes no sense to suggest that a minimal understanding of computers will empower an already technologically impotent citizenry. Computer literacy does not provide the public with the tools for wresting control of these technologies from the hands of corporate decision-makers. In fact, it is much more likely that a focus on minimal technical competence, as in CL, will lead to a sort of pseudocontrol, a false sense that one has power simply because one can make a computer do a little something. Real control of the direction the new technology will take involves political understanding, not trivial technical understanding, and it must focus on decisions which affect the design and use of large systems, not on the ability to create catchy little BASIC programs.

A few CL advocates are at least aware of this larger picture, but the overwhelming tendency is to ignore it. The trend in CL curriculum development is to turn away from what is derisively referred to as "computer awareness" (that is, a general overview of the social impact of computers) and to encourage instead a more hands-on, technical understanding. Basic to this tendency is the assumption that the control of a technology requires technological expertise. Control of nuclear energy in the hands of experts, however, proved dangerous in the case of Three Mile Island. People learned there that the experts did not really know what they were doing, that they did not genuinely consider the safety of the public as their top priority, and that ordinary citizens could confront and change the direction of a technology without having any technological understanding whatsoever. In the same way, control of computer technology by a few has created unmanned factories, offices of the future, useless gadgetry and games, "smart homes" and "electronic battlefields," all of which, it could be argued, lead to deterioration of people's jobs, skills, social relations, power, dignity, and even their chances of survival. Public debate on all of these transformations has been virtually nonexistent, and we must examine the public empowerment aspirations of CL in this context. We must ask whether CL is a movement which might help us confront existing policy, or whether it is in fact an extension of this policy, a vehicle for its dissemination, even a tool being used, often unknowingly, to further its public acceptance.

The content of CL courses now available contradicts any claim that they could possibly enlighten or empower anyone (unless "empowerment" is reduced to the keyboard familarity required to vote via videotex). Even if technical understanding were important for democratic participation, the minimal technical information available in such courses is many orders of magnitude removed from any significant understanding which might serve to enhance public deliberation. And any token attention to "social impact," in those courses that address it at all, is typically one-sided and delimited. For example, the New York State Association of Math Teachers, in its state-wide curriculum proposal, defines social-impact objectives in this manner: "The student will be aware of some of the major uses of computers in modern society ... and the student will be aware of career opportunities related to computers." The nontechnical components of CL courses generally are reduced to a cursory look at the history of computers (often ignoring the military contribution), a brief survey of benign computer uses, an unrealistic description of computer careers, and a gee-whiz glance at the marvels of the future. One popular CL course, now being introduced throughout the nation, is called Computeronics. Except for one or two comments about the frustrations of computer errors and a short parody of the dehumanized home of the future, the "Computers in Society" text of this course reads virtually as propaganda for the status quo. Job loss or social disenfranchisement are not mentioned, and the student is asked to "imagine that you are an executive," never an unemployed autoworker or assembler, when the effects of computerization are examined.

Even more disturbing was the attitude of teachers and trainers at a Computeronics teacher workshop I recently attended. Neither the teachers nor the trainers appeared very knowledgeable about computers or their impact, and there was a collective inclination to keep things light and uncomplicated. One trainer asked that we pretend not to know anything about computers so that he could practice his craft, and discussions about social questions were kept amusing and friendly, even as some real concerns were expressed. When one woman jokingly suggested we go down to the gym, get baseball bats, and destroy the micros surrounding us, the response was uncomfortable laughter. Teachers left that workshop with only the slightest knowledge of computer programming, with negligible understanding, of the social impact of this technology, and with very little desire to find out more. Yet such people as these, all nice folks, will be the ones conferring Computer Literacy upon millions of students. Not one participant appeared to realize the part he or she might be playing in the dissemination of such diluted, uncritical, uninformed, and possibly harmful education. This is hardly what Thomas Jefferson had in mind.

One further word about pseudocontrol. The computer differs from the TV and telephone in that, although it appears alien and menacing to the uninitiated, it can be tamed, controlled by the user, once some simple programming is learned. The possibilities for learning to control one's computer appear limitless because of the variety of functions it can be made to perform. Thus the home computer hobbyist enjoys a tremendous sense of power over his or her small piece of the technology: "When you program a computer, you feel a great deal of control and mastery" because "to program a computer is to enjoy power." The danger is that this sense of control, or pseudocontrol, becomes a substitute for real control, deluding one into thinking that one has mastered a technology when in reality one is only playing God with a chip of silicon.

This false sense of empowerment blocks any real participation in the social control of the technology as a whole. The result is a nation of individual computer masters who can't see the forest for the trees. The intensity of the debate about the impact of computer technology seems to have diminished in recent years, and discussions of its effect on human values appear to be out of fashion. If CL is truly a campaign for public enlightenment, one would have expected just the reverse, and this might tell us something about the real nature of CL. Is it possible that the failure, not the success, of CL might bring us closer to a collective understanding of where we are heading and what we might do about it?

• • •

CL is, in its practical claims, a bunch of nonsense, both hollow and full of danger, both ludicrous and grave. An examination of its specious content may alarm some readers, but probably not many. This is because almost everyone, including most CL advocates themselves, has already swallowed its faults of logic and distortions of reality without so much as a second thought. There is no question that the majority of those who are pushing CL into every corner of this country honestly believe that CL makes sense. There are some advocates of CL, however, who, it seems reasonable to assume, are using CL as a means to furthering their objectives at the expense (literally and otherwise) of a defensive American public. It is time to look at the weavers of the emperor's new clothes.

Hans Christian Andersen's weavers claim to be making cloth which is invisible to fools and incompetents. The swindlers' success requires a population which is sufficiently insecure about its intellectual competence to be willing to deny the obvious truth, a scenario not very different from the present state of affairs in America. Many Americans question their abilities and fear for their present or future jobs, to the point of being persuadable that what appears obvious to them (for example, that computers are troubling or dehumanizing) is false. The important thing is that oneself and one's children not be left behind.

As the country now agonizes over its presumed intellectual deficiencies, comparisons between our education and skills and those of the Japanese or Soviets proliferate in the press; one reads everywhere that we won't be able to "problem-solve" or "think critically" as well as our competitors or enemies unless we "create another Sputnik" and proceed full speed ahead. Add to this a climate of recession, loss of jobs to foreign industry, and high unemployment, and we are ready for the weavers: "The general context," writes one strong CL advocate, "that I think it is essential to assume, even if we have to engage in a deliberate suspension of disbelief in order to assume it, is an overarching national goal: to reverse the trend of decline of the U.S. relative to its main competition in productivity, prestige and leadership" (emphasis mine).

Enter High Tech. "America Rushes to High Technology For Growth," Business Week announces on a recent cover. Just as the promoters of the electrical and chemical technologies in the first decades of this century saw World War I as their great opportunity, so the promoters of computer technology are seizing this opportunity to establish their technology at the center of our economy. Only the acquiescence of the American people is needed: "It is clear that in the coming years we are going to retool our industry, and it should be made clear that we must, at the same time, retool ourselves." Enter computer literacy. But cui bono? Who might benefit most from such a massive "retooling" of the American people? Two obvious parties come to mind. First, there are the manufacturers and retailers of hardware and software, who envision an enormous

Communication and Education

educational demand for their wares. "We're looking at an infinite market," says the chairman of one such manufacturing firm. Anyone who is at all skeptical about CL usually comes to this answer first: CL is just a way to sell computers. This, then, is one not-so-hidden agenda behind CL.

A second party which stands to benefit from the push for CL is the education profession, in schools, colleges, industry, and small, profitable computer schools. As new graduate programs in computer education start up, as thousands of laid-off workers look to be "retrained," as millions of students need computer courses in order to graduate, as twenty-six million managers look reluctantly at the computers in their futures, as millions of teachers line up for in-service training, the realm of the educator has suddenly acquired a large and rich new province. "School administrators are laying their bets on a sure ticket to a better life for schools--technology." This, then, is a second agenda behind CL.

The content of CL is largely irrelevant for both agendas so long as demand for the hardware, software, and instruction remains high. This helps to explain how CL has spread so quickly despite its dubious content and justification. Many educators sincerely believe in what CL promises, and many sincerely want to provide the best possible CL curricula for their students. Nevertheless, very few have examined the assumptions and context of their effort and, given what they stand to gain, it is altogether understandable that they have not bothered. This is even more true for the manufacturers and retailers of computers and software; their business is selling products, and if CL expands their markets, who are they to question it? Educators, manufacturers, and retailers all follow agendas which have expanded the perceived need for CL among the American people. These groups are primarily responsible for the CL movement in this country. They have intensified high-tech fever, and have responded with predictable enterprise to the "needs" of a defensive population. They are, however, merely spreading someone else's vision of a new world.

It seems reasonable to interpret CL as propaganda which parades as public enlightenment, and to conclude that it means to create a populace that can comfortably accept the prospect of a computerized world. The common thread running through the various definitions of Computer Literacy encourages a suspicion that something like this is the program:

> The goal of CL should be to give as many of [the masses] as possible the sense of belonging in a computer-rich society.
>
> Give all people, at least, a minimal amount of computer knowledge that would enable them to become "computer comfortable."
>
> [CL leads] to a favorable or well-informed affective orientation.

[CL will enable people to] take reasonable positions on information-related issues.

[CL will help people to] understand the concept of compromise ... with respect to policy issues such as informational privacy and security.

Many individuals today are apprehensive about privacy, misuse, attitudes and automation in general. [CL] is the way to eliminate these concerns.

Training is a concrete basis for understanding the value of computers and ... leads to greater acceptance of other societal applications as well.

It is difficult to ignore the implication here. The weavers of CL's dubious cloth are the prime movers behind the computerized society itself, the fabricators of "high tech," "telecommunications," "information society," and "computer revolution." Catchwords such as these have convinced the nation that it is entering a social transformation which is both total and inevitable. Those corporate leaders and their ideological allies who mean to transform the workplace, the home, the school, and the functions of government into an efficient, highly controlled, and easily monitored technological marketplace, are the real originators of CL, if not by that name, because they need something like it to make their social transformation a reality. (Whether the transformation is taken to be conspiratorially organized, or largely a matter of implicit common interests, scarcely matters.) Whereas educators and computer merchants have only enlarged upon an existing demand, the makers of the Information Society, those who would transform our world to suit their needs, have perpetrated CL in order to ensure public acquiescence in their grand design.

How does the propaganda of Computer Literacy ensure this acquiescence? First, it introduces people to computers, gives them some hands-on experience, and deludes them into thinking that all computers are friendly and easily controlled because their little micro is so. In this way, CL mystifies in the name of demystification. The very act of making computers accessible conceals the more socially significant, and far less accessible, purposes of the technology. The one-sided presentation of marvelous computer uses in CL courses furthers this deception in the name of "awareness."

Second, as manufacturers and designers work to produce computers which are ever more user-friendly, so CL is used to "produce" people who are ever more computer-friendly. A person who is familiar with a school computer, or even better, one who has a personal computer at home, is far less likely to be suspicious of a computerized society than one who is uninitiated and scared.

This brings us to a third way CL ensures public acquiescence in the information society. It is used to psychologize dissent. Anyone who might for whatever good reason be reluctant to get involved with computers is called "computerphobic," which means that he or she is really afraid of computers out of mere ignorance. Few people who have been labelled computerphobic don't somehow believe it themselves. It is powerful stuff; those accused of fearing something new become disoriented as old truths lose ground. CL exists not only to inform but also to give such people an easy way out, when a more difficult way might lead them to the truth.

A fourth use of CL propaganda is to stifle debate and to depoliticize discussion. The focus on the technical, and the establishment of a carefully delineated arena for discussions of "social impact," render any genuine criticism illegitimate, even irrational. And the portrayal of the computer society as a given discredits any discussions of human values and dignity as being wishful thinking or nostalgic reverie.

The fifth influence of CL propaganda is perhaps the most effective. The unequivocal message of CL is this: computers are important, very important, and knowing about them is equally important. There is hardly a way that a society bombarded with such exhortations to become computer literate, as we have been, can continue to believe that knowing about computers might not be very important. Some of the hysteria of parents, schoolmen, and management results from this bombardment. One certain way to ensure public cooperation and acquiescence is to make people feel that they have no choice, and the CL campaign is designed to do just that. When a fervent appeal to national pride and prestige is added, and a resolve to overcome our foreign competition in trade and international leadership, it becomes hard to find someone who will even admit the possibility that all this computer talk may be exaggerated. Many people breathe a noticeable sigh of relief at such a suggestion, and many have thanked me for mentioning the unmentionable. But the relative unimportance of computer knowledge must be stated plainly and often before people can learn to hope that the picture of the future woven into the CL tapestry is, as yet, essentially a fiction.

The weavers of the emperor's new clothes wanted to line their pockets with gold. Those who weave the far-reaching strands of Computer Literacy want to redesign our world. It is especially troubling, therefore, to find that several of the more visible proponents of CL have historical associations with an ideology whose focus is military and whose methods are decidedly scientific and antidemocratic. Only a few pieces of the puzzle are yet in place, unfortunately. They include the author of "The Next Great Crisis in American Education--Computer Literacy," who is also a National Science Foundation convenor of national CL conferences. His work prior to the rise of CL included a study for the Army on "undergrounds in insurgent, revolutionary and resistance warfare," in which he states that "the most effective countermeasure is the use of immediate, overpowering force to repress the first signs of insurgency or resistance. Nations with a representative or constitutional form of government are often restrained from such action by moral, legal and social considerations." HumRRO, Human Resources Research

Organization, a major recipient of CL grants and also a convenor of national CL conferences, was founded by the Army in 1951 to "improve human performance through behavioral and social science research." It is unclear at this time what the connections may be between such backgrounds and CL, but the matter certainly warrants closer examination. Some agendas will remain hidden until then.

• • •

Hans Christian Andersen chose a child to break the spell of the weavers. Our story is different. We can hardly count on our children to point out the fraudulence of Computer Literacy. They are already too comfortable, for the most part, within the new world, and their fearlessness, often admired by a cautious older generation, could in fact be their greatest weakness. The naked truth must be declared by those who can still see it, so that we may still have a chance to choose our future.

It must be stated that computers are not the problem. A word processor would have facilitated the writing of this paper tremendously, and I would not reject a CAT scan at the appropriate time. Too often, however, when one intones the homily that "computers aren't harmful, people are," one is assuming that "people" are reasonable beings like us, or, if they are not, that they can be replaced. But things are not that simple, and the people who are forging the information society cannot readily be assumed to share our idea of what is reasonable. The distinction between computers and the people who control them once again becomes blurred, and Luddism takes on fresh appeal.

But the subject of this paper is not computers. It is Computer Literacy. Although the two are assuredly related, it is important that they be kept separate. One does not have to be "anti-computer" to choose to reject the Computer Revolution or to see through the transparent fraudulence of Computer Literacy. What is desperately needed at this time is the resurrection of critical debate, a renewal of public discourse about how computers might be understood and used in ways which enrich our lives. This would be the first step toward a truly computer-literate society.

THE REFERENCE LIBRARIAN WHO TEACHES:
THE CONFESSIONS OF A MOTHER HEN*

John C. Swan

This is in many respects an elaborate defense of the simple and time-worn practice of taking a library patron in hand and walking and working through the search process with that person. More than that, this is an assertion that this homely activity, conducted in the right spirit, can be the foundation for truly effective library instruction. Since the arguments concerning such instruction which follow may seem an odd mixture of the reactionary and the enthusiastic, I had better make it clear that they are conditioned by experience in a specific context. In many libraries, especially small, very active academic libraries in which professional versatility is a necessity even when it is not an unalloyed virtue, the reference librarian (in the singular) is also in charge of teaching others how to use reference tools, and by extension, the rest of the library. The performance of this dual role of reference and teaching encourages much overlapping of (and some conflict between) the two activities; it also brings one to see the deep connections between them--connections which transcend this small-college environment.

In his invaluable "Library Literacy" column in a recent RQ, John Lubans quoted an accusation from one of the disgruntled that serves here to sound the reactionary note: "BI--The moral majority of the library profession."[1] Jeremy Sayles amplifies this charge: "There is a continuous commotion about the evils of spoon-feeding, of dispensing information. We librarians are supposed to feel guilty if we give information to students. Yet, this is what we are prepared for: indeed, this is our function."[2] This reaction to the "library instruction juggernaut" is very understandable, even from one who, like Mr. Sayles, believes strongly in "a program of basic research skills to complement the traditional reference service."[3] But then, the juggernaut itself is understandable, considering the resistance, the hostility, and the inertia of librarians and faculty (not to mention students) which BI missionaries have had, and still have, to overcome. But even taking the passions of the struggle into account, there re-

---

*Reprinted by permission of the author and publisher from The Reference Librarian, 10 (Spring/Summer 1984) 55-66; copyright © 1984 by The Haworth Press, Inc. All rights reserved.

mains a basic disagreement about priorities. On the one hand, referring again to Sayles, "Library instruction, at best, is merely the overture to traditional reference service. It does not replace it; it complements and strengthens it."[4] Or, in a more recent statement, a response by two librarians to the controversial ACRL Bibliographic Instruction Section "Think Tank Recommendations," "Such instruction is not designed--nor should it be designed--to make the student user independent of the reference department. We need not make every student a reference librarian, though we can certainly make them more knowledgeable."[5]

On the other hand, the "Think Tank" itself provided the most assertive claim for the pride of place of BI in their rejection of "the notion of bibliographic instruction as a secondary activity of library reference departments, instead viewing it "as the very heart of the reference process."[6] As one who has been to the Mountain (Earlham) and communed with the Truth (Evan Farber's annual workshop) in this matter, I feel the force of the "Think Tank" claim. Indeed, armed with the appropriate clay tablets, we at Wabash have begun to put into effect, with modifications to suit our circumstances, a number of Earlham techniques for moving library research methodologies closer to the center of the students'--and faculty's and librarians'--consciousness. The innovations have begun to add considerably to our thriving program of one-shot course and assignment-related library tours. Working with faculty to develop assignments that require the students to create annotated bibliographies in a sequence of phases, and also working cooperatively to develop research assignments that encourage specific and intelligent use of reference tools, have begun to take us beyond what is possible in the one-shot program.

It is no reflection upon my experience in the Earlham workshop (although I eagerly and futilely looked for substantial flaws that would let me out of this painful change in life) that I still find myself among those who cannot jump into the Think Tank. (I ought to make clear that Earlham was not literally represented in the Think Tank group, although it has long been one of the most successful examples of an instruction-centered library.) BI just isn't the "very heart of the reference process," either for the librarian or the patron. The essence of the process is obviously the search itself, the use of the investigative skills in interplay with thought and experience, not the mere acquisition of those skills. For all the considerable good in them, the ACRL recommendations, at least the most overreaching of them, present the danger of separating the learning process from the using process. It is true enough that it is necessary to focus upon educational techniques and program planning,[7] but if BI is treated as an end in itself, a discipline for students to master, rather than a path to the mastery of real disciplines, then the vital link between searching and learning can be broken. The relentless earnestness and simplified abstractness of many BI exercises, especially those only tenuously related to real course needs, based on regimented preparation conducted, often, away from the points of use, can turn the searching adventure into the sterile pursuit of a flow-charted answer.

Constance McCarthy has provided an illuminating analysis of the way in which some users of the library are led to "underestimate the complexity of library systems" by "library instruction that stresses detail and permits easy success at the expense of realistic experience with library research."[8] This kind of misunderstanding can lead to patron guilt and frustration when the application of dutifully learned simple procedures doesn't pay off, but more seriously, it fosters the belief that the search for information is nothing more than obediently following the schematics set forth by the librarians and their guides. The assumption that the truth lies at the other end of a string of keywords and cross-references does yield results in many cases--there is never a shortage of simplified questions with simplified answers--but it also carries the danger of a flat and uncreative relationship with information and ideas. This is especially true for the many who find the library a rather foreign place to begin with, for whom any quick and easy pathway to an answer or to a paper topic is likely to be the end, rather than the beginning, of inquiry.

To be fair, it must be said that the Think Tank recommendations envision a much richer and more fully developed instructional process, although the language they choose to describe this vision is not always reassuring. "All sound instruction is based on the imparting of the basic tenets of a body of knowledge; all instruction should be conceptually based."[9] Fine words, supported by the collective wisdom of countless educators who have chosen to address students' capacity to understand in preference to their capacity to memorize. But what do they mean in light of the statement under the heading, "The Importance of Research":

> Bibliographic instruction should be based on knowledge of the social and intellectual characteristics of the academic disciplines which give rise to their different patterns of scholarly, bibliographic, and encyclopedic literature.... Instruction librarians should make explicit (and thus teachable) the tacit knowledge of experienced researchers and determine the concepts and techniques which should be taught.[10]

If this means we should master and then impart "sociology of knowledge," research networks, "deep structure" and metaphors of reference rather than, or even antecedant to, actual research skills, it could well lead to the alienating abstraction of one of the few learning activities that can be both concrete and conceptually stimulating at the same time.

For all their moments of insight and their structural elegance, the attempts so far to do this conceptual structuring, the ghostly paradigms cast up by McInnis[11] and Nitecki[12] (for instance) fail to put weapons for enlightenment into the hands of this teaching librarian. Even more chilling, but just as much in line with the Think Tank thought, is Keresztesi's argument that librarians should not seek "the solution in the acquisition of degrees in practice-oriented subject disciplines, but by preserving proudly our generalist posture, we should cultivate our own garden."[13] By "generalist" he does not mean the pseudo-polymaths that most of us in reference gradually become ("wizard" was Daniel Gore's term, I believe), with our efficient, reassuring and superficial acquaintance with vast, bleeding chunks of the world of organized knowledge. No, he means something more exalted and severe, the mastery of a real discipline, a "science of bibliography" in which we learn and teach the "topography" of the disciplines, each suitably arranged into multi-categorized "dimensions."[14] It is undeniable that there is a discipline of bibliography, just as there are several thriving varieties of information science, citation analysis, operations research, and sociologies of inquiry. It may well be that this "meta-librarianship" fits well into this world. But just as BI is not for the purpose of transforming the unsuspecting patron into a reference librarian, it is similarly irrelevant to turning out information scientists (although it should be a good start for both procedures, come to think of it). The metaphorical approach certainly can't provide the sense of the activities of research and inquiry that actual experience in subject disciplines can; it has yet to demonstrate its conceptual usefulness to the reference librarian who would also gladly teach.

Reference librarians are, the stereotype to the contrary, quite often eager to be helpful. Not only is that what we are paid for, but the "sitting duck" nature of the reference desk instills in many of its occupants the urge to demonstrate in public that they can be useful, even expert. Producing the requested information quickly, accomplishing this without letting the patron in on the false starts and dead ends, often effects a wonderful transformation of image: Sitting Duck becomes Eagle Eye. To befowl the image one more time, it must be confessed that the same motivation plays a role in the mother hen impulse. It is satisfying to watch the look of gratitude supplant that of anxiety as I lead the patron to the right places, clucking concernedly all the while. It must also be admitted that the "reference interview" that goes with this style is not always successful--just as mother hens can get in the way of their own offspring.

These confessions are not meant to deny the value of the mother hen approach, but to make it clear that, despite its efficacy, it has its dangers. In fact, the mother hen quality is extremely useful for both fulfilling the immediate needs of the patron and establishing a relationship of trust--always devoutly to be sought, of course, but especially necessary in a small college situation, where there is a particularly direct connection between this trust and the amount of business that comes the way of the reference desk.

Most relevant here, this nurturing behavior of the reference librarian has a direct impact upon the instructional role. The pedagogy of the connection rests on simple grounds, one of which is well expressed by Joanne Euster: "Bibliographic instruction at its most elemental level is simply one-on-one reference assistance."[15] This is the most compelling reason that the joining of reference and BI ought to be much more than the shotgun wedding it often seems

Communication and Education   173

to be. One-on-one instruction is only practical when there are time, resources, and staff or it, a less-than-common conjunction these days. However, it is my experience and my basic argument that the more that one-on-one approach can be carried over into group instruction (an even hard instruction, as some institutions conduct it), the more effective is the teaching.

Having made the claim that mother henning has something to do with teaching, I am obliged to put it into the context of the "information versus instruction" question; after all, mother hens of the reference species seem to be firmly on the "information" side of this debate. In his stimulating discussion of "alternative professional models," Brian Nielsen refers to the performance of reference work in sociological terms as a "core professional task";

> First of all, reference is a librarian role that involves a "professional-client" relationship, unlike other task areas such as cataloging, book selection, and administration, where the contact with library users is not often direct.... Reference work is also a specialty area in which the "application of special and esoteric knowledge," that criterion so important to achieving professional status, is patent: the public perception of the all-knowing reference librarian (which coexists with other, less flattering images) is testimony to this.... Still other qualities of reference work that give weight to its "core task" nature are that the work is not reducible to rules, it is difficult to measure, and its practice relies on intuition, hunches, and bits and pieces of information that only long experience and a retentive mind--not a textbook--can develop.[16]

The consequence of this professional identification has been to emphasize what Nielsen calls the "intermediary" aspect of reference, the librarian enhancing his status (re the Eagle Eye) by mediating between his resources and the patron, rather than providing the person with the skills to use those tools independently. The professional is encouraged in this practice by the fact that he/she really does, or ought to, know the ropes better than they can be taught within the constraints of bibliographic instruction. And the patron is usually there in the library for information rather than training, anyway. Nielsen argues well that the intermediary role is essentially limiting and, if used alone, is finally doomed to serve only an elite who can afford the services of the staff trained in that role:

> If librarians truly wish to work toward the best interests of their users, it is absurd to continue to advocate the old classic professionalism, which places users in a dependency relationship with librarians. Such a relationship does a disservice to users and ultimately retards the development of library services, of librarians, and of much library technology.[17]

The argument is convincing, but it does not foreclose the very important possibility that modified versions of the "old classic professionalism" can be combined with the teaching of library skills. Indeed, the most effective teachers, at least in terms of intimacy with the subject to be taught, ought to come from the ranks of these "intermediaries," reference librarians who have a working sense of what Elizabeth Frick has called a "basic art"[18] in our complex world of information, the art of literature searching. The force of that word "art" may not apply to the search in its expressive sense, but as an evocation of the thought, creativity, and reflection that goes into the best searching, it will do just fine.

In order to understand how a clearly intermediary approach to reference can also partake of the teacher's role, it is necessary to move beyond Nielsen's alternatives--and more is implied here than merely that reference librarians can also be instruction librarians. Janice Koyama, supporting Nielsen, has emphasized that:

> Extremists on either side are better directed to forge a new alternative role ... and to accept reference desk activity and bibliographic instruction as interrelated, compatible, and necessary for the future growth and continuing existence of both.[19]

This acceptance of the alternatives echoes the stance which Katz has taken, a position which has behind it a good deal of scepticism about the claims that have been made for BI. He believes that:

> the library user, and nonuser, should be given a choice. It is important to stress "given a choice." The user should have the option either (1) to learn how to use the library or any of its parts, or (2) not to learn how and still to expect a full, complete, and total answer to his or her question(s) from the reference librarian.[20]

It is important for the establishment of trust between the librarian and his patron that the latter feel that he does indeed have a choice. More than once I have seen a student withdraw that trust when his question evoked a lesson rather than an answer or a specific path to an answer.

Koyama's "new alternative role," I could argue, ought to be a rethought version of the old mother hen role; however, the alternatives of which it is made only partly express the notion of mother hen as teacher. In practice, this is not so much a set of alternating roles as a simultaneous combination. And this is not to construct a paradox, but to describe a teacher. Like the good teacher, the reference librarian who would teach something of his trade even as he connects questioner with answer must have a richer self-conception than that of information dispenser. He must be a role model.

Every good teacher is to some degree a role model, but this does not mean a model for teaching (except perhaps for those students who will themselves teach, and even bad teachers have served that function for generations of bad teachers after them). The teacher who succeeds in communicating with his students does present himself as a source of learned skills and knowledge, to be sure, but that role would have little communicative impact if the teacher did not also reveal the thinker and learner inside that teacher role, using, testing, applying the education and experience which he seeks to convey. In other words, the teacher who manages to make a difference is a role model as a learner for the students who learn from--or more precisely with--him.

This is hardly a fresh insight, but it is also hardly a guiding principle among librarians who find themselves attempting to communicate some portion of their research skills to single or multiple students. Not that it prevails among teachers themselves--Ivan Illich's well-known condemnation of the educational system could, with very little alteration, apply both to hard-nosed reference librarians and the most righteous of the BI crusaders:

> Schools are designed on the assumption that there is a secret to everything in life; that the quality of life depends on knowing that secret, that secrets can be known only in orderly succession; and that only teachers can properly reveal those secrets.[21]

Librarians often conceive of their professional role in essentially clerical and externally manipulative terms: they are paid for mastering systems of storage and retrieval according to outward descriptions and codes, but the actual content of what they manipulate is beyond their purview. Therefore, that which they seek to teach they also present in terms of these externals. Even on a one-to-one basis, this presents a formidable challenge to anyone who seeks to make this into an enlivening educational experience (not even considering the countless librarians and teachers of librarians who have been perfectly content with memorization of index titles and coverages). It just may be that the necessary life-giving principles will emerge from the aforementioned efforts of McInnis, Nitecki, Keresztesi, and the like. However, since these theoretical plumbings are more likely to lead to greater abstraction instead, it might prove more useful to learn from the success of those reference/instruction librarians who are not hampered by an outsider's relationship to the world of content. These include reference librarians who insist on remaining in touch, however superficially, with the literature which lies at the other end of their indexes. And they include mother hens who draw sustenance not only from their mothering but from the substance within the knowledge structures through which they guide their charges.

Pauline Wilson has drawn the distinction between the roles of the teacher and the librarian upon this external/internal basis:

> The teacher must have a good understanding of the content of that portion of the graphic record which he or she is

charged with disseminating.... The librarian, on the other hand, must have a different understanding ... an in-depth understanding of the graphic record as a structure, an entity.... The librarian does not disseminate content and does not disseminate by teaching but by means of library processes.[22]

It is possible for the reference librarian who also teaches research skills to accept this distinction simply by alternating between the two roles ("librarians sometimes teach").[23] However, it is much more liberating (potentially), and much closer to the complex reality of the librarian's actual research process if we discard this categorization and admit that content is very much in the librarian's domain.

We should teach the research process as an activity which does indeed offer the fascination and complexity that we ought to recognize in a "basic art." To do this we must draw upon the questions and the issues themselves; we can't stop at keywords and cross-references. This is not an argumentation for unnecessary complexity or mystification (no mother hen could ever mystify, except maybe with prose); there really are simple, straightforward questions and answers, and they are surely necessary in beginning BI. But the teacher's truth holds even from the start: To give a student or a class of students a genuine sense of the search, show them a searcher in action, grappling with content as well as index terms, ideas as well as citations. The reference librarian in particular has the excellent opportunity to serve as the role model, the expert learner demonstrating for the novice learner. This, by the way, is an opportunity that will be lost if conflict and specialization eventually put bibliographic instruction exclusively in the hands of library instructors who are responsible only for teaching and therefore develop their teaching routines at the expense of their own knowledge.

The reference librarian who consciously fulfills the function of the role model both as reference guide and as teacher must confront his research challenges, not as an expert in the content of the matter he searches, but as one skilled in the discovery and quick evaluation of that content. Very importantly, this requires the willingness to be vulnerable, not concealing those false starts and dead ends, being honest about what one understands and what one doesn't (sometimes especially difficult for wizards).

One of the basic sources of resistance to the belief that librarians must deal with content as well as structure is the clear impossibility of becoming a real wizard, of learning in any depth at all the content of the subject matter to which we provide access. But how many "real" teachers have in-depth knowledge of even their own fields in the modern age of information, except in cases of extreme specialization? Mastery of content is not the point, either for the reference librarian or, nearly always, for the persons for whom, with whom, the reference process is accomplished. What is relevant? Engaging the content in a meaningful way, an act which must be preceded by similarly meaningful search.

The unique pedagogical advantage of mother henning relates directly to this business of making the search meaningful. One of Carl Rogers' most creative (over)statements is to the point: "I have come to feel that the only learning which significantly influences behavior is self-discovered, self-appropriated learning."[24] In the light of this passage, the mother hen has a distinct advantage over the prescriptive instructor, Illich's teacher of "secrets." No one would deny that young chickens and young humans learn most naturally from role models; there is no reason this should not apply to library instruction. We who concernedly shepherd the patron through every step of the research course, sharing, sympathizing, worrying, have stepped at least part of the way out of the prescriptive role; we encourage the student's learning by self-discovery because we must go through it ourselves. We cannot deny that there are always the dangers of smothering or infantilizing our charges, but that means we must ply our trade with a healthy awareness--and mother henning is not the kind of role that excludes all other styles and approaches in those who adopt it, although it does serve as an excellent base of operations.

Despite the image and the natural dynamics of this approach, it is not an exclusively individual mode of instruction--most mother hens have a fair number of offspring exploring at the same time. The basic attitude of openness, the personal concern, and the sense of discovery may be difficult to maintain all the time, but a nourishing attitude is usually itself rewarded with nourishment. It is not difficult to adapt the attitude to classes of BI students, and its effects linger even when major logistical compromises are necessary. In my experience, it has been possible to use the individual approach with a group, using questions and research problems arising from the group, with more success than the canned demonstration, in spite of the preordained success and efficiency of the latter. However it is applied, against whatever obstacles of numbers, time, and resources, the mother hen style should have value in any library teaching context. When the spirit is right, it bears the seeds of trust, shared experience, and real library education.

References

1. Lubans, John, Jr., "Library Literacy," RQ, Fall 1982, p. 14.
2. Sayles, Jeremy W., "An Opinion about Library Instruction," Southeastern Librarian, Winter 1980, p. 199.
3. Ibid., p. 198.
4. Ibid., p. 200.
5. Lewis, David W., and C. Paul Vincent, "Reactions to the Think Tank Recommendations: A Symposium: An Initial Response," Journal of Academic Librarianship, March 1983, p. 5.
6. "Think Tank Recommendations for Bibliographic Instruction," College and Research Libraries News, December 1981, p. 395.
7. For a humane and practical view of the planning side, see Keith M. Cottam, "Avoiding Failure: Planning User Education," RQ, Summer 1982, pp. 331-33.

8. McCarthy, Constance, "Library Instruction: Observations from the Reference Desk," RQ, Fall 1982, p. 36.
9. Think Tank Recommendations, op. cit., p. 396.
10. Ibid.
11. McInnis, Raymond, "Do Metaphors Make Good Sense in Teaching Research Strategy?" in Cerise Oberman and Katina Strauch, Theories of Bibliographic Education: Designs for Teaching (New York: Bowker, 1982), p. 45-74.
12. Nitecki, Joseph Z., "An Idea of Librarianship: An Outline for a Root-Metaphor Theory in Library Science," Journal of Library History, Winter 1981, pp. 106-120.
13. Keresztesi, Michael, "The Science of Bibliography: Theoretical Implications for Bibliographic Instruction," in Oberman and Strauch, op. cit. p. 26.
14. Ibid., pp. 21-24.
15. Euster, Joanne, "Reactions to the Think Tank Recommendations: A Symposium: 'Full of Sound and Fury, Signifying' What?" Journal of Academic Librarianship, March 1983, p. 14.
16. Nielsen, Brian, "Teacher or Intermediary: Alternative Professional Models in the Information Age," College and Research Libraries, May 1982, p. 185.
17. Ibid., p. 188.
18. Frick, Elizabeth, "Teaching Information Structure: Turning Dependent Researchers into Self-Teachers" in Oberman and Strauch, op, cit., p. 193.
19. Koyama, Janice T., "Reactions to the Think Tank Recommendations: A Symposium: Bibliographic Instruction and the Role of the Academic Librarian," Journal of Academic Librarianship, March 1983, p. 13.
20. Katz, William A., Introduction to Reference Work, Volume II: Reference Services and Reference Processes, Third Edition (New York: McGraw-Hill, 1978), p. 261.
21. Illich, Ivan, New York Review of Books, 1971, quoted in Morrow's International Dictionary of Contemporary Quotations, Compiled by Jonathon Green (New York: Morrow, 1982), p. 360.
22. Wilson, Pauline, "Librarians as Teachers: The Study of an Organization Fiction," Library Quarterly, Volume 49, No. 2 (1979), p. 155.
23. Ibid.
24. Rogers, Carl R., "Personal Thoughts on Teaching and Learning," in William F. O'Neill, Selected Educational Heresies (Glenview, Illinois: Scott, Foresman, 1969), p. 210.

MINDS ALIVE: WHAT & WHY GIFTED STUDENTS READ FOR PLEASURE*

Susan I. Swanton

This analysis of the habits of gifted and other elementary school students who read for pleasure resulted from my own observations during my 18 years as a public library director and from experiences as a parent of a child who is gifted.

Four years ago, when my son Michael was accepted into the Gates-Chili School's GOAL Program for children tested as having academic potential, I noticed that a high percentage of the parents attending the GOAL orientation session were those I'd met years before in my evening preschool hours. From other parent meetings I'd attended, I knew this high percentage was unusual. Three years later, when my son's sixth grade teacher asked me to participate in the county conference for the gifted child, I jumped at the opportunity to test my hypothesis that there is a correlation between early childhood use of public libraries and academic achievement in later school years.

With the help of the teacher, Tina Shumway, I designed a questionnaire to be distributed throughout three school districts, to be completed by the 140 students in nine gifted/accelerated classes, ranging from third to sixth grade.

After the results of the first survey were tabulated, I decided to further test the results by surveying students in the regular classes. With the cooperation of five sixth grade teachers who distributed the survey to their students, I was able to obtain another 100 completed questionnaires for comparison with those received in the initial survey.

A total of 240 questionnaires were analyzed. These represented eight classes of gifted students from three Monroe County school districts (Gates-Chili, East Irondequoit, and Penfield), grades 3-8, and six regular sixth grade classes from the Gates-Chili Central

*Reprinted by permission of the author and publisher from School Library Journal, 30:7 (March 1984) 99-102. Published by R. R. Bowker Co. (a Xerox company). Copyright © 1984 by Xerox Corporation.

School District. Among these were 123 questionnaires from students in gifted programs, and 117 from students in regular programs. Because every student did not answer all questions, the percentages provided are based on the number of questions answered.

Survey Questions and Answers

Question 1. What type of books do you choose to read on your own for fun? (For example, not related to school assignments--okay to list titles and authors, too.)

For both the gifted student and the regular student, mysteries topped the list as the favorite type of book, and fiction generally placed second for the gifted and third for regular students.

The similarities end here. For the gifted students, science fiction books placed third and fantasy fourth. For regular students, comedy/humor placed second, and adventure fourth. Some categories (history, historical fiction, medieval history) were mentioned only by gifted students, while other categories (horror, war, and sad stories) were much stronger among regular students. Biography and animals were read more widely by regular students than by the more gifted; sports stories, surprisingly, were favored by the gifted.

When I asked this question of gifted members of the Kids Court panel at the Genessee Valley Gifted and Talented Educational Team's (GVGET) Conference, they said they liked science fiction and fantasy because of the challenge it presented, as well as its relationship to Dungeons and Dragons--a popular game.

The gifted child has a well-developed mind which needs exercising, and science fiction/fantasy has few if any present-day reference points, forcing the reader to stretch his or her imagination. On the other hand, youngsters who are considered average may still be attempting to master reading skills, which may explain why comedy/humor and adventure tales appeal so much more strongly to them.

TYPES OF BOOKS

	Gifted	Regular
Mysteries	43	47
Fiction	41	23
Science fiction	29	10
Fantasy	18	5
Sports	12	6
Comedy/humor	10	27
YA problem novels	9	13
Young romances	7	6
Animals/nature	7	13

History/historical fiction	7	0
Adventure	6	18
Medieval	6	0
Non-fiction	6	6
Biography	5	8
Scarey/horror	2	8
War	2	6
Sad stories	0	4

Question 2: Where do you get the books you listed in Question 1? (Check as many categories as apply to you but underline the major source of your fun reading.)

The majority of gifted children (52 percent) mentioned the public library as the primary source of recreational reading, almost three times as many as the next source, the school library (19 percent). Yet as many as 37 percent of the regular students listed the school library as their major source of recreational reading; 33 percent of the regular students listed the public library as a major source of recreational reading.

For other sources of recreational reading, the public library once again placed first for the gifted, and the school library first for the regular student. Bookstores were the second source for the gifted and public libraries second for regular students. School libraries place after the home as a source for recreational reading for the gifted.

Given the wide range of the gifted student's interests and reading skills, it follows that the public library, with its primarily adult-level collection, would be better equipped to meet their reading interests. It also follows that the school library, in targeting service to the majority of students, would better serve the needs of the regular student.

Among other sources of recreational reading, school book clubs were named by a number of students. One school in the Gates-Chili area had a "Reading is Fundamental" program before the school closed (due to declining enrollment). A number of students who transferred to another school mentioned that they missed the program. I believe very strongly in the value of kids owning their own books, and these comments reinforce that belief.

Traditionally the public library has served as a haven for the gifted child who is often urged by adults--parents and teachers alike-- to do extra credit projects and to satisfy his or her insatiable curiosity. Happily, the public library often becomes, in the words of one fourth-grader, "a ticket to some other place in this galaxy." Knowing this, public libraries should strive to work closely with their school districts to establish special programs to meet the needs of the gifted.

WHERE BOOKS ARE OBTAINED

	Gifted	Regular
Major source:		
Public library	32 (52%)	26 (33%)
School library	12 (19%)	29 (37%)
Home	11 (18%)	14 (18%)
Bookstore	7 (11%)	10 (12%)
Other sources:		
Public library	88	82
Bookstore	71	55
Home	60	69
School library	59	95
School bookclub	8	21
Friends	7	19
Teachers	4	2
Gifts	1	2

Questions 3 and 4: What is your very favorite book or author? Why is it your favorite?

Students as young as third graders--both gifted and regular-- listed Judy Blume as their favorite. Thereafter the favorite choices diverged. Lloyd Alexander and J.R.R. Tolkien were top choices for the gifted, consistent with the high ranking of science fiction and fantasy. Second and third choices for the regular student were Wilson Rawls' Where the Red Fern Grows and Jack London's Call of the Wild and White Fang, again consistent with the interest in adventure stories among regular students.

FAVORITE AUTHORS

	Gifted	Regular
Judy Blume	30	36
Lloyd Alexander	8	3
J.R.R. Tolkien	8	1
C.S. Lewis	6	0
Lois Duncan	4	0
V.C. Andrews	3	0
Laura Ingalls Wilder	3	1
Beverly Cleary	2	3
Where the Red Fern Grows	0	9
Jack London	0	5
S.E. Hinton	0	2
Poltergeist	0	2

Question 5: How important do you think reading is to your parents (or guardians)?

The majority of gifted students (73 percent) and of regular students (64 percent) felt reading was very important to one or both of their parents. In these homes there were lots of books and magazines to read at all times. But 33 percent of regular students thought reading was only somewhat important or not very important to their parents (versus only 19 percent of students in gifted programs). So the majority of children surveyed are getting a clear message from their parents that reading is or is not important. I've long felt that schools and libraries alone can't demonstrate that reading is vital if kids perceive that their parents rarely, if ever, read anything at home. Easy access to books in the home promotes good reading habits.

IMPORTANCE OF READING

	Gifted	Regular
Very important (especially to one parent)	48 (40%)	47 (40%)
Very important (to both parents)	40 (33%)	29 (24%)
Somewhat important	17 (15%)	30 (25%)
Important	14 (11%)	3 (3%)
Not very important	2 (1%)	6 (5%)
Unimportant	0	2 (2%)
English not spoken	0	2 (1%)

Question 6: When you were little, what sorts of activities did your parents (or guardians) do with you to encourage reading? (Check as many categories as apply, but underline the activity you enjoyed the most.)

The first part of this question asked which activity students enjoyed the most: 60 gifted and 72 regular students indicated their favorite activity was "being read aloud to."

As this response also turned up strongly in Question 10, I asked the gifted students who served on my Kids Court panel if they still enjoyed being read to, and received a clear division between those who did and those who did not, even within the same family. Those who still enjoy being read to, although they can all read very well on their own, said they appreciate the sharing aspect of reading aloud. One fourth-grade boy said, "I like the feeling my parents put into reading aloud. My mother will read [a passage aloud] very differently from my father, but I enjoy them both."

Those who didn't like to be read aloud to felt this activity separated them from the book, which they could read faster and get more from on their own. One teenager said, "[Being read to] makes me feel like I'm on the outside, and I'm watching the action from a distance when I want to get into the story."

I'm convinced it's all in learning styles and perception, since I had one younger boy in Kids Court who didn't like being read to, yet his older sister enjoyed it very much. If I were a teacher or a school librarian, I'd poll a class and respond according to the learning style preferred. I would also consider strongly the reciprocity in reading aloud, and give kids a chance to read aloud to other kids or members of their family.

The second part of Question 6 asked for multiple answers and covered all the activities parents conducted to encourage reading when their children were young. Slightly more of the regular students (58 percent) were read to or read aloud themselves to their parents when young, versus 49 percent of the gifted children. More revealing was the higher amount of contact the gifted child had with the public library as a pre-schooler (32 percent), versus 19 percent of the regular students. Storytime attendance, which requires regular weekly visits to the public library, was more than double for the gifted (13 percent versus only 6 percent for the regular student). Among the gifted, 25 percent indicated public library visits were a favorite activity, versus 17 percent of the regular students. I've long felt the earlier a public library habit is developed, the better, and these responses seem to bear that out.

I was also glad to see that owning books and magazines was highly valued. Appearing in the other category, getting their first public library card (generally about age 6) was considered memorable and I would encourage public libraries to consider giving more attention to that experience.

ACTIVITY I ENJOYED THE MOST

	Gifted	Regular
Parents reading to me	24 (40%)	36 (50%)
Reading to my parents	11 (18%)	13 (18%)
Parents buying me books or magazines to own	10 (17%)	11 (15%)
Parents taking me to storyhours	9 (15%)	3 (4%)
Parents taking me to visit the library	6 (10%)	9 (13%)

Communication and Education

ACTIVITIES THAT ENCOURAGED READING

Parents read to me	88 (27%)	99 (34%)
Parents had me read to them	69 (22%)	72 (24%)
Parents took me to public library	62 (19%)	39 (13%)
Parents enrolled me in storyhours	41 (13%)	17 (6%)
Parents bought books and magazines for me	50 (16%)	55 (19%)
Other	9 (3%)	11 (4%)

Question 7: When you were little (ages 4-7), what were the types of books you remember liking best?

Dr. Seuss and fairy tales were the top two choices for both gifted and regular students. Several types of books mentioned are not usually available in public libraries in our locale. I would encourage librarians to acquire more Disney titles, comic books, Golden books, as well as the less frequently mentioned Richard Scarry titles, Hardy Boys and Nancy Drew series, and pop-up books.

EARLY CHILDHOOD BOOKS

	Gifted	Regular
Dr. Seuss	32	37
Fairy tales	22	16
Animal stories	10	13
Picture books	8	3
Comic books	7	4
Golden books	7	2
Walt Disney titles	6	7
Easy readers	6	3
Winnie the Pooh	5	0
Curious George	4	10
Beverly Cleary	4	0
Monster stories	4	1
Fantasy	4	0
Funny stories	3	8
Nursery rhymes	0	5
Bill Peet	2	5
Judy Blume	0	3
Peggy Parish	0	3

Question 8: How many books do you own?

The answers to this question were very revealing. Of the gifted students, 35 percent owned 100 books or more versus only 19 percent of the regular students. Only 2 percent of the gifted children owned under 10 books, but 13 percent of the regular students owned fewer than 10 books.

I asked members of the Kids Court about the pleasures of owning one's own books. The majority very much preferred to own their own books. A minority preferred to borrow from the library or from friends. "Why clutter up my room when I can get the book again from the library whenever I want?" responded one teenage girl. Yet others wanted their own books so they could make notes or underline in the book, or just for the pleasure of owning and rereading a favorite title. One sixth grade boy, a student in the GOAL program, had read his Lord of the Rings trilogy three times!

The value and pleasure of owning books is something schools and school support groups, like the PTA, can promote by organizing book fairs and promoting programs such as Reading Is Fundamental. For years public libraries in our area have distributed lists of suggested Christmas book purchases for children: schools could help distribute those lists as Christmas reminders.

By promoting library use at all levels, and promoting home ownership of books, schools and public libraries can do much to help enhance each child's home environment. We should look on both steps as providing a good atmosphere for encouraging interest in reading.

NO. OF BOOKS OWNED

	Gifted	Regular
Over 100	43 (35%)	22 (19%)
Between 10 and 100	74 (61%)	78 (67%)
Under 10 books	2 (2%)	15 (13%)
Other (usually shared with family members)	3 (2%)	2 (1%)

Question 9: In comparison to other activities you do for fun (watch TV, play sports), what do you like best about reading?

Both gifted and regular students viewed reading as pleasurable for reasons of relaxation/quiet, fun/enjoyment, and imagination/education/mind involvement.

More gifted students pointed out the reasons I grouped together under the freedom and flexibility of reading: freedom to take a break whenever you want, to read (or reread) at your own speed, and the portability of books to almost any location.

Regular students favored slightly more than gifted students the reasons of satisfying personal interests, good when alone or bored, or for action and suspense. Enjoying reading for feelings of accomplishment was a reason that appeared only among regular students, and there were more "nothing or no answer" for this question among regular students than among the more gifted. (The one gifted child who said: "None, I like my computer better," was honest in his response!)

Most students, gifted or regular, gave positive reasons for preferring reading and frequently were critical of television and movies: "You can't pick the shows put on the air"; "[In a book] there aren't any commercials when a good part is coming"; "There's more detail in the book than in the movie." Television and movies do not compare favorably with the freedom of reading. So much for the influence of mass media.

ENJOYMENT OF READING

	Gifted	Regular
Freedom and flexibility of reading	31	15
It's relaxing/quiet	24	18
Involves your mind/imaginative/educational	22	18
It's fun/enjoyable	18	15
It's real/feel you are there/identify with	10	8
Action/suspense	7	9
Satisfies my interests	6	11
Good when bored/alone	6	8
Escape from reality	5	5
Gives me feelings of accomplishment	0	5
More variety than movies or TV	0	3
Provides more detail than movies or TV	0	2
Nothing or no answer	1	9
Other	0	2

Question 10: What advice would you give to teachers/librarians/parents to encourage kids to read more?

There were similarities in advice given by both gifted and regular students for many categories: read more to kids (17 gifted/17 regular); let kids pick out their own reading (12/12); have more reading games or projects (10/9), and more library tours or booktalks (7/7).

Some differences emerged--there were more pleas to "supply more books of interest to kids" from the gifted (10/8) and more requests from regular students (5/19) for teachers, parents, and librarians to "show more what can be learned from reading."

Only the gifted children suggested "remove modern distractions" and only regular students suggested "give more reading homework," and "have more silent reading time in school."

A number of creative solutions offered in the other category were: "more nudity in books"; "advertise more"; "have more questionnaires"; "make books more fictional"; and "provide quieter classrooms."

I showed the questionnaire results to the group of gifted children in Kids Court, and they summed up their advice: "go by what kids like to read; don't force or assign a particular book." They liked having a choice of books to complete a reading assignment and they were very much against parental selections. One teenage girl told me how her mother had lost credibility for making reading suggestions by choosing too many of her own childhood favorites now dated and boring in her daughter's eyes. The advice was clear: trust kids to select their own reading materials.

The Role of Schools & Libraries

In examining these survey results, and after reading both the current bestseller Megatrends by Naisbett, and Barbara Heyn's 1978 book, Summer Learning and the Effects of Schooling, I have my own advice on how we can work together to best prepare our children for the coming transition "from the Industrial Age to the Information Age." (Incidentally, I urge all teachers to read at least Chapter 9 of Summer Learning and the Effects of Schooling, entitled "Reading, libraries, and summer achievement".) As an educator doing a study of the Atlanta, Georgia, area, Heyn found that "more than any other public institution, including the schools, the public library contributed to the intellectual growth of children during the summer" (p. 177). Her study showed the greater a child's use of the public library for reading over the summer, the more vocabulary and reading skills the child retained when starting school in the fall, especially if the child came from an underprivileged background.

School districts everywhere should view the public library,

Communication and Education

along with the school library, as an integral part of every school's educational team. Because of escalating taxes and declining purchase power, it has become very important to work together to maximize use of all community resources.

Ways of Cooperation:

1. Schools should know what summer reading programs their local public library offers and actively promote student participation in them.

2. As a part of the annual preschool census survey, information on what parents can do to help prepare their three- and four-year olds for school should be included: specifically, mention the value of reading aloud to children, the value of giving children their own books, and include recommended bibliographies of currently available, low-cost, or paperback titles for purchase consideration, and emphasize the benefits of public library use, whether for storytime programs and weekly visits or for selecting bedtime reading. Encourage parents to be aware of the role model they provide their children on the value of reading; if the child never sees his or her parents reading, the child will wonder why mastering this skill in school is so important.

3. Encourage your school librarian to do booktalks to entice more reading; a good suggestion is to do booktalks before school holidays so kids know they can enjoy reading without the pressure of daily homework. If the school librarian doesn't have the clerical support staff to free him or her to do booktalks, lobby for more support staff. Suggest the possibility of a team approach to booktalking--in our area, sometimes two public librarians or one school librarian and one public librarian prepare a joint presentation. I've also worked with teachers who had a strong interest in science fiction to promote booktalks--I presented ten titles and the teacher presented another ten.

4. Especially at the third- and seventh-grade levels, push for field trips to the public library. Perhaps the public library could book a feature film related to a school curriculum topic and then give the class a tour of the library and an opportunity to select books of their own choice. We've done this for several classes in Gates; "The Hobbit" is a favorite feature film on which to focus a tour.

5. Public libraries should work actively with area schools to provide the above services, and should strive to be in frequent contact with schools, especially with their best natural ally, the school librarian. In our area we've even written and been awarded a joint grant as a focus for school-public library co-operation.

6. Public libraries should advertise widely all childrens' programs and services in the schools.

7. They should also make obtaining a first library card a special event, perhaps by giving the child a free bookmark or other appropriate giveaway as a reward/enticement.

The real gift of public librarians and school library media specialists to the children who will be tomorrow's readers is to expose them to the huge variety of human expression in print. Children are already "minds alive"; they will continue to grow in their reading development if we, the adults, give them the open, diverse environment to explore and the freedom to discuss, without age or role barriers, the ideas encountered in their reading explorations.

CRITICAL DECISIONS: REFLECTIONS ON THE CHANGING ROLE OF A CHILDREN'S BOOK REVIEWER*

Elaine Moss

In the course of about twenty years in children's book reviewing I made a series of decisions. Looking back, I can see that I started out the way most people do: I received books for review--and reviewed them. But whether it was my temperament or the challenge of getting books to children in a largely indifferent world or a mixture of the two, I don't know; for some reason conventional reviewing became not enough for me. I might have become what is commonly known as a critic. But I don't think I did.

After serving my apprenticeship as teacher, librarian, publisher's reader, and mother (the last was the most important by far), I did start my more public life in children's books as a newspaper critic for The Times (London). But with the parlous state of adult knowledge about children's books at that time--and it still exists now--newspapers hardly seemed to be the place for serious discussions of children's book trade issues or for academic criticism. Yet both began to creep into that Times page. Surely, the space that is given to children's books should be used positively to help parents and teachers get a grasp of the basic principles of choosing with children the books they will enjoy.

So I began to ask myself what The Times page was doing, and why. Who was reading what was written? What was the effect? Were the hordes of children out there a jot better off because of it? Or were they, possibly, marginally worse off because of the widening gap between the critics' choice of books and what real children want to read? Did these children get books? If so, what--and how? If not, why not? With questions like these assailing me, I couldn't settle for the quiet (well, relatively quiet) life of the so-called quality press critic. I began to look at aspects of the children's book world, to learn by experience, and to use what I discovered as an integral part of what I wrote: the historian in me, I now suppose, thirsting for field work.

---

*Reprinted by permission of the author from Horn Book Magazine, 60 (April 1984) 170-177. Copyright © 1984 by Elaine Moss.

The first step was to leave The Times, a prestigious newspaper, and take over an occasional column in The Sunday Mirror, which is anything and everything but. Here was a massive audience --and massively indifferent, if some people were to be believed. Certainly you write for readers of a tabloid quite differently from the way you write for readers of The Times. It is really very easy to write about books for the quality press, for you are mainly talking to people of your own background and education about something that should be of automatic interest, even if it isn't always so.

But for The Sunday Mirror you have to think about hooking your readership, stimulating people, and sending them off not to a bookshop but, in all probability, to one of a large chain of stationers and booksellers--like our W. H. Smith's--where they will find the right books for their families. You have to write simple but arresting prose; there is no room for convoluted subsidiary clauses in an opening sentence that mustn't exceed nine words. And, above all, you have to guard against disappointment and disillusion on the part of the book-seeker, for the first steps in using books with children are hard and people are easily discouraged. So, unlike my predecessor in the job, who had written sparkling throw-away little pieces on the current new children's novels submitted for review by hopeful publishers (but unlikely to be found in ninety percent of the book outlets in this country because hardcover fiction is difficult to sell), I decided to work backward.

Ever pragmatic, I went to a large W. H. Smith store and made a list of the best of the new books they stocked: paperback picture books, fiction, and colorful information books. And it was from these that I chose my books for review: for instance, the James Reeves anthology, A Golden Land (Hastings); stories about Mrs. Pepperpot; and Raymond Briggs's Father Christmas (Coward). I did not prostitute myself, I promise you; but I sallied forth into this new world under banner headlines, such as "Paperbacks to Keep 'Em Quiet" or "Bloomin' Christmas Here Again," which might make you blush unless times have changed--and I rather suspect they have.

It was at this period, in 1973, that by great good fortune I was invited by a group of social workers and teachers in London's Dockland to help set up a children's book stall in the Saturday market in Whitechapel High Street. There was no bookshop in that vast area, nowhere children could even see new books, let alone buy them. With that stall we proved, through blazing summers and perishing rainy winters, that if the right books are easily accessible and you are prepared regularly on Saturdays to stand around between the eels and the cauliflowers, you make friends, influence people, and sell books. Some books. Which one? Why? You begin to value the best of the easy-reading series that critics never write about or the paperback classics like Alice in Wonderland, for which one child saved up for a month. You know you need multicultural books, not because activists say so but because not to have them is an offense to many of the families who come to look at the books as well as a limitation on your ability to reach them with stories. And you learn the value of knowing what's inside a book if you want to sell it.

Communication and Education

At this time I had already embarked upon the ten-year marathon of Children's Books of the Year, so I knew what was inside the books. No "real" critic, I fancy, would have taken on that job. I didn't actually take it on, though; it just happened. For some years the National Book League had chosen annually what it called "500 Children's Books" for a traveling exhibition. The choice could be arbitrary and haphazard because there was no annotated catalog through which the selectors had to justify their choices or balance their selections. When I was called upon to assist the NBL in the choice of fiction (three weeks in which to choose two hundred titles), I began to ask awkward questions to which I received very dusty answers. Finally, someone said in exasperation, "Well, if you want to be responsible for the whole selection and write an annotated catalog, go ahead!" That, they thought, would silence me. Instead, it opened the way for me eventually to turn the "500 Children's Books" touring exhibition into the catalog and exhibition which came to be known in 1970 as Children's Books of the Year.

It is not for me to evaluate that exercise. It provided a service, I think, in presenting busy teachers and librarians with a personal (and fallible) choice of about three hundred new books from a publishing year producing about three thousand. The catalog provided an annotation for each book, which--because it explained why the title was included and evaluated plot, style, and likely readership-- could not be thought of as criticism in the intrinsic sense. My aim was to be helpful to those who bought books for children's libraries-- or for families--by offering them what I hoped was informed comment. And in order to be able to offer informed comment, I suppose I thought it was my duty (although it was really my pleasure and delight) to broaden the base of my experience with children's books through every opportunity that came my way.

The first opportunity was that of meeting the public through a Children's Books of the Year exhibition in the Albemarle Street gallery of the National Book League. But would anyone come? The opening exhibition was very low-keyed and experimental. The books were on trestle tables, while I or the NBL staff hovered discreetly. It immediately became obvious to us all that a selected annual exhibition for professionals, parents, and children (with storytellers, artists, competitions, and a bookshop) would draw crowds. August is, of course, the tourist season in central London, and to our surprise and delight we discovered that many people began to key their holiday to our fortnight. Soon study groups also became part of our program.

But I am supposed to be considering critical decisions--not exhibitions. In retrospect, however, I can see how much of the ten years I was responsible for Children's Books of the Year added to my education as a commentator. It was a thrilling opportunity to be in that gallery every day, not only watching people looking at books (often with the catalog in their hands) but answering, or trying to answer, a million and one questions on every aspect of using books with children.

I remember the large, silent, patient-looking man from Ghana, who came in two days running and spent hours in the picture book section before introducing himself to me as Ghana's Minister of Education and asking advice about starting a simple picture book publishing program. (Two years later at Bologna on one of those heart-rendingly empty Third World stands I saw his first books.) There were the teacher-librarian from Prince Edward Island who told me I was her best friend, although we had never set eyes on each other until that moment; and the head of a comprehensive school in Hong Kong who greeted me with the words "the two ends of the lifeline come together at last." Each one had a story of book-life in other places to tell--a missionary from India, a teacher from Mexico, a delegation of Colombian printers (would pop-ups ever catch on, they wanted to know), and mothers and fathers of English-speaking families from Italy and Iceland, Singapore and Malta.

Then there were the specific requests. Books for deaf children, which put me in touch with a scheme for adapting the texts of ordinary picture books for children with impaired hearing. The problem of the eight-year-old gifted reader who needs more difficult material but is not emotionally ready for ten-plus novels. The younger child in a family who has overtaken the older one in reading. And, inevitably, the child who is brought remonstrating to a book exhibition: He doesn't read; his mother thinks he should; here he is; make him! This was the only situation I would gladly have ducked because with both parties present and books silently protesting that force-feeding will result in permanent disability on the part of the fed, there is nothing one can do. Of course, many of the conversations were about broken pencils (we ran competitions), getting lunch, the best way to the British Museum from Piccadilly, or where was the loo. And hundreds and hundreds of questions about finding just the right book to give to someone special. When you think about it, this is really the end to which all practical children's book criticism is directed--through librarian, bookseller, teacher, and parent.

My favorite Children's Books of the Year story, like Wanda Gág's Millions of Cats (Coward), is about the agony of choice, a choice of cats, too. A very serious nine-year-old girl started to talk to me about picture books about cats. She was, she said, trying to choose one for her sister, who adored cats. She was sure, very sure, of the kind of book she was looking for. In her words, "They must be lovely cats, and the story mustn't be sad." It was the year of Graham Oakley's debut with The Church Mice (Atheneum); I thought she might find Samson appealing. But no. "My sister wouldn't be able to stand the picture of Samson the cat tied up in all those cords by the mice." Understandable. Then, Mouse Trouble by John Yeoman and Quentin Blake (Macmillan)? "But the farmer tries to be cruel to the cat!" So, at my wits' end I suddenly thought of Orlando the Marmalade Cat (Transatlantic Arts), a new edition of which had appeared that year. "How about Orlando?" I asked hopefully. The girl looked carefully through Kathleen Hale's enchanting, untidy pages and then said with a sigh of relief. "Yes, yes; this will do." I was delighted. And as she walked away, I asked casually, "How old is your sister?" She smiled, looked up at me trustingly, and said, "Promise you won't laugh if I tell you? She's twenty-one."

It is tempting to imagine that my interest in picture books for older readers stemmed from that conversation, but I must be honest. I don't think it did. I think that in writing the annotations for the Children's Books of the Year catalog and, above all, in setting out the books as physical objects in the exhibition, I became acutely aware that lumping picture books together as the first fiction category automatically implied that they were for the early years only. I began, therefore, placing Anthony Browne's humorously surrealist picture book about snobbery, A Walk in the Park (Atheneum), in fiction for the eight-to-eleven-year-olds and Russell Hoban and James Marshall's delicious teenage frolic, Dinner at Alberta's (Crowell), where it truly belongs and where it is now appreciated in daring schools--with fiction for ages eleven to fourteen, even though it looks like an easy reader for seven-year-olds. Were we really to allow the physical form of a book to cut it off from its best potential readership? It seemed a pity.

This was the moment when at the ripe old age of fity-two, in the middle of my ten-year stint with Children's Books of the Year and busy as always with reviews for the Times Literary Supplement and other journals, I was presented with a now-or-never opportunity to get a worm's eye view of children and books. Would I like to be the Inner London Education Authority's first chartered librarian in a primary school--just one day a week, as an experiment? I have to confess that, like the proverbial fools, I rushed in. Why else, I asked myself, looking for a pattern as always, had I qualified in my twenties both as a teacher and as a librarian?

I could talk all day about my six years at Fleet Primary School, but I will restrict myself to a quotation from a lecture I gave, called "The Dream and the Reality: A Children's Book Critic Goes Back to School" and published in Signal. The passage is about fiction for the "middle" reader: It describes life as it is--the reality, not the dream--and what I learned from it:

> If you can hear the distant roll of thunder, it is the pounding of thirty-five pairs of intimidating feet running, jumping down the stone staircase from the classroom above where a teacher has just said, "Go down quietly to the library." Thirty-five kids--and only ten chairs, the little upholstered ones, so comfortable for those who actually sit and read. Nobody needs chairs in order to change library books, but the class nabobs bag them immediately and thenceforward glide on the chairs' iron runners towards the lowest shelves, unless forbidden to do so. When you suggest a Betsy Byars to a good reader who likes humorous books and get the reply "Can't reach the B's, miss, they're on the top shelf and 'e'll take my seat." you have either to become conspiratorially involved in gang politics (by handing him

The Eighteenth Emergency) or (time, oh time!) break it up.

Once the chair problem is sorted out and the terrible business of getting the right tickets back in the respective books despatched ... what do these nine-year-olds read? The answer is anything from I'll Teach My Dog 100 Words (how good at the Beginner Book stage to have a dog who knows less words than you do) to Lord of the Rings.

Soon I begin to recognize the postures of kids at the bottom of the ladder ("Books is good to 'it 'im over the 'ead wiv'") and at the top ("Which one comes after The Children of Green Knowe?"). I realize that a tactful reorganization of the library could result in a useful physical mingling of slow-learners with high-flyers--absolutely essential if those in the middle, who are seldom given the attention they deserve, are not to fall into a tempting but destructive habit. That habit, induced by a wish to identify with the good readers rather than with the strugglers, is for the child quietly to choose an impressive-looking novel that he has no hope of reading because it is far too difficult but that he believes gives him a certain status....

What was lacking at Fleet five years ago was a large, bright, clean collection of good in-between fiction--Beverly Cleary's Ramona, Cathering Storr's Clever Polly, Alan Coren's Arthur books--that could be read to some and by others, that were potentially common coin, a unifying force in a competitive world. That was a section of the library we built up, to the great advantage of almost everyone in the school. And the experiment of creating a high-on-the-wall Gold Star picturebook section (for Tintins and Asterixes as well as the more sophisticated picture books by Michael Foreman, Raymond Briggs, Anthony Browne, Anno and others) subtly undermined all kinds of artificial barriers among staff and children alike.

That children from seven to eleven need, enjoy, and profit from picture books was proved beyond doubt. In two articles called "Them's for the Infants, Miss," also published in Signal, I have described that picture-book project in detail; and in Picture Books for Young People 9-13: A Signal Bookguide I extended the articles into what, with some trepidation, I venture to call a work of simple criticism--although being mine, it is criticism of a positive, practical, and promotional kind.

I mention these pieces of writing for two reasons. In the first place they were the result of direct experience giving rise to theory, the practical running alongside the formulating principle. So much that is written about children and books is either hatched in the isolation of the academic incubator or written by librarians in retirement during that pleasant afterglow when blinkered teachers and disruptive children are memories one can smile over, not frustrations that make one despair. Secondly, if these writings have any value for readers, you have to thank Nancy Chambers for them, not me.

Communication and Education

The subtitle of Signal is Approaches to Children's Books. She wanted commentary as one of the approaches, so I became, willy-nilly, the Signal "fool"--in the sense of the medieval court jester, who in a light-hearted way draws people's attention to serious issues.

In a recent article in the Times Educational Supplement Neil Philip, a young and respected critic, surveys the world of children's books and remarks on its ever-widening range, its disparate audience, the diverse ways in which children's books are used, and the "hotly contradictory" perspectives from which they are viewed. His is a distinctive voice of the eighties, recognizing that children's books will survive in their rich diversity only if they are seen in relationship not just to the literature of their day but also to the idea that all children need to be catered for. Reading his piece I began to wonder whether, all unawares and following my own instinct, I hadn't after all been a children's book critic--of this new strain, only working away in the decade before it became respectable. I shall watch new developments from my armchair with interest.

REFEREEING AND THE EDITORIAL
PROCESS: THE AHR AND WEBB

Margaret F. Stieg

Refereeing is central to scholarly communication, a process which has attracted more and more attention in the last decade.[1] It is one of the most important elements in determing what will be published and what will not be. Refereeing is used as a synonym for peer review and evaluation, although the term "refereeing" is usually reserved for the evaluation of articles rather than that of books.

The referee has been aptly described as the gatekeeper.[2] His primary function is to judge the quality of an article, to decide whether it meets the standards of a given journal. Presumably, his thorough knowledge of the literature of the subject enables him to determine whether an article is sufficiently new to justify publication. He may, in the course of making his judgments, recommend changes. By doing these things, the referee relieves the pressure on editors and lends stature to the resulting publication.[3] The need for effective gatekeeping is all too evident. More than a decade ago the British physicist J. M. Ziman wrote of his own field:

> Not only is there too much scientific work being published; there is much too much of it ... the need to get recognition by publication forces each of us to shout a little longer and louder so as to be noticed at all in the gathering, swelling crowd of voices.... The result has been a proliferation of semi-literate, semi-scientific, half-baked and trivial material which threatens to swamp the whole system.

This article is an attempt to examine in depth the operation of the refereeing system in the field of historical periodicals. Almost all writing on refereeing has been done by natural scientists, psychologists, or sociologists; this examination may therefore show if the process is significantly different in a discipline which bridges the social sciences and humanities. The case method has been used in the hope that it will reveal some of the informal as well as formal facts and considerations and that it will show the interrelation-

---

*Reprinted by permission of the author and publisher from Scholarly Publishing, 14:2 (February 1983) 100-122; ©1983 by University of Toronto Press.

ships of the various aspects of refereeing. Some of the fundamental questions can be put as follows: Who should decide what is published? What should be the qualifications of referees? On what basis should decisions be made? Where do the responsibilities of the referee lie -- to the journal, to the discipline, to the author, to the reader? What role should the referee fill? Should there be refereeing at all?

The American Historical Review (AHR) was selected for detailed investigation. Like other journals whose refereeing has been studied, it is a journal of unquestioned importance in its field. More historians in the United States subscribe to it than to any other single journal. Founded in 1895, it is the oldest scholarly American historical journal and has set standards for the profession and for other historical journals. Despite an editorial disclaimer that it does "not stand at the top of a pyramid of scholarly prestige, automatically to be tried first by an ambitious author before he moves on to a lesser journal" most historians in the United States would not agree. One would-be contributor said that publication in the AHR was worth a Mass.

Practical considerations also made it an excellent choice for study. The records of the AHR through 1971 are on deposit at the Library of Congress, open by permission to the qualified researcher. [6] Those of 1969 were selected for analysis because they are almost if not quite complete. They represent a year that is not atypical in any way and are the most recent nearly complete records currently available. Using 1969 made possible a check on what happened afterwards, both to articles accepted and to those rejected. Records for 193 articles rejected in 1969 and 17 accepted, most published in 1970, were found. [7]

There is no doubt that the practice of refereeing has been spreading. Although other motives may be present, such as the desire to prevent overly restrictive control of a journal by an editor or editorial board, refereeing is fundamentally a response to the advance of specialization a phenomenon shared by all fields of knowledge and areas of endeavour. The relationship between specialization and refereeing is very clear in the field of history. The earliest scholarly historical periodical, the Historische Zeitschrift, did not boast even an editorial board until 1896, nearly forty years after its founding. All evaluation was done by the editor and his assistant. When the American Historical Review was founded in 1895, it had a board of editors, representing various fields of history, which the managing editor used to read and review submissions; the board members were the referees. This pattern in which editor and editorial board decided what was to be published was adopted by most of the major historical scholarly journals subsequently founded in the United States, such as, for example, the Mississippi Valley Historical Review (now the Journal of American History) and the Journal of Southern History. Only after the second world war, when specialization ran rampant, did the outside referee, necessary to supplement the competences of the members of the board of editors, become a regular feature of scholarly historical periodicals. Before the outside referee became an accepted institution, editors might have to go to extraordinary lengths to achieve the same result. In 1941 Louis Pelzer, editor of the Mississippi Valley Historical Review, invited Francis Wiesenburge "to serve temporarily on our board of editors" so that Wiesenburge could review a paper.[8]

The use of outside referees, although increasing, is by no means universal or automatic among historical journals. Only a minority (12%) of all historical journals responding to a recent survey have the principal evaluation done by a referee.[9] Some of the others used referees, but only as one element in the decision-making process. Canadian and American journals were much more likely to use outside referees to make the principal decision than those published elsewhere, a difference that is also characteristic of scientific journals.[10] Among scholarly historical journals, 32% of American and Canadian journals had the principal evaluation done by a referee, as opposed to only 11% of those published elsewhere.

In 1969 R. K. Webb was editor of the AHR. He was a specialist in nineteenth-century British history, a graduate of Oberlin College whose Ph.D. was from Columbia University. Most of his teaching career had been at Columbia and he had left there as a full professor to become the AHR's editor. This was his first full year in the position; he had taken over from Henry Winkler, also a specialist in British history, but of the twentieth century, in the spring of 1968.

The members of the editorial board were all leading scholars in their fields, notable for the quality and quantity of their publications. Two went on to become presidents of the American Historical Association. They shared similar backgrounds and experience; seven of the ten had received their doctorates from Ivy League universities. Five of the ten were employed by Ivy League universities and the remaining five by universities in other parts of the country.

The seventy-two outside referees used in 1969 were similar in many respects to the members of the editorial board. They too had predominantly received their doctorates from Ivy League universities, although they were now employed by a more diverse group of institutions. Like the editorial board, too, they were publishing scholars, although their writings tended to be somewhat narrower in scope than those of board members. These small variations do not, however, alter the general impression that the AHR was controlled by professional, academic historians who were leaders of the field.

The authors of the articles submitted in 1969 to the AHR were a heterogeneous group. The majority, of course, were history professors at American universities. Ten were instructors, fifty assistant professors, thirty associate professors, and forty full professors. Their institutions ranged widely, from small colleges, public or private, even a technical school or two, to older state and private universities. There were a few submissions from faculty members at schools noted for strong graduate programs in history, but they were very few. Except for a very few British and Canadian scholars, all the potential contributors were Americans or affiliated with universities in the United States. Only a handful of submissions came from women. At least twenty-five were from individuals with no academic affiliation, and another seven can be identified as having been written by students. This non-professional group is testimony to the fact that history can be and often is an avocation, practiced by amateurs. It helps explain disparities between rejection rates of leading journals in the natural sciences and this leading journal in history. Successful research and writing in, for example, physics is almost never an amateur activity.

The articles submitted to the AHR in 1969 varied considerably in subject and treatment as well as in authorship, although the vast majority dealt with some aspect of American or modern European history. A number were not, strictly speaking, even articles, but brief notes, or essays on topics like "What's wrong with history?" Most were traditional political or diplomatic history; only one attempt at psychohistory was sent in that year. This distribution pattern of articles reflected the interests of American historians--for example, the few articles submitted in the history of science corresponded to the relatively few historians in that field.

A comparison of the characteristics of the rejected articles and would-be contributors with those of accepted articles and successful contributors shows little difference. Perhaps, proportionally, slightly more articles on social and economic history were published than were submitted, but it was a slight disproportion. In background and affiliation, the successful contributors were similar to the unsuccessful professional historians. They were employed at a wide variety of institutions, from the Ivy League to new state universities and colleges. Their degrees did tend to be from distinguished institutions, but not invariably. One had not yet completed his doctorate.

Once the articles were received and read by an assistant editor who recommended outside readers, their paths diverged. Webb commented in an editorial that, beyond the less than one-tenth of submissions that were actually published, only a further two-tenths were worth serious consideration. [11] He himself read and dismissed without further evaluation 120, or 62%, of the 193 rejected. The frequency with which he as editor acted as sole arbiter provides the greatest possible contrast to the refereeing practices of the sciences. In journals of the natural sciences evaluation by an outside referee was by that time almost automatic.

After this initial screening Webb then decided to whom an article was to be sent for refereeing, further enhancing his power to influence and shape the final product. Those articles which did receive further consideration after his initial reading followed no set pattern. Most frequently an article would go either to one member of the board of editors or to one outside referee. That one opinion (plus Webb's) was sufficient for refusal. Some of these articles

Webb in fact had no serious interest in; he would often send an unacceptable article out to a board member for comment principally to give himself a knowledgeable opinion to quote in his letter of rejection. [12] When he used more than one reader, he could be doing it because the first reader considered the article in question worth pursuing but was not himself knowledgeable enough to give a definitive opinion. He could want a second or third opinion to resolve doubts or questions raised. In some cases the manuscript would go out to two readers at once. Generally speaking, it is fair to say that two readers were an indication of his real interest in an article. Then, after considering all the reports, Webb would make the final decision.

The AHR did not use the blind assessment that has been proposed and sometimes used in other fields. The referee usually knew the name of the author, although the author was not told that of the referee. Occasionally, from comments made or a paucity of appropriate reviewers, an author must have been able to guess, but he was never told officially.

The editorial board did much of the refereeing. It did not, as might be expected, exist to provide a semi-knowledgeable opinion, a first opinion before manuscripts were sent out to a specialist. Occasionally it did do just that, but more often a member was just another referee, perhaps somewhat more dependable than the general run. Webb worked some harder than others and relied especially on David Donald, Henry May, and Peter Gay. Several, like Tom Jones, an ancient historian, were in fields in which articles were rarely submitted. At least one board member seems to have been avoided to some extent. His judgements tended to be rather harsh-- he himself referred to his 'sceptical' mind--and number of articles in his field were sent to another member whose field was close to his.

The prominence of the editorial board in refereeing indicates some significant facts about the nature at that time of scholarship in history. Most writers on refereeing have assumed that the appropriate qualification for a referee is that he be the leading, expert on the particular subject. [13] But these writers have been natural scientists, sociologists, or psychologists. Specialization in history had not yet proceeded so far that it required a specialist on the same topic to discern what was wrong or what was right with an article. Greater breadth, a slightly different perspective--assuming a general knowledge of the subject--may even have been a positive advantage, enabling a reader to see what was missing. Historians tend to mature late, and the best history is likely to be that based on the widest reading and experience.

Outside referees were selected in various ways. Usually the assistant editor made some kind of recommendation, relying partly on a file of prospective readers. Webb himself probably chose many from among his personal acquaintances. A relatively high proportion of outside referees were Columbia-related. There was a similarly high proportion from the Washington, DC, area where the AHR office was located. This is not surprising. Anyone who has ever organized anything knows that what is wanted is people whose judgment can be trusted and who can be depended upon to do the job. Such knowledge comes only with personal acquaintance. The outside referees were far from being a closed clique, however. Several were suggested by a member of the board who had read the manuscript; others were suggested by scholars who were refusing a request to serve as referee. (By far the most usual reason for such refusals was lack of time.) In at least one case a just-accepted contributor was asked to evaluate an article in his field. Occasionally there would be some overlap with other periodicals. More than one referee had already read the article concerned for another journal when Webb made his request. These cases, it should be noted, almost always involved articles that had been returned for revision on a first evaluation and were being resubmitted.

It was noticeable that if an article posed a direct challenge to the work of another scholar, that scholar was not asked to be its referee. This is a delicate issue, because the principle of refereeing is to seek the most knowledgeable referee. It is not a universal practice. One article submitted to the AHR had earlier been sent to another journal which did send it to the established authority on the subject, whose work the paper's findings brought into question on an important point. Abuse of just such a refereeing request was one element in a recent academic scandal.[14]

The length of time it took to make a decision on an article primarily depended on how many referees were used. If an article was read by Webb alone before being rejected, it was usually returned in less than five weeks from the time the author sent it off. The range for this situation was a low of 2 days to a high of 95, but in fairness to Webb it must be said that the maximum figure was a distinct aberration. When the article was read by one outside reader, the range was between 21 and 136 days, with an average of 58. For two or more readers, the range was 49 to 154, the average 83. Accepted articles had the highest average, 94 days, a result of the fact that they were likely to have the most readers. Although these periods would be unacceptable to physicists, complaints from historians about the slowness of the process, even inquiries about a manuscript's fate, were rare. One scholar who had submitted an article in 1968 complained because his article had been returned in two weeks and he had not felt that the referee could possibly have done a thorough job in such a short time.

Webb was very conscious of the frustrations of delay and endeavored to keep them to a minimum. He would send follow-up letters if a reader had an article for a month without returning comments. He was helped by the fact that his editorial board was almost invariably conscientious. Some factors, however, were beyond his control. Often his first choice for a referee would refuse to review a manuscript and he would have to try again, having lost two or three weeks. The person he wanted might be difficult to reach, on vacation, or abroad. Webb was also hampered by an illness of his own in the late fall of 1969 from which he was slow to recover, and by an illness of his secretary immediately thereafter.

Delay is the single most frequently identified problem of refereeing. [15] Because establishing priority is so important in the natural sciences, particularly if two natural scientists are working on the same problem simultaneously, the problem is most acute there, but all journals suffer from slow referees to some extent. [16] Several writers have gone so far as to use the term "malpractice" about delay. That is strong language, but considering the stakes perhaps not too strong.

Over the years, editors of the AHR have made various attempts to provide guidance to authors and referees on its standards. The founders of the journal had looked for contributions that were fresh and original in treatment, that were the result of accurate scholarship, and that had distinct literary merit. [17] In 1939 a review committee accepted a policy of publishing "only such articles as throw light upon what has been done before, or suggest new and fruitful fields of historical study and advance significant new historical interpretations."[18] The editor in 1955 informed prospective authors that acceptance came most often when

> sound research into primary resources brings change or new interpretations and when the results of this research are couched in clear and precise English. At this time the Review particularly welcomes essays which attempt to answer for specific fields the questions, "Where have we been, where are we now and what are the obstacles facing us?" The chances of acceptance for this or any kind of essay will be considerably enhanced if the author has constantly in mind the question "Will the reader want to turn the page?"[19]

In the light of his experience Webb himself in 1970 made the most specific statement on standards. He described the true scholarly article as "confined to a carefully argued thesis, complete in itself, provocative in interpretation, and productive of further work by others." Taking the humbler virtues of good scholarship for granted, he concentrated on the need for breadth of appeal and insisted that articles not be "communications addressed by specialists only to fellow specialists." He listed certain types of articles that were not usually acceptable: detailed accounts of minor diplomatic transactions (in his rejections he usually phrased this "single" diplomatic transactions); articles in local history in which a central relationship to broader historical concerns was not made explicit, primarily biographical studies of second-rank or lesser figures; articles summarizing books about to be published or unrevised chapters from dissertations or books; most articles on methodology per se; and routine articles summarizing the "state of the argument" on a particular theme of scholarly debate. [10] Otto Pflanze, the present editor of the AHR, reaffirmed Webb's policy when he took over.[21]

None of these statements really contradicted any other. Putting them together yields the following model for an AHR article in the Webb period. It was an article that dealt with an important topic in a sophisticated, provocative, and original fashion, that was complete in itself, that exhibited thorough research in appropriate sources and knowledge of other relevant scholarship, that was logically argued and well-written, and that had broad appeal. It is noticeable that, with the exception of the broad appeal, this statement could stand as a general definition of a good historical article. With a change in the portion relating to sources, it could stand as a list of desiderata for almost any kind of scholarly article.

It is, indeed, not the norms of scholarship that are so different in the different disciplines, but their application and interpretation. Social and natural scientists use slightly different words from historians; they talk in terms of the significance of an article, the quality of research methodology, the analysis, the completeness and relevance of background literature, and the quality of writing.[22] Obviously, these are the same broad categories used by historians for evaluation, although different disciplines would rank the various qualities differently. Natural scientists, for example, stress replicability of research techniques, originality, mathematical precision, and coverage of the literature; social scientists stress logical rigor, theoretical significance, and applied significance.[23]

Hard as the various editors of the AHR tried, with the exception of Webb's list of unacceptable types of articles they could not be very specific about what they looked for in an article. Referees themselves had to develop more particular, more definite measures to apply. The grounds on which the AHR referees criticized articles fall into several identifiable categories. The most frequently given was some variation on the theme that an article was not appropriate to the AHR. Nearly one-third of the articles rejected were considered too narrow or too specialized for a journal which, as the publication of a broad-based organization, wished its articles to have wide appeal. Many other articles were not, in Webb's often used phrase, the "major scholarly article" the AHR published; some were too slight, some not scholarly enough, some not historical, others were not even articles but essays, notes, or speeches.

Once that very large group that was totally unsuitable was eliminated, the remainder of unpublished articles was rejected because of some inadequacy in execution. Referees criticized articles because they were not important enough. They expected articles to have a large scope and a sophisticated treatment. They expected them to do something new. One article, for example, was described as 100% derivative. The judgment on another was that the political group analyzed in it was shown to be what it had always been thought to be; the supposedly "innovative" method had first been used in 1918. Almost any article on Frederick Jackson Turner stood an especially good chance of being rejected because it was so hard to say something fresh on this frequently treated historian.

Less often given as a reason for rejection was inadequate research in sources. Occasionally an individual would miss an important relevant collection the reader knew about. The author might also fail to show sufficient knowledge of context, either of other scholarship on the subject or of other relevant events. One Englishman who submitted an article on a historian of the medieval period earned the comment, "Like so many English historians, he prefers to ignore what Americans and other historians wrote."

A large number of articles were considered poorly written, probably a more serious drawback in history, many of whose practitioners still considered it a form of literature, than it would have been in other fields. Some of these were poor in the fundamental sense of style, but a larger number were logically flawed. Logical failures were naturally individual, but those cited by referees included diffuseness of purpose, lack of balance, use of arbitrary categories, looseness in definitions, the setting up of straw men, promises of more than was delivered (another way of saying overambition), fundamental misconceptions, overly simplistic analysis or absence of analysis, and insufficient development of the material. One hapless article was dismissed with the comment, "It begins with complete irrelevance and continues with considerable unimportance."

Referees also displayed concern over tone. In one case one referee found an author's argumentative stance refreshing, and another, reading the same piece, found it offensive. In all other cases, however, authors were criticized if they were not calmly judicious.

A closely related problem was that several articles evaluated the work of former, still living, presidents of the American Historical Association. Webb felt strongly that the AHR should not publish articles attacking these colleagues. He also had some difficulties over Jack P. Greene's article "Political mimesis: a consideration of the historical and cultural roots of legislative behavior in the British colonies in the eighteenth century."[24] This piece was to a certain extent a criticism of the work of Bernard Bailyn, a member of the board of editors. Bailyn was not asked to evaluate it, but after it was accepted Webb felt obliged to send it to him. Bailyn objected to the article and asked to publish a response to it in the same issue in which it appeared. Rather reluctantly, Webb allowed this somewhat unusual procedure and the article, a comment by Bailyn, and a reply by Greene to Bailyn all appeared at the same time.

The last reason for rejection had little to do with the quality of the article but related strictly to editorial convenience. The need to achieve balance forced the refusal of a number of submissions because articles on the same or closely related topics had just been published or accepted. This was not invariable: one referee successfully urged the acceptance of Roland Sarti's article "Fascist modernization in Italy: tradition or revolution?"[25] even though it would be published very soon after another article on Fascist Italy.

The referee pointed out that a good deal of research was then being done, belatedly, on that subject.

The evaluations of articles published by the AHR provide suggestive contrasts with the evaluations of those that were rejected. Praise was likely to be in such terms as "adds new dimension," "documentation thorough," "significant theme with contemporary relevance," "original," "stimulating," or "avoids special pleading." "Interesting" was a favorite. If an article was criticized at the same time as it was praised, it was usually because the referee found its reasoning unclear or its writing poor.

Although the reasons cited by referees were more precise than the vague generalities of the various editorial statements, they were far from any absolute state of exactness. They were not the mathematical and technical criteria of the natural sciences, and only a few were similar to the less defined logico-theoretical standards of the modern social sciences. Many, like sophistication and importance, were highly subjective. Probably most important was "breadth," a rather special requirement of the particular journal. Ultimately, these standards were a matter of opinion. How provocative, broad, or original did an article have to be to be provocative, broad, or original?

Webb appreciated helpful suggestions for improvement that could be passed on to an author, but he made no systematic effort to obtain such advice; unequivocally, the primary function of the referees' comments was to assist the editor to make up his mind. It is, however, very difficult to get any clear impression of just how their comments influenced his opinion, because often a referee's comments would be partially praise and partially criticism. Rarely was there any straightforward recommendation for rejection or acceptance, and even if there was, Webb could always disagree with the reasoning of the referee. It is often impossible to tell what weighed most with him.

Because the sequence of events varied so much from article to article, it is impossible to detect any recurring pattern. Occasionally an early reading would raise just enough doubt on a piece Webb felt strongly about, either positively or negatively, for it to be sent out for additional criticism. There were cases in which articles that received initially favorable readings were rejected and cases of articles that were unenthusiastically reviewed being accepted.

In the marginal cases the factors which most often swayed Webb's decision were breadth of appeal and newness. One very favorably reviewed article on French party history was sent back to the author with the advice that he consider the contemporary British political situation and make the article of more interest to a general readership, although even so it was rejected on its next round. More than one article received a similar suggestion that it be broadened. The two published articles that had received the most mixed reactions from referees were accepted because Webb took seriously his mandate to broaden the interests of the journal. One was accepted because, as Webb explained to a referee whose opinion he was overruling, he hoped it would inspire better work, the other because the AHR published little of the type of history of which it was an example. Later in his editorship, Webb became even less tentative, and there are a number of examples of new types of history to be found in the AHR's pages. His successor described the period of his editorship: "Under Webb's leadership the Review was receptive to new kinds of historical investigation and to the controversies they spawned. He was, writes the editor of another publication, an 'imaginative' editor who 'provided leadership for other journals in a difficult time.'"[26]

Studies in the sciences suggest that the ratio of acceptance to rejection is related to the nature of the criteria used for judgment.[27] The figures presented by Harriet Zuckerman and Robert K. Merton in a (if not the) seminal study on the subject of refereeing seem to provide evidence to support this conclusion.[28] The authors presented a table showing rejection rates in various fields ranging from 90% in history, 86% in language and literature, and 85% in philosophy to 24% in physics, 22% for geology, and 20% in linguistics. These figures are based on a very limited sample, and the three journals used for history must have been journals like the American Historical Review and the Journal of American History, the top of the line, so to speak. Not many scholarly historical journals have such a high rejection rate.

The range of the rejection rates in the different disciplines is so striking that these figures have often been quoted.[29] Zuckerman and Merton themselves attributed the variation to how well institutionalized the norms of the respective disciplines were, institutionalization being defined as agreement on what constitutes adequate scholarship. Such lack of agreement is undoubtedly part of the problem, but there are real differences in the natures of the journals and the traditions of the fields which need also to be taken into account.

If one compares the AHR with the Physical Review,[30] the top of its particular line and the journal which Zuckerman and Merton studied in some detail, some obvious differences appear which suggest that the institutionalization of norms is not the only reason for the disparity in rejection rates. The articles in the Physical Review tended to be very short, approximately two or three pages; those in the AHR were long, averaging about twenty pages. Even allowing for the vagaries of type faces and sizes of pages, these are real variations. A much smaller proportion of the AHR was devoted to articles: in volume 56 (1950-1) 25%, in volume 74 (1968-9) 23%. The space of the Physical Review was almost wholly given to articles; it did not carry any of the book reviews which occupied the bulk of the space of the AHR and gave only a few pages to letters and to the proceedings of the American Physical Society. There was also a considerable difference in size. The 1950 volume of the Physical

Review had 3920 pages, the 1970 volumes, then in four series, 19,255 pages. Compare these with the 276 pages of volume 56 (1950-1) of the AHR given to articles and 427 pages of volume 74 (1968-9). There were somewhat more physicists than historians, but the difference in numbers did not begin to approach the difference in length of articles or size of journals.[31] These figures do not explain all the difference among Zuckerman and Merton's percentages, but they demonstrate that the internal dynamics of physics and history are dissimilar. It should also be noted that rejection rates have risen in the sciences since Zuckerman and Merton collected these figures.[32]

The ultimate test of an editorial system is whether or not it publishes the right articles. A study of the journal Social Problems concluded that, because there was a high degree of agreement by pairs of referees on acceptance and rejection, it did.[33] No such easy answer is possible on the AHR's choices, given the lack of consistency in procedure and usually mixed evaluations. It is possible to consider, however, the related question of whether the standards of the system were applied even-handedly. The whole system, after all, was based on the exercise of intellectual conviction--what some might call prejudice.

By and large, the answer must be that the system operated fairly. When a referee had some kind of personal involvement, he tried to make it clear. One qualified a generally unfavorable evaluation with the comment that he found all Western U.S. history acutely boring and largely irrelevant and that the article ought probably, therefore, be sent to a Western historian. Another explained that he favored a different article which dealt with events he had himself experienced because he agreed with the author's interpretation. Political bias was less often a factor than political activists would allow. Some writers have found that political bias exists in refereeing,[34] but at times on the AHR radical politics may have helped rather than hindered the chances of an article: in 1969 Webb very much hoped to publish some New Left history so that he could avoid seeming too conservative. Nor did personal connections help. The editor may have more frequently been enthusiastic about articles from his friends and former students, but this did not mean that they received preferential treatment. They were sent out for refereeing and got rejected and accepted on the same basis as other articles.

There is an appearance of institutional bias; among accepted articles, the backgrounds of authors and referees were often similar. Such similarities are not necessarily, however, evidence of skulduggery, but the result of the system of graduate education in history. Distinguished institutions were able to attract and select the best applicants; they were oriented to producing research-minded scholars. It is hardly surprising that their graduates were doing what they had been prepared to do.

Fortunately for the AHR, its system seemed to be generally acceptable to both successful and unsuccessful contributors. The pressure, present in some fields, to expand referees' comments into a form of continuing education did not exist. Nor was there any great dissatisfaction with slowness, although authors would doubtless have been happy if the process could have been shortened. The nature of historical inquiry is such that there would be little point and less opportunity for a referee to hold back an article to give himself or a student an opportunity to publish first on the same subject, blunting the impact of the paper being refereed. Such abuses have been cited by scientists[35] but historians are less vulnerable. Even if two historians use the same source material, they rarely approach it with the same questions. Nor do priority and novelty have the same importance as in the natural sciences.

AHR editors received very occasional complaints from individuals who could not see how their articles were any narrower than ones which had been accepted, but there were also those who expressed their gratitude for criticism. A few rejected contributors argued with the judgments; one, for example, complained that the reader had missed the point of what he was trying to do and informed Webb that the AHR ought to be publishing articles which, like his, used computer applications. Another author made a point of informing Webb that his article, rejected by the AHR, had been published in the Journal of Southern History, implying that the AHR just might have made a mistake.

In fact, approximately one-half of the 193 articles the AHR rejected in 1969 were eventually published in other journals.[36] Webb himself often recommended submission to one or another journal. He had a fairly standard list of suggestions: the Journal of American History for American history, French Historical Studies for French, Journal of British Studies or an English historical journal for British history, Central European History for German, and Political Science Quarterly for almost any political history. The list of journals in which these articles were actually published is much wider.[37] It included the more specialized historical journals, but it also included interdisciplinary journals, periodicals in other disciplines, and reviews aimed at the intelligent general reader. If an article was going to get published, it was most likely to be published within the two years following its rejection by the AHR.

The list of journals publishing the rejected articles reveals a great deal about the nature of history and historical scholarship. The sheer numbers confirm that history is not a close-knit discipline. After the AHR there was no single journal to try. That so many articles could find publication after rejection by the AHR--many of them rejected because of supposedly inadequate execution--indicates that standards are not absolute nor control over the channels of communication very tight. The wide disciplinary range of the journals illustrates in one way the fact that every subject has a historical dimension. Several were general interest periodicals, attesting to the wide audience history enjoys; it is not limited to scholars. The fact that only two of them were journals published outside the United States, Britain, or Canada shows how parochial historical scholarship is; only British, Canadian, and American historians did much reciprocal publishing in one another's journals.

For those articles which did get published in the AHR, it was a guarantee of wide dissemination, if not of scholarly fame and fortune. Citation, an important measure of scholarship, was sure to follow. The AHR, according to the Social Sciences Citation Index Journal Citation Reports, is the most frequently cited historical journal.[38] Even when that figure is adjusted to take account of the AHR's long years and many published articles, it is still among the most frequently cited, a fact confirmed whenever historians' sources are studied.[39] It is also cited widely. Those journals in which citations to it appeared in 1978 included many foreign journals and covered a wide disciplinary range.[40]

The general satisfaction with its refereeing procedures would make the AHR somewhat unusual today. Journals in many other disciplines have been under pressure to make changes. Implicit in many recommendations is a desire for greater formalization of procedures. A survey of members of the American Psychological Association in 1970 showed that the five most desired improvements were that measures should be taken to ensure speedier review of articles, that referees should be asked to supplement their criticism with helpful suggestions, that publication criteria should emphasize more strongly the total significance of an article rather than simply its technical soundness, that referees should be required to be familiar with articles or other material specifically cited as being important background material in the manuscript being reviewed, and that there should be more journals publishing very brief reports with short publication lags.[41]

Some suggestions have been more radical than others. The desire for different types of journals, for instance, has been met in some fields. Physical Review Letters was founded to provide quicker publication for short pieces than Physical Review could. Physics Today was begun to give a place for commentary on the field and for larger, integrative writing. The American Sociologist was designed to fulfill the same purpose in sociology as Physics Today did in physics.

The most frequent suggestions for change in recent years revolve around whether or not referees should continue to be anonymous. [42] The arguments in favor of having referees sign reports are fairly obvious; if your name is attached to something, you are more likely to do it properly.[43] A signature puts limits on opportunities for malpractice. Counter-arguments are equally obvious; it is easier for the referee to be tough and unsentimental if he is unknown, easier for the reader to accept criticism if the referee has not been identified.[44] One writer compared anonymous refereeing to the secret ballot;[45] open votes are fine for unimportant issues, but secrecy is essential on those that matter. Some editors have argued that referees would be unwilling to serve if they had to face the prospect of combat.[46] This last was the reason Webb gave one rejected author when the author requested the names of his referees in order to discuss his ideas further with them.

In recent years some journals have experimented with making the process more open. For example, the Bulletin of the Geological Society of America instructs its referees: "It is the reviewer's privilege to remain unknown to the author, but we hope this privilege will be exercised only in very special cases."[47] Authors are also sometimes given the option of choosing their referees.[48] As an alternative to fuller disclosure, equal anonymity has also been proposed; authors would remain as anonymous to referees as referees to authors.[49] These experiments thus far, however, seem to have been limited to journals in the natural sciences; the Journal of American History is one of the few historical journals which now use blind refereeing.

The AHR's refereeing system represented one successful set of answers to the basic questions of refereeing posed at the beginning of this article. Its particular answers derived from its own goals and from the traditions of historical scholarship. They contrasted suggestively on many points with those given by journals in the natural sciences.

There was to be refereeing, but only to a limited extent. Every submission was not automatically sent out to a referee. The editor had a very large role. This centrality of the editor was probably the single largest difference between the AHR and journals in the natural sciences. Webb took a very direct hand. He made many decisions himself--and not only in the actual acceptance and rejection of articles. He used his referees to advise rather than to decide, which meant he had much more opportunity to give the journal a distinctive point of view. This pattern was in the great tradition of famous editors of historical journal: Heinrich von Sybel and Friedrich Meinecke of the Historische Zeitschrift, Gabriel Monod of the Revue historique, J. Franklin Jameson of the American Historical Review, and Marc Bloch and Lucien Febvre of the Annales. These men all had a well-recognized impact on the development of historical scholarship.

Another area of considerable contrast was the function of referees. The AHR referees were clearly selecting rather than weeding, a pattern which resulted from a fundamental difference in purpose of the AHR from that of natural science journals. The AHR's greatest emphasis was on its book reviews, not its articles. This assessment was reflected in the apportionment of space; the AHR gave much more room to book reviews than to articles.

The differences between the AHR and journals in the natural sciences were smaller on the questions of what the qualifications of referees should be and on what basis they should make their decisions. Refereeing, after all, serves the same fundamental purpose in any field in which it is used: simplistically stated, it confers scholarly validity; it discriminates between "good" and "bad" scholarship. The referees used by the AHR were not required invariably to be experts in the identical subject area of the article. The standards they had to apply were somewhat less well-defined than in the sciences. Although good historians were doubtless as agreed as natural scientists upon general principles, the historians had greater latitude in interpretation.

Refereeing has become an integral part of the knowledge industry. It performs an essential function, If it did not exist, a substitute would have to be created. But it must not become a false god. Too many journals have used it indiscriminately in an attempt to assert a claim to scholarship, since too many academics have a rather fuzzy conviction that refereeing equals scholarship.

Refereeing must not be allowed to take the place of wise editing. It has the strengths and weaknesses of the committee approach. Without the personal elements of taste and a point of view, essential in scholarship, whether humanistic or scientific, a journal is likely to become homogenized, noted more for its dullness and lack of coherence than for anything else. Such a journal is not much of a contribution to true scholarly communication. The 1969 AHR shows how judicial use of the practice by an intelligent editor produced an academically valid, but also stimulating, volume.

References

1. Scholarly Communication: The Report of the National Enquiry (Baltimore and London: Johns Hopkins, 1979)
2. Diana Crane, "The gatekeepers of science: some factors affecting the selection of articles for scientific journals," American Sociologist 2 (November 1967), pp. 195-201
3. Frank T. Manheim, "The scientific referee," IEEE Transactions on Professional Communication PC-18 (September 1975), p. 190
4. J. M. Ziman, "The light of knowledge: new lamps for old," Aslib Proceedings 22 (May 1970), p. 188
5. "Articles for the AHR: an editorial," AHR 75 (October 1970), pp. 1577-80
6. Unless otherwise indicated, all data are derived and all quotations taken from these records. To avoid invasion of privacy, exact attributions will not be made. Most of the individuals concerned are still living, and rejection (or acceptance) is a sensitive matter. The referees accepted their assignments with the understanding that they would be anonymous, and even though the records have been opened, it seems unnecessary to change that.
7. According to the editorial "Articles for the AHR," approximately 250 articles were submitted to the journal each year during this period. Records on five articles published in 1970 and presumably accepted in 1969 were not in the files. Probably records of some rejected articles were also missing.

8. Nebraska State Historical Society, Organization of American Historians Collection, Series One, Box 103: Louis Pelzer to Francis P. Wiesenburge, 4 October 1941.
9. During the winter of 1979-80 a questionnaire was sent to approximately four hundred journals listed in Ulrich's International Periodicals Directory. All those listed in the history section with circulations of over 1000 were included, plus a selection of those with under 1000 circulation and some journals from other sections that were clearly historical. About half the periodicals were U.S. and Canadian. A response rate of slightly over 50% was obtained. They included all types of historical periodicals: local, broad scholarly, highly specialized sholarly, and popular.
10. Manheim, "The scientific referee," p. 190; F. T. Manheim, "Referees and the publications crisis," Eos 54 (1973), p. 532
11. "Articles for the AHR," p. 1580
12. For example, Robert K. Webb to Bryce Lyon, 27 March 1969 (Library of Congress, American Historical Association Collection, Box 575)
13. For example, Duncan Lindsey, The Scientific Publication System in Social Science (San Francisco: Jossey-Bass, 1978); Norval D. Glenn, "The journal article review process: some proposals for change," American Sociologist 11 (August 1976), pp. 179-85
14. Lawrence K. Altman, "Columbia's medical chief resigns; ex-associate's data fraud at issue," New York Times, 9 August 1980, sec. 1, pp. 1, 8
15. Mark Azbel, "Soviet vs. U.S. referees," Physics Today 32 (October 1979), p. 98; Mark Azbel, "PRL versus JETP," Physics Today 31 (December 1978), p. 82; William M. Easson, "Prompt review--early publication," Journal of Clinical Psychiatry 40 (1979), 331-5; Marc H. Hollender, "Authors, editors and referees," Journal of Clinical Psychiatry 40 (1979), 331-5; A. Jack Meadows, "The problem of refereeing," Scientia 12 (1977), p. 791; Hyman Rodman, "The moral responsibility of journal editors and referees," American Sociologist 5 (November 1970), p. 351; Scholarly Communication, p. 47
16. It is interesting to compare standards. Eight to ten weeks seems to be normal in the social sciences, while physicists consider a month slow. Azbel, "Soviet vs. U.S. referees"; Azbel, "PRL versus JETP"
17. J. F. Jameson, "The American Historical Review, 1895-1920," AHR 26 (October 1920), p. 8
18. Editor's note, AHR 61 (October 1955), pp. 253-64
19. Ibid.
20. "Articles for the AHR"
21. "New editor talks about AHR," AHA Newsletter 14 (December 1976), p. 2
22. J. M. Chambers and Agnes M. Herzberg, "A note on the game of refereeing," Applied Statistics 17 (1968), pp. 260-3; Janet M. Chase, "Normative criteria for scientific publication," American Sociologist 5 (August 1970), pp. 260-5; Duncan Lindsey and Thomas Lindsey, "The outlook of journal editors and

referees on the normative criteria of scientific craftsmanship," Quality and Quantity 12 (March 1978), pp. 47-8; Michael J. Mulkay, "Norms and ideology in science," Social Science Information 15 (1976), p. 638; Jacob Neufeld, "To amend refereeing," Physics Today 23 (April 1970), pp. 9-10; Richard Nisbett, "A guide for reviewers; editorial hardball in the '70s," American Psychologist 33 (May 1978), pp. 519-20; Erwin O. Smigel and H. Laurence Ross, "Factors in the editorial decision," American Sociologist 5 (February 1970), p. 21; Richard D. Whitley, "The operation of scientific journals: two case studies in British social science," Sociological Review 18 (July 1970), p. 242

23. Chase, "Normative criteria for scientific publication," p. 263
24. AHR 75 (December 1969), pp. 336-60
25. AHR 75 (April 1970), pp. 1029-45
26. "New editor talks about AHR"
27. Chase, "Normative criteria for scientific publication," pp. 264-5
28. Harriet Zuckerman and Robert K. Merton, "Patterns of evaluation in science: institutionalization, structure, and function of the referee system," Minerva 9 (1971), p. 77
29. For example, Manheim, "The scientific referee," p. 190
30. The years compared were 1950 and 1969, the years covered respectively by Zuckerman and Merton and by this study.
31. The sponsoring organizations, the American Historical Association and the American Physical Society, had respectively 5200 members and 7000 members in 1950. In 1970 the AHA had grown to 16,000 and the APS to 27,232.
32. Manheim, "The scientific referee," p. 191
33. Smigel and Ross, "Factors in the editorial decision."
34. Stephen I. Abramovitz, Beverly Gomes, and Christine V. Abramovitz, "Publish or politic: referee bias in manuscript review," Journal of Applied Psychology 5 (July-September 1975), pp. 187-200
35. Meadows, "The problem of refereeing," p. 791; Joseph Gillis, "Discussion," in Scientific Information Transfer: The Editor's Role, edited by Miriam Balaban (Dordrecht: D. Reidel, 1978)
36. The poor condition of bibliographical control in history makes it inevitable that some were missed. The Social Sciences Citation Index, Social Sciences and Humanities Index, and Writings on American History were searched through 1975. Individual unindexed journals were also checked in some cases. Occasionally a source would list an item as having been published but not given a citation good enough to enable identification of the journal. Thanks to a computer error, one article was erroneously attributed to the International Nursing Review. This listing means that the article must have been published, as bibliographers do not create entries out of nothing, but did not permit its location. The absence of complete texts also led to some uncertainty.
37. The following journals published articles rejected by the AHR in 1969. If the journal published more than one such article, the number of articles follows the title in parentheses. Africa Today; American Academy of Political and Social Sciences

Annals; American Academy of Religion Journal; American Oriental Society Journal; American Philosophical Society Proceedings; American Quarterly (2); California Law Review; Canadian-American Slavic Studies; Canadian Slavonic Papers; Catholic Historical Review; Central European History (3); Church History (2); Columbia Journal of World Business; Comparative Studies in Society and History; Economic History Review; English Historical Review (2); French Historical Studies (3); Historical Journal (2); Historian (6); History Teacher, History and Theory; Huntington Library Quarterly (2); Illiff Review; Illinois Historical Society Journal; Institute of Studies of the USSR, Munich, Journal; International Behavioral Scientist (2); International Journal of Middle Eastern Studies; Journal of American History (6); Journal of Asian Studies; Journal of British Studies; Journal of Economic History (2); Journal of Individual Psychology; Journal of Negro Education; Journal of Negro History; Journal of Southern History (2); Journal of the West; Journalism Quarterly; Maryland Historical Magazine; Mid-America (3); Negro Education Review; Negro History Bulletin; New England Quarterly; New-York Historical Society Quarterly; Phylon (2); Political Science Quarterly; Prologue; Review of Politics; Revue d'histoire diplomatique; Russian Review; Slavic Review; Social Science; South Atlantic Quarterly; Survey; Virginia Quarterly Review; Victorian Studies; World Affairs

38. Eugene Garfield, comp. and ed., SSCI Journal Citation Reports (Social Sciences Citation Index, 1978 Annual, vol. 6) (Philadelphia: Institute for Scientific Information, 1979)
39. Arthur M. McAnally, "Characteristics of materials used in research in United States history," Ph.D. dissertation, University of Chicago, 1951, p. 135; Clyve Jones, Michael Chapman, and Pamela Carr Woods, "The characteristics of literature used by historians," Journal of Librarianship 4 (July 1972), p. 143
40. Garfield, SSCI Journal Citation Reports
41. Yvonne Brackbill and Frances Korten, "Journal reviewing practices: authors' and APA members' suggestions for revision," American Psychologist 25 (October 1970), pp. 937-40
42. Alfred Romer, "Protection of authors: the case for anonymous referees," Physics Today 44 (April 1976), p. 397
43. R. Douglas Wright, "Truth and its keepers," New Scientist 45 (1970), pp. 402-4; R. Mirman, "For open refereeing," American Journal of Physics 43 (September 1975), p. 837
44. Manheim, "Referees and the publications crisis," p. 536
45. Ibid., p. 534
46. "In defense of the anonymous referee," Nature 249 (14 June 1974), p. 601
47. Manheim, "Referees and the publication crisis," p. 534
48. Heinz K. Henisch and Rustum Roy, "Refereeing rectitude," Physics Today 30 (May 1977), pp. 104-5
49. Manheim, "Referees and the publications crisis," p. 536; William C. Davidov, "Comment on protection of authors: case for anonymous referees," American Journal of Physics 45 (January 1977), p. 102

Part III

THE SOCIAL PREROGATIVE

THE PUBLISHING CULTURE AND THE LITERARY CULTURE*

Ted Solotaroff

As a literary editor in a trade publishing house I lead a sort of double life. Much of my working days--and often most of my evenings and weekends--are spent with manuscripts of fiction, poetry, and intellectual prose that, more often than not, the industry that employs me regards as marginal and counterproductive until proved otherwise. Hence it is incumbent on me to foster this proof by doing what can be done to help these manuscripts become estimable and profitable. This means scrutinizing every sentence, responding to every point, suggesting any possible way the work can be made stronger, more interesting, more accessible, sometimes going through two or even three versions of a manuscript until it is as effective as the author can possibly make it. This also means playing an active role in the publishing process of distributing and marketing books by addressing its problems, talking its language, playing its game. The more unique a book is, the more one-of-a-kind, which are the only books I'm really interested in acquiring and working with, the less likely the industry is to know what to do with it or for it. In other words, if you want to be involved with such a book, you had better be prepared to chaperon it every step of the way and to create just the right aura for it in its physical appearance, its catalog and jacket copy, its words of welcome from other authors, its press release, which may help to get it reviewed, and its advertising copy, if you can manage to get any money to advertise it. In short, I am partly a practical critic who works more closely with a text than even a scholar does and partly a promoter of unlikely prospects, a bond salesman in an increasingly problematic market.

This partly explains why, between editing the American Review and the books I do, I have gone through four publishing houses in thirteen years. For during this period my double life has become more difficult, the split between the two cultures I work in more pronounced. Several major seismic developments have been separating these two archipelagos and making navigation between them more precarious. Put another way, as long as the literary culture and the publishing culture were adjacent to and facing each other, as they

---

*Reprinted by permission of the author and publisher from Library Quarterly, 54:1 (January 1984); copyright © 1984 by The University of Chicago. All rights reserved.

traditionally have been, they could reflect and implement each other's aspirations and needs, the pen yearning for the press, its public modality, as it were, the press, on the other hand, yearning for the fine pens that enabled it to move upward in society from a trade to a profession. By far, the most important development in trade publishing in recent times has been the transforming impact of the corporate mentality and methods as, one by one, the major publishing houses have been taken over by conglomerates or have become conglomerates themselves. At the same time, one by one, or rather ten by ten, the independent booksellers have been losing out to the giant marketing chains such as B. Dalton and Waldenbooks. Instigating and underwriting these developments has been the rapid expansion of the mass market for books, which, like any other mass market, operates by means of standardizing the product and the demand for it. The much-reported "blockbuster" phenomenon in book publishing can be viewed as the industry's effort to come as close as possible to producing and relying on brand-name products. So too the burgeoning "lines" of written-to-order romances and, lately, soft-core pornography that hog the racks in airports and drugstores.

These three interrelated forces work like pincers, narrowing the scope and prospects of literary and intellectual publishing. The publishing corporation as distinct from the traditional publishing house, works, breathes, and wills like any other big business, at least at the management level. Its paramount concern is not the value of its product but the value of its shares which is keyed to its short-term profits, the number and profitability of books it sells rather than the quality of the books it sells. This tailoring of the product to the demand is more pronounced in paperback publishing, where the silent hand of the mass market is more coercive, but it inevitably affects hardcover publishing as well, both as the supplier of the reprinters and as a merchant looking for its piece of the action in the mass culture: that is, the books that service broad consumer needs or merely consumerism itself, that is, the need to keep buying or preparing or just wishing to buy that has turned the shopping mall into the church where so many Americans worship each weekend. This explains the shift, visible in most publishing houses, to consumer-oriented titles: the proliferation of cookbooks and diet books, self-help books, investment guides, crafts manuals, advice books on all stages of the life cycle.

Publishing for the shopping mall inevitably transforms the house that undertakes it by altering not only its procedures but also its functioning values; to borrow David Riesman's famous terms, it shifts these values from inner-directed to other-directed [1, pp. v-vi]. The traditional publishing house characteristically bore the name of its founder--Norton, Holt, Harper Brothers, Knopf, Morrow, Dutton, Farrar Straus, Simon and Schuster, and so forth--and developed along the lines of his vision, taste, and interests and those of his successors, who were chosen to maintain the house's established identity. Its functioning values tended to derive from a kind of idealized self-image of its founders, which, though adapted as it might be to later conditions and revised by subsequent directors, still maintained a remarkable continuity. The main reason for this was that the identity of the publishing house was protected from the fluctuations of taste and trend: profits were expected to be modest and variable given the nature of the business. Thus Alfred A. Knopf was free and able to develop a list of high international standing. Publishing for Knopf, a cultivated German Jew, was a means of joining his two cultural worlds at a high level, just as he personified this integration in his life-style and deportment. He is supposed to have said that he did ' not like to publish authors whom he would not like to invite to dinner.

One can trace much the same continuities through the other houses. For example, Harpers Brothers, for a century or more, bore the impress of its commitment as a book and magazine publisher to acting as an arbiter of American culture, particularly its political and social concerns. And, until fairly recently, it still tended to be the publisher of record, providing a forum for many important political figures and airing many important issues. Or again, publishers like James Laughlin and Barney Rosset, though they did not name their houses after themselves, still stamped their lists of authors with their own signatures. The scion of a steel fortune and a poet himself, Laughlin was the highest kind of patron, the one who supported his authors by publishing them, and he devoted New Directions mainly to discovering and disseminating the canon of the modern tradition in literature. Similarly, Rosset, an Irish Jew with a bohemian streak, made Grove Press into a kind of clearing house for the international avant-garde of the 1950s and 1960s. Though Laughlin and Rosset continue to publish, their houses are attenuated shadows of their former selves, leaving a large haunting absence in trade publishing of the risky, the experimental, the extreme literary work-- the book that as often as not ushers in the future. This function has mainly passed to the small-press movement and increasingly to the university presses, where much of our innovative and difficult literature leads a dispersed and marginal existence.

Though Mr. Knopf has faded from the scene and his house has been owned by a series of conglomerates, it stands as one of the exceptions to the rule that such ownership leads to a dilution of identity, a loss of cultural mission, and a transformation of values by which the good but unusual book becomes marginal, and the bad, derivative book, in which, typically, a gimmick meets a fad, becomes highly commercial.

Why is this so? What happens when a conglomerate takes over a publishing house? Let us begin with a hypothetical example. Telcom, a far-flung media empire of newspapers, magazines, and television and radio stations, decides it wants the prestige and scope of owning a New York publishing house. It acquires Harbinger House, a venerable publisher of mostly quality books that has been hard hit by high interest rates, soaring manufacturing and overhead costs, and the depressed economy and badly needs the cash flow that Telcom is all too willing to supply. Then, in order to have both feet in the ring, as they say, Telcom buys Premium Books, a full-line paperback house, as well. For a time not much changes. The chief ex-

ecutive officer (CEO) of Telcom is content to let his new acquisitions
run along in their accustomed and experienced ways. He has some
fourteen subsidiaries under his wing and may find himself phoning
room service in the morning to recall what city he is in. However,
the profits of both houses remain flat in his terms: Harbinger around
7 percent, Premium around 12 percent, roughly one-half and two-
thirds, respectively, of the overall profit levels of Telcom.

To "coordinate" his new trade-publishing operation, to fit it
more symmetrically into Telcom's organizational chart, and to "goose"
its management, the CEO sets up a new division and places it under
the management of a Telcom executive who has no experience in publishing but was very successful in running the marketing division of
Telcom's TV stations. This executive moves in with his team of
financial and marketing analysts who quickly discover that trade publishing is a very irrational and uncertain way of doing business. For
example, only 12 percent of Harbinger's list is responsible for 78
percent of its profits. Except for 2 titles, fiction books sell significantly less well than nonfiction books, and, of the latter, consumer-
oriented books far exceed those of general interest, with the exception
of biographies, though there it is necessary to distinguish between
historical ones and celebrity ones. And so on and so forth. Title
by title, category by category, editor by editor, the lists of both
houses pass through the computer and produce the crystal-clear conclusion that the profit picture could be immediately and dramatically
improved by publishing more books with a high return on investment
and fewer books with a low one. Also, Premium's picture would be
a lot rosier if it did not have to buy those expensive books from
hardcover houses but rather from Harbinger and if it dropped all
titles moving at a lower rate than a thousand a month and bought
only those titles that could be expected to move at a higher rate.
A Ludlum or a Carl Sagan comes high, but that is where the investment should be; acquiring James Michener and doing him in both
editions is a license to print money; it is almost as exciting as picking
off a competitive rival by a tender offer that cannot be refused.

What is likely to happen to the two houses' lists is obvious.
At Harbinger, poetry is cut back to a few established authors; literary criticism pretty much departs, as does drama. Quality fiction
comes under the marketing manager's scrutiny: Does it have a page-
turning plot; sympathetic characters; a clear, lively, unfancy style;
a topical subject; erotic interest? Is it, in short, a book that he
himself likes to read? Collections of stories are highly dubious unless the author has been consistently published in the New Yorker.
Each work of political and social criticism is similarly subjected
to the standard of popular appeal: Is its point of view fashionable
and palatable, immediately accessible, striking, controversial? Is
its author, in short, likely to be invited to appear on the Phil Dona-
hue Show? If not, is it likely to be adopted in college courses? So
with psychology, biology, economics, religion. What is the market,
and how do you reach it? All this has a subtle conditioning effect
on even the more independent, venturesome, quality-minded editor.
He finds that his value to the house has become quantified: his salary

and overhead are now expected to produce x times their total in the
net sales of the books he acquires. This pressure, as well as the
changed atmosphere of the house itself, affects the way he reads,
judges, and even edits manuscripts, his attention and influence imperceptibly but determinately shifting from the characteristics that
make a book unique to those that make it marketable.

Fortunately, though, there are still countervailing winds that
can help to keep him on his particular course. Even commercialminded publishing does not lend itself all that readily to the kind of
controls that corporate managers like to employ to tailor the product
to the market. The reading tastes and interests of the book-buying
public still tend to be more individualized than any computer can
track. Once you get past the proven best-selling authors and the
trashier categories and lines of pop writing, you are in a gray area
of crude comparisons, hunches, and surprises. Also, American book
publishing still operates in a very big and diverse country that has
been educating a lot of people. That is why even the beleaguered
editor at Harbinger House remains haunted by the tutelary spirit of
art and ideas. For the literary or intellectual work that strikes it
rich can strike it very rich indeed, and for years to come. First
novels may generally lose money, but how would you like to have
passed up Catcher in the Rye, Catch-22, The Naked and the Dead,
or Invisible Man? A writer whose first four novels did not sell is
hard to justify to the salesforce and bookstore buyer, but how would
you like to have turned down The World According to Garp, The
Adventures of Augie March, or The French Lieutenant's Woman? So
all but the most shortsighted eidtors and publishers tend to maintain
a margin of imagination and venture capital for at least a few of
those strange, disturbing manuscripts that do not fit in anywhere but
may turn out to have been written by the next Tom Robbins or Sylvia
Plath.

Nonetheless, the current marketplace makes it more difficult
to establish the one-of-a-kind book, for the pressures I have been indicating that operate in the publishing houses are even more onerous
at the other end of the process. Two major developments in bookselling are at work here. The first is the spectacular growth of the
bookstore chains, such as B. Dalton and Waldenbooks, which control
about 20 percent of the market and deeply influence the rest of it.
A recent article in Publishers Weekly carried the following description
of the Waldenbooks mentality: "All [of its top executives] strongly
support the mass merchandising concept (that is, of treating books
like a product in the same way a manufacturer would merchandise
a bar of soap). Hoffman [the president], who views romance titles
with as much respect as literary works, experienced the selling power
of mass merchandising techniques when he was an executive at Bell
& Howell...." [2, p. 37]. The way profitability is reckoned at
Walden and Dalton is quite literally on a "sales per square foot
basis." This means that a book will be ordered or not on the basis
of its sales predictability and will remain in the store or not on the
basis of its sales performance, in which it competes with every other
book in the store as either a frontlist (recently published) or a back-

list item. The acceptable rates of sale are fed into a central computer, and if a book does not quickly meet them, it is replaced. The book by a relatively unknown author that does not have a substantial first printing and advertising budget either does not get into the chain bookstores at all or its few nominal copies are lost in the shuffle of the best-sellers and the traffic of the category consumer books.

An even more ominous phenomenon is the advent of the discount bookstore chains, such as Crown Books and Barnes and Noble, that narrow the market even further by restricting their inventories to current books that have a rapid turnover and books being remaindered. The main trouble with both kinds of chains is not that they exist (no one in publishing is opposed to selling as many books as possible) but that they make it increasingly difficult for the independent bookseller to survive unless he turns his store into the same kind of high-volume discount operation as the chains. This is a serious loss for quality publishing because the independent bookseller provided the specialized advice and service to readers, including a congenial atmosphere for browsing, that gave the one-of-a-kind book the chance to reach its limited but nonetheless dependable audience. As an outpost as well as conduit of the literature culture in most communities, the endangered and indeed vanishing condition of the independent bookseller vitiates the principal alternative to the mass merchandising of books and its distorting and withering consequences and implications for the publishing culture. As one of my colleagues puts it, quoting a poet you are unlikely to find in any shopping mall, "The best lack all conviction, while the worst / Are full of passionate intensity" [3, p. 215].

I began by speaking of the widening gulf between the publishing culture and the literary or even literate one. For if the former is advancing steadily into the mass culture, the latter is retreating to a significant extent from it into the confines of the university. I have noted that an increasing amount of literary and intellectual publishing is being taken on by the university presses. At the same time, most of our novelists, poets, and critics depend on teaching as their principal livelihood, as do our more significant writers in most other fields. One can say that this is all to the good in that it has solved the age-old problem of how serious writers are to live, particularly in a society where one has to earn fifteen thousand dollars a year just to survive--about three times the average earnings of published writers.

One way this has been accomplished is by developing programs in creative writing. In 1952 when I was looking for a writing program there were exactly two to choose from: Iowa and Stanford. Today, at last count, there are close to 500 schools that grant B.A.'s and M.F.A.'s in writing, and their numbers increase every year because they are very popular. Indeed, formerly the tail of an English department, the writing program now tends to wag the dog. The course in writing lyric poetry is oversubscribed, while the course in the Elizabethan lyric has been dropped because only a handful of students

The Social Prerogative 225

were signing up for it. When I asked a friend of mine who teaches fiction writing at a Texas university what his students were writing, he glumly replied, "Mostly imitations of Star Trek." The proliferation of writing students seems to me partly a function of our much-noticed age of narcissism and partly a function of the shrinkage of distance between the writer and the consumer that is fostered by the mass market. But even the gifted young writer, the one with a future, may well find himself on a track that leads from a writing major, to one of the graduate workshops, and on to a position of teaching writing himself. This means that what he increasingly knows most about is campus life, which means that most sectors of specific public experience are closed off to him. One can chart in many if not most of the oeuvres of our leading fiction writers a movement from a concern with the people and piece of the world they came out of to either a preoccupation with the university ambiance and their life within it or else a preoccupation with some master fantasy or simply with innovations in technique. The marketing manager who says to me, "Who wants to read another novel about a professor who is screwing a student and fighting with his colleagues?" has a point. Or another apocalyptic, black-humor novel, or another collection of plotless stories with characterless characters. Also one can see in the regnant school of academic criticism, structuralism/deconstructionism, a further stage in what Ortega y Gasset termed "the dehumanization" of literature [4], one that removes even the author from the text by disconnecting his circuitry of meaning and thereby gives the text an independent, arbitrary, and hermetic existence waiting to be inhabited by the critic. None of this seems to me very useful for a viable and significant literary culture. Meanwhile the perplexing, ominous, distressed common life of our society goes on: real people coping with bewildering changes. Amid the steady stream of escapist trash, proliferating from year to year, one looks for the literary works that have some sense of necessity in them, that can matter to readers because they help them to understand their lives and to bear them better.

I recently published at Harper and Row a collection of short stories called Shiloh, a first book by a forty-year-old writer named Bobbie Ann Mason [5]: no advertising or publicity and a distribution of 2,200 copies, which meant that roughly one out of three bookstores had a copy of it. But despite all of the adverse circumstances that I have been charting and grousing about, the book began to catch on. The stories deal mostly with contemporary women and their families in small towns in western Kentucky who find that they have slipped the moorings of the traditional rural folkways and are trying to figure out where to turn next. All across the country, in the cities and towns and campuses, reviews turned up--not so much reviews as hands raised in welcome and recognition. These wry, sad, respectful stories are now in their fifth printing. And much the same success, for many of the same reasons, is about the descend upon a Chicago writer named Joan Chase, whose first novel, During the Reign of the Queen of Persia [6], is also a one-of-a-kind book on a theme pressing for expression: the rivalries and bondings among three generations of women on a farm in Ohio. It is no accident that both books are by mature women, for women writers today have a genuine subject and a passionate constituency, and a really gifted writer--an Alice Walker, Alice Munro, or Anne Tyler, a Lynne Schwartz or a Marilynne Robinson--is able to surmount the obstacles that the conglomerates and the bookstore chains and the mass culture itself place between her and her readers. So what it comes down to, I guess, is that editors like myself can only insist and persist so much; we need the right books, those that speak forcefully to our private imaginations and public concerns, for only they can join once again the literary culture and the publishing culture, if only here and there, and keep the two from being pulled completely asunder.

References

1. Riesman, David. "Preface." In The Lonely Crowd: A Study of the Changing American Character, by David Riesman in collaboration with Reuel Denny and Nathan Glazer. New Haven, Conn.: Yale University Press, 1950.
2. Frank, Jerome B. "Waldenbooks at Fifty." Publishers Weekly 223 (April 29, 1983):36-41.
3. Yeats, William Butler. "The Second Coming." In The Collected Poems of W. B. Yeats. New York: Macmillan Publishing Co., 1934.
4. Ortega y Gasset, José. The Dehumanization of Art, and Notes on the Novel. Princeton, N.J.: Princeton University Press, 1948.
5. Mason, Bobbie Ann. Shiloh and Other Stories. New York: Harper & Row, 1982.
6. Chase, Joan. During the Reign of the Queen of Persia. New York: Harper & Row, 1983.

GOVERNMENT SECRECY*

Richard Schmidt and Cecile Shure

I. Richard Schmidt

The late Chief Justice of the United States, Earl Warren, once commented that he did not believe the First Amendment to the Constitution of the United States would have stood a chance of being adopted at the time of America's celebration of its Bicentennial.

Thanks to the inherent wisdom of our founding fathers, we were not faced with that problem during the Bicentennial observance nor are we in the year of Orwell, 1984. However, in contemporary America, controversy around the role of a free press in the United States continues to ebb and tide, and seemingly always on stage in the theatre of controversy is the question of the free flow of information versus the right of privacy.

A relatively recent study of the National Readership Project, sponsored by the American Society of Newspaper Editors, the American Newspaper Publishers Association, and other press groups, stated:

> One of the dominant traits of modern society, particularly since Vietnam, is a general concern with one's self, a turning away, in a sense, from large, complex issues that seem beyond the reach of individual thought or action. As one reader complained, "Editors live in one world--and I live in another. They're worried about the Middle East, and I'm worried about meeting my bills."

This appeal to the right of privacy vs. the free flow of information has apparently encouraged the current administration in Washington to move in many areas to restrict the public's right to know. Not only do the organizations that I represent in a professional capacity find this alarming but I must state that, advocacy aside, I personally find it very disturbing.

---

*Reprinted by permission of the authors and publisher from Newsletter on Intellectual Freedom, 33:5 (September 1984) 129, 159-169; copyright © 1984 by the American Library Association.

I start with the premise that no government, including ours, "loves" a free press. At best, governments "tolerate" a free press.

I recognize that the press today is a favorite target of many Americans in all walks of life. As author Victor Lasky testified on December 8, 1983, in Washington before the Citizens Choice National Commission on Free and Responsible Media, sponsored by the U. S. Chamber of Commerce, "Just rap the media in any speech in any city in America, and you'll get applause." Press organizations are well aware of the truth of this statement but nevertheless they shall continue to advocate the cause of the free flow of information and the basic rights of free speech and free press guaranteed under the First Amendment to our Constitution.

A few of the examples of anti-disclosure activities that have been proposed in the last three years are:

(1) The effort to amend the Freedom of Information Act to make it more of a shield for government than a sword for the public.
(2) To use the Federal Privacy Act as a new tool for government secrecy by claiming that virtually any document containing an individual's name may not be released to the public.
(3) Expansion of the government's authority to classify information for "national security" reasons.
(4) Deemphasis of the declassification of historical documents and other information that no longer warrants continued classification.
(5) A proposal under National Security Division Directive-84 to impose lifetime prepublication review on literally thousands of government officials.
(6) To make use of public access laws more expensive and time consuming for the public.
(7) To further restrict the dissemination of nuclear information, even that information customarily in the public domain.
(8) Increased government efforts in all aspects to manage news and to prevent the press from reporting on major government actions such as the invasion of Grenada.
(9) Registration of films from foreign countries dealing with issues of public interest.
(10) Denials of visas to selected foreign nationals.

All of these steps have been taken with at least tacit public approval. The question that keeps recurring to me is why does the public not only approve but even applaud measures to deprive them of information concerning the operations of their government?

Martin Pawley, the British author and historian, has stated:

> Western society is on the brink of collapse--not into crime, violence, madness, or redeemed revolution, as many would believe--but into withdrawal. Withdrawal from a whole system of values and obligations that has historically been the basis of public, community, and family life. Western societies are collapsing not from an assault on their most

cherished values, but from a voluntary, almost enthusiastic abandonment of them by people who are learning to live private lives of an unprecedented completeness.

We must keep in mind that government is one of the most powerful of all forces, and it has the ability to take away liberty. To me, therefore, it is more important than ever that the press be allowed to be the watchdog of government, to record its misfeasances and malfeasances.

This national desire for privacy was not always so apparent. At the end of World War II, as a result of the aftermath of information restrictions which had been imposed because of our nation's involvement in that conflict, Congress and the public became concerned by the federal bureaucracy's limitation of access to the public of administrative information.

In 1955, the House of Representatives created a special Subcommittee on Government Information, chaired by representative John E. Moss of California, which held a series of exploratory hearings on the availability of information from federal departments and agencies. In the Senate, Senators Thomas Hennings and Edward Long of Missouri, chairing subcommittees on the judiciary, also began to review the government information access issue.

Congress itself displayed a sense of frustration in being unable to obtain information from the Executive Branch, which was constantly invoking claims of official secrecy and assertions of executive privilege. As a result of this study of over a decade, the Freedom of Information Act was signed into law on July 4, 1966. It is interesting to note that during legislative hearings on this measure no executive department or agency spokesman expressed support for the measure. It was truly a bipartisan effort on the part of Congress to open up channels of government information to the public.

In 1972, Congress held oversight hearings on the administration of the Freedom of Information Act, and the House Committee on Government Operations concluded, "The efficient operation of the Freedom of Information Act has been hindered by five years of footdragging by the federal bureaucracy, ... obvious in parts of two administrations."

Again in the 93rd Congress, in 1974, a move was made to strengthen the Freedom of Information Act by amendments offered once more on a bipartisan basis. The legislative history discloses that during the course of House and Senate Committee hearings on FOIA amendments, no executive branch department or agency offered testimony in support of the proposals. Despite this, the amendments were adopted by a 383 to 8 record vote of the House and a 64 to 17 roll call vote in the Senate.

On October 17, 1974, President Gerald Ford vetoed the bill, arguing that it would affect adversely the retention of military or intelligence secrets, would compromise the confidentiality of investigatory law enforcement files, would unreasonably burden agencies by imposing specific response time, and was otherwise "unconstitutional and unworkable."

In November, the House overrode the President's veto on a 371 to 31 vote, the Senate overrode the veto the following day by a vote of 65 to 27.

I wish we could state that Congress had struck its blow for freedom of information and continued to support the concept. However, in the fall of 1980, a House-Senate conference committee amended the Federal Trade Commission Act to exempt from the Freedom of Information Act large areas of FTC documents relating to such fields of consumer interest as pricing policies, product safety and truth in advertising. This measure was passed without hearings of any kind in either house.

In June 1981, another conference committee exempted large areas of documents held by the Consumer Product Safety Commission. This exemption, again implemented without notice or hearings, affects such matters of public interest as product-safety data and warranty information.

In July 1981, once more without hearings, Congress amended the Omnibus Tax Bill to exempt from disclosure under the FOIA the auditing standards and rules adopted by the Internal Revenue Service. In the 97th Congress, more than twenty bills were introduced to restrict access to government records.

Samuel J. Archibald, now a professor at the University of Colorado School of Journalism, was one of the chief staff members of the House Committee on Government Information that conducted the study leading to the passage of the original Freedom of Information Act in 1966, and also directed the Library of Congress study in 1972 which led to the 1974 amendments strengthening the Act. Archibald, along with others, has decried efforts to emasculate the Freedom of Information Act stating, "Too bad--just when we've got it working well; too bad--just when the federal government is beginning to learn to live with a democracy in which the people who mean to be their own governors are arming themselves with the power knowledge gives." Archibald, who has spent some time studying this phenomenon, states in a new study the following facts:

(1) Federal agencies are doing a much better job of administering the Freedom of Information Act than they did before the 1974 amendments which were designed to end their bureaucratic footdragging.

(2) The press and public interest groups have become freedom of information bedfellows. As a result, the Freedom of Information Act finally has become an effective weapon to enfore the people's right to know.

(3) The federal agencies which are leading the fight to emasculate the Freedom of Information Act are those which, as a result of greatly increased press and public use of the law, have suffered the most public ridicule as their administrative failures and foulups have been disclosed.

Archibald also states that political conservatives who were major supporters of the early Freedom of Information Act have now in many instances become the major opponents of the law which makes the freedom of information ideal into a reality.

Archibald has pointed out that conservative support for the Freedom of Information Act and its amendments in 1974 came from those conservatives who opposed big government, who opposed concentration of power in Washington. They wanted the Freedom of Information Act as a tool to dig out the corruption and incompetence that they believed to be the cancer of the federal bureaucracy.

He asks the question whether the current conservative political support to amend the Freedom of Information Act in the Senate of the United States comes about because it is now "their government; it will become, to a large extent, their bureaucracy. The federal records are now their records; the Freedom of Information Act might now be used to expose their shortcomings."

I submit that the attacks today upon the Freedom of Information Act are in many respects a thrust from a different direction by those who have been unable to go as far as they wished in developing stronger and stricter rights of privacy.

William Hornby of The Denver Post, a past president of the American Society of Newspaper Editors, has stated:

> Our passion for privacy in this age of great worry about individualism can be directed into unwholesome channels by those interested in the cause of secret government.

Hornby sums up the press's attitude as follows:

> The arteries of information in this country are gradually closing. They are being closed by people who don't believe in a democratic society and its open processes. They are being closed by an even more complex technology which makes access to information more difficult. They are being closed by the growth of attitudes among the general public, which do not include fervent support for freedom of information processes that we know to be vital.

One of the current arguments against the Freedom of Information Act is that it costs the taxpayers too much money. The administration is complaining that it costs somewhere between fifty and sixty million dollars per year to administer. This in indeed a large figure, even by today's monetary standards; but let's keep it in perspective. As stated in an editorial in The Miami Herald, this is still less than the amount of money that the Pentagon spends each year on marching bands. It is also the same as the price tag for two Army AH-64 helicopters. As Michael Gartner, president and editor of The Des Moines Register, stated, "That seems a paltry price to pay for freedom."

On January 27, 1984, the United States Senate by voice vote passed S. 774, the so-called Freedom of Information Reform Act. The bill has now moved to the House of Representatives and is before the Subcommittee on Government Information of the House Committee on Government Operations, chaired by Congressman Glenn English of Oklahoma. Congressman English has commenced hearings on the bill and has stated he will proceed in a thorough and deliberate fashion, but not a dilatory fashion.

Although S. 774 is a much improved product over the Administration's original proposals, it still contains many features which press and public interest groups find objectionable. These objections have been presented with vigor to the House committee.

The CIA has, over the past few years, requested a blanket exemption from the Freedom of Information Act, despite the fact that, as admitted by former CIA director Admiral Stansfield Turner at an appearance before the 1980 convention of the American Society of Newspaper Editors, the CIA has never lost a case in the courts where it claimed that something was classified and therefore could not be released.

The CIA has now modified its request to ask for an exemption for reviewing "operational files." A bill exempting the CIA from reviewing "operational files" was passed earlier this year by the Senate and the House Select Committee on Intelligence. It is now before Congressman English's Subcommittee on Government Information.

Hodding Carter, III, writing in The Wall Street Journal in an article entitled "Less Freedom of Information Means Less Freedom," stated from his experience as an Assistant Secretary of State in charge of State Department FOIA responses, that there is admittedly information which should be kept secret that is occasionally made public. But, Carter stated, such information "is made public invariably in ways which have nothing to do with the Freedom of Information Act."

On March 11, 1983, President Reagan issued National Security Decision Directive-84. It has two purposes: to bind all officials with access to what is called Sensitive Compartmented Information (SCI) to a lifetime censorship system and to broaden the use of polygraphs in government to investigate leaks. After hearings in both the Senate and the House on this proposal, Congress placed a moratorium on its implementation until April 15th 1984.

On February 29, 1984, hearings were held before the House

The Social Prerogative

Post Office and Civil Service Committee on H.R. 4681, introduced by Congressman Jack Brooks of Texas. This bill would prohibit pre-publication review and random polygraph examinations for all government agencies except the CIA and NSA (National Security Agency).

Richard Willard, Assistant Attorney General testified at those hearings that the President had "suspended" and "withdrawn" those provisions of NSDD 84 concerning pre-publication review and polygraph exams for "leaks." The Administration also promised to give Congress 90 days notice in the event they plan to reinstate the pre-publication and polygraph provisions.

I find it most interesting that five Republican members of the House of Representatives Committee on Government Operations, in a report issued November 22, 1983, concerning the lifetime pre-publication review procedures ordered by the Reagan Administration, stated:

> ... we agree: (1) that there is no evidence presented to the Committee to indicate that there exists a serious problem of former government employees divulging compartmented information through published materials; (2) that a compelling overriding governmental need for prior restraint has not been established; and (3) that the few instances of unauthorized disclosure do not, on balance, justify or warrant the imposition of a lifelong censorship system.

On March 20, 1984, Robert C. McFarlane, President Reagan's National Security Advisor, wrote to Congresswoman Patricia Schroeder stating the Administration would not reinstate the pre-publication review and polygraph provisions of NSDD-84 during this session of Congress and will not do so in the future without notifying the House Post Office and Civil Service Committee at least 90 days prior to their effective date.

On April 21, 1984, Mr. McFarlane responded to a further inquiry from Mrs. Schroeder stating that the Defense Department has proceeded separately from NSDD-84 and that other executive branch departments were operating under an earlier version (Form 4193-Dec. 1981).

In the meantime, Congressmen Jack Brooks, Chairman of the House Government Operations Committee, and William D. Ford, Chairman of the House Post Office and Civil Service Committee, requested the General Accounting Office to investigate the status of existing pre-publication review agreements.

On June 11, 1984, GAO reported its findings. A questionnaire was sent to all agencies and offices handling classified information except for the CIA and the National Security Agency. They were asked to reply within 15 days. Six weeks after the request, all but eight (8) agencies had responded. The non-responding agencies were the U.S. Arms Control and Disarmament Agency, Department of Energy, Environmental Protection Agency, Interstate Commerce Commission, Department of Justice, Office of Management and Budget, U.S. Trade Representative and the Executive Office of the President.

The 43 agencies that did respond disclosed some startling facts. Most agency employees who had access to SCI (Sensitive Compartmented Information) already had signed non-disclosure agreements (the Dec. 1981 Form 4193 or a similar one) prior to President Reagan's suspension of the provisions of NSDD-84 dealing with prepublication review. As of Dec. 31, 1983, GAO reported that more than 120,000 had signed. DOD reported that 156,000 military and civilian employees had signed agreements. Twelve agencies reported that current employees must sign prepublication review agreements regardless of whether they have SCI access. The GAO report states that prepublication review procedures cover 3,423,418 agency employees. GAO says DOD exercised pre-publication review of 10,088 books and articles in 1983 compared to 2,784 in 1981. The other 11 agencies reported they reviewed 34 books in 1983 and 5,461 articles as compared to 19 books and 4,814 articles in 1981.

So now we find that the President's suspension only addressed the particular pre-publication contract under NSDD-84. His suspension has not affected the continued use of the Form 4193 contract.

Another interesting statistic from the GAO report shows there are over 2.6 million Federal employees and more than 1.3 million contractor employees with security clearances. About 10 percent of all federal employees have top secret clearances--that is more than 1/2 million persons, and 42%, or over 2.1 million, have secret clearances.

Faced with this directive restricting their writings for the rest of their lives, scholars and journalists who have served their nation ably as federal appointees might have said, "No thanks." And why not? Why should such people jeopardize their future livelihoods in the bureaucratic morass that this directive would mandate? This directive, in short, would tend to deprive the federal government--and thereby the American people--of the intellects that are often at the cutting edge of socially beneficial thought.

Obviously an informed opinion, such as that which a former government official might beneficially offer the public, could be based on facts about which he had obtained knowledge during his career in government. Whether such an official, out of the many thousands covered by this order, would venture an opinion if there is any doubt about the application of the order, remains to be seen.

One need only look to American newspapers today, particularly the Op-Ed pages, to see the numbers of columns and stories that are originated by former government officials who, by these comments, bring before the American public important issues of the day and

The Social Prerogative

allow a healthy and robust debate concerning important public policies. If an administration can censor the comments and criticisms of its predecessors, the potential for political mischief is frightening.

Another item that has caused great concern to the press was the refusal to allow press coverage in the initial stages of the U.S. incursion into Grenada last October. The American Society of Newspaper Editors, along with other press organizations, protested the Administration's restrictions on U.S. press coverage of the invasion. ASNE stated:

> It is deplorable for Americans to be depending on Radio Havana as a major source of news during the first few days of the invasion.... We understand fully the military need not to telegraph any invasion in advance. We do not understand the refusal to allow U.S. reporters to go to Grenada with our troops. From D-Day in 1944 through the Korean and Vietnam wars, U.S. reporters have been at the front with U.S. armed forces without endangering military security.

Ironically enough, the U.S. Department of State notified the office maintained by the Cuban government in Washington, as well as the Soviet embassy, of the fact that our military invasion of Grenada was about to take place, requesting that the Cubans and Russians make no resistance and therefore avoid bloodshed. They suggested those Cuban construction workers with their 45-caliber shovels be removed! This notification was of course an automatic notification of all the Cuban and Russian news outlets, which immediately proceed to notify the world of the U.S. action.

Jerry W. Friedheim, executive vice-president of the American Newspaper Publishers Association, who served as Assistant Secretary of Defense for Public Affairs in the Nixon administration, is a person with vast experience in military information. Friedheim stated:

> The excuse given for this news blackout has been concern on the part of some U.S. military commanders over the 'safety' of journalists. Such an excuse is insufficient reason to prevent correspondents from covering an important military operation. There have been many U.S. war correspondents who--like Ernie Pyle in World War II-- risked and gave their lives accompanying American forces so that the American people might know what their armed forces were doing--and not doing.

Friedheim went on to say:

> It is particularly sad and disturbing that the 'safety' excuse should [be] resorted to, when it has been for years one of the key schemes used by the Soviet Bloc in UNESCO forums to support measures which provide government

control over the flow of information. This sort of excuse is completely inappropriate for American officials to use in a free society.

Ironically enough, the Administration recently served notice of the U.S. intention to withdraw from Unesco, citing as a primary reason Unesco's attacks on press freedoms. Friedheim went on to say "We are also mystified at the actions of U.S. military officers who picked up several American correspondents on Grenada after the invasion had begun and transported them to a U.S. navy vessel offshore, where they were held essentially incommunicado."

The news organizations further stated, "We think senior government officials must remember that for years professional journalists and professional public officials have been able to find ways to provide both troop security and the flow of information which an open society demands."

President Reagan, in an interview with Gannett Company executives published on December 15, said the Pentagon made the decision to bar reporters. He said he did not even know of the ban until U.S. forces invaded Grenada on October 25. David Gergan, who last year resigned his post as White House communications chief, stated that "there were some mistakes on our part, including the failure to involve our press people in the loop of those briefed on invasions plans."

As a person connected with the American press, I, too, am aware that the general public did not initially support the press position in this matter. A Cable News Network phone-in program with Daniel Schorr produced 4-to-1 support for governmental secrecy in Grenada. Larry King's radio show on Mutual Broadcasting showed a 75 to 25 percent support for the Reagan Administration's secrecy. A poll by The Los Angeles Times conducted on November 12-17, 1983, showed 52 percent approved of press exclusion.

Some of you have perhaps read Lou Harris' column in a recent issue of the Columbia Journalism Review in which he states that by December 1983, 65 percent of the American public was convinced that "a small group of reporters should have been allowed to accompany the troops when they invaded Grenada in order to report it to the American people." Apparently, there has been a turnaround in public opinion.

Under pressure from the press, the Department of Defense appointed a commission under retired General Winant Sidle, composed of both civilian and military members. The Sidle Commission recently filed its report with the Pentagon and we await the Secretary of Defense's decision. General Sidle announced at the beginning of the hearings that the commission had reached the unanimous conclusion that the press should be allowed to accompany U.S. forces on military incursions, subject to proper safeguards for national security and protection of military safety.

The Social Prerogative

Columnists Jack Germond and Jules Whitcover have called this administration "deft" in taking advantage of hostility toward the press. The Reagon administration, they wrote, achieved a policy assuring that the public heard only what the government wanted it to hear. They wrote, "The public is allied with the government against a group whose job in this society is to give the public an independent accounting of government's deeds."

Letters to the editors of newspapers throughout the country have shown some interesting and to me frightening themes. Many of these have stated, "The press is unpatriotic and caused us to lose in Vietnam." Others write to say, "We don't believe anything you report anyway so we would rather hear only what our government has to say."

As one of our editorial writers stated, "It is hard for me to accept the notion that there are a lot of people out there who would blithely trade our tradition of a free and independent press for the managed information system favored by totalitarian regimes around the globe, but the evidence points that way."

Senator Patrick Leahy of Vermont made some thoughtful comments on the floor of the Senate concerning the Grenada problem. He stated:

> War presents special problems for a democracy. Since the Civil War, all Presidents in times of war have made an attempt to cooperate with the press in order to promote an open society, while preserving a secure one.
> This time no accommodation was made. No reporters accompanied the invasion force, though it would have been simple--and acceptable--to include reporters in the invasion force, but to embargo their stories until the need for surprise no longer existed. After the invasion had begun, some censorship would have been understandable where the release of information might have jeopardized lives.
> Instead of that kind of accommodation, what the American people got was stonewalling. Even when the administration conceded on Wednesday that reporters should be allowed to come to Grenada, reporters were not allowed to leave the island until after the completion of President Reagan's speech Thursday night. The only film footage of the invasion was that of the Defense Department, and that was only released in time to be aired after his speech was over.
> President Reagan was right when he said that Americans stand shoulder to shoulder when we are threatened. But the President has forgotten why. We stand shoulder to shoulder because of trust. And the sad truth is that this administration does not trust the American people to judge the facts firsthand.

The White House has announced the press may not be excluded from future military operations--if there is a nuclear war the press will be the first to be invited!

Sociologist and political scientist Edward Shils, reviewing the history of Western man's struggle for freedom in his book entitled The Torment of Secrecy, wrote:

> The struggle for constitutional government, for the extension of the franchise, and particularly for the freedom of the press ... was directed against privacy in government. Almost as much as the extension of the franchise is constitutional restraint on monarchical absolutism, publicity regarding political and administrative affairs was a fundamental aim of the modern liberal democratic movement.

In his book, Gulag Archipelago, Aleksandr Solzhenitsyn describes the ultimate in governmental privacy when he tells of the frantic search by relatives of persons who have disappeared in the hands of government, going from jail to jail to be told, "nobody here by that name," or "never heard of him."

With all of the screaming and shouting that is currently going on to clamp down on freedom of information and access by the press and public to records and governmental procedures, I would hope that all of us would remember the words of James Madison, enshrined on the building bearing his name at the Library of Congress: "A popular government, without popular information, or the means of acquiring it, is but a prologue to a farce or tragedy; or perhaps both. Knowledge will forever govern ignorance; and a people who mean to be their own governors must arm themselves with the power which knowledge gives."

II. Cecile Shure

I appreciate the opportunity to be here with you today. I'm a book lover and in bringing up three children, my priority was books over anything else. Today, prior to this session, I was in the exhibit hall and had a wonderful time--I've got bags full of posters and things like that!

I also was looking at some of the computer services that are being made available to libraries. It was very exciting--for a while --to think of these wonderful opportunities in a free society. You have access to computers and high technology to teach, to grow, to learn, to provide information, and this is what it's all bout. But I was brought back to reality very quickly because many of the systems and many of the data bases that I saw on the free market in our open society are the very ones that the Soviet Union will do anything to get. And unlike the Americans, the Soviets don't have to go before the Congress for budget processes; their priority is defense. They may not be able to do everything, but they can do anything and what they want they get, with the first priority being for defense. We use a CAT Scan for heart patients, they use it for defense.

Two experiences that I've had come to mind (I'm going to be

The Social Prerogative

weaving in many of the things I've seen in the last few years while working on the whole question of international technology transfer.) The first thing that came to my mind was the IBM computers. Now, the Soviets have developed their own large computer that is comparable to the IBM 360. As a matter of fact, we know they got it from Western technology--they were attending a fair and were caught taking pictures. The interesting thing is that the Soviet software begins with a welcome to the IBM 360! So clearly they are taking our software and putting it to use.

A more recent example is something you probably read about in the newspapers in late December. In both Hamburg, Germany, and Stockholm, Sweden, ships were stopped on their way to the Soviet Union with components for a VAX computer, one of the most sophisticated computers in the world. Had the Soviets gotten that computer, they would have gained the technology to run anti-ballistic missile systems. Now, they are fantastic at reverse engineering. And what they would have done was run that computer system, learned how it worked while they developed an anti-ballistic missiles fire fighting system. So, there is a very basic dichotomy--we want to share with and grow and provide education, but we also have to live with the reality that the Soviet Union wants our technology and wants it for other than peaceful and educational purposes.

I want to present a hypothetical, but true, scenario. It addresses our situation.

We've had a student exchange program with the Soviet Union. The Soviet student comes to America on a scientific exchange. He's 38 years old, he's a Ph.D. nuclear physicist. He comes to America and goes to one of our universities. He can travel unrestricted. He can speak to anyone. He can have access to our American libraries, and subsequently, to our journals, publications, software, and data bases. He studies alongside our American scientist who is on the brink of discovering advanced technology which can in the future have defense implications.

The American student going to Russia, on the other hand, is age 24, and is working on his master's degree, in history or art. He cannot travel outside his host city; he cannot read or study anything beyond the designated discipline for which he came to Russia. He has no access to scientific data and he is not allowed into scientific labs.

Once home, the Soviet returns to his highly-valued government-sponsored job. And he brings his newly gained knowledge to the Soviet government labs where it is used to meet the needs of the Soviet government--again, defense is the primary goal. The American returns, goes back to his university and continues to work on his dissertation. The U.S. government does not have any requirements.

A true case in point: A group of Soviet visitors asked to visit the Lockheed factory--they wanted to see the L1011, a commercial airliner. Shortly thereafter, the Soviet Union made a breakthrough in a long-desired capability with transports for military use. The breakthrough was a result of knowledge gained during their visit. How? Each one of those Soviet visitors was wearing sticky shoes, and as they walked through the plant, they were able to pick up the metals on their shoes--the very metals that gave them the breakthrough to gain the technology.

Many students from Third World countries or countries with ties to the COMECON, or Soviet bloc countries, have very different goals and, therefore, very different sensitivities towards protecting our technology. Often, the purpose of studying in the United States is to gain skills specifically to bring back to their countries. And this is occurring during a period of time where more and more defense and dual use research is being conducted in the academic and free world environment. No longer do defense contractors have a monopoly on research; much of it is going to the universities. Particularly with diversification and with commercial work in high technology, it is often more valuable to get the research done in the universities.

Dick [Schmidt] mentioned a conference where an American was stopped from giving a paper by the Air Force. A conference two years ago this summer basically kicked off a lot of what is going on today. It was a conference for the Society of Photo Optical Instrumental Engineers, more commonly known as the SPIES conference. Two days prior to the conference, 120 papers were pulled by the Defense Department, the reason being that this conference was both an international conference and a classified conference back-to-back. There were several Soviets attending and it was believed after a review of the titles of the papers to be presented that these 120 papers had data which could provide information to the Soviet Union. Now, interestingly enough, there were existing DOD regulations about prepublication review and about attendance at conferences by contractors. But in each and every case, including papers written by government workers, the papers had never been submitted to the government for any kind of review.

After the conference, when things simmered down--and after a lot of bad publicity for the Defense Department--the papers were reviewed. It turned out that there were very few that would have been pulled. But unfortunately in this circumstance, there was a lot of rash reaction from people who had not followed the regulations. There was one good thing that did come about as a result, and that was a study which I'll get to in a minute.

I'd like to give you an example of conferences that I attended in the last two years where the interests of the Soviet Union to gain our information and our technology were very apparent to me. About a year and a half ago, I was asked to go to Pakistan to attend a Third World conference about the Indian Ocean area. Among the countries represented besides Pakistan were India, Sri Lanka, and Nepal, in addition to the Russians and the Chinese from the People's

The Social Prerogative

Republic of China. As a delegate to the conference, I was one of eight Americans--six were academics, and most were acquainted with the Soviet "professor" who also was there. The Soviet professor had stayed in their homes and had a very close relationship. The Americans were very proud that they went beyond the politics of America and could share with other scientists. This Russian scientist was considered special because he, himself, questioned the Soviet Union.

As a delegate, I was met at the airport and taken into the VIP lounge where I picked up my luggage. Interestingly, the Soviet professor was coming in at the same time I was. He was met by the Soviet Ambassador to Pakistan--something that one would not expect the average professor attending a conference to encounter. The next day, the Soviet made an attempt to approach me. Now I was the only woman delegate there and the Soviet asked me where I worked. I reminded him, that had he read the book, he would have known I was the only woman delegate and, yes, I worked for the Defense Department. In the course of events, the Soviet did attempt to invite me to the Soviet Union and then asked me what my soldiers would think. There was an example of an attempt--and it was not just an innocent attempt. Again, I remind you that the ambassador just doesn't come out to meet professors.

More recently, in February, I was on a USIA tour through Europe. It happened, by the way, at the time the blacklist came out; I was rather amazed that I was not on the blacklist--but I was not and I was there. My first stop was in Vienna. I no sooner arrived than I started getting phone calls in my hotel room from a strange man asking me to meet him, and saying that he had seen me in the hallways. When I called the concierge to complain about giving out my room number, I was told I was asked for by name.

My last stop was Brussells and the third secretary of the Soviet Embassy showed up at my speech. He went up to the embassy representative and said, "I received this invitation, is it all right that I'm here?" I was told not to divert from my speech and I did show several slides which showed targets that the Soviets were after in our technology fields. At the end, the Soviet walked up to the Embassy representative and said, "Your American expert is really quite an expert. She only made one mistake." The mistake was a very simple one. I was referring to a factory instead of a capability and he mentioned it--slip of the tongue more than a mistake. It was tantamount to admitting that what I was saying they were after was for real.

So, therefore, the reason for the controls.

Following the incident of the conference, in January, 1982, then Deputy Director of the CIA Admiral Bobby Inman addressed the American Association for the Advancement of Science and spoke of the hemorrhage of technology to the Soviet Union, referring to the academic world as being part of it. The information going over, he stated, is as damaging or as sensitive as the hardware itself. A month later, Inman testifed at a Senate subcommittee hearing--my old committee, as a matter of fact, the Permanent Subcommittee on Investigations--and reiterated this. The two incidents--the SPIES conference and Inman's testimony--caused a great deal of concern among the academics. It gets back to what Dick Schmidt was talking about--who's going to want to work for the Defense Department if there's going to be such control.

As a result, Dale Corsen, President Emeritus of Cornell University, headed up a nineteen-member panel called the Scientific Communication and National Security Panel. They did a very intense study; as a matter of fact, they were given government money and also were privy to quite a few very highly classified documents. The study did conclude that there was a lot of loss of technology, but it also questioned the extent of the role that academia or scientists play in this. This has been a problem; no one has really been able to identify how much has gone out to the Soviet Union and in what way. This particular panel concluded that controls are necessary. But they expressed a great deal of concern about the degree of control and the potential of curbing innovation through control.

They also established criteria for controls. The four criteria they established were, first, that the controlled technology should be developing rapidly, and, second, that it should be identifiable and have direct military application or dual use. (For those who don't know what dual use is, let me explain. In the past, one could determine that an item was strictly for defense purposes. In recent years, many innovations have gone on the commercial market and it's only been later that a defense application has been discovered. In recent testimony on the Hill, Assistant Secretary of Defense Richard Pearle actually brought in an Apple Computer and suggested it be on the control list because the army is using it for training in Europe.) The third criterion was that acquisition by the Soviet bloc could give them a significant breakthrough in a very near term, and the fourth, that the information could not be obtained from any other friendly nation.

The report was accepted, and recently a followup was written. It was not very complimentary on how the Defense Department was following the initial Corsen report. As a matter of fact, Paul Gray, president of MIT, and the presidents of Cal Tech and Stanford met with Secretary of Defense Weinberger in January and April on the whole question of the pre-publication review and the censoring of non-classified material.

What has been going on in the Defense Department? A steering committee on technical data bases was established to look into many of the things the Corsen panel brought up. There's also a defense university panel that is looking into many of these issues. A DOD directive is coming out which has not yet been approved-- DOD 540XX--but is going to be an amendment to the FY84 Defense Authorization Act. This will allow the Secretary of Defense to withhold data subject to the export control laws.

The Social Prerogative

I'd like now to talk briefly about this committee and the five subcommittee panels under it. Subcommittee One is looking into contractual provisions. The area of interest is the use of contracts to control direct and indirect participation in research projects, publication or public dissemination of research results, and research projects only partially funded by DOD. Subcommittee Two is on visa controls, which, again, is something Dick raised. Interestingly while the Defense Department is still working on its subcommittee, in May, 1983, Undersecretary of State William Schneider concluded an interagency study and proposed some very tough new visa laws. He indicated that action can now be taken on a visa solely on the basis of the potential for technological loss.

Subcommittee Three is technological monitoring and the areas of focus are the identification and monitoring of rapidly emerging and changing technologies. What is an "emerging technology?" How is it defined? And what will the list be used for--controls or investments? Subcommittee Four is concerned with scientific conferences and trade shows and, again, the focus is the establishment of procedures for identifying conferences and showing where potential technology transfer problems exist. They want to establish criteria for control of attendance at the targeted scientific conferences or trade shows--and, believe me, this kind of conference [ALA Annual Conference] is one that could be of the same interest, particularly as you go out to your exhibits and look at the technology.

Subcommittee Five is concerned with publication and presentation of research papers. Here again its concern is with the procedures for review of papers being considered for publication or public presentation, and variations in procedures for papers written by DOD employees, by defense contractors, and by defense-funded research scientists.

I want to report on the status of all these committees' work, as of three days ago. The subcommittee on visas has coordinated and published a directive, but it's not yet gone out publicly. The subcommittee on conferences has proposed directives but these are still not out. The subcommittee on contracts--still no report. Subcommittee on publications--the final report is ready for approval.

Why are we so afraid of conferences if we feel we are not giving the scientists or the Soviet Union classified material? I think many people fear that the Soviets will come into these conferences and informally gather information on a one-to-one basis, picking up bits and pieces. It's very, very clear that they spend a lot of time checking out conferences, reading and seeing what's being given in public places. Let me give an example. The American Defense Preparedness Association Plastics and Chemical Job Symposium was advertised in our local journals and in local magazines. It was held at the Four Seasons Hotel in the Lake of the Ozarks in October, 1983. The Old Crows Electronic Warfare Technical Symposium was held at Virginia Beach. Now, everyone knows that Aviation Week is widely read in the Soviet Union. It goes on Washington newsstands on Monday and they say the first two copies are on the first airplane going to the Soviet Union. By the time it gets there, it's translated into Russian. And every time you open up Aviation Week, there's a list of every one of these technical conferences. So even if they're not attending because it's classified, they have all the access in the world to go into these environments and learn as much as they want.

Last summer, the University of Michigan at Ann Arbor held a symposium on flow visualization and in Seattle, they hosted a conference on propulsions. Among the foreigners were two Czechoslovakians--they attended both, they knew both of these conferences were being held. One was stopped when he requested to go to a presentation on wind tunnels at the first conference.

I think the key point here is the awareness that these conferences exist and the locations and the openness of them certainly become a source for the Soviet Union and its bloc members to travel freely in the United States and gain access. No one monitors their conversations and the Americans often do not even recognize that they're being asked leading questions.

Now, the Freedom of Information Act, it would appear, is too obvious a channel for the Soviet Union to employ--they immediately would be identified as Soviets looking for information. A Washington Post article in September, 1983, indicated than an attorney, Paul Rosa, conducted a search which turned up no evidence the Soviets were using the FoIA to gather information. Based on that article one could conclude they don't find it worthwhile. But the potential for the Soviets to have mastered the art of subterfuge in gaining information, such as using a waged researcher to do their bidding, or out-and-out bribery, surfaced just days later.

Right after the Washington Post article appeared--and I don't know whether it was timed for that or not--there was an arrest and a Soviet spy was expelled. His crime was using a third party, an American student, to gain valuable information. The Soviet told the American that he needed help in getting the material because the Americans didn't like Russians and wouldn't let him come to the meetings to get documents.

Recently, a deputy assistant secretary of defense, Edie Martin, testified in Congress that the Defense Department was going to rescind and back down on this gray area, the dual use area, in establishing controls. This was quite a shock to people; it was a revelation that perhaps the administration was backing down on control. But I think what's more important for everyone to recognize is the role of the Export Administration Act. The Export Administration Act was started in 1948 as a method for the United States to control our valuable assets during wartime. The Act sort of limped through the sixties and stayed intact without many changes. But in, I think, 1971, Senator Jackson and Congressman Vanick came up with the Jackson-Vanick Amendment which was one of the first

The Social Prerogative 245

attempts to control technology and exports to the Soviet Union.

Today, the Export Administration Act is in limbo. It expired in September, 1983. It was extended for two weeks. Reagan then imposed the Emergency Economic Powers Act to keep it in place for fear that if it died, and there were no controls, there would be an open field for the Soviet Union to get all the technology they could. Right before the Congressional recess there was an agreement to extend the Export Administration Act until February, 1984. Since then, it has again been in limbo and again the subject of Hill hearings and many, many debates.

I think the bottom line, and the thing to be most aware of, is the fact that the Export Administration Act has become the focus of concern about Soviet attempts to get our technology and how controls aimed at stopping this are applied. So when Dick [Schmidt] talks about rescinding NSDD 84, and we talk about a deputy assitant secretary rescinding the gray area, I want to remind you that the debate has not gone away. There is still the reality that the Soviet Union and the bloc countries set a priority on gaining access to our data bases, our technology, everything they can get.

In closing, I'd just like to bring it back to your world, and, frankly, all of our worlds. What you're dealing with as librarians is the right to read and an open press. One might ask how far do we go or how far don't we go? What I've tried to do today in a short time--and hopefully, I haven't confused you too much--is to lay out the dilemma that we face: the technology that we use for peace, the Soviets want for defense. And as important as it is for us to have the technology we need to grow, to share, and to innovate, we have to look for that fine balance and understand that the controls are not meant to stop Americans from moving on, but that the Soviets use the same information for their defense and their aggressive acts.

Thank you for your time and for listening to a different picture of the issues, and for letting me lay out some of the actions that are being taken in the Defense Department. I think it's very clear that the Defense Department is trying to deal with the academic world, with the scientific world, to find some kind of solution so that there can be some balance in this issue.

NUCLEAR HOLOCAUST AND PUBLIC POLICY*

Joe Morehead

One year before the destruction of Hiroshima and Nagasaki by atomic bombs, the Danish nuclear physicist and Nobel Laureate Niels Bohr sent identical letters to President Roosevelt and Prime Minister Churchill in which he spoke of "a weapon of unparalleled power ... which will completely change all future conditions of warfare." Accordingly, in Bohr's words, nuclear weapons have become a "perpetual menace to human society."[1]

Alas, the weapons used on Japan in 1945 appear by present standards almost as children's toys in a halcyon age of nuclear innocence; they have been downgraded to "tactical" instruments today. No one knows the exact number of nuclear warheads that exist in the world at any given time, but an authoritative United Nations study issued in 1981 place the number at between 40,000 and 50,000, "the combined explosive power of which is believed to be equivalent to that of more than one million Hiroshima bombs or, to put it differently, some 13 billion tons of TNT, which represents more than 3 tons for every man, woman and child on earth."[2] More recent figures indicate that at least six nations--the United States, Russia, Britain, France, China and India--have some 43,000 atomic weapons. The superpowers, of course, dominate; the United States has "about 26,000 nuclear weapons, the Soviet Union about 14,000." This country's "long-range strategic warheads equal 3,700 megatons; Russia's total 6,100 megatons. It takes 50 Hiroshima-type atomic bombs to equal 1 megaton, the equivalent of 1 million tons of TNT.... Scientists estimate that if all the nuclear weapons in the world were detonated, the force would equal 10 trillion tons of nuclear explosive power."[3]

In the intense colloquy that characterizes the nuclear weapons issue, statistics and comparisons, though odious, have a symbolic dimension. For example, it is important that words like "megaton" acquire a picturesque coloration. As British expert Solly Zuckerman points out, "If one could concentrate into one focal point and one focal moment all the destruction which Britain suffered in the Second World War, the picture would not be as bad as the one that needs to

---

*Reprinted by permission of the author and publisher from The Serials Librarian, 8:3 (Spring 1984) 7-24; copyright © 1984 by The Haworth Press, Inc. All rights reserved.

The Social Prerogative 247

be conjured up when one talks of the explosion of a single megaton weapon over a city."[4] Jonathan Schell asks us to visualize "the consequences of the detonation of a one-megaton bomb, which possesses eighty times the explosive power of the Hiroshima bomb, on a large city, such as New York." We become, in our mind's eye, witness to the instant death of millions, winds of 400 miles per hour, the melting of everything made of metal or glass, and the spectacle of corpses charred beyond recognition. Within an area of sixty-one square miles "the people of New York would be burned, battered, crushed, and irradiated in every conceivable way." But this is a small scenario. There is no inherent limit on the size of nuclear weapons. Twenty-megaton bombs are not uncommon in nuclear arsenals; the Soviet Union once detonated a sixty-megaton bomb. When the United states detonated a fifteen-megaton hydrogen bomb, obscenely codenamed Bravo, at Bikini Atoll in 1954, the heat and blast pulverized the coral, debris was dispersed twenty miles into the stratosphere, and radioactive fallout descended upon an area of 7,000 square miles. As Schell notes, "Part of the horror of thinking about a holocaust lies in the fact that it leads us to supplant the human world with a statistical world; we seek a human truth and come up with a handful of figures."[5]

What follows is a brief synopsis of the human and statistical world of nuclear war, selective abstracts of the vast literature on public policy and nuclear weaponry. Participants in this sorrowful dialog include individuals, groups, and government officials from presidents to minor but often influential functionaries. Some have learned to love the Bomb, others have not reached that spiritual plateau. It is, perhaps, a minuscule measure of our maturity that, four decades after Trinity,[6] the world is "thinking about the unthinkable" with an urgency not hitherto evinced.

Federal Government Publishing Activities

Central to the nuclear war debate is the ability of this nation to cope with the effects of a nuclear attack. What to do when the Bomb arrives forms a part of what the federal bureaucracy calls "comprehensive emergency management," a relatively recent concept and program that deal with "major life-threatening emergencies in the United States." Primary responsibility for this kind of planning resides in the Federal Emergency Management Agency (FEMA), which was established by President Carter's Reorganization Plan No. 3 of 1978.[7] This reorganization consolidated in one agency the activities of the Federal Insurance Administration, the United States Fire Administration, and the Defense Civil Preparedness Agency, as well as other existing federal programs such as community weather emergency plans, earthquake and dam safety programs, the emergency broadcast system, coordination of emergency warning, and federal response to terrorist incidents. Over 2,000 employees staff ten FEMA regions and the agency's Washington headquarters.

Few question the need for an agency at the federal level to manage, anticipate, and respond to major civil emergencies such as floods, fires, terrorism, radiological accidents, and severe storms. But when FEMA issues pronouncements on the management of nuclear attack, it enters a new dimension, a Twilight Zone where directives acquire a bizarre incredulity. Later in this account I will comment specifically on this aspect of FEMA's role in public policy.

The 1982 Serials Supplement to the Monthly Catalog identifies two FEMA periodicals: Disaster Information and Emergency Management. The former, issued irregularly and classed in FEM 1.9 (Depository Item 216-A-4), reports federal and state cooperation in programs for flood control, protection of museum treasures, public health disaster plans, community relocation, and the like. Emergency Management, on the other hand, began as a quarterly in the Fall of 1980 (FEM 1.16; Depository Item 216-A-10) but was discontinued in 1982 by the Office of Management and Budget pursuant to President Reagan's "War on Waste" ukase.[8] During its short life, the periodical carried some interesting articles on the medical consequences of nuclear war, crisis relocation planning, emergency broadcasting, and other apposite topics. In addition, FEMA publishes an annual report to the President and other series, a number of which are available to depository libraries and for sale through the Superintendent of Documents.

The responsibilities of FEMA have been growing. Executive Order 12148 (July 20, 1979) assigned to the agency functions formerly vested in subunits of the Department of Housing and Urban Development and the General Services Administration.[9] 44 CFR 323.1 is a federal policy directive "on the use of resources in the period immediately following a nuclear attack on the United States." Appendix 1 to Part 323 provides a long list of "essential survival items" arranged by seven major groups and includes everything from alcohol to tents. A superficial reading of federal directives might lead to the conclusion that the industrious officials of FEMA have everything well in hand.[10]

Presidential Rhetoric: Truman to Reagan

The annual volumes of the Public Papers of the Presidents of the United States (GS 4.113; Depository Item 574-A) provide a chronology of thoughts and vocal expressions of our chief executives. It is appropriate to begin this account with Harry S. Truman. In July, 1945, Truman traveled to Potsdam, Germany, to confer with Churchill and Stalin on the matter of occupation zones and administrations for German territory. While in Potsdam, he received secret word that American scientists had successfully tested an atomic bomb for the first time. On his way home, Truman gave the fateful order to drop an atomic bomb on Japan, and nuclear war was born.

On May 11, 1946, Truman was awarded an honorary degree at Fordham University. In his acceptance remarks he averred that

"Civilization cannot survive an atomic war. Nothing would be left but a world reduced to rubble. Gone would be man's hope for decency. Gone would be our hope for the greatest age in the history of mankind--an age which I know can harness atomic energy for the welfare of man and not for his destruction."[11] Here is an expression, to be repeated again and again, of commingled hope and fear in the face of the awesome scientific achievement that harnessed the power of the atom.

In an address before the United Nations General Assembly on the peaceful uses of atomic energy in 1953, Dwight D. Eisenhower considered the perilous state of the United States-Soviet Union relations. Must we, he stated, forever confirm "the hopeless finality of a belief that the two atomic colossi are doomed malevolently to eye each other indefinitely across a trembling world"? And he added a prophetic note, one that has been conveniently ignored by many in the Reagan administration: "But let no one think that the expenditure of vast sums for weapons and systems of defense can guarantee absolute safety for the cities and citizens of any nation. The awful arithmetic of the atomic bomb does not permit of any such easy solution. Even against the most powerful defense, an aggressor in possession of the effective minimum number of atomic bombs for a surprise attack could probably place a sufficient number of his bombs on the chosen targets to cause hideous damage."[12]

Eisenhower's successor, John F. Kennedy, also addressed the General Assembly of the United Nations. The time was 1961 and the occasion was the death of Dag Hammarskjold, the revered Secretary-General of the UN from 1953 until his death in a plane crash in 1961. Kennedy used this occasion to comment on the death, not of one man but of civilization. "Today, every inhabitant of this planet must contemplate the day when this planet may no longer be habitable. Every man, woman and child lives under a nuclear sword of Damocles, hanging by the slenderest of threads, capable of being cut at any moment by accident or miscalculation or by madness. The weapons of war must be abolished before they abolish us."[13]

By 1964 this nation had a limited nuclear test ban treaty with the Soviet Union. Lyndon B. Johnson issued a statement on the reopening of an 18-nation Committee on Disarmament in Geneva on January 21, 1964. Noting that further steps must be taken, Johnson expressed United States determination "to reduce the risks of another worldwide war, a war in which the first hour might be measured in terms of how many hundreds of millions are killed." He proposed that "both sides stop all production of the fissionable material that is used in nuclear weapons. This country and the Soviet Union already have produced enough explosive force to equal 10 tons of TNT for every man, woman, and child on the face of the earth. We have already announced that we are cutting back our production. We are willing to shut down more plants if and when the Soviet Union does the same, plant by plant, with inspection on both sides."[14]

Richard Nixon was wont to define the U.S.-U.S.S.R. conflict

as one involving self-interests and spheres of influence. In a report to Congress on United States foreign policy for the 1970s, he opined that if "some nations define their security in a manner that means insecurity for other nations, then peace is threatened and the security of all is diminished. This obligation is particularly great for the nuclear superpowers on whose decisions the survival of mankind may well depend."[15]

After Nixon's departure from the Oval Office, Gerald R. Ford in 1976 addressed the nation on radio, in which he triumphantly proclaimed progress in peace. Working "from a position of strength," he said, "we have sought to reduce tensions in the world and to avert the threat of nuclear holocaust. Early in my administration, I met with Secretary Brezhnev in Vladiovostok to begin negotiations to limit nuclear armaments. Today those negotiations are 90 percent complete." However, later in that same address he insisted that "To preserve the peace, we must be willing to pay the price for a mighty military force."[16] The paradox that has informed the history of the arms race is reiterated in the conjunction of these statements.

At a White House reception for Pope John Paul II in 1979, Jimmy Carter affirmed the need to "wrest the fateful lightning of nuclear destruction from the hands of man. We must successfully conclude our nuclear arms agreement, and in this continuing effort we must find a way to end the threat of nuclear annihilation in every nation on Earth. The age of nuclear weaponry can either be long or short, as we choose."[17]

Commentary by current presidents is found in the Weekly Compilation of Presidential Documents (GS 4.114; Depository Item 577-A) until they are reprinted in the Public Papers series. Much of Reagan's energies during his first two years in office anent the nuclear peril have focused on the "growing threat to Western Europe which is posed by the continuing deployment of certain Soviet intermediate-range nuclear missiles." Naturally, we must counter with our deployment of land-based Cruise missiles and Pershing II missiles in the countries of our European allies. "The essence of U.S. nuclear strategy," Reagan stated in 1981, "is that no aggressor should believe that the use of nuclear weapons in Europe could reasonably be limited to Europe. Indeed it is the joint European-American commitment to share the burden of our common defense which assures the peace." [18]

Like his predecessors, Reagan acknowledges that "any use of nuclear weapons would have the most profound consequences. In a nuclear war, all mankind would lose. Indeed, the awful and incalculable risks associated with any use of nuclear weapons themselves serve to deter their use." Ah, this is the point at which the paradox of the nuclear arms race approaches absurdity. The consequences of actually using our nuclear arsenals are so "incalculable" that their sheer existence deters. But, by the same grisly logic, we must stockpile these weapons in greater and greater number to preserve the rationale of the irrational quest. Thus it is perfectly "rational" for Reagan to affirm that "the only answer to these (Soviet missiles pointed at Western Europe) is a comparable threat to Soviet threats, to Soviet targets; in other words, a deterrent preventing the use of these Soviet weapons by the counter-threat of a like response against their own territory."[19] Ergo, Western Europe must be turned into a nuclear fortress. It is no wonder that educators and health service personnel are discovering more and more children who have an apprehension that the world "could be annihilated by a chain of events that adults cannot control," a pervasive sense of what Yale University psychiatrist Robert Jay Lifton calls "radical futurelessness."[20] The nuclear theologians argue that greater risk means greater deterrence, that raising the stakes of a nuclear confrontation is the only way to insure that neither side will play. But when Soviet and NATO missiles are poised, millions of Europeans "huddled at ground zero will not even have time to find out whether those blips on their sensors indicate an enemy attack or an electronic malfunction. East and West will have only eight minutes grace, and war could be more likely than ever."[21]

Nevertheless, Reagan is clearly committed to what President Ford called a "mighty military force," if might can be expressed purely in dollar amounts. His five-year projections for military spending begin with $238 billion in fiscal year 1984 and rise to $377 billion in fiscal year 1988, for a quinquennial total of over $1.5 trillion. Personnel costs in these estimated expenditures are high, but a not insignificant amount will be used for the submarines, fighters, bombers, missiles and other instruments of war, many to be equipped with the most sophisticated nuclear weaponry that the ingenuity of the human mind can design.[22] With the production of each new weapon by the nuclear powers, this beautiful blue-green planet, the only world we know, is placed in greater jeopardy, and the words of Prospero in Shakespeare's luminous valedictory drama, seen in a new and terrifying context, haunt our consciousness:

> The cloud-capp'd towers, the gorgeous palaces,
> The solemn temples, the great globe itself,
> Yea, all which it inherit, shall dissolve;
> And, like this insubstantial pageant faded,
> Leave not a rack behind.

Civil Defense

While it is difficult to imagine how any nation could survive a nuclear holocaust, FEMA officials are responsible for the reification of this macabre abstraction. Because relatively optimistic scenarios are devised, the language of civil defense plans often assumes a sanguine, almost cheerful, cast. Thus an official of the old Office of Civil Defense (1961-1972) suggested that one of the benefits of a nuclear attack would be to "alleviate some of the factors leading to today's ecological disturbances that are due to current high-population concentrations and heavy industrial production."[23] Although verbal horrors of this sort are mercifully few, the typical euphoria of civil defense pronouncements engenders almost universal scorn and derision among the populace.

Nevertheless, any civil defense efforts concerning nuclear war must presuppose survival. The Reagan Administration in 1982 proposed a $4.2 billion, seven-year plan designed to minimize the effects of a nuclear assault. Speaking before a group of civil defense coordinators in Jackson, Wyoming, in September, 1982, FEMA administrator General Louis Giuffrida stated that the federal government is "legally and morally obligated to prepare a plan which can predictably increase the chance of survival for a significant number of American citizens."[24] Civil defense, of course, is not a new idea; many of us remember the schoolhouse drills of the 1950s and early 1960s "that had (children) diving under their desks against the day when a fireball seared the sky."[25] There was a time, too, when constructing backyard shelters was almost de rigueur. But these activities became largely dormant for two decades; attempts to revive them are now meeting with less than public enthusiasm.

Writing in the Spring, 1981, issue of Emergency Management, Drs. William K. Chipman and B. Wayne Blanchard try to state the case for civil defense planning. "Everyone agrees that a nuclear war could be an unparalleled disaster. But it need not be an unmitigated disaster. It is the responsibility of government to take those reasonable steps which can greatly mitigate, even though they cannot eliminate, the deaths and suffering that would result from a nuclear disaster."[26] The exercise in mitigation consists of two basic components: evacuation and shelter. I will confine my remarks to these points.

Evacuation

Evacuation, jocularly known as the "head-for-the-hills" approach, is called "crisis relocation" in federalese. Quite simply, it involves transporting those living in "high-risk areas" (places where there is a large concentration of people and strategically important areas like missile sites and airfields) to "host communities"--safer areas where nuclear weapons are less likely to be targeted. Plans drawn up over the years have achieved a fairly high degree of specificity. One checklist suggests that the relocatees bring with them not only the necessities of food, clothing, sanitation and medical supplies but also "important papers" such as social security cards, insurance policies, stocks and bonds, deeds, wills, savings accounts books, credit cards, and cash.

With 145 million Americans on the road, traffic is likely to be somewhat congested. Thus, "If you get caught in a traffic jam, turn off your engine, remain in your car, listen for official instructions, and be patient." If your car experiences mechanical difficulties or if you run out of gas, "move your car to the side of the road

The Social Prerogative 253

out of traffic lanes to allow traffic to continue. Service to stalled autos will be available during the evacuation period. Leave your hood up as a sign that you are stalled, and you will be assisted as soon as possible." All contingencies are accounted for in tranquil, unruffled prose. "If you have no private means of transportation, public transportation will probably be provided to move you to your reception area. If you are physically unable to get to transportation, make arrangements to be picked up and be transported to your reception area."[27] The instructions continue in this vein, the dreamlike serenity of a pleasant reverie, creating the impression that crisis relocation is an activity resembling nothing more than a holiday outing with its minor inconveniences and overheated automobile engines. "Crisis relocation," according to Drs. Chipman and Blanchard, "can greatly improve the odds for both individual and national survival. Analyses indicate that by the end of the first day, 60 to 70 percent of the total U.S. risk population could be evacuated; by the end of the second day, 80 to 90 percent; and by the end of the third day over 95 percent."[28] Thus do FEMA officials prophesy the successful evacuation of America in one-half of the hexahemeron, the six days required for the creation of heaven and earth, of the light and starry firmament, of fish and fowl and beasts and the lilies of the valley, of Adam and Maiden.

Shelter

Evacuation plans are based on a series of assumptions so optimistic that many federal, state and local officials are embarrassed when confronted by the media and skeptical anti-nuclear groups. The concept of shelter, however, has fared somewhat better. Perhaps this is due to intermittent accounts of a small number of citizens who in recent years have undertaken protective measures of their own. Calling themselves "survivalists," they have built little fortresses in remote areas of the country, filling their shelters or cellars with canned foods, medicines and guns. But for most people there will be neither time nor opportunity to proceed to shelters. Many believe that the idea of adequate shelter in a nuclear holocaust is as outrageous as the idea of evacuation on a large scale. Nevertheless, the feasibility of shelter is alive and well in certain Washington circles; one must give proponents of this method of surviving nuclear war their day in court.

Robert Scheer is a national reporter for the Los Angeles Times; a former editor of Ramparts magazine, he is a frequent contributor to magazines and has been nominated six times for a Pulitzer Prize in journalism. Thomas K. Jones, appointed by Ronald Reagan as Deputy Under Secretary of Defense for Research and Engineering, Strategic and Theater Nuclear Forces, is an outspoken advocate of the efficacy of shelters against nuclear attack. In an extraordinary interview with Jones, Scheer recorded the official's "celebration of the shovel and primitive shelters as the means to nuclear salvation." After reading Soviet civil defense manuals that advocated digging holes in the ground, Jones became an enthusiastic advocate of the method.

"If there are enough shovels to go around, everybody's going to make it," Jones said. "You can make very good sheltering by taking the doors off your house, digging a trench, stacking the doors about two deep over that, covering it with plastic so that rain water or something doesn't screw up the glue in the door, then pile dirt over it." Jones waxed particularly rhapsodic over the beneficent qualities of dirt. "You've got to be in a hole.... The dirt really is the thing that protects you from the blast as well as the radiation.... It protects you from the heat. You know, dirt is just great stuff.... It's the dirt that does it."[29]

Laurence Beilenson, author of The Treaty Trap and other books that have been published by right-wing presses, is on a first-name basis with Ronald Reagan. Differing with Jones's views on civil defense, Beilenson favors "underground skyscrapers" in lieu of evacuating American cities. As he told Scheer, "When the atom bomb was first invented we should have dispersed our population. We should have gone underground. We should be one story above, twelve underground."[30]

Others outside of government, like Jonathan Schell, have a different vision of shelters. Schell notes that the firestorm caused by a nuclear blast "renders shelters useless by burning up all the oxygen in the air and creating toxic gases, so that anyone inside the shelters is asphyxiated, and also by heating the ground to such high temperatures that the shelters turn, in effect, into ovens, cremating the people inside them."[31]

Official statements paint a hopeful picture of shelter living. "In most cases the fallout radiation level outside the shelter would decrease rapidly enough to permit people to leave the shelter within a few days." Indeed, "people soon might be able to leave shelter for a few minutes or for a few hours at a time in order to perform emergency tasks." As for survival, "enough food and water would be available after an attack to sustain our surviving citizens.... Most of the nation's remaining food supplies would be usable after an attack.... Water systems might be affected somewhat by radioactive fallout, but the risk would be small, especially if a few simple precautions were taken.... Milk contamination from fallout is not expected to be a serious problem after an attack.... In summary, the danger of people receiving harmful doses of fallout radiation through food, water or milk is very small."[32] But Schell offers quite another scenario. In a full-scale attack, he avers, "there would in all likelihood be no surviving communities ... everyone who failed to seal himself off from the outside environment for as long as several months would soon die of radiation sickness. Hence, in the months after a holocaust there would be no activity of any sort, as, in a reversal of the normal state of things, the dead would lie on the surface and the living, if there were any, would be buried underground." If Schell's vision of a nuclear holocaust appears unnecessarily harrowing, it seems at least closer to the potential power of the Bomb than the sunny statements of government functionaries who speak of nuclear conflict as if it were scarcely more threatening

The Social Prerogative 255

than the heartbreak of psoriasis. After all, we do have comprehensive scientific studies of the consequences of Hiroshima and Nagasaki. [33]

Plans to protect the artifacts of civilization and its denizens, whether by antimissile missiles, evacuation or shelter, partake of the Theater of the Absurd. As Otto Friedrich notes, "It is absurd ... for governments that spend billions of dollars on the weapons of destruction to spend almost nothing on defending their own citizens from attack. Bomb shelters are absurd, but the lack of bomb shelters is also absurd. The idea of evacuating major cities in a time of crisis is absurd, but if such evacuations may save millions of lives, then the absence of any serious evacuation plan is absurd." Moreover, to build defensive missiles or bomb shelters, to initiate large-scale "practice" evacuations, "is by definition provocative and threatening. It implies a dangerously increased readiness to fight, because it reduces, no matter how slightly, the absurdity of war. In absurdity, therefore, lies safety. That statement, too, is absurd."[34]

The Ideological Conflict

Our array of apocalyptic armaments, more dreadful than any Dr. Strangelove fantasy, is designed in theory to respond to a surprise attack. The memory of Pearl Harbor still remains strong. But for the Russians, too, the great wound left by modern history is surprise attack. The fierce march of the Germans in 1941 was as unexpected a catastrophe for the Soviet Union as the Japanese naval attack half a year later was for the United States. Democratic America and Marxist Russia abandoned their differences, fought a just war, and extirpated the moral cancer of Nazism. Those who have traveled in the Soviet Union return with a strong sense that the Russian people yet remember the horror of war.

But we cannot, we dare not, gainsay the immense differences between the superpowers. From the grotesque revelations of The Gulag Archipelago to the possible complicity of high Soviet officials in the attempted assassination of a Pope, there are powerful reasons to distrust Soviet intentions. Moreover, the Soviet system allows no public expression of anti-nuclear sentiment among the Russian people. Save for the solitary cry of the underground dissident, there is no evidence of a Soviet citizenry protesting the Bomb. There is no Union of Concerned Soviet Scientists, no Soviet Physicians for Social Responsibility, no Soviet Women's Action for Nuclear Disarmament. Thus the efforts of the people of the United States are blunted. While we have strong support to end the insanity of the arms race from the clergy, scientists, physicians, businessmen, parents, etc., there is no measurable counterforce to the Russian leadership, which remains as paranoid and obdurate as our leadership. Public opinion in the free countries must bear the burden of public pressure on all governments. But the silence of the people behind the Iron Curtain places our government at great risk in attempting any significant unilateral action, and it permits the hawks in the Administration and in the Congress to carry the day.

Despite the seemingly insurmountable ideological chasm that separates the United States and the Soviet Union, the contemplation of nuclear holocaust transcends all differences and all facile shibboleths like "Better dead than Red." Nuclear war must be perceived in eschatological terms. "The new metaphysics of war makes this configuration: nuclear bombs preside, in a dark, speculative way, over the human imagination of war. Nuclear is to conventional war what the monotheism of the avenging God was to the old amiably human and relatively harmless idolatries of polytheism. The wrath of God becomes the dread mushroom and megadeath and firestorm -- totality, cessation. It is not relative, like the old wars, but absolute, the utter blank of extinction."[35]

Unfortunately, there are countervailing influences to the dread of nuclear destruction, forces which seem to pose too great a technological temptation. Quite simply put, making the Bomb is so damned "cost-effective" for the superpowers and, indeed, for any nation with an advanced industrial capacity. Jack Ruina, an MIT engineering professor who has served on presidential science advisory committees and as an adviser to the National Security Council, and who was a former director of the Defense Department Advanced Research Projects Agency, stated the issue in this way: "What does it cost to make a bomb, delivered? $10 million? If for $10 million you can do $10 billion worth of damage, if you get a thousand-to-one ratio against you, then the defense has to be so fantastically good -- I'm talking about defense of cities. This was not the case before nuclear weapons." Ruina draws an analogy. "The Mount St. Helens eruption was the equivalent of a 10 megaton bomb in its single big explosion. It did $2 billion worth of damage, and it occurred in the middle of nowhere. With nuclear weapons, the superpowers can destroy a thousand times more than it costs to do the destruction." [36]

Figures like this cast grave doubts on all the civil defense plans hatched by FEMA and other government officials. The picture of people driving along on untouched roads and across bridges to a safe haven in the country summons a reaction best expressed in black humor. In 1982 a plan concocted by the United States Postal Service drew media attention as it was ridiculed by members of a House of Representatives Subcommittee on Postal Personnel and Modernization. The 300-page document set forth contingency plans for a "limited nuclear conflict." Among the fatuities were "about 2,000 emergency change-of-address forms" which have already been stocked in each post office except very small ones. "What good will that do?" asked one member of the subcommittee. "There will be no addresses, no streets, no blocks, no houses." The subcommittee wanted to know "how in the world the mail could be delivered with the destruction of the country's infrastructure," that pompous federalese word for roads and bridges. The postal officials who testified before

The Social Prerogative 257

the subcommittee lamely responded that "Our plans have to assume there would be something available for us. If there is not, there is nothing we can do."[37] Shortly after the press had their fun with this proposal, an anonymous wag penned the following piece of apposite doggerel. Entitled "The Armageddon Rag," it is to be sung to the tune of "Oh, What a Beautiful Morning."

> Oh, what a promise they made us,
> they swore that they never would fail.
> If the bomb hits some fine summer morning,
> you'll still get all your junk mail.
>
> All the houses will turn into rubble,
> all the ozone will turn into dew.
> But the mailmen will still do their duty,
> your phone bill will always get through.
>
> You might think this is all utter nonsense,
> you might think we're perverting the facts.
> But the post office says it's not fooling,
> and you'll still have to pay all your tax.[38]

Next Time, No Brains

In October, 1982, the National Conference of Catholic Bishops made public the proposed draft of a controversial letter on nuclear arms, the opening paragraph of which framed the issue in theological terms. "In the nuclear arsenals of the United States or the Soviet Union alone, there exists a capacity to do something no other age could imagine; we can threaten the created order. For people of faith this means we read the Book of Genesis with new awareness; the moral issue at stake in nuclear war involves the meaning of sin in its most graphic dimensions. Every sinful act is a confrontation of the creature and the Creator. Today the destructive potential of the nuclear powers threatens the sovereignty of God over the world He has brought into being. We would destroy His work."[39] But whether the universe was created by a deity or by a mysterious confluence of chance and necessity, it is one whose fundamental substance contains the energy with which we are able to extinguish ourselves. It is probably inevitable that, after millennia of scientific progress, we have "wrested from nature the power to make the world a desert or to make the deserts bloom."[40] But it would be hypocritical to charge the scientific community with sin or moral turpitude, for the scientific enterprise is inexorable, the search for truth; and it began, not with Einstein but with Euclid and Archimedes. Over the millennia, the awesome truth lay in waiting for us. Events obliged us to translate that truth in one terrible moment in the early morning hours at Alamogordo on July 16, 1945. "People were transfixed with fright at the power of the explosion. Oppenheimer was clinging to one of the uprights in the control room. A passage from the Bhagavad-Gita, the sacred epic of the Hindus, flashed into his mind."

> If the radiance of a thousand suns
> were to burst into the sky,
> that would be like
> the splendor of the Mighty One--

Yet, when the sinister and gigantic cloud rose up in the far distance over Point Zero, he was reminded of another line from the same source:

> I am become Death, the shatterer of worlds.

Sri Krishna, the Exalted One, lord of the fate of mortals, had uttered the phrase. But Robert Oppenheimer was only a man, into whose hands a mighty, a far too mighty, instrument of power had been given."[41]

That the achievement of the intellect, that great glory of the human species, should bring us to the certain possibility of destruction on a planetary scale prompted Ian McHarg to create a poignant fable: "The atomic cataclysm has occurred. The earth is silent, covered by a gray pall. All life has been extinguished save in one deep leaden slit, where, long inured to radiation, persists a small colony of algae. They perceive that all life but theirs has been extinguished and that the entire task of evolution must begin again-- some billions of years of life and death, mutation and adaptation, cooperation and competition, all to recover yesterday. They come to an immediate, spontaneous and unanimous conclusion: 'Next time, no brains.'"[42]

The Choice

In 1946 the United States exiled natives of the Bikini atoll so that nuclear-weapons tests could be conducted. From 1946 to 1958 this country detonated twenty-three atomic and hydrogen bombs over the atoll, an isolated group of islets lying some 2,500 miles south-west of Hawaii. "Nuclear explosions in the lagoon had vaporized three islets.... Radioactive waves had covered the islands at one point, killing off all animal life except one hardy variety of rats." In 1972, after a massive United States effort to restore the atoll to habitability, the Bikinians were allowed to return home. Six years later, however, "new radiological tests by American technicians showed higher-than-normal amounts of strontium, cesium and plutonium in the islanders' bodies from their eating food grown on the islands and fish caught in the lagoon. Once again they were forced to leave." Thus the Bikinians "have been shunted from island to island" in the sprawling Marshall Islands archipelago, "with little chance of returning anytime soon to their beloved atoll because of lingering radiation."[43]

Accordingly, what is one to make of an official government document that discusses radiation sickness brought on as the result of a nuclear attack? "Symptoms," the document says, "of radiation sickness (include) headache.... If the patient has headache ... give him one or two aspirin tablets every 3 or 4 hours (half a tablet for a child under twelve.)."[44]

I have deliberately juxtaposed the plight of the wandering Bikinians and the aficionados of the "aspirin solution" to demonstrate what is real and unreal about the nuclear colloquy. The authors of the document exist on a plane quite beyond irony. The treatment of the effects of nuclear war in the official literature as if it were just another emergency is itself a sickness--a disease of the soul, a moral malady.

The patent need for government to euphemize the full consequences of nuclear war is itself perilous; it results in a distortion of clarity of thought and the language by which that thought is conveyed. Thus, when President Reagan announced in November, 1982, that he had decided to "emplace 100 MX missiles ... in superhard silos in a closely-spaced basing mode at Francis E. Warren Air Force Base near Cheyenne, Wyoming," he referred to this new intercontinental ballistic missile system as "Peacekeeper."[45] Indeed, the convoluted syntax of "Nuketalk" is replete with exotic and bizarre words, phrases and acronyms. At this writing the MX basing system has not yet been resolved, but the issue has already spawned verbal indignities like "fratricide theory" and "DensePack" (called "Dunce-Pack" by critics of the scheme). MAD, the acronym for "mutual assured destruction," arose from the 1972 ABM Treaty with the Soviet Union, in which strategic balance insures that neither side is able to gain a decisive advantage by attacking first. NUTS, or "nuclear utilization target selection," characterizes the use of nuclear weapons against specific targets in limited-war situations. "Decaptation" refers to a nuclear strike targeted to destroy Soviet political and military leaders and their centers of command and communications. SIOP (pronounced "sigh-op") stands for our nation's doomsday plan for nuclear war--the Single Integrated Operation Plan--controlled by the President and executed by the Joint Chiefs of Staff. The gobbledegook of words and acronyms, especially those that are humorous, masks the enormity of nuclear holocaust; like the Newspeak of Orwell's Nineteen Eighty-Four, these pernicious expressions are designed to obscure the harsh reality they connote.

One could assemble a chrestomathy of passages denouncing the Gehenna of nuclear war, but a growing consensus indicates that time is running out and our future must be measured in deeds, not words. Unfortunately, redoubtable forces impel us toward the abyss. Behind the political leaders and generalissimos resides a bevy of lesser-known bespectacled consultants and technicians. War planning groups like the Committee on the Present Danger advise strategies to "increase the risk of nuclear war in order to keep peace.... They pay no heed to the mounting ground swell for a nuclear freeze. Public demonstrations do not deter them." Détente, according to these pundits, "is impossible because the USSR is incapable of change.... The military's central role in Soviet life makes it reach outward to maintain its power--international stability is a danger to the Soviet system because it would eliminate external tensions and focus attention on the need for internal reforms. The demand upon the military to hold the non-Russian nationalities in check by force will continue despite generational changes in Soviet leadership and efforts toward détente." Accordingly, the advisers "believe that until American policy takes this into account, it will be repeatedly frustrated as the Soviets protect and further their imperial interests."[46]

Zuckerman identifies another influence in the nuclear arms race, the quiet, almost anonymous technician. According to Zuckerman, "it is the man in the laboratory, not the soldier or sailor or airman, who at the start proposes that for this or that reason it would be useful to improve an old or devise a new nuclear warhead.... It is he, the technician, not the commander in the field, who starts the process of formulating the so-called military need. It is he who has succeeded over the years in equating, and so confusing, nuclear destructive power with military strength, as though the former were the single and sufficient condition of military success. The men in the nuclear weapons laboratories of both sides have succeeded in creating a world with an irrational foundation, on which a new set of political realities has in turn had to be built. They have become the alchemists of our times, working in secret ways that cannot be divulged, casting spells which embrace us all. They may never have been in battle, they may never have experienced the devastation of war; but they know how to devise the means of destruction."[47]

There is no doubt that the superpowers "hold fundamentally incompatible views of world order, the organization of society and the individual's role in it." Therefore, Russia and the United States will be engaged in a competitive struggle "for as far into the future as anyone can see." It is foolish to hope that we can "bring about the end of the Soviet system and erase all economic and political differences between our nations." However, thoughtful voices argue that we can both coexist while pursuing peaceful competition ... to forge a relationship that rechannels our competitiveness into peaceful and productive activities." An arms race in an attempt to "bludgeon Moscow into policy changes won't work and could be counterproductive." Instead, we "should give the Soviet Union a stake in peace, which we are best prepared to give through trade." The "carrot and the stick" analogy is useful in this context. "We have far more carrots that they do, and as long as they adhere to their flawed economic system, we always will." Moscow has a stake in increased trade, as we do. The carrots of trade and related peaceful devices will, in the long run, work far better than the sticks of nuclear armaments. Indeed, it was Richard Nixon who said recently: "We've got to get over our disillusionment with détente and put aside the notion that the Soviet Union is an outlaw nation and must be so treated."[48]

Beyond détente, peaceful coexistence, mutually beneficial trade, athletic competition, cultural and scholarly exchanges, even a nuclear weapons freeze, lies nuclear disarmament. At this point in the dialog, a chorus of voices sounds the familiar refrain: such a notion represents simple-minded idealism, fuzzy thinking, bleeding-heart sentimentality, Communist-inspired treachery. But is the alternative, the present condition, any less preposterous--the capacity of each side to destroy the inhabitants of the earth forty times over? In his moving jeremiad The Fate of the Earth, Jonathan Schell stated the choice: "Two paths lie before us. One leads to death, the other to life.... Either we will sink into the final coma and end it all, or, as I trust and believe, we will awaken to the truth of our peril, a truth as great as life itself, and, like a person who has swallowed a lethal poison but shakes off his stupor at the last moment and vomits the poison up, we will break through the layers of our denials, put aside our fainthearted excuses, and rise up to cleanse the earth of nuclear weapons."[49]

References

1. Comprehensive Study on Nuclear Weapons (New York: United Nations, 1981), p. 145.
2. Ibid.
3. U.S. News & World Report, December 6, 1982, p. 58.
4. Solly Zuckerman, Nuclear Illusion and Reality (London: Collins, 1982), p. 29.
5. Jonathan Schell, The Fate of the Earth (New York: Knopf, 1982), pp. 36, 47-50.
6. The first atomic bomb was detonated at the Trinity test site, near Alamorgordo, New Mexico, on July 16, 1945.
7. 43 FR 41943, 92 Stat. 3788, 5 USC 101 et seq.
8. Weekly Compilation of Presidential Documents, April 24, 1981, p. 447; see also OMB Press Release 82-25, "Reform 88: Elimination, Consolidation and Cost Reduction of Government Publications" (October 6, 1982).
9. 44 FR 44790-96, which includes a useful FEMA organization chart at page 44796.
10. See Title 44 of the Code of Federal Regulations (October 1, 1981), pp. 429-433.
11. Public Papers ... Harry S. Truman, 1946, pp. 245-46.
12. Public Papers ... Dwight D. Eisenhower, 1953, pp. 816-17.
13. Public Papers ... John F. Kennedy, 1961, p. 620.
14. Public Papers ... Lyndon B. Johnson, Book I, 1963-64, pp. 172-73. The "ten tons of TNT for every man, woman, and child" may reflect the Johnsonian penchant for hyperbole. However, at ratios of the magnitude of 3 or 10, the results would be the same.
15. Public Papers ... Richard Nixon, 1970, p. 122.
16. Public Papers ... Gerald R. Ford, Book III, 1976-77, p. 2762.
17. Public Papers ... Jimmy Carter, Book II, 1979, p. 1831.
18. Weekly Compilation of Presidential Documents, October 26, 1981, p. 1181.
19. Weekly Compilation of Presidential Documents, November 23, 1981, p. 1275.

20. "Kids with Nuclear Jitters," Newsweek, October 11, 1982, p. 117; See also Dr. Helen Caldicott, "Growing Up Afraid: The 37th Summer of the Bomb," Family Weekly, August 8, 1982, pp. 4-7.
21. Newsweek, January 31, 1983, p. 14.
22. The New York Times (city edition), February 1, 1983, p. A17.
23. Schell, The Fate of the Earth, p. 7.
24. Riverton Ranger (Wyoming), September 13, 1982, p. 9.
25. Newsweek, April 26, 1982, p. 31.
26. William K. Chipman and B. Wayne Blanchard, "Civil Defense and the Medical Consequences of Nuclear War," Emergency Management (Spring 1981), p. 3.
27. U.S. Defense Civil Preparedness Agency, Protection in the Nuclear Age (Washington: Department of Defense, February 1977), pp. 51, 54-55.
28. Chipman and Blanchard, p. 5.
29. Robert Scheer, With Enough Shovels: Reagan, Bush and Nuclear War (New York: Random House, 1982), pp. 18-19, 23.
30. Ibid., pp. 101-02.
31. Schell, The Fate of the Earth, p. 49.
32. Protection in the Nuclear Age, pp. 7-9.
33. Schell, The Fate of the Earth, pp. 5, 60.
34. Otto Friedrich, "The Bomb ... And Beyond," Playboy 29 (September 1982): 192.
35. Lance Morrow, "The Metaphysics of War," Time, May 17, 1982, p. 88.
36. Scheer, With Enough Shovels...., pp. 81-82.
37. The New York Times (city edition), August 13, 1982, p. A26.
38. Albany Times-Union, August 15, 1982, p. B4.
39. The New York Times (city edition), October 26, 1982, p. A20.
40. Adlai Stevenson, Speech, Hartford, Connecticut, September 18, 1952.
41. Robert Jungk, Brighter than a Thousand Suns: A Personal History of the Atomic Scientists (New York: Harcourt Brace Jovanovich, 1958), p. 201.
42. From Design with Nature, published for the American Museum of Natural History by the Natural History Press, 1969.
43. U.S. News & World Report, October 18, 1982, pp. 48-50.
44. Protection in the Nuclear Age, pp. 57, 68.
45. Weekly Compilation of Presidential Documents, November 29, 1982, p. 1515.
46. Jerrold L. Schecter and Leona P. Schecter, "The War Planners," Esquire, January 1982, p. 69.
47. Zuckerman, Nuclear Illusion and Reality, pp. 105-06.
48. Donald M. Kendall, "Give Moscow 'Carrots,'" The New York Times (city edition), February 9, 1983, p. A31.
49. Schell, The Fate of the Earth, p. 231.

THE THREAT TO LIBRARY CIRCULATION RECORDS:

A CASE STUDY*

Richard Rubin

The call came on April 11, 1983. The Office of the Summit County Prosecutor telephoned the Akron-Summit County Public Library in Akron, Ohio, to request the circulation records of an inmate residing in the county jail. The prosecutor was informed that based on the library's "Confidentiality of Circulation Records Policy" the circulation records could not be released. Two hours later, the library received a subpoena demanding that it produce the requested records.

On the morning of April 12, 1983, the Assistant Prosecutor arrived with a process server to obtain the records requested in the subpoena. The Assistant Prosecutor was informed that the library could not comply with the subpoena at that time and that a motion would be filed in court to quash the subpoena.

Five hours later, the process server returned to the library and served the Assistant Director and the Library Director with a court order demanding their appearance in court in ten days to show why they should not be held in contempt of court for impeding a criminal investigation.

Within a 24 hour period, the library had become subject to the investigative and enforcement powers of the county prosecutor, normally its legal defender. While adhering to ALA and internal library policy, the administrators of the library had seemingly changed from law-abiding citizens and now faced contempt of court citations and possible jail terms.

When a library receives a request for circulation records from a governmental or investigative agency, a constellation of issues immediately arises. Many libraries may find themselves unprepared to deal with these issues in the initial, pressure-filled moments when the request comes.

*Reprinted by permission of the author and publisher from Library Journal, 109 (September 1, 1984) 1602-1606. Published by R. R. Bowker Co. (a Xerox company). Copyright © 1984 by Xerox Corporation.

Library policy

An orderly response to a request for circulation records requires that the board, administration, and staff know the adopted policy of their library on the confidentiality of such records. When an established policy is communicated to the staff prior to a request for circulation records, the chance that a staff member might comply with a request which the administration or board would resist is diminished.

In Akron, the library had adopted, with minor modifications, the ALA policy on the confidentiality of circulation records. The policy was communicated to all staff and supervisors on numerous occasions. The policy, as modified, is as follows:

> The Akron-Summit County Public Library specifically recognizes that its circulation records and other records identifying the names of library users with specific materials are confidential in nature. No such records shall be made available to any agency of state, federal or local government, or to any individual not specifically authorized by the Librarian-Director for legitimate business purposes, except pursuant to such process, order, or subpoena as may be authorized under the authority of, and pursuant to, federal, state, or local law relating to civil, criminal, or administrative discovery procedures or legislative investigatory power.
> Upon receipt of such process, order, or subpoena, the library's officers will consult with their legal counsel to determine if such process, order, or subpoena is in proper form and if there is a showing of good cause for its issuance in a court of competent jurisdiction. If the process, order, or subpoena is not in proper form or if good cause has not been shown, the library will insist that such defects be cured.

Although the policy on circulation records is directly applicable to this situation, other library policies may have implications for the protection of readers or viewers in the library. Such ALA policies and documents as the Freedom to Read Statement, the Freedom to View Statement, the Policy on Governmental Intimidation, the Library Bill of Rights, the Resolution on Prisoners' Right to Read, and Administrative Policies and Procedures Affecting Access to Library Resources and Services, may directly or indirectly influence the library's decision on whether or not to comply with a request or subpoena.

The law and the prosecutor

Even if your library has adopted all of these ALA policies, they are simply the internal policies of the library and have no legal standing. This does not mean that they are useless. It means that while the library may be upholding broadly-accepted First Amendment values, the prosecutor may be using specific local and state statutes to procure the circulation records. In Akron, the prosecutor cited the Ohio Public Records Act. This act, which is based on the Federal Freedom of Information Act, implies that all records kept by a public institution are open to the public unless specifically exempted by state statute. In Ohio, library records are not exempted. According to the ALA Office of Intellectual Freedom, only 21 states have enacted exemptions for library records.[1]

Apart from the Ohio Public Records Act, the Prosecutor's Office is vested with specific powers to investigate criminal activity. These powers are considerable and may even supersede protections which have been explicitly written into public records acts for library circulation records. In November 1979, for example, a prosecutor requested circulation records from the Des Moines Public Library, Iowa. The library refused and the case reached Iowa's Supreme Court. The court ruled that even in the face of an express exemption in the Iowa statute, the specific powers of the prosecutor overcame this exemption and the court ruled in favor of the prosecutor.[2]

Refusing the request of a prosecutor or any investigative agency may subject the library to formal attempts to obtain the information desired. By issuing a subpoena, the prosecutor demands that the library produce the records identified in the subpoena. The prosecutor has no obligation to offer the reasons for his demand or to provide any additional information to the library. It should also be noted that individuals can be named in the subpoena and the named individuals are subject to criminal penalties for failing to abide by the subpoena. A subpoena is considered an important part of the legal arsenal for investigating criminal offenses and carries with it a sense of compulsion backed by judicial enforcement powers.

"Show cause" orders

Refusal to comply with a subpoena is unlikely to be greeted by the prosecutor with enthusiasm. As a next step, the prosecutor may ask a judge to issue a court order for those individuals named in the subpoena to appear for a public hearing to explain why they have not produced the requested records. This order is called a "show cause" order. If the library fails to convince a judge that it has good cause to resist the subpoena, and if the library refuses the judge's order to produce the records, it will likely result in the individual(s) named in the "show cause" order being found in contempt of court. Contempt of court may result in a jail sentence of indeterminate length.

Both ALA policy and Akron's specific policy require that the prosecutor show "good cause" for the circulation record request. In order to reach this point, the library was, in essence, required to resist the subpoena to force the prosecutor to explain the reasons for his request. The hearing, therefore, represented two forces: the prosecutor asking the library to show "good cause" for refusing to comply; the library asking the prosecutor to show "good cause" as to why such records should be made available. From a purely legal point of view, however, the fate of the library rests with the judge. "Good cause" is whatever the judge determines it is.

Preparing the defense

The process of making a decision on the release of circulation records involves numerous variables which must be carefully weighed. The first step in the process is to make sure that competent legal counsel is available.[3] The legal issues are complex and few librarians are sufficiently knowledgeable to weigh them and their consequences in the absence of experienced attorneys. Although the final decision may be based on philosophical rather than legal grounds, knowledge of the legal aspects of the case is invaluable.

The legal counsel can, for example, explain the meaning of legal instruments and technical actions; explain the exact process by which the library may appeal a subpoena or court order; and provide a contact point with the prosecutor and judge for clarification, negotiation and, possibly, settlement of the controversy. The legal counsel can explain the penalties for noncompliance; review the existing case law and assess the chances for winning an appeal; review the consequences of compliance or appeal in terms of the library's ability to protect circulation records in the future or liability to the institution if privacy rights are violated; provide a defense of the library in a court of law; and provide legal advice to the librarian(s) who become vulnerable to fine or incarceration.

It is also important to note that the information process works both ways. Even competent counsel may not be conversant with library issues. It is important that a library be prepared to educate its counsel on the professional character of a circulation records controversy. To this end, the Akron administration prepared a notebook for each attorney which summarized and elucidated the philosophical and legal grounds for refusing to release circulation records. The notebook contained the following items in the following order:

1) A chronology of events up to the point the attorneys entered the case;

2) Policies adopted by the Board of Trustees of the library; Confidentiality of Circulation Records Policy, the "Library Bill of Rights," and the Freedom to Read Statement;

3) Other related ALA policies: the Resolution on Prisoner's Right to Read, the Policy on Confidentiality of Library Records, the Administrative Policies and Procedures Affecting Access to Library Resources and Services, Restricted Access to Library Materials, and ALA's Policy on Governmental Intimidation;

4) Copies of pertinent Ohio laws: the Ohio Public Records Act, the Powers of Boards of Library Trustees, and an Attorney General's Opinion on public records in Ohio;

5) Three pertinent law articles: "Libraries, Librarians, and First Amendment Freedoms" by Robert O'Neil; "Constitutional Law: Individual's Right to Disclosural Privacy As Limited by the Public Records Act" by George Hays III; and "Surveillance of Individual Reading Habits: Constitutional Limitations on Disclosure of Library Borrower Lists" by Mark Wilson.[4]

By providing this material to the attorneys the administration formed a common foundation for discussing the critical issues behind the library's reluctance to comply with a subpoena or court order.

Involving the board

There is little doubt that a matter as serious as the potential incarceration of the library director requires the concentrated attention of the library board. It is best to assume that the board members, although supportive, might also require a review of the particular philosophical and constitutional issues surrounding a circulation records dispute. Consequently, the materials and information provided to the attorneys must also be provided to the board members. Before meeting with the board, however, it may be necessary to check with the state "sunshine laws" to ensure that meetings with the board to discuss the circulation records issue can be private.

During meetings with the board, members must be free to ask questions and to express their misgivings so that the director is able to assess the degree of support that will be available. It is also important that counsel be present to answer all questions concerning legal issues that may arise.

There is little doubt that a strong relationship of trust is important between the library director and the board in such a controversy. The pressure of impending court actions, and the potential for public exposure and debate require clear internal communications and decisions that are arrived at jointly with full discussion of the possible consequences of the actions taken.

Obtaining the facts

Communication between the prosecutor, judge, and library may be established prior to a public court appearance. In Akron, legal counsel forged a vital link in this communication process. Although the prosecutor's office was reluctant to provide specific information, various pertinent facts did come to the attention of the library: 1) The inmate was charged with numerous criminal offenses including rape. 2) The inmate, during commission of some of these crimes, quoted specific ideas associated with well known people or religious movements. 3) The prosecutor was specifically interested in material the inmate requested on Gandhi, Occultism, François Villon, Christianity, and Islam.

Because the circulation records requested by the prosecutor were for a period of time during which the inmate was already incarcerated, the library surmised that the circulation records were not direct evidence in the commission of a particular crime. Rather the records were being used to corroborate the fact that the inmate held certain beliefs or interests. The library also determined that the case involved very serious criminal offenses and that the prosecutor had, at least, ostensible if oblique, grounds for wanting to see the inmate's library requests.

The library's attorneys learned that the prosecutor considered the evidence important and would seek "jail terms" for the individuals named in the subpoena if they refused to comply.

Aside from the facts available on the criminal case, it was also necessary for the library to obtain the facts concerning the circulation records which were the subject of the subpoena. To this end, the library director obtained the actual circulation records in question. In addition, because the jail service used a unique circulation system, a detailed account of how the circulation records were created, handled, and maintained was also obtained.

Public relations

Court orders and court appearances are, of course, public matters. As such, they may become subject to media coverage. The public relations impact on a library's image in a circulation records controversy is significant and unpredictable.

The impact will vary, depending on which alternative the library chooses. The decision as to who one defines as the "public" with which one is concerned will also influence the results. The library could be viewed as a defender of the First Amendment or it may be perceived as an obstructor of justice, particularly in a case involving a serious crime.

The public relations officer must be involved from the beginning in the deliberations on the issues. In this way, if a public statement is required, the officer has the fullest possible understanding. The role of a public relations officer in an intellectual freedom controversy is really two-fold: to help assess the potential public relations impact for the board and administrators' decisions and to explain to the public the underlying reasons for the library's decisions.

There is always the danger that the principles of intellectual freedom may be sacrificed to image. Because a library depends on levies and taxpayers to maintain library service, the library's image certainly has a tangible significance. Nonetheless, public relations, like all aspects of library service, exists to support, not corrupt, the principles of free and open access to library materials.

In a real sense, the notion of the "public" in this type of controversy can also be extended to the library staff. Staff members may vary significantly in their understanding of the library's relationship to First Amendment issues. Opinions may differ among the staff as to the correct course of action and many of these opinions may be formed on the basis of limited and unreliable information. The public relations officer must provide clear instruction to the staff members to make no comments to the press or public concerning the case. If procedures governing the staff's relationship with the media are not already a part of library policies, then a memo clearly stating the expectations of the administration in this area is advisable. Some aspects of the deliberations must remain confidential, but the staff should certainly be informed of the general nature of the controversy, the legal actions taken, and the reasons for taking them.

Challenging the subpoena

Underlying the deliberations of the Akron's Board and Administration was a strong commitment to protecting the First Amendment rights of the library user. There was a concomitant concern that turning over the records would set an unhealthy precedent which might encourage additional requests from law enforcement agencies or even private citizens or groups. As a consequence, most of the library's deliberative time was committed to finding lawful and effective means of resisting the subpoena. Basically, the library had two avenues of defense. It could argue that substantive legal and constitutional issues would be raised in complying with the subpoena. It could also argue that there were technical grounds for refusing to comply.

The chances for success

The Board, Administration, and legal counsel agreed that a request for circulation records was of legitimate First Amendment concern especially if patrons became hesitant to read or view certain materials because they feared public exposure or censure. However, it was also realized that the court would attempt to balance the degree to which First Amendment rights were affected with the need for a prosecutor to perform his obligation to investigate and prosecute criminal offenses.

At least two issues worked against the successful use of such a First Amendment defense in Akron's case. First, the case involved the unusual circumstance of an inmate in jail. It seemed unlikely that the judge would be convinced that turning over the inmate's circulation record would deter the average citizen from checking out library materials. Second, the case involved very serious criminal offenses. It again seemed unlikely that the judge would interfere in the evidence-gathering process on the basis of a hypothetical projection that library use would be curtailed. As a consequence, legal counsel expressed little confidence that the library would win its case on these grounds.

The library could alternatively argue that the inmate's right to privacy was being violated. Counsel pointed out that the library would be required to argue that the inmate had an "expectation of privacy" when he requested the library materials. Although in the normal library setting this argument could be effectively made, the setting in the jail was substantially different. The inmate wrote his book requests and reading interests on a form and handed it to jail personnel. It was the jail personnel that transferred the form to library staff. The written requests had the inmate's name on them and were open to view. Under these circumstances, it would be very difficult to argue that the inmate assumed his requests were private.

Finally, the library could argue that circulation records are not public records as defined in the Ohio Public Records Act. However, a 1980 Ohio Attorney General's Opinion on the Ohio Public Records Act stated in part: "Unless made confidential by law [italics mine] all records maintained by a governmental agency that are necessary to the agency's execution of its duties and responsibilities are public records..."[5]

As noted earlier, no provision protecting the confidentiality of circulation records is present in Ohio law, and, certainly, the records were being used in the "execution of its duties" to provide library service to the county jail. It appeared, therefore, that arguments concerning the Ohio Public Records Act were destined to fail.

Challenges on technical grounds

The library could challenge the subpoena arguing that the request was not specific enough, or that the subpoena was incorrectly written. The lack of specificity in the request was of particular concern because the library wanted to prevent a "fishing expedition" by the prosecutor into the general reading habits of library patrons.

Counsel was quick to point out that the resolution of technical problems, such as a misspelled title, even a narrowing of the request for the records, all could be accomplished very quickly by the judge at the time of the court hearing. This approach, therefore, provided little assistance even in delaying the hearing. Although these legal maneuvers might have temporarily kept the Administrators out of jail, it did not eliminate the fact that if the library lost its appeal, the impending jail sentence of the court would have to be served.

Consequences of court appeals

Based on conversations between library counsel and the judge, it was predicted that the library would not receive a sympathetic ruling on the constitutional issues. Acknowledging the likelihood that the library would lose at the "show cause" hearing, and that the director and assistant director might be sentenced to jail, it was necessary to identify the possible actions that the library's attorneys could take in appealing an order to turn over the circulation records. The attorneys pointed out that the Des Moines Public Library had already appealed its case to the Iowa Supreme Court and lost. The attorneys noted that the Iowa case was stronger than Akron's case in several respects including the fact that the circulation records requested were not for one person, but for any persons who took out books in a certain call number. Thus, many innocent parties were involved in the investigation.

In addition, the material requested was not evidence in a criminal prosecution because no individual had yet been arrested. Rather, it was merely for a general investigation. It was felt that, should the Des Moines case be appealed, the U.S. Supreme Court would more likely act to protect circulation records in these circumstances rather than in one in which prosecution of a heinous crime was imminent.

Although the process of appeal increases the opportunity to have a favorable ruling, it is important to remember that as the appeals reach higher levels in the judicial system, the applicability of the ruling extends over greater and greater geographic area. If, for example, Akron were to appeal to the Ohio Supreme Court and the court ruled that Akron's circulation records were public records, that ruling would apply to all public libraries in the state. Notwithstanding the opinion of the Ohio Attorney General, it was still possible that in a future and stronger case, the library could obtain a sympathetic court ruling extending at least partial protection to circulation records. Compliance with the subpoena in this particular case would localize the threat to circulation records rather than jeopardize libraries throughout the state.

Making the decision

Based on the facts in the case, the attorney's dim assessment of the library's success in court and the potential for further damage to the privacy of circulation records throughout Ohio, the library decided, with considerable reluctance, to comply with the subpoena. It was necessary, therefore, to make attempts to minimize any undesirable consequences that compliance with the subpoena could create. It seemed clear, based on the attorney's observations, that neither the judge nor the prosecutor would relish the idea of sentencing the administrators of the library to jail and that they would respond positively to reasonable suggestions from the library concerning the content of a court order to turn over the circulation records.

The library had three major concerns: 1) ensuring that the prosecutor was more specific concerning what records he desired; 2) obtaining the recognition from the court and prosecutor that there is substantial constitutional support for a policy of confidentiality of circulation records; and 3) ensuring that compliance with the subpoena will have no precedential value if future requests were to arise.

A draft of a court order which dealt with these concerns was provided by the administrators, board, and counsel to the judge and the Prosecutor's Office. With their approval, the following language became the substance of the court order:

> The court recognizes the importance of the claim of the Akron-Summit County Public Library that its circulation records are confidential. The Court further recognizes that the First Amendment and privacy claims raised by the Akron-Summit County Public Library are substantial.
> Based upon the agreement of the prosecutor and counsel for the Akron-Summit County Public Library, photocopies of the following documents are ordered to be produced:
> "All lists of books requested by John Smith for the period February 17, 1983 to the present which relate to the following topics: Gandhi, Occultism, François Villon, Christianity and Moslemism."
> Any information in documents produced which does not relate to any of those five categories may be whited out or otherwise obliterated so that Mr. Smith's other book requests will not be revealed.
> Given the extraordinary circumstances involved in this request, the order to the Akron-Summit County Public Library requiring that these records be produced is of no precedential value in future litigation involving the confidentiality of library circulation records. [6]

A lingering uneasiness

By conforming to ALA and local policy on the confidentiality of circulation records, delaying compliance, and demanding a hearing, the library achieved concessions which would not otherwise have resulted. Perhaps most important was the recognition by the court that substantial First Amendment and privacy claims support a confidentiality of circulation records policy. These results were not, however, achieved without a good deal of time, emotional drain on the participants, and money. [7] The absence of an exemption for library circulation records in the Ohio Public Records Act created serious problems for the library in its attempt to protect the reading and viewing habits of library patrons.

There is, also, an inevitable and lingering uneasiness which will forever be associated with this event; a feeling that the principles of free speech were, to some degree, compromised because the legal system failed to fully accommodate the rights of individuals to seek out the ideas of their choosing without governmental intrusion.

The Social Prerogative 273

Epilogue

Early in May, the inmate went on trial in the criminal courts of Summit County. The defendant was charged with aggravated robbery, kidnapping, and rape. The victims testified that the defendant discussed religion with them and mentioned Gandhi. The library director testified at the trial verifying that the record given to the prosecutor was, in fact, the circulation record in question. During the trial, the defendant claimed that he was not subject to earthly laws and refused to defend himself or permit his court-appointed lawyer to defend him. The jury deliberated for two hours. On May 10, 1983, the defendant was convicted on 18 criminal charges. He was sentenced to six years on two robbery charges and to 110 to 385 years on the remaining charges. [8]

On July 15, 1983, the U.S. Supreme Court refused to hear the appeal of the Des Moines Public Library. [9]

References

1. American Library Association, Office of Intellectual Freedom, Newsletter on Intellectual Freedom, January 1984, p. 5.
2. Public Library Board of Trustees of Des Moines v. Dan L. Johnston, Polk County Attorney and Gerald Shanahan, Chief, DCI, State of Iowa, 1981. Because of this ruling, the American Library Association is recommending that laws exempting circulation records include a section which provides that records can only be subpoenaed if a "compelling reason" can be demonstrated by the prosecutor. This places a much greater burden on the part of the prosecutor to show why the circulation records are necessary.
3. When a library is confronted with an intellectual freedom controversy, there are several organizations associated with the American Library Association that can be contacted for both legal advice and financial assistance. Explanations for the purpose of each of these organizations can be found in the Office of Intellectual Freedom Memorandum, July 1983.
4. Robert O'Neil, "Libraries, Librarians and First Amendment Freedoms," Human Rights 4 (1975): 295-312. George Hays III, "Constitutional Law: Individual's Right to Disclosural Privacy As Limited by the Public Records Act," Stetson Law Review 10 (1981): 370-395. Mark K. Wilson, "Surveillance of Individual Reading Habits: Constitutional Limitations on Disclosure of Library Borrower Lists," American University Law Review 30 (1981): 275-331.
5. Ohio Attorney General's Opinion, 80-096.
6. Order from Judge Reece, Case No. CR 83-02-0232.
7. Total cost of attorney's fees exceeded $2,950.
8. Akron Beacon Journal, May 10, 1983, p. C.1.
9. Publishers Weekly, July 15, 1983, p. 13.

SPREADING THE WORD:

THE BILLION DOLLAR CHRISTIAN BOOK INDUSTRY*

Audrey Eaglen

An astute and dedicated follower of The New York Times Book Review "Bestsellers" column may have noted an unusual entry in the hardcover bestseller list on September 11, 1983. The nonfiction title popped up, in fifth place no less, and just as quickly went off the list in the next issue of NYTBR; but that is not what made the title unusual. What did is the fact that it was published by Thomas Nelson Publishers, a religious publishing house which claims to be the "world's leading Bible publisher," and produces such giants for the bible-buying world as The Open Bible, The New King James Version, and The Good News Bible, huge sellers all. The book which made the list in The New York Times Book Review, however, was not a bible, but a self-help book called Tough Times Never Last But Tough People Do, by Robert H. Schuller, a radio/TV evangelist whose weekly programs claim a listening/viewing audience in the millions.

Schuller's book exemplifies the "new breed" of religious books being published by a little-known (to many Americans and, if my experience in speaking to groups all over the U.S. is any indication, practically unknown to most librarians) segment of the publishing world: the Christian book publishing industry, an industry which in 1982 reached the status of a billion dollar business--no small potatoes in anyone's book.

Religious books have been published in the United States from colonial times on. The first printing press to appear in the colonies was brought from England by the Reverend Jose Glover in 1638 and set up in Cambridge, Massachusetts. In 1640 Glover's press produced The Whole Booke of Psalmes, which quickly became a bestseller not only in the colonies but in the mother country as well, and went into a number of editions. And when other colonial printers set themselves up in business, religious/liturgical tracts were their stock in trade; in fact, Cotton Mather in 1713 sought (and failed) to have enacted a law that would prevent sellers of books from selling any but "books of piety" to villagers and farmers. When Mathew Carey, the first important publisher in the new United States, set up

---

*Reprinted by permission from Collection Building, Winter 1984, pp. 48-52.

The Social Prerogative 275

shop in 1790 in Philadelphia, the first two books he produced were a Douay (Roman Catholic) and a Protestant bible, both of which were successful enough to enable him to begin publishing non-religious books by American and British writers. His star salesperson in the field, a "hawker," or one who traveled to outlying areas to sell books to farmers and others who lived on the frontier, was a fellow known as Parson Mason Locke Weems, who wore a preacher's outfit on his sales calls, ostensibly to inspire the customers' trust and encourage them to accept his authority as to which books they should buy.

Joshua B. Lippincott set himself up as a publisher in 1836 and specialized in religious books so successfully that he became known as "the Napoleon of the book trade." Other publishers such as Harper Brothers (now Harper & Row) followed Carey, and while most of them, like Carey, branched out into general publishing, the publishing of religious books was (and in the case of Harper & Row, among others, still is) an important part of their business, so much so that religious books dominated publishing well into the 19th century.

It was not until after the Civil War, however, that religious books began to be published by companies that specialized in that field. One of the first of these was Fleming H. Revell of Chicago, who, in 1869, began to publish a religious newspaper and soon branched out into publishing sermons and tracts in book form; among his most successful titles were the works of a popular evangelist of the time, Dwight L. Moody, whose books were bestsellers of the period. Another religious publishing house established during this era was the Morehouse Publishing Company, later renamed Abingdon-Cokesbury Press, whose avowed purpose was "to encourage the writing of distinguished books in the broad field of evangelical Christianity," and a spate of others soon followed, many of which are still in existence today.

But the modern Christian publishing industry is a far cry from what it was in the nineteenth and the first half of the twentieth centuries. No longer is title output restricted to tract and treatise, or learned exegesis of scriptural texts. In fact, while Christian book publishers still see their primary role as evangelistic, or one of preaching the gospel and converting the unconverted, many of the books they produce today can only remotely or indirectly be interpreted as "evangelistic" in the strict sense.

A look at the four-color ads of Bookstore Journal, a 200 (or more) page, glossy paper journal issued monthly by the Christian Booksellers Association, reveals ads for such titles as Great Composers and Their Influence and Dream Thief (a science fiction novel), published by Crossway Books; Love's Silent Song, described as a frontier romance, and a whole series of "Rhapsody Romances" (Harvest House); Heroes of the NFL (Here's Life Publishers); Festive Breads of Christmas (Herald Press); Making TV Work for Your Family (Bethany House); and even one called The Messies Manual; The Procrastinator's Guide to Good Housekeeping (Fleming H. Revell).

Clearly, while most of the religious houses' titles to deal directly with religion in one form or another, many of these same houses are branching out into the secular, even if it is with only positive, "up-beat" inspirational and self-help titles. That there is a market for such books is attested to by the growth of the industry: from a $250 million business in 1970 to today's present billion dollar a year level. The growth of the Christian book industry is shown by responses to a questionnaire sent out to 32 of the top religious publishers a year ago, as reported in Publishers Weekly. In 1981, those 32 publishers (of the more than one hundred in the business) did more than $360 million in business. In 1982, this climbed to $390 million, and projections for sales by 1987 indicate that they will reach an annual volume of $680 million.

For the most part, the books produced by the Christian book publishers are sold through approximately 6,000 religious bookstores throughout the United States, of which about half belong to an organization known as the Evangelical Christian Publishers Association (ECPA), an organization whose "roots go back 10 years, to a Minneapolis booksellers convention when several religious publishers decided that they weren't getting the attention they deserved [because] the large chains ignored them, the media didn't understand them [and] the National Book Awards didn't even recognize religious books."[1] Furthermore, the publishers themselves recognized that they did not really understand their market and thus were probably not marketing their products in the most effective ways.

As a result of that meeting, the ECPA was born, and now boasts of some 50 member publishing houses. Its function is to bring a degree of professionalism to the Christian publishing business, and this is accomplished through ECPA's research, consumer profiling, trend monitoring, member surveys, and whatever else is necessary. In that sense it is similar to the Association of American Publishers (AAP), with the fundamental differences being in the ECPA's size and its adherence to a nine-point "Statement of Faith," which affirms the Christian commitment of the ECPA members. How well the ECPA has done in its decade of existence is shown first by the incredible growth of the industry in a decade when other areas of publishing were bemoaning the effects of cuts in federal money, a series of recessionary periods, and generally flat sales. Second, and perhaps even more telling, is the fact that the large chain bookstores have begun to expand their religious book sections to sell more Christian titles, and the nation's major book wholesalers now routinely stock them--not to mention the fact that both Publishers Weekly and Library Journal currently devote almost entire issues on a regular basis to religious books.

The ECPA's executive director, Ted Andrews, was quoted recently in PW as defining the association's goal for the 1980's as "reaching out and expanding the market to the secular audience," a goal which seems highly likely given the progress that has been mentioned above. But one aspect of the secular market which remains largely untapped by the ECPA or Christian book publishing in general is the library market; only a few of the hundreds of Christian titles published in the United States each year ever appear on library shelves. Why?

In the first place, much of the fault lies with the religious book publishers themselves. Several years ago, as president of the Young Adult Services Division of ALA, I proposed a program for the San Francisco Annual Conference, dealing with religious publishing, and wrote to dozens of religious houses asking them for catalogs, samples for display, etc. The response was overwhelming; the publishers not only sent informative giveaways, but many went to great effort and expense to ship their books to San Francisco, set up displays, and staff them. Almost without exception their reaction was two-fold: first, surprise (astonishment even) that anyone in the library field was interested in their materials, and second, as a corollary, chagrin at having never themselves thought of investigating the possible library market for their products. They did not include libraries in their catalog mailings and only infrequently, if ever, advertised their wares in general publishing and library journals, so in one sense librarians could hardly be blamed for not purchasing their materials.

On the other hand, libraries have a long tradition of being highly selective when it comes to books of a religious nature, and certainly do avoid purchasing books that are viewed as evangelical in nature. Books that proselytize or appear to proselytize, as it were, are explicitly or implicitly restricted from purchase by many if not most libraries' selection policies (although in many selection policies the language is so murky and so ambiguous that one wonders how anyone can tell what is permissible for purchase and what is not; for example, see Library Acquisition Policies and Procedures, by Elizabeth Futas, Oryx Press, 1977). And most books on collection development are of little help either, to wit, Bonk and Magrill's Building Library Collections:

> Another category which is liable to be troublesome is the ... religious "self-help" book. Some of these are characterized by lack of good taste, by sweeping and unfounded generalizations, by suppression of all details which do not support the author's thesis. The style is often a nauseous blend of weepy bathos and the most superficial sentimentality. It is precisely this category of religious literature which is liable to be most in demand rather than the scholarly histories of religion, the treatises on theology, or the collections of sermons. If librarians operate on the theory that the library must supply whatever its patrons demand, regardless of quality, they will find a good part of the budget for religious literature being spent on materials of no real worth or permanent interest. The librarian who wishes to build a collection which represents intrinsic worth would find such a situation distressing and will be much less friendly to the cheaper kind of popularization. The solution to the problem--or the compromise which is ar-

rived at--will depend on the librarian's conception of the purposes of the library.[2]

Katz,[3] on the other hand, and Evans[4] both ignore the issue entirely and no entry dealing with religion or religious books appears in the indexes to their books on collection development. Given Bonk and Magrill's apparent hysteria and Katz's and Evans' indifference toward the whole thing, the librarian faced with patrons who request books that they may have seen in the local Christian bookstore--or even B. Dalton or Waldenbooks stores--may be hard pressed to decide whether or not to purchase materials; and in this case, the authorities are of little or no help.

What then is the librarian to do? First, of course, it behooves him or her to find out exactly what the Christian publishers are publishing in the 1980s. A great deal of their output is "religious" only in the sense that the books' writers make no secret of their faith and are not at all shy of letting others know it. A good example was found in my area (Cleveland, Ohio) recently when Andre Thornton, a star outfielder for the Cleveland Indians baseball team, wrote a book about his tragic experience in the late 1970s, in which his young daughter and his wife were killed when Thornton lost control of his van on the icy Pennsylvania Turnpike.[5] According to Bonk and Magrill, the book should not have been purchased: it's not all that well written, it is "weepy" and sentimental, and it is concerned in large part with how Thornton's faith pulled him through his personal crisis. But it was in demand by library patrons, many of them. Should we not have purchased it? (Of course we did, and a number of copies at that.)

In a sense, Thornton's book epitomizes the problem librarians face in deciding to add certain "religious" books to their collections. His book is, of course, religious in its outlook, and a testament of his beliefs, ergo, at least indirectly, proselytizing. On the other hand, libraries have bought thousands of copies of Joni by Joni Eareckson, a paraplegic girl, which is also a near-bathetic tale of a tragedy and of the sustaining religious faith of its protagonist--but Joni is published by Bantam, not some esoteric Christian house in Oregon (although it was originally published by Zondervan, one of the largest Christian publishers).

Do such books proselytize? Christian publishers answer that almost all books that express a viewpoint do, whether their topic is abortion, nuclear freeze, Watergate, or the Middle East. Rarely is a book on these and other controversial topics not written from a point of view--and a point of view that the author obviously wishes to persuade others to accept. In the face of this argument, it is not so easy to explain why Christian books are criticized for being polemical, and a book like Seymour Hersh's The Price of Power is not.

Whatever librarians' decisions may be about buying many of the titles that are being published by the Christian publishing houses today, it goes without saying that there is a large--very large--

The Social Prerogative

group of readers out there who up to now have been willing to fork out their own money to buy the books they want to read and want their children to read--to the tune of a billion dollars in 1982; and this segment of the publishing industry continues to grow at a rate that many other kinds of publishers can only envy.

Sooner or later, librarians are going to have to face up to a hard decision: whether to begin to meet the needs of a very large portion of the population who want to read books by Janette Oke, Robert Schuller, James Dobson, and Charles Swindoll--a group of readers who number in the millions and have as much right to find "their" books on library shelves as do readers of Irving Wallace and Wayne Dyer. Meanwhile, the Okes and Schullers and Dobsons and Swindolls continue to write books that sell--often in millions of copies--and obviously find a vast readership. It is to be hoped that libraries will soon stop shortchanging these readers and offer them the same level of service that they offer to others, guided by the Library Bill of Rights, which clearly states that "Books and other library resources should be provided for the interest, information, and enlightenment of all people of the community the library serves" --even "born-again" Christians.

Note: While this column deals with Christian/Protestant publishing, the same holds true for the published books of any other religious denomination, and there are many, as a look at the size of Bowker's Religious Books In Print will attest.

References

1. Publishers Weekly, September 30, 1983, p. 58.
2. Bonk, Wallace John and Rose Mary Magrill. Building Library Collections. Fifth ed. Metuchen, N.J.: The Scarecrow Press, 1979, p. 79.
3. Katz, William A. Collection Development: The Selection of Materials for Libraries. New York: Holt, Rinehart and Winston, 1980.
4. Evans, G. Edward. Developing Library Collections. Littleton, Colo.: Libraries Unlimited, 1979.
5. Thornton, Andre. From Triumph to Tragedy. Eugene, Ore.: Harvest House, 1983.

OUR COMMISSION, OUR OMISSIONS*

Eric Moon

In the history of American government the batting average of national commissions is not such as to produce many Hall of Fame candidates. For the most part commissions have acquired a deserved reputation as delaying devices, mechanisms for inaction, or fronts for presenting, with contrived impartiality, the views of whatever administration is currently in power.

The civil rights model

One shining exception to this sad record for many years was the U.S. Commission on Civil Rights. Under administrations of both parties it stood firm and independent, strongly espousing and fighting for the principles inherent in its name. Then along comes a celluloid cowboy from the West, three commissioners whose dedication to civil rights could scarcely be faulted are dismissed, and a "neoconservative" (to use the term applied by the current chair, Clarence M. Pendleton, Jr.) fifth column is established. As we moved into 1984 we witnessed the Orwellian spectre of the Commission advocating the denial and total reversal of much that its distinguished predecessor had ever represented.

The obituary of the Commission as believers in civil rights had known it was written, vividly and appropriately, by Mary Frances Berry (one of the original Reagan targets, later reinstated as part of a dismally unsuccessful "compromise"): "The Civil Rights Commission has become a twin of the civil rights division of the Justice Department, and the bank of justice, as Martin Luther King used to say, is now bankrupt. The Civil Rights Commission is no longer the conscience of America on civil rights. I despair for women and minorities in this country."[1]

NCLIS and Reagan

In 1981 President Reagan attempted, illegally, to dismiss three mem-

---
*Reprinted by permission of the author and publisher from Library Journal, 109 (July 1984) 1283-1287. Published by R. R. Bowker Co. (a Xerox company). Copyright © 1984 by Xerox Corporation.

The Social Prerogative

bers (all of them women, and one a former President of the American Library Association) of the National Commission on Libraries and Information Science (NCLIS). Looking back, this appears uncannily like a preview of the successful experiment which transformed the Civil Rights Commission from a decent and generous Dr. Jekyll into a malevolent Mr. Hyde. Actually, in the case of NCLIS the Administration's plan misfired badly: after many protests the Senate sat on the President's recommendations, the process of investigation and confirmation had to begin all over again, and the three "fired" Commissioners wound up serving an extra six months beyond their originally allotted terms.

Among those who best expressed the fears aroused by this arbitrary White House raid on NCLIS was Frederick Burkhardt, the first, and perhaps most distinguished, chair of the Commission. Testifying before a Senate committee, he warned that the premature dismissals violated Congressional directives specifically designed to "insulate the Commission from shifting political winds," and cited three precedents (two Supreme Court decisions and one district court ruling) to support his contention that "There are some offices that by their nature and function are meant to be independent of control, direction and interference from the President."[2]

This event, despite its ominous ramifications, elicited no great outpouring of comment or criticism in the library press. It may well, however, have exacerbated some of the doubts and uncertainties about the Commission's direction and purpose that have rumbled, mostly below the surface, in many areas of the library profession since NCLIS became a legal entity.

Early doubts about NCLIS

Reporting on the first NCLIS press conference, back in the early 1970s, for example, LJ commented that "Both the makeup of the Commission and the tenor of its first utterances suggest that libraries will be of peripheral concern,"[3] and pointed to the absence among the Commission's membership of anyone concerned with the information problems of children and youth, anyone from the publishing industry, anyone concerned with the information starved urban poor, anyone from the Office of Education or the American Library Association ... and so on.

The makeup of the Commission continues to be a problem of serious concern. Throughout the dozen or more years of NCLIS, perhaps only Clara Jones, former director of the Detroit Public Library and former ALA President, could truly be described as a member drawn from the mainstream of librarianship, a person widely known and respected in library circles and deeply involved in professional activities. Over those years, too, ALA has had a consistently dismal record in gaining representation on the Commission.

Political naïveté

Today, for the first time, two librarians, both women, front for the Commission. On the staff side, Toni Carbo Bearman serves as Executive Director. Serving as chair of the Commission (the first woman and first librarian in this seat), is Elinor Hashim from Connecticut, a former public librarian who is now a special librarian. I asked the politically astute Hashim why she thought ALA was so ineffectual with its nominations for the Commission. Her response, in essence, was that too few librarians are actively involved in politics (and certainly in the Republican camp), that ALA puts forward too many names each year, and with little regard for their political affiliations. She was talking about political naïveté. Her analysis is shrewd and on the button. And I speak as a left-wing Democrat who has been nominated at least twice to a very right-wing Republican administration.

Another early critic of the Commission was Dan Lacy, surely one of the most respected voices from the book world. In the midseventies when NCLIS unveiled its first, and only, basis policy and program document, Toward a National Program for Library and Information Services: Goals for Action, Lacy criticized the report for "its primary emphasis not on strengthening the resources of individual libraries but on largely electronic networking." Said Lacy: "One had the impression that the report was seeking problems for the solution rather than the other way about."[4] His comments found little support because in this NCLIS had jumped on a bandwagon already occupied by many leaders of the profession. The vehicle remains crowded today, but the resources of many libraries are in poorer shape than when Lacy made his comments.

By the mid-'70s John Berry saw NCLIS as one of "three potential sources of library legislative leadership." His other choices were, obviously, the ALA Washington Office and, curiously, Librarian of Congress Daniel Boorstin. "The problem with NCLIS," however, said Berry, "is that we are not yet sure to which library body that arm is connected" ... and "before we accept the well-intentioned leadership of such an agency, we'd better be sure we can influence the results."[5] In the next few years there were some who began to wonder whether the arm was connected to a library body at all.

Private forces

For example, in 1980 two leaders in the Illinois Library Association questioned "the oblique direction the National Commission ... has been taking with regard to its constitutional charge," and declared that " ... private interests have been allowed to be the overwhelming force in the conduct of the Commission."[6]

This apprehension gathered steam when the Commission, in early 1982, issued its Task Force report on Public/Private Sector Interaction in Providing Information Services.[7] Carol Tauer, a

The Social Prerogative

professor of philosophy in Minnesota, said: "When I first tried to read the report ... I was dismayed. Frankly, I couldn't figure out what it was all about ... the Task Force report was nearly incomprehensible to me.... There must be a hidden agenda, I thought.... It occurred to me that perhaps the Task Force had been assigned the task of formulating an information policy that would be consistent with Reaganomics."[8] And, in the best balanced and most thoughtful article yet to appear on that report, Patricia Schuman concluded that the approach advocated by the NCLIS Task Force was "simplistic, but dangerous."[9]

Over the years of the Commission's existence, LJ has been by far the most frequent and insistent critic of its directions, purposes, and motives. Most of the quotations above have been drawn from its pages because there is little elsewhere in the library press other than regurgitations of NCLIS press releases as news. When I was commissioned to prepare this assessment of NCLIS past and present, I suspect that the editors of LJ knew I shared some of the doubts and concerns that they have repeatedly expressed.

Before coming to any conclusions in print, however, I set off in search of more balance, to test some of my gut feelings against the views of knowledgeable people who are or have been deeply involved with the Commission and its work. Some of their views are reflected in what follows, although few of them are identified; many would not have talked so freely had their comments been for attribution.

Bureaucratic styrofoam?

So where stands the Commission in relation to the library field today? Is it friend or foe, giant or pygmy, advocate or fifth column? Is it a leader, a catalyst, an honest broker (the Commission is fond of those last two terms)--or just another layer of bureaucratic styrofoam, in place to deaden noise and impact? How do those who are or have been involved with the Commission see its role, its mission, its purpose?

The two women, Elinor Hashim and Toni Bearman, who stand on the bridge of the Commission as it sails into whatever future lies ahead for libraries and information services, are clearly and emphatically agreed upon one point: the limitations of NCLIS, its inability to do all that its critics or its proponents would wish of it. With a total staff of ten and an annual appropriation hovering consistently around $700,000, NCLIS is clearly not in much more than the rowboat class among the vessels of the Federal Fleet. Even though that budget is cushioned by something like $200,000 from other sources (contracts such as one with the Department of Commerce for about $66,000, and "in-kind services" such as the loan of two professional librarians from IBM), a disproportionate amount of the Commission's effort the past few years has had to be expended on insuring its own survival.

The only increase

Some political cynics have seen the constant pressure from the Office of Management and Budget as a calculated device to keep the Commission in line with Administration policies and objectives. Hashim denies this strenuously. She points to the fact that this year the Administration, for the first time, has recommended an increase in the NCLIS budget. Even though the increase is minuscule, any increase in the present Washington climate can be fairly judged a minor miracle. It is, I think, the only increase proposed by the Administration for any library program in the past year.

This does perhaps support the view, propounded by one informed observer, that NCLIS has been gradually winning the support of individuals in government, proving its worth agency by agency, and has gained sufficient political backing that it can now be regarded as pretty well established. This is not to say that all threats have vanished, but that NCLIS security is more nearly normal on the federal agency hazard scale.

No degree of security, however, seems likely to convert the Commission into the kind of advocacy or lobbying leader that some of its critics want it to be. It still sees itself primarily, as it was set up to be, as an advisory body, providing informed and "independent" information when and where it can along the labyrinthine corridors of government. My strong impression is that it has done, and continues to do, that job rather well--if one accepts the limitations it seems to place upon its interest-range. A recent example of its growing acceptance as a source or gatherer of information is the request made by a Senate Committee that NCLIS develop technical advice on the reauthorization and redesign of the Higher Education Act as it impacts on libraries.[10]

Issues for NCLIS

But whatever successes it has had in this direction, there are many who are not satisfied, who want NCLIS to act rather than react, to be more up front on serious issues with strong potential effect on libraries and librarians. Among such issues which came up repeatedly during our interviews were: 1) The continuing incursions by the current Administration upon access to and dissemination of information. Even the ALA Washington Office, which for years has made almost a fetish of "bipartisanship," has issued three chapters in a continuing chronology of government misdeeds in this area.
2) The standards proposed by the Office of Personnel Management, which would severely downgrade federal library and information positions, the fallout from which could be expected to reach into all areas of the profession. One observer commented that NCLIS had been "supportive" on this matter but had not exercised much influence. When I asked Elinor Hashim about the OPM issue she seemed to confirm that observer's evaluation. "We couldn't come out as strongly as we wished," she said. 3) The OMB Budget Circular

A-76 which, if its proposals were adopted, would result in more and more federal library services being contracted out to private companies. Again, one of our interviewees said, "NCLIS has never gotten involved in this." 4) The emerging campaign for a National Lending Right. Here is a case where the Commission could get in early and formulate some common sense approaches and attitudes before the debate sinks to the level it achieved during the British battle on the same issue.

If issues of this scope and import have failed to turn the Commission on, what has it been doing all these years? I asked everyone I talked to: "What do you think has been the Commission's greatest single achievement?" All of them, without exception, answered, "The White House Conference in 1979." Which leaves one with the old political question: "What have you done for me lately?" I also asked, in deference to the President's campaign rhetoric, "Are libraries better off, or worse off, than they were before the Commission?" That, of course, is a loaded (not to say unfair) question, given the variety of forces that have had an impact on libraries in the past dozen years, so it's no surprise that no one was prepared to declare that things are rosier now than they were pre-NCLIS.

Information without evaluation

One of the proud boasts of the Commission is that it has assembled, in the form of Task Force reports and other commissioned studies, a vast repository of information and testimony related to specific areas of library and information services. And so it has. But it is in connection with this "achievement" that some of the real problems and questions begin to come to the surface. Information without assessment and evaluation, leading to concrete policies and positions, is not necessarily particularly valuable; it is, perhaps, no more than what the information technologists call "raw data." It is when one asks what the Commission has learned from all this paper, and what positions have evolved from its accumulation, that one finds oneself immersed in a miasma of uncertainty. As Marilyn Gell Mason notes, "Although NCLIS ... and other federal agencies have sponsored numerous reports and held countless planning meetings, it is not clear what these efforts have accomplished."[11]

According to Hashim, it is only since she assumed the chair that NCLIS members have been asked to vote on specific recommendations made by reporting Task Forces. Previously it seems to have been policy for the Commission not to take positions on anything, but simply "receive" whatever was presented to it. "The Commission now feels an obligation to decide on report recommendations," says Hashim.

If this is one small step toward clarification of its positions, and away from such marshmallow phrases as "catalyst," "honest broker," "forum" and "resident expert" to describe the Commission's

apparently amorphous view of its role, there was an even firmer
stride in January this year when NCLIS issued its statement on "Libraries and Information Skills in Elementary and Secondary Education." This firm statement in support of school libraries was issued
in response to "an important void" in reports such as A Nation at
Risk, prepared by the National Commission on Excellence in Education. Said the NCLIS statement: "A major criterion for the determination of excellence at any college or university is the quality of
its library and information resources; and, yet, NCEE omitted any
such criteria from the determination of excellence in elementary and
secondary schools."[12]

In talking to Bearman and Hashim (separately) I applauded
this public affirmation of the value of school libraries and asked
whether similar statements would be forthcoming on the contribution
that public and other types of libraries made to education. One said
yes. The other said no, the school libraries statement was it.
NCLIS may not yet be familiar enough with advocacy to have learned
that a united front is helpful.

NCLIS & Unesco

Another recent example of NCLIS position-taking, one which offers
some refutation of the claim that NCLIS is under the thumb of Reagan
administration policies, occurred at the ALA midwinter meeting last
January in Washington, D.C. ALA's International Relations Committee was battling in the ALA Council for a resolution in favor of
continued U.S. participation in Unesco and deeply regretting the
President's decision to issue notice of U.S. withdrawal from membership in that body. To the microphone came Elinor Hashim to
report, surprisingly to some, that the Commission supported the
intent of this resolution.

[Apparently those who were surprised had a point, or that
presidential thumb was in motion after Midwinter. On May 21, long
after Eric Moon wrote the paragraph above, Sarah G. Bishop, the
Acting Executive Director of NCLIS, prepared a statement on the
NCLIS role regarding Unesco. According to that statement, NCLIS
"reviewed its dual responsibility as secretariat for the U.S. National
Committee for the Unesco General Information Program (PGI) and
official advisor to the State Department on matters relating to the
program." According to the Bishop statement, NCLIS has been
asked by the State Department to "1) encourage full and active U.S.
participation in the Unesco/PGI for the remainder of the year; 2)
monitor any changes in the program during the year; and 3) draft a
proposal for alternative mechanisms to accomplish the objectives of
the PGI, should the U.S. carry out its intent to withdraw from
Unesco...." Bishop also reports that in an April resolution on the
subject, NCLIS said that "... if the U.S. does actually withdraw from
Unesco, NCLIS will adhere to official U.S. policy." The statement
adds that, "The Commission is deeply committed to the objectives
of the PGI and will continue to help further them through whatever
means are available."--Editor]

Public vs. Private Sector

If there are critics who are unhappy about the Commission's inaction on issues, there are others who believe that the Commission has developed positions (even if rather mistily) that they regard as pernicious and in opposition to policies espoused by both the White House Conference and the American Library Association. One insider we talked to felt that there has been a pronounced negative policy change, that NCLIS has "reneged on the long-range plan" presented in the old blue book[13] without replacing it with any new plan.

These kinds of doubts about where the Commission really stands are most virulent in relation to the two most pervasive and powerful issues involved in library and information services today: the respective roles of the public and private sectors, and the application of fees for various services in libraries.

On the first of these, the NCLIS report, Public Sector/Private Sector Interaction ..., was perhaps the most controversial document yet to emerge from NCLIS, and it heightened the fears that a policy direction had developed--and that it was distinctly in favor of the private sector. The reappointment (yet again) of Carlos Cuadra, unquestionably the most ardent and perhaps most able and influential Commission supporter of the private sector, exacerbated those fears and seemed, to the fearful, to have added confirmation of a growing conformity between the views of the Commission and the Administration as to the respective roles of the public and private sectors.

The Commission, nevertheless, declares that it has as yet taken no firm public positions on this issue. There are many who disagree, including some we have quoted earlier in this article. Another whose opinion seems unequivocal is Marilyn Gell Mason who, as former director of the White House Conference, is certainly familiar with Commission currents. She says: "Even NCLIS, the agency responsible for the White House Conference and thought to be sensitive to the public need for information, has issued a report that recommends the shifting of responsibility away from the public sector to private industry."[14] Earlier in the same volume she notes: "... there is no doubt that the administration's actions have resulted in a deliberate shift of power from the public to the private sector." [15]

Also, among those we interviewed, one person with close connections to NCLIS declared flatly, "The Commission has moved toward the interests of the private sector." Another said, "I feel that in the Commission the private sector view has prevailed," attributing this result, at least in part, to the imbalance in the Commission's membership, and added, "With the Reagan appointments continuing ... the imbalance will probably continue."

NCLIS on fees

When we raised the question of fee-based services with both Hashim and Bearman they declared absolutely that to date the Commission has taken no position. Indeed, incredibly (to this observer at least), they indicated that the Commission did not have enough facts to take a position and that they were considering a "literature search" to find out what was happening in relation to fees in libraryland. This would be hilarious if the issue were not so vital to the future of library services and to the public good. Given years of constant and loud debate on this issue in all corners of the profession, one has to wonder whether the Commission has been locked in a very remote ivory tower or whether it is being evasive in the best political manner.

One Commission document which brought the fee issue into the full glare of the spotlight was the recent Report of the Task Force on Library and Information Services to Cultural Minorities.[16] Only a month before its appearance the Commission issued another Task Force report on Community Information and Referral Services.[17] That one NCLIS had happily "received, accepted and endorsed" at its meeting in April 1983, apparently without reservations.

Unprecedented rejection

By contrast the Commission reacted strongly to the report from the Cultural Minorities Task Force and even seemed to take some pains to dissociate itself from the recommendations therein: "It is important to note that this is a report to the Commission from an independent Task Force.... We have not assisted the Task Force substantively in the preparation of the report...."[18]

The foreword by the chair Elinor Hashim notes that the Commission endorses "the majority of the 42 recommendations in this report," but "we have declined to support eight of the 42 recommendations at this time."[19] Three of the eight rejected recommendations dealt with financial barriers to information access, and two of these addressed the fee question directly.[20] The Commission's response to these three was: "The Commission supports, in general, the concept of 'free' basic library service. However, in order to take advantage of the enormous power of technology, it may be necessary to pass on certain related costs to users."[21]

As John Berry notes in an LJ editorial on this report, the NCLIS-sponsored White House Conference had voted that "...all persons should have free access, without charge or fee to the individual, to information in public and publicly-supported libraries." Similar positions have been adopted by the NCLIS precursor, the National Advisory Commission on Libraries, by the American Library Association, the Public Library Association, and numerous state and national organizations. "In that sense the NCLIS Task Force recommendations echo widely accepted principles of public library service."[22]

We asked E. J. Josey, the chair of the Cultural Minorities

The Social Prerogative   289

Task Force, how his group had reacted to the rejection of eight of
its recommendations. He was clearly upset that neither he nor any
member of the Task Force had been informed about the rejections
and learned about them only after the report was in print. "We were
given no opportunity to respond," he said, "not even given a chance
to explain more fully why the recommendations were made." He
added: "Once again minorities were treated as minorities." To the
best of our knowledge, the Commission's response to this report is
unprecedented, and it's possible, again, that lack of experience
with position-taking may have contributed to the Commission's dis-
courtesy in not even informing the Task Force chair of its actions
prior to publication.

NCLIS no shows

Not all of the blame for the uncertainty about the Commission's role,
activities and positions (if any) can be laid at the door of the Commission itself. The press coverage of its activities over the years
has been lamentable. The library press hardly ever shows up at
Commission meetings, we were told by both Hashim and Bearman,
even though these meetings are open and attempts are made to hold
them in conjunction with or adjacent to meetings of library or information associations. It should perhaps be noted, in passing, that
one prominent library periodical editor, some years ago, was fired
for, among other things, being apparently too interested in reporting
what the Commission was doing.

   If the library press can be faulted for inattention (and here one
might except Berry, who has maintained a steady editorial barrage
of questions and criticisms), the profession itself has not been much
more active in Commission watching or pushing. Both Hashim and
Bearman acknowledged that Bob Wedgeworth and Eileen Cooke both
maintained a steady top-level ALA contact with the Commission, but
both bemoaned the fact that few librarians ever attend Commission
meetings or otherwise make much direct contact. Certainly the ALA
Council, usually involved in a feast of parliamentary minutiae, has
paid little or no attention to the activities of NCLIS.

   A year or so ago Bob Wedgeworth spoke to me (and I believe
to one of the annual dawn breakfast gatherings of past ALA presidents)
about his concerns over the dwindling content of both Membership and
Council meetings at ALA conferences. I asked everyone I interviewed
about the Commission how they would react to the idea of ALA calling
upon the Commission to send representatives for a public exchange
of views at an ALA membership or Council meeting. The Commission could receive ideas and input directly from more librarians at
such a session, and, one hopes, this might lead to some constructive
consideration, by ALA Council particularly of Commission activities
in major issue areas that affect us all. The response to this suggestion was positive, indeed enthusiastic, and both Hashim and Bearman said they would welcome such an opportunity.

Simmering discontent

One person I talked to about the Commission said that one reason for the Commission's increasing tilt toward private sector interests was that they had done a better job of getting their views across and that the library field had done comparatively little to lobby or pressure the Commission effectively. Said this person: "Either ALA doesn't think the Commission is important (which is sad), or it believes that it can't influence it (which is equally sad), or it is simply apathetic."

If there is a prevailing discontent with, or unease about the Commission in the library field--and I think there is--it is not enough for it just to simmer below the surface; it should be communicated strongly and effectively. If the Commission advocates or supports positions which are in opposition to widely held beliefs in the profession, ALA should make it clear that it will not support the Commission uncritically and unconditionally at budget time.

Like the Commission, the American Library Association, and its policy-making body, the Council, have been criticized in recent years for lack of leadership. Here is an area where leadership could, and should, be demonstrated. The Commission is in a very prominent position to affect library services, for good or ill, and it deserves, at the very least, our scrutiny and forceful attention. It seems to want it. Let's see that it gets it.

References

1. New York Times News Service Story, Jan. 18, 1984.
2. "Burkhardt challenges White House for terminating NCLIS appointments," LJ, June 15, 1982, p. 1166.
3. "National Advisory Commission Meets the Press," LJ, January 15, 1972, p. 139.
4. "Memos to NCLIS," LJ, November 15, 1975, p. 2107-14.
5. Berry, John, "NCLIS: Accountable to Whom?" LJ, January 15, 1976, p. 297.
6. Simpson, Betty J. and Deborah Miller, "NCLIS and the Private Sector," LJ, June 1, 1980, p. 1240-41.
7. National Commission on Libraries and Information Science. Public Sector/Private Sector Interaction in Providing Information Services, GPO, Feb. 1982.
8. Tauer, Carol A., "Social Justice and Access to Information," Minnesota Libraries, Summer 1982, p. 39-42.
9. Schuman, Patricia Glass, "Information Justice," LJ, June 1, 1982, p. 1060-66.
10. "NCLIS committee to seek input on HEA revision for Congress," LJ, March 15, 1984, p. 526.
11. Mason, Marilyn Gell. The Federal Role in Library and Information Services. Knowledge Industry Publications, 1983, p. 133.
12. NCLIS. "Statement on Libraries and Information Skills in Elementary and Secondary Education." Approved unanimously by the Commission, January 6, 1984.

The Social Prerogative   291

13. NCLIS. Toward a National Program for Library and Information Services: Goals for Action. Washington, D.C., 1975.
14. Mason, op. cit., p. 147.
15. Ibid., p. 99.
16. Report of the Task Force on Library and Information Services to Cultural Minorities, Washington, D.C.: NCLIS, 1983.
17. Community Information and Referral Services. Final Report to the National Commission on Libraries and Information Science from the Community Information and Referral Services Task Force. Washington, D.C.: NCLIS, 1983.
18. Minorities Task Force Report, p.v.
19. Ibid.
20. Ibid., p. vii.
21. Ibid., p. viii.
22. "NCLIS and Fees," LJ, November 15, 1983, p. 2110.

WOMEN, POWER, AND LIBRARIES*

Patricia Glass Schuman

Professional women hear a lot these days about the things mother never taught us. Still, there are things mother and father did teach us--and now we need to look at them as well. One significant lesson we learned was that it was not considered "proper" for women to discuss money, sex, or power. It really isn't "nice" to think about any of these things, or to admit that you want or have any of them.

"Power is America's last dirty word," says Rosabeth Kantor in her Men and Women of the Corporation. "People who have it deny it, people who want it do not want to appear to hunger for it; and people who engage in its machinations do so secretly." Power is a particularly distasteful word to most women. In an informal survey of my women friends, I asked what terms came to mind when they heard the word "power." The most common responses were: manipulation, control, dominance, ruthlessness, coercion, and anger.

The double bind

"Power tends to corrupt. Absolute power corrupts absolutely." We usually drop the word "tends" from that famous statement and just say, "power corrupts." This view of power is certainly not confined to women. Men often find the raw concept of power somewhat repugnant. To women, however, the concept of power--of being powerful--is almost a societal taboo. Witness the clichés by which women's power has always been masked:

> "The hand that rocks the cradle rules the world."
> "The iron hand in the velvet glove."
> "The woman behind the throne."

These clichés may have been used historically to soften the news that women do have power, but they also imply a power of almost awesome proportions. This is the double bind--the myth of female weakness and female strength.

─────────
*Reprinted by permission of the author and publisher from Library Journal, 109 (January 1984) 42-47. Published by R. R. Bowker Co. (a Xerox company). Copyright © 1984 by Xerox Corporation.

Images of the magical fertility goddess or the all-powerful mother abound in literature and history. Throughout history (and mythology) man has feared and worshipped her power. Joseph Campbell claims, in The Mask of God, that women's mythic power "... has been one of the chief concerns of the masculine part of the population ... to break, control, and employ it for its own ends."

From the beginnings of time, women have been taught to submit, to give up their power. This in itself is an admission that women have power. In her Man's World, Women's Place, Elizabeth Janeway points out: "In mythic identification of power and weakness, women immolate themselves as a sign of strength. They are the givers. But how can one give if one does not possess riches and substances.... Here is the paradox: women are weak because they can be strong only through giving. They are strong because they give what is needed, and this assures that their dominance will continue." Of course women's power has usually been private power, power within the family. The age-old power bargain states, in part, that "men rule the world, women rule the home."

During the past 20 years, women have made great strides-- though not nearly great enough--in our struggle for equal rights and opportunity; in our fight to change the terms of the bargain. Yet we remain largely a powerless group--a majority not well organized, nor powerful enough to pass the Equal Rights Amendment.

The conditioned response

Our lack of knowledge and understanding about power is largely a conditioned response. I am President of my own company. I'm told that I am the first women to be nominated for treasurer of the American Library Association. LJ's editors obviously thought enough of this article to publish it. Yet how do I want the reader to view me? Certainly not as "powerful." I want you to like me. To think I'm "good." Women are products of a compromised power group, taught to perceive ourselves as submissive, rather than as wielders of power and influence. Intellectually I know better, but emotionally....

I'm trying to get past my conditioning because I think it is essential that we understand power--understand what it is and where it comes from and how and when to use it.

The widening gap

Why be concerned about women and power? Much of the library profession is female--part of the power structure. We're concerned, obviously, because the gains of the women's movement notwithstanding, women still have a long way to go. To put it in simple economic terms: in 1955, women earned 64.3 cents for every dollar men earned. In 1978, we earned 60 cents for every dollar. The earning gap is widening. Women have to work nine days to gross the same amount of money men do in five. Even those of us lucky enough to be "exceptions" are still grappling with the personal and emotional problems that come from trying to change very strong conditioning.

Women, as a group in our society, are still largely powerless. Women librarians are even more so. We may be members of a "women's profession," but the reality is that women hold only 15 percent of the directorships of libraries that belong to the Association of Research Libraries, 25 percent of top posts in library education, and only a third of the directorships in major public libraries. Even then, these positions are not in the largest and most prestigious institutions. Salary data also demonstrate that regardless of position or type of library, women continue to earn less than men. The gap widens at the highest levels.

Despite more than a decade of activism, there has been no clear improvement of the status of women in librarianship. The profession continues to evidence a clear pattern of dual career structures. Recent research and analysis by Kathleen Heim, Leigh Estabrook, and others suggests that salary discrimination exists, even when allowances are made for personal, career, and professional variations. There is segregation by type of library, with almost half of the men in the profession working in academic libraries. Women clearly dominate library services for schools and children. "Men hold major administrative positions in all types of libraries nearly three times as often as their proportion of the total work force would suggest, while women cluster in the lower levels of the organizational hierarchy," according to Heim.

Women librarians clearly lack economic power, but even more important, we lack structural power--the power to change and improve our institutions and our society.

Power defined

In order to achieve and use power, we must first define it. Max Weber's simple definition is a good starting point: "Power is the possibility of imposing one's will upon the behavior of other persons."

A person has power when she has the ability to mobilize resources (human and material), to apply negative or positive sanctions in order to get something done, to have her interest felt, to have effect on the decision-making process.

Power can be given, taken, assumed, inherited, vested, won, lost, used, abused, feared, and respected. Power comes with certain roles--mother, director, boss, expert.

Individuals and groups seek power to advance their own interests, to extend to others their personal and religious or social

The Social Prerogative

values. They use it to win support for their economic or social perception of the public good.

Power is neither moral nor immoral in itself, though it can be used for good or ill. As the late Saul Alinsky observed, "Power is an essential force always in operation either changing circumstances or opposing change--a gun may be used to take or save a life, to enforce slavery, or to achieve freedom. The morality of the use of power is not in the instrument but in the user."

How power works

It is important to understand how power works, what differentiates those who exercise power from those who are subject to it, before dealing with the ethics of its use. Where does power come from, how does it grow, how is it transferred and used?

Sociologists, psychologists, management consultants, economists, and others have attempted to classify the types and sources of power. In a fascinating discussion in his recent book, The Anatomy of Power, John Kenneth Galbraith defines three main types of power and where they come from:

Condign Power enforces submission through the threat of adverse unpleasant, or painful consequences--power by punishment.

Compensatory Power assures submission through affirmative rewards by giving something of value, like money.

Conditioned Power wins submission by changing belief, through persuasion, education, or social commitment to what seems "natural, and right." The submission reflects the so-called "preferred" course.

Individuals subject to power which uses punishments or rewards for enforcement are aware of their submission to it. However, conditioned power, relying upon belief, is subjective, neither those exercising it nor those subject to it are always aware that it is being exerted. We just know that "God is on our side." Advertising is a prevalent form of conditioned power, though not as reputable a form for teaching socially acceptable views as our educational system. "Power is served in many ways," says Galbraith. "No service is more useful than the cultivation of the belief that it does not exist."

Of course, all of these forms of power are interrelated. For example, although the reputation and use of condign power--punishment--has greatly declined in modern societies, its aura survives. For those who once possessed it as a "right," the image (conditioning) is still a factor in winning submission. "The husband, parent, teacher, and sheriff all have authority now in consequence of a past association with the right to inflict punishment."

One of Galbraith's major theses, of crucial importance to

women, is that power in modern society is moving, through social and economic forces, from condign physical enforcement and compensatory monetary rewards to an ever-increasing reliance on the use of conditioned power, the power of belief. Of course those subject to this conditioned power are rarely aware of it. Submission to it usually reflects what we view as a "proper," "reputable," "acceptable," or "decent" behavior. We obey the law. We pay taxes. We accept the mores and taboos of society.

Another important point Galbraith makes is that: "something in the exercise of masculine authority must be attributed to the superior access of the male to condign power, to the greater physical strength of a husband and its use to enforce his will on a physically weaker and insufficiently acquiescent spouse. And no one can doubt the frequent efficiency of compensatory power, of reward in the form of clothing, jewelry, housing, entertainment. These have long and adequately demonstrated their utility in securing feminine compliance with masculine will."

Male power and female submission have relied much more completely, however, on the belief since ancient times that such submission is the natural order of things. "Men might love, honor, and cherish; it was for long accepted that women should love, honor, and obey." Granted, relief from the compensatory power wielded by men has been sought through the development of employment opportunities for women and by publicizing employment discrimination that keeps women in subordinate jobs. A major part of the effort has had to be "the challenge to belief--the belief that submission and subservience are normal, virtuous, and otherwise appropriate roles for women."

The sources of power

Of course, all of these ways of enforcing power--reward, punishment, and conditioning--play various roles in the exercise of power. The question is, "What provides access to power, what allows its exercise?" Galbraith has three basic answers: personality, property, and organization. These are the ultimate sources of power. They almost always appear in some kind of combination and each relates to a type of power.

Galbraith contends that in modern society organizations (unions, governments, corporations, public agencies, special interest groups) are the key source of power, though certainly inter-related with other power sources. He quotes scholar, Charles Lindblom, to make his point: "Some people believe that wealth or property is the underlying source of power. But property is itself a form of authority created by government."

Galbraith uses the professional football team as a metaphor. The team, he says, uses all the sources and instruments of power and it is accepted that success depends on the effectiveness of their

The Social Prerogative

use. It uses the personality of the coaches and the more spectacular or effective players. It takes property, resources to support a major team. Most of all, the highly sophisticated organization of the teams and the game is essential.

The instruments of enforcement are the threat of condign rebuke from teammates, coach, and fans. The promise of compensatory power resides in the high salaries. Above all there is the highly developed training and conditioning required to win. "The team most strongly combining all of these elements of power will win; it will gain the submission of the opposing team. As in sport, so in life," says Galbraith. Men know this. How often do we hear women use the terms "end-run" or "teamwork" or say "There goes the ballgame?" That's not to say that we should.

Power for what?

The football team may be an analogy to the "norm" of how power is exercised. The dilemma for women is whether we want power in its usual form and for its usual ends. Power is neither moral or immoral, it depends upon how it is used. To make a choice is to exercise power. If the choice is an effective one, it alters the status quo, it can change the distribution of power. There are no ethics inherent in power itself; there are only the ethics of the people who wield power. The key questions are: What do we want power for? How much do we have? How much do we want? How much risk are we willing to take? On what--or whose--terms?

The illusion of power

Does power mean being the director of a library, more prestige, more money? Do we want to "buy in" on the societal terms men have set up and thus reap the rewards of power? Will we submit to "organizational goals," or will we enlarge and change them? If we want power, we must be aware of the danger of having the "illusions" and trappings of power, without the impact. To quote Galbraith once again, this time on modern corporations and public agencies like libraries:

> ... there is the illusion of individuals in these organizations that they have and are using power. As personality gives way to organization, there is inevitably a wider participation in the exercise of power. What once expressed the will of the boss is now the product of bureaucracy--of conference and committee and proposals passing up through the organizational hierarchy for modification, amendment, and ratification. In the older business enterprise, submission was to the owner; his word, as it was said, was law. In the modern large corporation, submission is to the bureaucratic processes in which many participate. The boss, as he may still be called, is the agent of those who

instruct him; the power he is presumed to exercise is at least partly the endowment of those who, sensitive to his vanity, attribute to him an authority that, were it real, would be disastrous. The modern corporate title expresses the reality: the chief executive officer--the CEO--is only the chief among those with executive authority. As with the modern corporation, so with the public agency. It, too, concentrates power and then distributes it among the individual participants.

The illusion of power is very seductive. I founded my company seven years ago, on a shoestring. We couldn't afford an office, so we worked out of my apartment. I had been a librarian and editor before that--all middle management positions. Suddenly I was a "president." Much to my amazement, as soon as I started calling myself "president," I began to be offered jobs as "president" of other publishing companies, positions no one would have dreamed of offering me three months earlier. I was the same person, with the same talents. Only the title had changed.

Illusions of power can also result from political and special issue organization. Just by forming an organization, making a speech, issuing statements, having meetings, we can create the illusion that we are exercising power, when in reality we are just spinning our wheels--marking time, feeling good, while others still hold the reins of power. We need to be able to distinguish between this illusion and the practical effect--the results any such organization has.

Organizing for power

Women also face danger in the power arena when we attempt to take and use power only as individuals--thinking that we are "different" than other women. We think we are somehow better, smarter, and more talented. We can stand alone. We don't need "organized" power. How many times have you heard other women disavow the "feminist" label? Letty Cottin Pogrebin, in a recent New York Times article, discussed several important and strong women who say they agree with feminist goals, but choose to disavow their feminism. She quotes Chris Craft, the TV commentator who sued the station that demoted her for being too old, unattractive, and not deferential to men: "I hate being categorized. Objectivity has always been my goal. If I said I'm a feminist, I'd never get another job as a reporter. I mean no slap against feminism, but this is my battle and mine alone."

Pogrebin suggests that women "resist being categorized because despite more than a decade of women's movement activism on everything from child care to homemaker's rights, the category 'feminist' still conjures for many an image of a narrow, negative fringe group. I can vouch for the power of those preconceptions. I stand five feet, four inches tall. At virtually all my lecture appearances, believe it or not, someone says, 'I thought you'd be bigger. Each of us who calls herself a feminist testifies that feminists come in all sizes, races, marital states, and sexual persuasions. Admission to our 'category' is by commitment only."

Pogrebin compares Craft's desire for objectivity to Gloria Steinem's civil rights parody of the equal time rule: "O.K., we've heard from the black victims; now let's get the attack dog's side of the story." It's absurd to suggest that there are two sides to the denial of human rights to anyone. "Being a feminist--in favor of women's rights--should not stigmatize a woman; it should mark her as a person with rudimentary human concerns and female self-interest."

Using power

We run other risks, as well, in attempting to use power. One is exhibiting the classic behavior of the powerless--using whatever power we do gain in an oppressive way. In work situations, women are often said to hoard what little power they are given. Sometimes we think we need to do it all ourselves, to prove something. Often we don't delegate.

Rosabeth Kantor describes powerless people as those who supervise closely, focus on rules and procedures, are less willing to delegate, are territorial, attempt to hold on to the small "scraps of power" they may have. Contrast that with Carl Rogers' description of powerful people: "People who trust their own power do not need to have power over others. They are willing to foster and facilitate the latent strength in the other person. Constructive power can be released when people accept their own inner strength." Too often we see ourselves as the recipients of the benefits of power, rather than as a part of the power system. We see ourselves as the recipients of the benefits of networks, mentors, sponsors, and the like--rather than as those who pass on and share power.

Power & librarianship

Women are members of a class that is perceived as powerless. As librarians, we are members of a profession that is perceived as powerless. The sociologists call librarianship a "semi profession" because librarianship evidences three characteristics that are predominantly female: First, within the hierarchy of all occupations/professions, librarians are low in status, prestige, and income. Second, administrative positions are usually held by men. Third, men earn more than women when at equal levels of occupational and professional development.

We are, for the most part, an institution-based profession. Our goals and our services center around an institution over which we often have little control. Libraries are hierarchical institutions. Rarely do librarians have much to say in their workplace regarding hours, schedules, physical plant, or other conditions which effect the quality of their work.

We tend to do things for the people we serve. We rarely do things with them because we perceive ourselves as having little power to share.

Redefining power

The old cliché "information is power" has new meaning in a society that is rapidly changing from an industrial base to an information base. Over 50 percent of our Gross National Product is devoted to the production and distribution of information. Daniel Bell calls this a post-industrial society. Others say we're in the "age of information." If information is, or is rapidly becoming, one of the more effective tools with which to wield power, then the lack of it implies powerlessness. Librarianship is a profession ethically dedicated to the organization and dissemination of information--the dissemination, therefore, of knowledge and power. Our impact on existing and developing power structures could be massive. We can make a difference, changing who is information rich and who is information poor. In order to exploit this impact to its fullest, as women and as librarians, we must redefine power ourselves.

Forget Max Weber's definition of power as "imposing one's will on others." Let's redefine power as the ability to get cooperation. By that definition we have power when we can gain access to resources, information, and support and we mobilize these effectively to get things done. Rather than viewing power as something done to us, let's examine it as something we can use.

Remember there are no ethics of power. Power itself is neutral. Power can be used for either positive or negative ends. The use of power does not always have to result in a situation where "if I win, you lose." There is not just one "piece of the pie" to be shared among those of us who are the most dominant and aggressive --not unless we are willing to buy into a hierarchical system. It is a system within which much of the power is illusory--and we must not lose sight of this fact.

Unfortunately, as the members of a power-compromised group, women have few role models. Because of the position of women in society it is unlikely that any of us have escaped without some trauma to our self-perceptions. When we do have a chance to exercise power, we sometimes don't recognize it, we are sometimes frightened of it, and often we don't know how to use it. The problem is not ability, or opportunity, but an understanding and appreciation of the elements of power.

Despite the hierarchy and the ordained authority we may or may not have in our immediate workplace, there are many ways we can exercise power. The power we have is not ours through the

The Social Prerogative

authority of a title alone. We exercise power through friendships, personal traits, perceived expertise, confidence, status, seniority, and interpersonal skills. We have many more opportunities to exercise it than we realize. We are powerful not only when we control resources (money, personnel, equipment) and time (schedules, assignments). We are also powerful when we have access to people--supporters, backers, allies. We have power when we have control of, or access to, information. We have power when we understand how the system works and we have political access to it.

In order to gain and use power, women must join together, in an organized effort, for common goals. To operate only on "good will" and "principle" is not enough. What are these common goals? How can feminist power differ from the norm? Can we use power creatively, constructively, in life-enhancing ways? Will we use it to empower others?

Power: changing the terms

How will we respond to the existing power establishment? Galbraith observes that the common response to an unwelcome exercise of power is to build a countering position of power. Usually we meet like with like, force with force, social conditioning with social conditioning. Yet consider the power--the impact--of those who have successfully refused to use power by traditional methods: Martin Luther King's nonviolent resistance, Gandhi's use of Satyagraha. They changed the world by refusing to "buy in" on the usual terms. Realizing that there was no effective way to meet the power structure on its own terms, they changed the terms.

If we--as women and as librarians--accept the power bargain on the terms of the conventional wisdom of the hierarchy, we are subject to the dangers of what Warren Bennis terms "collective immorality." When moral, "good" people get together to make decisions for organizations, in order to preserve the values and goals of the institution, they often go against their individual ideals and principles. Loyalty is often held to be the highest good by an organization. Those who put the organization first in the narrowest sense, those people who unquestioningly follow the course perceived to be best for the organization, are often its most highly prized employees. Talent, ingenuity, innovation, intelligence, and creativity run a poor second in many organizational value systems.

That demand for loyalty, for adherence to the orthodoxy is perceived as the only way the organization can survive. Our first advice from the lawyer who drew up the papers to incorporate Neal-Schuman was: "Remember, your business is an entity unto itself. It's not an extension of you--it's something separate, something that has to be protected at all costs--even at the expense of the individuals involved." There are many valid reasons for protecting an organization, but unswerving and unquestioning loyalty is also the stuff from which both mediocrity and totalitarianism are made.

Joining the powerless

Do we, as women, want to change our positions in libraries and in the world or do we want to change librarianship and the world? It has often been said that men are more effective when manipulating "things," but women are more effective when working with people. When we buy into the power structure of the hierarchy, with its punishments, rewards, and conditioning, we may think we have gained power, but in the end we are once again joining the ranks of the powerless. We may obtain personal gratification by "joining up" and offering unquestioning loyalty to the organization, but that route will leave us powerless to bring change or have real impact.

Merely replacing the male administrators with female administrators does not change the power structure. The key to truly feminist power lies in changing the terms of the existing power structure, not in becoming part of it. Women have discovered several effective routes to bring this change. We must build on them, even though they all involve challenges to the ways we traditionally value work and people, and to the ways in which people relate to each other. The new routes to using power to bring change begin with defining and confronting basic, yet neglected, issues of power and control.

Sharing power

To rescue our institutions, our libraries, from their debilitating foundations in traditional hierarchical authority, will first demand change within ourselves. We will not achieve true participatory power as long as we unquestioningly accept existing authority as legitimate. We will not be able to achieve the new forms of power as long as we remain content with the status quo, even when that status quo gives us a small share of the existing authority. This fundamental shift in the terms of power not only requires restructuring our work-places, but also reeducating ourselves to a full awareness of the alternatives to the power assumptions that we now accept as reality--as the "way things are" and are supposed to be.

Networking is one fine example of a channel women are using to reach around existing power structures. Networks cut across institutional and hierarchical lines, offering open access to people, resources, and issues. There is no authority or leader at the top, as in conventional organizations. In a network, each individual is at the center. The routes to sharing power are direct; traditional boundaries disappear. Through networks we share power; we expand power. We empower both ourselves and others. We don't climb over others up some hierarchical pecking order.

Women have found the law to be another effective route to changing the terms of power. We didn't manage to pass the Equal Rights Amendment, but we have made progress in many areas of law. For example, there has been tremendous progress on the issue of comparable pay for comparable worth. Our progress toward acceptance of the concept that pay be equal not just for the same job, but for all jobs that call for comparable skills, effort, and responsibility has clearly changed the terms of power.

The current job market is rigged against women, who are concentrated in historically underpaid fields. These fields systematically pay less than male-dominated ones. The recent ruling in Tacoma, Washington found "overt and institutionalized discrimination" in the state, thus reinforcing the doctrine of comparable worth that the Supreme Court acknowledged in 1981. The questions here go much deeper than the issue of whether or not librarians compare in worth to garbage collectors. Are librarians serving children or in schools worth as much as history bibliographers or online searchers?

A third route we have travelled since the beginning of the modern women's movement is consciousness raising. Frankly, I thought I was beyond all that, at least in terms of my professional life, until I started to examine my own reactions to power--how much I have, how much I use, and why and how I use it. I discovered how far I still have to go--not only to understand power, but even to feel comfortable using it. My discomfort with power is a clear result of my own conditioning, conditioning most women share.

Understanding power, feeling comfortable with it, and using it constructively is a building and learning process. Networking, consciousness raising, organized action, and pressure to change existing structures and laws are tested routes to power, valuable tools that we have at hand. We live in a world where the mind, through the pen, is literally more powerful than the sword. With it we can rewrite the terms of power--not only for women, but for all human beings.

Total power, omnipotence, is not available to any of us, nor would we want it. Our current impotence, our lack of power, is equally unacceptable. We can be, to coin a word, "partipotent." As women, we cannot accept the current terms of power which allow it to be concentrated in the hands of a few. Our task is to recast those terms and to share the power we gain. When we share power we empower others. When we share it, we bring power to all who are the victims of its traditional misuse.

Bibliography

Alinsky, Saul D. "Of Means and Ends," Union Seminary Quarterly Review, January 1967, p. 107-124.
Campbell, Joseph. The Masks of God: Primitive Mythology. Morrow, 1967.
Galbraith, John. Anatomy of Power. Houghton, 1983.
Heim, Kathleen. "The Demographic and Economic Status of Librar-

ians in the 1970's, with Special Reference to Women," in Advances in Librarianship, Vol. 12. Academic Pr., 1982.
Heim, Kathleen, ed. The Status of Women in Librarianship: Historical, Sociological, and Economic Issues. Neal-Schuman, 1983.
Heim, Kathleen M. and Leigh S. Estabrook. Career Profiles and Sex Discrimination in the Library Profession. ALA, 1983.
Janeway, Elizabeth. Man's World, Woman's Place: A Study in Social Mythology. Morrow, 1967.
Kantor, Rosabeth Moss. "Power Failure in Management Circuits," Harvard Business Review, July-August 1979, p. 65-75.
Pogrebin, Letty Cottin. "Hers," New York Times, September 22, 1983, p. C2.
Rogers, Carl. On Personal Power. Delacorte, 1977.
Weber, Max. Max Weber on Law and Economy in Society. Harvard Univ. Pr., 1954.
Weibel, Kathleen and Kathleen M. Heim. The Role of Women in Librarianship 1876-1976: The Entry, Advancement, and Struggle for Equalization in One Profession. Oryx Pr. (A Neal-Schuman Professional Book), 1979.

"HUCKLEBERRY FINN" AND THE TRADITIONS OF BLACKFACE MINSTRELSY*

Fredrick Woodard and Donnarae MacCann

All great literature transcends yet at the same time mirrors the values of its times. Such is the case with Mark Twain's The Adventures of Huckleberry Finn. The novel has been the focus of controversy. In the midst of much heat but little light, it has become clear that close analysis of the book in terms of the messages it gives on issues of race remains to be done. It is to help fill that gap that we present the article below. We hope that teachers will share with their students the insights it offers.

Scholars and other commentators have generally maintained that Mark Twain's The Adventures of Huckleberry Finn is a broadly humanistic document. Twain's ability as a humorist and stylist, his effective satires and his advocacy--at times--of improved conditions for Black Americans have contributed to this judgment.[1]

However, in spite of the countless analyses of Huck Finn, the influence of "blackface minstrelsy" on this story is either barely mentioned or overlooked entirely, even though the tradition of white men blackening up to entertain other whites at the expense of Black people's humanity is at the center of Huck Finn's portrayal of Jim and other Blacks. This dimension is important to a full interpretation of the novel and should be considered essential to any classroom analysis of the book.

Minstrel performers were an important cultural influence in the last century. They were featured in circuses and other traveling shows, as well as in the afterpieces and entr'actes of the formal, "high art" theaters. In 1843, four white actors, the Virginia Minstrels, created an entire evening's entertainment of minstrel routines. By the middle of the 19th century more than 100 professional troupes in "blackface" were touring the U.S., with some performing in the

*Reprinted by permission of the authors and publisher from Interracial Books for Children Bulletin, 15:1-2 (1984) 4-13; copyright © 1984 by Council on Interracial Books for Children, Inc.

White House.[2] According to sociologist Alan Green, the minstrel caricatures were so compelling to white audiences that "anyone after the early 1840s who wished to portray a humorous Negro on the stage had to conform to the minstrelsy pattern, and that included Negroes themselves."[3] By the latter part of the century, guidebooks for amateur performers were available to the general public.[4]

Minstrel actors blackened their faces with burnt cork and wore outlandish costumes. They swaggered about the stage boasting nonsensically about minor accomplishments or fabricating tales of grandiose deeds; they had riotous celebrations; they mutilated the English language; and they quarreled vehemently over trivial issues.

Nineteenth century American minstrelsy drew upon European traditions of using the mask of blackness to mock individuals or social forces. The conventions of clowning also played a part, since clowns in many cultures have blackened or whitened their faces, exaggerated the appearance of the mouth, eyes and feet, used rustic dialects, and devised incongruous costumes. Clowns have filled a variety of social and aesthetic functions, but U.S. blackface performers have been unique in their singleminded derogation of an oppressed group. In the U.S., aspects of African American culture were incorporated into the minstrel routines in a highly distorted form. The resulting ridiculous or paternalistic portrayals of Black Americans were particularly appealing to the white theater-going audience.

Educators who teach Huck Finn as a literary and historical bench mark need to recognize how Twain used minstrelsy and how he himself was, to some extent, socialized by it.

Twain called these blackface minstrel routines a "joy." "To my mind," he said, "minstrelsy was a thoroughly delightful thing, and a most competent laughter-compeller...." He described the broad dialect as "delightfully and satisfyingly funny."[5] As to the typical violent quarrels between two minstrel protagonists, Twain wrote:

> ... a delightful jangle of assertion and contradition would break out between the two; the quarrel would gather emphasis, the voices would grow louder and louder and more and more energetic and vindictive, and the two would rise and approach each other, shaking fists and instruments and threatening bloodshed.... Sometimes the quarrel would last five minutes, the two contestants shouting deadly threats in each other's faces with their noses not six inches apart, the house shrieking with laughter all the while at this happy and accurate imitation of the usual and familiar negro quarrel....[emphasis added][16]

The notion that these stereotypical portrayals were realistic was commonplace. Carl Wittke, an early historian of minstrelsy, speaks of "Jim Crow" Rice, a popular white ministrel performer,

The Social Prerogative 307

as having "unusual powers as a delineator of Negro character."[7] These caricatures, so enjoyed by whites, moved from the stage to the pages of popular fiction and, eventually, to radio, movies and TV.

Twain wrote his laudatory remarks about minstrelsy in 1906, just four years before his death. Like many other authors, he was apparently influenced by this tradition throughout his life, even as he argued for more humane conditions for Black Americans and Africans.

Twain and Stage Performances

Twain's own career as a stage performer gave him a close tie with minstrelsy. Stage performances were a major source of income and status for Twain, and these performances were often based on "readings" of his works, a "lecture" style that was extremely popular at that time. Twain counseled a friend: "Try 'Readings.' They are all the rage now."[8]

Twain's performances point up his willingness to shape his message to his audience. On winning audience approval, Twain himself said: "No man will dare more than I to get it."[9] Following one performance, a Chicago critic wrote: "There is nothing in his lectures, for he very properly sacrifices everything to make his audience roar, and they do."[10]

It is not surprising to find that episodes in Huck Finn which read like skits in a minstrel show were probably written after most of the novel was completed, and at a time when Twain was planning a return to the stage with a new tour. These episodes--"King Sollermun," "Balum's Ass," "how a Frenchman doan' talk like a man," Jim's "rescue" by Huck and Tom Sawyer--would fit neatly into a Twain-style lecture tour, and it seems quite likely that they were created with the taste of theater audiences in mind.[11]

The novel's concluding farcical scenes--in which Huck and Tom concoct a nonsensical plan to help Jim, the runaway slave-- insured the book's success on and off the stage. As Twain wrote his wife about reading these rescue scenes: "It is the biggest card I've got in my whole repertoire. I always thought so. It went abooming...."[12]

The Minstrel Content

The depiction of Blacks in Huck Finn matches those of numerous minstrel plays in which Black characters are portrayed as addle-brained, boastful, superstitious, childish and lazy. These depictions are not used to poke fun at white attitudes about Black people; Jim is portrayed as a kindly comic who does act foolishly.

Early in the story, for example, Tom Sawyer moves Jim's hat to a nearby tree branch while he is sleeping. When Jim wakes he claims that witches put him in a trance and rode him over the state; he then elaborates this story several times until he finally claims that witches rode him all over the world and his back was "all over saddleboils."

Throughout the book, Jim is presented as foolish and gullible, given to exaggeration. After Jim and Huck get lost in the fog, an event Jim "painted ... up considerable," Huck tells Jim their frightening experience was only a dream. Jim believes him, even when he sees evidence that the experience was real:

> He had got the dream fixed so strong in his head that he couldn't seem to shake it loose and get the facts back into its place again right away.[13]

Twain has already established that Huck fulfills the role of a youthful, "unreliable" narrator; however, these comments about Jim seem accurate because they are backed up by Jim's own befuddled statements and actions. For example, Jim exclaims: "Is I me, or who is I? Is I heah, or what is I? Now dat's what I wants to know."

Similarly, when the Duke and Dauphin come aboard the raft, Huck sees that they are "lowdown humbugs and frauds," but says it "warn't no use to tell Jim," who is childishly proud to serve royalty.

Chapter eight is like a whole series of minstrel routines. First Jim explains how he speculated in stock, but the stock--a cow--died. Then he invested in a banking operation run by a Black swindler and lost more money. He gives his last dime to "Balum's Ass; one er dem chuckleheads, you know. But he's lucky, dey say...." Balum's Ass gives the dime to the church when he hears a preacher say "whoever give to de po' len' to de Lord, en boun' to git his money back a hund'd times."

The closing chapters serve a thematic purpose as Twain strengthens his attacks on the violence and hypocrisy of adult "civilization." Jim is a convenient instrument in the concluding burlesque, but his docile behavior reinforces his role as a dimwit--and hence as an audience pleaser. Jim could have walked away from his confinement many times, but he acts only under the direction of the white children--the implications being that he so dotes on the children that he will sacrifice his survival to their games, that he is helpless without white assistance and that he can think only on a child's level.

The farcical rescue scenes point up the unequal nature of the Huck/Jim relationship, but it is not the only time that Twain treats Huck and Jim as less than equal partners. For example, Huck makes no effort to find Jim after the raft is run down by a steamboat and the two are separated. He doesn't grieve over Jim's apparent death and doesn't express any relief when the two are reunited, although Jim nearly cries because he is so glad to see Huck alive.

The Social Prerogative

Literary critics calling Jim the novel's one and only noble adult are usually focusing on Jim's kindness toward Huck and Tom. With that image in mind, critics credit Twain with a broadly liberal perspective, but in fact, the "sympathy" that Huck Finn evokes for Jim is part of what minstrelsy is all about. "Stage Negroes" were shaped by their creators, according to Alan Green, so that they would be viewed sympathetically. Who would not feel affection for a "permanently visible and permanently inferior clown who posed no threat and desired nothing more than laughter and applause at his imbecile antics"?[14] Blacks had to be a source of hilarity for whites, says Green, in order for whites to cease feeling guilt and anxiety.

It's true that Jim is admirable because he is not an inveterate schemer, like most of the other people in the book. Jim also often makes more sense than other characters. For instance, when he argues with Huck about how Frenchmen talk, Jim is the more logical. But this debate "plays" like the dialogue in a minstrel show because Jim has the information-base of a child (i.e., Jim believes English to be the world's only language).

African American Speech Ridiculed

When Twain was working on The Adventures of Tom Sawyer in 1874, he wrote noted author and editor William Dean Howells, his literary advisor, about his technique: "I amend dialect stuff by talking and talking and talking it till it sounds right."[15] The "right" sound, however, was the sound of a white person playing a "stage Negro" --a sound that fit white expectations. The mock Black "dialect" in Huck Finn turns the humor into caricature and makes Jim's every appearance stereotypical. Jim's language is largely made up of either so-called non-standard words or so-called "eye dialect"-- words that look peculiar in print, as when "wuz" replaces "was." This eye dialect reinforces the notion that a character is stupid rather than merely poorly educated.

When Huck and Jim are both satirized in the chapter on having "a general good time," the language tends to isolate Jim as a fool. Huck reads from books salvaged from a sinking steamboat and we see the highly nonsensical result of his learning experience in a country school. Jim's garbled impression of the Scriptures is similarly revealed, and there is a nice give-and-take between the two vagabonds throughout the whole scene. But while we can easily laugh at Huck's very human confusion in this episode, it is more difficult to see the human side of Jim because of the exaggerated dialect. For example, Jim says:

> A harem's a bo'd'n-house, I reck'n. Mos' likely dey has rackety times in de nussery. En I reck'n de wives quarrels considerable; en dat 'crease de racket. Yet dey say Sollermun de wises' man dat ever liv'. I doan

take no stock in dat. Bekase why: would a wise man
want to live in de mids' er sich a blim-blammin' all de
time?[16]

The Aborted Anti-Slavery Storyline

Jim's attempt to escape slavery contributes a strong element of suspense in the early part of the novel, and Twain has an opportunity to comment on that institution. To a certain degree Twain offers a comic/serious protest against slavery, although we must remember that this issue had been decided by the Civil War some 20 years earlier. There are some brilliantly ironic stabs at slavery, but the plot line that focuses on Jim's escape is scuttled when the Duke/Dauphin burlesque takes over. This plot change occurs at the very moment Jim and Huck might have escaped in a newly acquired canoe. Instead, Huck goes in search of strawberries and then performs one of the most illogical acts in the story: he brings the false Duke and Dauphin to the raft he and Jim are living on. If the original plot line had remained important, good-hearted Huck might have sympathized with the desperate con men and he might have rowed them to some safer location, but it is hard to believe that he would suddenly contradict all his efforts to keep Jim out of sight.

Twain scholar Henry Nash Smith argues that the escape plan is aborted because Huck and Jim are virtually the captives of the Duke and Dauphin.[17] The text does not support this thesis, however, since Huck and Jim ignore several opportunities to follow through with their original plan while the Duke and Dauphin are working their confidence tricks on the river towns.

When Tom Sawyer reenters the story, Huck helps him carry out the farcical, futile escape plan. Because Jim's escape is not actually a high priority, Tom and Huck play at heroics based upon Tom's favorite adventure stories, affording Twain an opportunity to satirize such tales. When the boys actually release Jim, armed slavehunters are on the premises and the "rescue" has no chance of success. "The unhappy truth about the ending," writes Leo Marx in The American Scholar," ... is that the author, having revealed the tawdry nature of the culture of the great valley, yielded to its essential complacency."[18]

Jim is, in fact, finally free because his owner dies and frees him in her will. Thus his liberator turns out to be a slaveholder, the very sort, writes Leo Marx, "whose inhumanity first made the attempted escape necessary."[19]

The fact that Huck decides to "go to hell" rather than turn Jim in--to make, in other words, an eternal sacrifice for Jim--is often treated by critics as a superb evocation of anti-slavery sentiment. But to reach this interpretation, readers must not only ignore the characterization of Jim; they must also arbitrarily withdraw their attention from Twain's thematic and narrative compromises throughout the last fifth of the novel. Since Huck's concern for Jim all but disappears in the farcical "rescue" sequence, and since it is finally a slaveholder who is presented as the true rescuer, the "going to hell" pronouncement seems more closely related to Twain's many satirical commentaries on religion than to an overriding interest in the slave question. (In the incomplete novel "Tom Sawyer's Conspiracy," Twain uses Tom and Huck brilliantly as a means of debunking religion, while Jim is again a minstrel side-kick.)

Because Huck Finn is very contradictory as an anti-slavery work, it is important for readers, and for teachers especially, to examine the larger context of the "freedom" theme. This means pinpointing the text's cultural biases--the white supremacist beliefs which infuse the novel and which are not difficult to discover in a close reading. Notions of racial and cultural superiority appear in Huck Finn in the various ways that Twain undercuts Jim's humanity: in the minstrel routines with Huck as the "straight man," in the generalities about Blacks as unreliable, primitive and slow-witted, in the absence of appropriate adult/child roles, in Jim's vulnerability to juvenile trickery, and in the burlesqued speech patterns.

The Term "Nigger"

One of the most controversial aspects of Huck Finn is Twain's use of the term "nigger." As with every detail of the novel, the term needs to be examined in relation to its context. Huck uses "nigger" as it was used by white people to ridicule Blacks. When Huck says, "It was fifteen minutes before I could work myself up to go and humble myself to a nigger," he is rising slightly above his cultural conditioning by making an apology, but at the same time the reader sees him caught up in that bigoted culture by his use of a label that whites understood as pejorative.

A serious problem arises, however, in the fact that Jim refers to himself and other Blacks as "niggers," but the self-effacement inherent in his use of this term is not presented as a Black survival tactic. If Twain did not recognize the Black American use of such language as part of the "mask" worn to disarm whites, he was, like Huck, caught unwittingly in the bigoted system that he could not always transcend. If he understood this strategy, but left out any hint of this awareness in order to please a white audience, then he compromised his literary integrity.

These are necessary distinctions for sophisticated adult readers, but most young readers cannot be expected to make such distinctions. Children cannot usually respond to such loaded words with detachment and historical perspective. Whatever the purpose and effect of the term "nigger" for Twain's original white audience, its appearance in a classroom today tends to reinforce racism, inducing embarrassment and anger for Blacks and feelings of superiority and/or acts of harassment by whites.

It is important here to note Twain's use of irony. Some statements which seem blatantly racist are the most highly ironic. For instance, when Huck responds to Aunt Sally's query about an accident, "Anybody hurt?" with the statement, "No'm. Killed a nigger," a double layer of irony strengthens Twain's commentary. Aunt Sally replies, "Well, it's lucky; because sometimes people do get hurt," and the reader can easily discern the social conditioning behind Huck's denial of Black humanity, as well as the extraordinary indifference that makes Aunt Sally's idea of "luck" a bitterly ironic indictment of slavery. Similarly, one of the most potent comments on slavery occurs when Jim threatens to steal his own children and Huck responds:

> Here was this nigger which I had as good as helped to run away, coming right out flatfooted and saying he would steal his children--children that belonged to a man I didn't even know; a man that hadn't ever done me no harm. [20]

These ironic, "topsy-turvy" features are perhaps the easiest to teach in an English class.

Twain's Perspective

When looking at Huck Finn, it is important to consider Twain's upbringing and milieu. Twain himself emphasized the importance of early "training." Significantly, he lamented the fact that his mother would never abandon her support of slavery, but he defended her by saying, "Manifestly, training and association can accomplish strange miracles."[21] Huck himself emphasizes the importance of how people are "brung up." Tom was not "brung up" to free a "nigger" unless that slave was already legally free; the Dauphin was not "brung up" to deliver lines from Shakespeare properly; and kings, says Huck, "are a mighty ornery lot. It's the way they're raised." While Twain was in some respects a renegade, he was also "brung up" in a period in which opposition to slavery was a controversial position, and in which sensitivity to other issues of racial injustice was severely limited. In his autobiography, he writes:

> I was not aware that there was anything wrong about [slavery in my schoolboy days].... No one arraigned it in my hearing; the local papers said nothing against it; the local pulpit taught us that God approved it; if the slaves themselves had any aversion to slavery they were wise and said nothing. [22]

When Twain first went to New York in his late teens, he was apparently shocked by the sight of Blacks who were not slaves and wrote his mother:

> I reckon I had better black my face, for in these Eastern States niggers are considerably better than white people. [23]

The Social Prerogative

Several years later, when the Civil War broke out, Twain's sympathies were with the South, and he enlisted in the Confederate Army. His decision to quit after two weeks of soldiering seems to have had more to do with a new job opportunity out West than with any change of heart about the justice of the Confederate cause.[24]

Slavery aside, Twain's writings include many statements about Black Americans which reflect the prevailing white racist attitudes of the 19th century. In his autobiography, he mentions Uncle Dan'l, a slave on his uncle's farm, as the "real Jim." Uncle Dan'l, says Twain, was patient, friendly and loyal, "traits which were his birthright."[25] In Huck Finn, the racial bias of the statement that Jim was "white inside" is so extreme that it seems ironical. Yet, when Jim is commended as an "uncommon nigger," this is not unlike Twain's praise of his own butler as no "commonplace coon."[26] (William Dean Howells provides some insight on Twain's attitudes in this regard when he writes that Twain preferred Black or Asian butlers "because he said he could not bear to order a white man about." [27])

Twain amused colleagues by using the same caricatured speech he ascribed to Jim. He wrote his publisher:

> I's gwyne to sen' you di stuff jis' as she stan', now; an' you an' Misto Howls kin weed out enuff o' dem 93,000 words fer to crowd de book down to one book; or you kin shove in enuff er dat ole Contrib-Club truck fer to swell her up en bust her in two an' make two books outen her.... I don't want none er dat rot what is in de small envolups to go in, 'cepp'n jis' what Misto Howls say shel go in.[28]

Those claiming that Twain became a staunch advocate of social justice for Blacks usually cite his essay titled, "The United States of Lyncherdom," written in 1901. However, Twain decided not to publish this anti-lynching essay in the North American Review as he originally intended, because "I shouldn't have even half a friend left down there [in the South], after it issued from the press."[29] Instead, he chose to bury his indignation by placing the manuscript with papers he designed for posthumous publication.

Moreover, the essay's content, not Twain's timidity, is the important problem. It reveals Twain's deep-seated prejudice rather than his "de-southernization," which it is said to represent. Twain condemns lynching primarily because it is not due process, but he ignores the principle of due process in his discussion of a particular case. His arguments are based upon an unsupported presumption of Black guilt. He writes: "I will not dwell upon the provocation which moved the [lynchers] to those crimes...; the only question is, does the assassin take the law into his own hands?" And, in arguing that lynching is not a deterrent to crime, Twain supports the very myth that the KKK promulgated to justify its attacks--that Blacks threatened white women. He writes:

... one much talked-of outrage and murder committed by a negro will upset the disturbed intellects of several other negroes and produce a series of the very tragedies the community would so strenuously wish to prevent; ... in a word, the lynchers are themselves the worst enemies of their women.[30]

Twain's Ambivalence

Like many of his white contemporaries, Twain clearly had ambivalent attitudes about Blacks. On the other hand, we see his efforts to help Black college students financially, to aid a Black college, to publicly support the reputation of Black leader Frederick Douglass and to speak out boldly and progressively (e.g., there is a "reparation due," said Twain, "from every white to every black man"[31]). Yet he could not shake off some persistent white supremacist notions. In Huck Finn, Twain's ambivalence is recorded in the degrading minstrel elements on the one hand and in the anti-slavery theme on the other. (We must remember that the period following the Civil War and the abolition of slavery was one of intense racial conflict in this country as repressive forces sought to reinstate the "benefits" of slavery. Repressive "Jim Crow" laws, exploitative practices, terrorist activities designed to deprive Blacks of their voting and other civil rights--all were part of the climate in which Twain lived and wrote. These historical realities should be included in any classroom discussions of the work.)

Twain specialists have not generally provided much help to those concerned about the book's biases. For instance, Charles Neider, in his Introduction to The Selected Letters of Mark Twain, notes the offensive racism of Twain's frontier humor, but this does not prevent him from calling Twain the "Lincoln of our literature" and the "Shakespeare of our humor."[32] Perspective has quite a lot to do with what is classified as comic, and there are basic questions that cannot be passed over. Funny to whom? Funny at whose expense?

In The Grotesque Essence: Plays from the American Minstrel Stage, Gary Engle refers to minstrelsy as cruel, grotesque, monstrous and racist, and says it caricatures Blacks as "lazy, ignorant, illiterate, hedonistic, vain, often immoral, fatalistic and gauche." But, in spite of this, he calls Jim a "sympathetically drawn version of the minstrel clown."[33] Engle justifies minstrelsy by claiming that it purged the "American common man" of insecurity and blessed him with the "laughter of affirmation"--"By laughing at a fool, a nation can safely and beneficially laugh at itself."[34] Clearly, he is viewing the nation as a white society exclusively.

It is unfortunate that in extolling a work of literature, most critics feel they must endorse it in its entirety and, in effect, support its biases. Not surprisingly, Black author Ralph Ellison is one of the few commentators who has been critical of the minstrel tradition in Twain's works. It is Jim's stereotypical minstrel mask, notes Ellison, that makes Huck--not Jim--appear to be the adult on the raft. [35]

Literary historian Donald Gibson made the following statement about teaching Huck Finn to high school and college students:

> It should be shown to be a novel whose author was not always capable of resisting the temptation to create laughter through compromising his morality and his art. In short the problem of whether to teach the novel will not exist if it is taught in all its complexity of thought and feeling, and if critics and teachers avoid making the same kinds of compromises Mark Twain made. [36]

"All its complexity" must, of necessity, include the book's racism and its ties to the minstrel tradition. If students learn about this aspect of Twain's work, they will increase their capacity to understand Huck Finn.

This is an abridged version of a slightly longer essay to be published in 1985 by Scarecrow Press, Inc., as a part of the second edition of Donnarae MacCann and Gloria Woodard's The Black American in Books for Children.

References

1. Twain's talent for vernacular innovation, regional portraiture, mythic associations and other novelistic features could be discussed here, but they have been commented upon extensively in works by other critics. The problem in Twain scholarship is to bring about some balance between discussions of craft and discussions of content.
2. Gary D. Engle, The Grotesque Essence: Plays from the American Minstrel Stage (Baton Rouge: Louisiana State University Press, 1978), pp. xvi-xvii, xix-xx.
3. Alan W. C. Green, "'Jim Crow,' 'Zip Coon': The Northern Origins of Negro Minstrelsy," The Massachusetts Review, V. 11 (Spring, 1970), p. 394.
4. In the partially completed novel "Tom Sawyer's Conspiracy," Tom Sawyer goes to his aunt's garret to find "our old niggershow things" and plan a "nigger" disguise. Blacking-up kits, as well as performance manuals containing sample skits and lyrics, were widely sold to the general public.
5. Mark Twain, Mark Twain in Eruption: Hitherto Unpublished Pages About Men and Events, ed. Bernard De Voto (New York: Harper, 1922), pp. 110, 115.
6. Ibid., p. 113.
7. Carl Wittke, Tambo and Bones: A History of the American Minstrel Stage (New York: Greenwood reprint, 1968; original published in 1930), p. 25.
8. Paul Fatout, Mark Twain on the Lecture Circuit (Bloomington: Indiana University Press, 1960; reprinted, Gloucester, Mass.: Peter Smith, 1966), p. 190.

9. Justin Kaplan, Mark Twain and His World (New York: Simon and Schuster, 1974), p. 69. In the first lectures in 1866, Twain used a mixture of what Kaplan calls delightful "statistics, anecdotes, edification and amusement, humorous reflection delivered after a delicately timed pause, something that passed for moral philosophy, and passages of gorgeous word painting." In 1884, Twain adopted the format Charles Dickens used in public readings. His style became a blend of telling and acting episodes from his books (Kaplan, pp. 68, 128).
10. Fatout, p. 106.
11. The approximate times when different parts of the novel were written are discussed in Walter Blair's "When Was Huckleberry Finn Written?" (American Literature, March, 1958, pp. 1-25); in David Carkeet's "The Dialects in Huckleberry Finn" (American Literature, November, 1979, pp. 315-332); in Franklin R. Rogers' Mark Twain's Burlesque Patterns (Dallas: Southern Methodist University Press, 1960, pp. 139-140); in Michael Patrick Hearn's The Annotated Huckleberry Finn (New York: Potter, 1981), p. 111.
12. Rogers, p. 148.
13. Clemens, Samuel Langhorne (Mark Twain), Adventures of Huckleberry Finn: An Authoritative Text, Backgrounds and Sources, Criticism, 2nd edition by Sculley Bradley, Richard Croom Beatty, E. Hudson Long, Thomas Cooley (New York: W. W. Norton, 1977), pp. 71-72.
14. Green, p. 394.
15. Charles Neider, ed., The Selected Letters of Mark Twain (New York: Harper & Row, 1982), p. 84.
16. Clemens, p. 65. The dialect in a typical minstrel play reads as follows: "It 'pears dat de Lawd, after he done made Adam and Eve, sot 'em in de Garden ob Edem, dat de Lawd he Tol' em bofe dat dar was a sartain tree and dat dey musn't eat none of eet's fruit...." (William Courtright's The Complete Minstrel Guide, Chicago: The Dramatic Publishing Co., 1901, p. 83.)
17. Henry Nash Smith, Mark Twain: The Development of a Writer (Cambridge: The Belknap Press of Harvard University Press, 1962), pp. 113-137.
18. Leo Marx, "Mr. Eliot, Mr. Trilling, and Huckleberry Finn," The American Scholar, V. 22:4 (Autumn, 1953), p. 433.
19. Ibid.
20. Clemens, p. 74.
21. Charles Neider, ed., The Autobiography of Mark Twain: Including Chapters Now Published for the First Time (New York: Harper & Row, 1959), p. 30.
22. Ibid., p. 6.
23. James M. Cox, Mark Twain: The Fate of Humor (Princeton: Princeton University Press, 1966), p. 7.
24. Twain scholar John C. Gerber has explained how Twain tried to justify his withdrawal from the Confederate Army in an essay Twain wrote in 1885 entitled, "The Private History of the Campaign That Failed." Twain introduced fictional content into his explanation that would help him pacify his Southern critics. (See Mark Twain: Selected Criticism, ed. by Arthur L. Scott,

Dallas: Southern Methodist University Press, 1967, pp. 281-282.)
25. Neider, Autobiography of Mark Twain, pp. 5-6.
26. Arthur G. Pettit, Mark Twain and the South (Lexington: University of Kentucky Press, 1974), p. 104.
27. William Dean Howells, My Mark Twain (New York: Harper, 1910), p. 34.
28. Pettit, p. 128.
29. Kaplan, p. 194.
30. Maxwell Geismar, ed., Mark Twain and the Three R's: Race, Religion, Revolution--and Related Matters (Indianapolis/New York: Bobbs-Merrill, 1973), p. 34.
31. Edward Wagenknecht, Mark Twain: The Man and His Work (Norman: University of Oklahoma Press, 1967, 3rd ed.), p. 222.
32. Neider, Selected Letters, pp. 2, 5.
33. Engle, p. xxvi.
34. Engle, pp. xxvi, xxviii.
35. Ralph Ellison, "Change the Joke and Slip the Yoke," Partisan Review, V. 25:2 (Spring, 1958), pp. 215, 222.
36. Donald Gibson, "Mark Twain's Jim in the Classroom," English Journal, V. 57:2 (February, 1968), p. 202.

SELECTION AND CENSORSHIP: A REAPPRAISAL*

Lester Asheim

To buy or not to buy, that is the question. None of us can escape either of those responsibilities if we really see ourselves as professionals charged with serving the entire community through the institution for which we are the appointed gatekeepers. Thirty years ago I wrote:

> To the selector the important thing is to find reasons to keep the book. Given such a guiding principle, the selector looks for values, for virtues, for strengths, which will overshadow minor objections. For the censor, on the other hand, the important thing is to find reasons to reject the book. His guiding principle leads him to seek out the objectionable features, the weaknesses, the possibilities for misinterpretation....
> The selector says, if there is anything good in this book let us try to keep it; the censor says, if there is anything bad in this book, let us reject it. And since there is seldom a flawless work in any form, the censor's approach can destroy much that is worth saving.[1]

The reason it may be desirable to explore once again the differences between selection and censorship is the fact that in today's climate some serious thinkers, and more importantly many opinion leaders (who unfortunately are not always the same people), are raising the question: "Why should arrogant librarians be allowed to impose their preferences on materials that are purchased with other people's money?"

The key distortion in this attack is the underlying assumption that the approach librarians take to selection is based upon their own preferences, that books that are not bought are those the librarian happens not to like or care about, and that the collection is a direct reflection of the librarian's own pet peeves, preferences, and prejudices. I cannot say unequivocally that a library collection contains none of the books that the librarian likes to read, but I think I can

---
*Reprinted by permission of the author and publisher from Wilson Library Bulletin, 58 (November 1983) 180-184; copyright © 1983 by the H. W. Wilson Co.

say that any library in which any kind of professional selection policy is in effect (whether written or not) will contain many works that the librarian does not like or agree with. What the collection reflects is the librarian's view of what readers and users want and need, whether the librarian likes it or not. The librarian's bias is that the collection should be unbiased. But an unbiased collection is precisely what many censors disapprove of.

Which leads us to an interesting dilemma. Selection is as much involved in building a collection that responds to the whole community as in building a collection that caters only to the interest of a special group. To make sure that there is something for everyone, which sounds like "anything goes," requires just as tight a control over purchases as special purpose selection. For one thing, there is only so much money, which means that not everything can be bought; there is only so much space, which means that everything that is published or released in other formats cannot be added. The librarian's duty is to see that the available money and space are used in the best interests of all those who are present or potential users of the library. But while money and space require that selection be exercised, they do not determine which individual items be selected. That is where the librarian's judgment enters.

A representative institution

In these days of mass media, Nielsen ratings, blockbusters, and bottom lines, the library has a unique responsibility. The mass agencies of communication think in terms of large, faceless audiences. The common denominator, not the individual differences, becomes the criterion. A library, on the other hand, strives to assure that while the interests of the majority are being met, the interests of the many minorities are being protected. It is characteristic of American democracy that the individual, the special case, has rights too, and the public library is one of American democracy's most representative institutions.

So what we are saying, when we resist the removal of materials that have been selected for the library's collection or take exception to the restriction of materials that have already passed the test of relevance for a particular library, is not that questions may not be raised about the librarian's choices. It is that one segment of the library's total constituency should not be permitted to interfere with another segment's rights and that it is part of our responsibility to protect the rights of all.

The removal of materials threatens the democratic balance that the total collection is meant to represent, and while it is sometimes difficult to bleed, fight, and die for one book in a collection of thousands, there is a long-standing principle involved that should not be heedlessly overlooked in the heat of a momentary reaction to a single word, a private prejudice, or even a strongly-felt provocation. What we are saying is not that a member of the public does not have the right to express his or her opinions of our professional judgment, but rather that there should be a due process, taking all of the pertinent considerations into account, before a professional judgment is overthrown.

The right to choose

The response of the censorious, when a demand to remove an item from the collection is not immediately carried out, is: Why should this material, offensive to me, be rammed down my throat? Why are the morals of Las Vegas forced upon the citizens of Pleasantville?

These questions fall wide of the mark. The material picked out for repression sits in the library along with thousands of other books that the censor does not oppose. And there they all do, indeed, sit--approved or not--until someone chooses of his or her own volition to use them. The preponderance of books in a library are beyond criticism by any standard, and if shelf-space were a guarantee of wide public attention, not even the most censorious could complain.

The problem, of course, is not that certain books are forced on readers, but that readers make choices, and sometimes those choices do not coincide with the choices that the censorious would prefer them to have. It is the other person's right to choose that is being questioned by the censor, for even if librarians wanted to force the use of certain materials, they do not have the power to do so. As Samuel Goldwyn is purported to have said: "If the public doesn't come, no one can stop them." The grammer is a bit fractured, but the point is clear: when people have freedom of choice, they exercise it, and neither availability nor hype can make them choose any item they do not wish to choose.

Clearly, the problem is not that readers are coerced by librarians into using certain materials, but rather that people--given democratic freedom of choice--do not always choose as we would like them to. The censor's solution is to take away their freedom of choice. The social responsibility of the library is to preserve freedom of choice, and the selection policies of the librarians are designed to foster it.

If there is to be a confrontation between librarians and some members of the society, then the issue should be properly stated. The issue is broader than Catcher in the Rye or Huckleberry Finn or Brave New World. It is the right of the people in a democracy to have access to the widest possible variety of choices and freely to choose for themselves, on the basis of their own judgment. And notice that proviso: for themselves. Not for everybody else.

The Social Prerogative

Limiting special interests

In the program "Are Libraries Fair?" held during the ALA conference in Philadelphia last year, Cal Thomas, vice-president of Moral Majority, urged that libraries open up the book selection process to the public. There's nothing wrong with the general principle that ways should be found to learn from patrons about their wants and interests, to tap their satisfactions and their complaints and to be responsive to them. An informal system already works to provide that kind of feedback constantly to the librarian. But in the end, after one patron demands that a certain book be banned and another person insists that a certain book be bought, someone has to be responsible for the interests of the library's entire public, not just the interests of those who are vocal. And that is where librarians are called upon. Because by training, by experience, and through the exercise of professional skills, they are able, as particular interest groups often are not, to recognize and respond to those interests that differ from their own.

For the most part, those who would remove materials are motivated by the best of intentions; to keep what is right and to remove what is wrong, as they see it. I do not question the strength of their conviction nor the sincerity of their belief. But they tend to approach the library's collection as a case of "either/or" when to be truly responsive the library's motto must be "not only/but also."

I do not mean to suggest that any inquiry about the justification of a library's purchase is ipso facto censorship. What I am talking about are the actions that have been taken: the removal of books or parts of books, often in the form of theft or vandalism: the occasional but nevertheless actual burning of some library materials; the imposition of restrictions and barriers that reduce the number of ideas to which users may have access. The legal actions brought and the removal of librarians from their positions for doing what they were hired to do are a justifiable reason for concern not only about the specific instances themselves, but even more because of the "chilling effect" (a concept recognized by the courts) on future selection and freedom of access. Remember that the freedom we are talking about is not only our freedom to disseminate ideas; equally important is the public's freedom to receive ideas.

The one thing that reassures librarians that they are probably doing something right when they get into disagreements about the collection is that the protests are as vehement from the Left as they are from the Right, from the pro-somethings as from the anti-somethings. Each special interest group thinks its ideas are underrepresented while all others are overrepresented. It is seldom that any group can make the case that its ideas are not represented at all. The most they can say is that their perception is that ideas of which they do not approve appear to be more heavily represented than those they'd like to promote. And what is disturbing is that it almost invariably comes down to "let's get rid of" rather than "why don't you add?"

New words, old music

At least that's how it used to be, but today some of the censorious groups are getting more sophisticated. They have found, to their dismay, that the direct censorship and removal of materials is now frequently condemned, not only by librarians and other such humanistically-tainted types, but even by many of their own neighbors and fellow-citizens for whom they presume to speak. As a result, they have begun to alter their tone and--at least in the statements they make for public consumption--deny any desire to censor or remove materials. The aim, they say, is only to add the materials they favor in sufficient quantity to bring about a balance that is not now there.

They are also making tactical changes, such as adapting some of the arguments of the American Civil Liberties Union to their own purposes and, in the state of Washington at least, changing the name of the Moral Majority to the Bill of Rights Legal Foundation. It is a smart move, and if they really follow their new rhetoric, things may be looking up. I may be forgiven, I hope, in having some reservations about the sincerity of the new look, which, on the basis of past performance, could turn out to be more skillful public relations than a real change of heart.

Meanwhile, the change in rhetoric may be salutary both for them and for us. For the, because if they find themselves obliged to practice what they now publicly preach, it could change their approach to the materials that carry ideas. And for us, because if they begin to practice what they preach, we may have to do so as well.

We may have to listen to some of their complaints more seriously and look more carefully at what we do in the light of what they say we do. Up to now, we have been able to take refuge behind wisecracks, a sense of our own self-righteousness, and the assurance that the extremist groups are sure to go just far enough beyond reason to bring ridicule onto their own heads. Making the opposition look ridiculous is a delightful ploy; it is even better when the opposition makes itself look ridiculous with no help from us whatsoever. When the Mothers Against Smut, or some such group, a few years ago created a smut wagon filled with examples of obscenities from books and other sources and drove it around town for everyone to examine, they ended up in the pokey, quite rightly, for disseminating obscene materials. One always gets a certain satisfaction in seeing the biter bitten.

The put-down makes us feel good, of course, but such wisecracks as "The Moral Majority is neither moral nor a majority, and the New Right is neither, either," even if they convey a truth or a partial one, are an inadequate evaluation of the power of those groups. What's more, our satisfaction at getting a laugh can divert us from whatever may be worthy of consideration in what the opposition is saying. I suggest to you that we should pay more attention

The Social Prerogative 323

to those who attack our purposes and our practices for two reasons: because so many people do and because we should be prepared to answer those attacks, if we can.

Asking the right questions

I hope you don't think I've gone over to the enemy by suggesting that they might, in some instances, just possibly be right. If, on occasion, they are correct in some of their accusations, we ought to be glad for their help in putting us back on any track from which we may have inadvertently strayed. They have already learned from us and have altered their tactics as a result. Do we now have something to learn from them, something that goes beyond the simple alteration of tactics to a reaffirmation of our basic principles? Insights and truths turn up in all kinds of odd places and contexts.

Phyllis Schlafly (if you'll pardon the expression) back in 1981 suggested a test of libraries to her followers that we might ourselves adopt. In her article, "How to Improve Fairness in Your Library," she supplies a list of forty-eight titles that she feels local public libraries ought to have on their shelves in the categories of pro-life (meaning anti-abortion), pro-defense, pro-family, and pro-basic education. Her charge to her readers is to take this list and check it against their public library catalogs to see how many of them are there and then put the pressure on to add all the ones that aren't in the collection. She even adds a little list of pro-lib books as a check. Notice how sure she is of the library's bias; she's betting that few libraries will have any, or very many, of her preferred list.

ALA's Office for Intellectual Freedom took Schlafly's advice and tried to check the extent to which the titles she recommends are missing from libraries. As you can guess, it is much harder to establish factual evidence than it is to make broad, condemnatory generalizations, but a check was made of the holdings reported in the OCLC bibliographic network, which admittedly is not a very good source of information about small and medium-sized public libraries. On the basis of that quick and dirty survey, it appears that of the two titles Schlafly thought should be in all libraries (one written by her and one about her), 425 libraries in twenty-five states and the District of Columbia held a copy of one title, and 559 libraries in forty-six states and the District of Columbia held a copy of the other. Several of the other titles made an even better showing; several did less well.

This doesn't prove much except that Schlafly rather overstated her case. What we cannot yet prove is that libraries do give just as much attention to the prejudices on Schlafly's side as they do to the prejudices on other sides. I like to think that a really thorough search of library holdings would show this to be true, because if it is not, librarians have some explaining to do.

The balanced collection

The key is balance, which does not necessarily mean an equal number of titles on every subject. But even a term like "balance" may not mean the same thing to different people. In his Moral Majority Report for March 1983, Jerry Falwell expands upon Phyllis Schlafly's suggested campaign to check libraries for conservative titles, to which he appends a much larger list of books that he thinks should be in in the library. "If they don't put our books up," he says, "then take the liberal books down." In other words, balance to Falwell means a selected sample of titles from all other points of view as against the entire list of his recommendations.

But the librarian's responsibility is to identify interests and to make judgments with the entire collection and the entire community in mind, not just that part of it with the largest constituency or the loudest voices or the most intimidating threats. It sounds easier than it is, but that is true of all responsibilities. To make decisions, to make them for sound reasons, and to be able to defend them when they are questioned are characteristics of professional judgment that I like to think go with the librarian's territory.

The balanced collection, of course, will never completely satisfy the groups who want their own point of view more prominent. Against the more familiar complaints on the far Right--too much material on sex, too much material that is anti-religious, not enough material on the virtues of free enterprise and state's rights--there is the other extreme: not enough on sex, not enough material critical of the traditional religionist position, too much material "of interest to investors and business people."[2]

In other words, no subterfuge is going to avoid offending someone, and no amount of yielding to complaints is going to stop everyone. All we accomplish by giving in to such pressure is to shift the source of the complaints from those who want the material removed to those who want it retained and expanded. Which suggests that librarians may just have to take more responsibility for defining the nature of the collection, achieving balance as they see it, and be prepared for the denunciations. Have we known all along that any decision of any importance will offend someone, and have we then chosen to offend only those we think have the least power to retaliate?

An answer to the censor

In 1774 Edmund Burke was speaking to a group of citizens prior to an election and reminded them, "Your representative owes you, not his industry only, but his judgment; and he betrays, instead of serving you, if he sacrifices it to your opinion."

Remember that in its eighteenth-century connotation, "your opinion" meant "your approbation." If we substitute the word librarian for representative, we find an answer to those who feel that as keeper of a publicly-supported institution, the librarian must defer to every complaint of pressure from a taxpayer: "Your librarians owe you, not their industry only, but their judgment; and they betray, instead of serving you, if they sacrifice it to curry your favor."

Librarians and users are in this together. We have a responsibility that goes with our title; they have a responsibility to try to see the total picture, not just their own segment of it. Both of us still have a lot to learn about the provision and dissemination of ideas, particularly when that entails, as it often does, not a clash between right and wrong, but among many rights. Seen in that light, ours is an important role that has implications far beyond any one item in the library or any one uncomfortable confrontation that we would prefer to avoid. Our responsibility is the defense of access to ideas, to information, esthetic pleasure, to recreation in its literal sense of re-creation, and to knowledge or at least to the process that leads to knowledge.

So it really is not the one book or the one viewpoint that is at issue here, but the defense of ideas that is our concern. I still believe that the best solution to the problem of access is to add positively to the store of ideas, not negatively to reduce it.

References

1. Lester Asheim, "The Librarian's Responsibility: Not Censorship but Selection," in Frederic Mosher, ed., Freedom of Book Selection (Chicago: ALA, 1954), 95-96. Originally published in Wilson Library Bulletin, 28 (September 1953) 63-67.
2. Sanford Berman, "Inside Censorship," Wisconsin Library Bulletin (Spring 1977), 2124.

THE "ADULTERATION" OF CHILDREN'S BOOKS*

Jo Carr

Freedom of subject matter is matched with freedom of style. There are still people, no doubt, who imagine a children's writer as one cruelly limited in vocabulary. Such people cannot have opened any recently published children's books. They might have found, had they done so, an exuberance of language too seldom present today in the matter-of-fact pages of the adult novel with its drab, tape-recorded dialogue. [1]

Pete lumbers up to the reference desk at the local library. He asks the librarian where he can find information on epidemics for a paper he's been assigned. The reference librarian helps him, and he settles down with a pile of books. They are thick books. The print, peppered with footnotes, is only occasionally relieved by a photograph or a drawing or a chart. He tries to make sense out of the pages in front of him, but he doesn't read very well and begins to feel overwhelmed almost immediately. Before long he has "turned off" in self-defense. He copies down some information from an encyclopedia and leaves the library. Although he might have originally approached the reference desk with a flickering of curiosity about epidemics, this flicker has been effectively extinguished--partly by the volume and complexity of the information in the books, partly by the bland writing in the encyclopedia. Pete will probably be in no hurry to come back to the library.

If, by some lucky mistake, Pete had found himself in the children's room, he might have discovered Melvin Berger's Disease Detectives. Having once opened it, he would have been sufficiently intrigued to follow the string of clues and questions leading to the solving of Legionnaire's Disease by the Disease Control Center. This book, while giving clear and complete information, might at the same time have successfully kindled that original flicker of curiosity.

Or, same scene, same library: This time it is Mrs. Mackenzie who is heading for the fiction shelves to find a book by Norah

---

*Reprinted by permission of the author and publisher from Library Journal, 109 (September 15, 1984) 1729-1732. Published by R. R. Bowker Co. (a Xerox company). Copyright © 1984 by Xerox Corporation.

Lofts. She says she likes Norah Lofts because her books have a
story and they make you feel good and they aren't pornographic.
Mrs. Mackenzie admits that the writing is dismal, but what is she
to do? She has tried John Updike and Thomas Pynchon and Anthony
Burgess, and, well, we all know how difficult their books are.
Furthermore, they are all so depressing! Doris Lessing is good,
or was, until she started getting complicated. Margaret Drabble is
fine, but there aren't anywhere near enough books by her. And
since she can't find writing she really likes, she has no choice but
to read Norah Lofts. Or, as an alternative, she is forced to read
mysteries that have been written masterfully by P. D. James, even
though she doesn't really like mysteries.

If, once again by mistake, Mrs. Mackenzie had wandered
into the children's room, she might have found All Together Now by
Sue Ellen Bridgers. At once she would have been mesmerized by
the compelling story of a fragile friendship between a young girl and
a retarded man twice her age. Following the unfolding of the plot,
Mrs. Mackenzie would have absorbed a kind of gentleness that could
have cast a pleasant glow over her household chores for weeks to
come, to say nothing of enjoying writing so accomplished as to shame
Norah Lofts right off the shelf.

It is unfortunate that these two scenarios are fictional, that
a real Pete and real Mrs. Mackenzie would probably never have this
happy experience in a real library. As a result, they--and all of
us--may be missing books that rival the best in adult collections.
Children's books are not just for children anymore.

Not that the idea of children's books for adults is really new.
Children's librarians have always believed what C. S. Lewis once
said: "I am almost inclined to set it up as a canon that a children's
story which is enjoyed only by children is a bad children's story."[2]

Crumbling walls, looming barriers

What is new is the extent of adult appeal in today's children's books.
Sheila Egoff has suggested that the child reader may have been forgotten by those who are writing and publishing for children today.
In her important May Hill Arbuthnot lecture in 1979, Egoff comments:
"The sad fact is that contemporary children's literature, whether for
its virtues or its faults, seems to be moving perilously close in tone,
in theme and language to the adult world."[3] She speaks of children's literature as a garden, until recently protected from adult
problems by a wall of considerable height. Now, she says, the
wall is down. Since childhood itself has become vulnerable, it is
hardly surprising that children's books would have become in many
cases indistinguishable from adult books.

Curiously enough, while the wall has been crumbling around
Egoff's garden of children's literature, another wall continues to loom
over the same books. The actual difference between adult and chil-

dren's books may be getting fuzzier, but library collections have failed to reflect this. In libraries, access is nothing if not partite. John Rowe Townsend, a critic of children's literature in England, says: "Books are, in fact, continually finding their way on to the children's lists which, in another age, would have been regarded as general fiction. Abetted by their editors, writers for children constantly push out the bounds of what is acceptable. Yet because of the great division these writers, and their books, are probably more shut off than ever from the general public."[4]

What is the division, and why is it so formidable? Townsend claims: "Arbitrary though it is, the division [between adult and juvenile publishing] has become sharper in the present century. The main reasons have been the expansion of school and public libraries for children, and corresponding changes in the book trade. On the whole, I believe that the children's library has been a blessing to authors and publishers as well as children. The growth of a strong institutional market has eased some of the cruder commercial pressures and has made possible the writing and publication of many excellent books which otherwise could never appear. But it has hardened the dividing line between children's books and adult books into a barrier, behind which separate development now takes place."[5]

The barrier is indeed there. Try to persuade a high school student, like Pete, that America's Endangered Birds might tell him as much about whooping cranes as a duller, longer book in the adult section. Or try convincing a fiction addict, like Mrs. Mackenzie, that a book by K. M. Peyton might be a better "read"--and far better written--than Arabella by Georgette Heyer.

The definition of "children" is actually part of the problem. Although librarians in public schools usually think of children as those in elementary school and below, most public librarians define childhood as ranging in age from pre-school through intermediate school; in other words, through grades 8 or 9. To some extent, the public library's perception of young teenagers as "children" has caused more than a fair share of the difficulty.

The children's room of every public library, while serving these children from pre-school through grade 8 or 9, also houses two kinds of adult books: those so well written they can be appreciated by anybody who can read, adult or child; and those that are not for children at all. Both kinds are found in fiction and nonfiction. (For a discussion of "adulteration" in picture books, see the article on teenagers and picture books in the October 1980 Wilson Library Bulletin.) The two forms of "adulteration" can be spotted immediately in juvenile nonfiction collections, as will be apparent when we return to the library which Pete has just left.

"Adulterated" nonfiction

Now it is Mrs. Herman at the reference desk. She is looking for

The Social Prerogative

information about cathedrals before she leaves on her French tour. With the help of the reference librarian, she finds books on cathedrals, but--like Pete--she doesn't read too well and feels somewhat daunted. She suddenly identifies strongly with the child who said about the book he was reading: "This book tells me more about penguins than I want to know." What Mrs. Herman really needs is David Macaulay's book Cathedral, a book for children. Line drawings, showing each stage in the construction of a cathedral--from inside out, outside in, upward, downward, close up, far away-- clarifies by sheer graphic skill. No wonder some art history professors have made slides of this book for college lectures.

Then there is Mrs. Herman's neighbor who is curious about the nest outside her kitchen window. She would be fascinated by a children's book, Window into a Nest, in which superb photographs give a detailed, day-by-day account of what is happening. Or if her neighbor is interested in what is developing inside the egg, the book to find would be A Chick Hatches by Joanna Cole, with photographs by Jerome Wexler. The subject could not be more clearly explained, never mind the third-grade reading level.

The children's shelves are filled with books like these: lively, accurate, clear. Franklyn Branley, a fine science writer for children, has explained why this may be so. It is only when he must explain a subject to children, he says, that he realized he doesn't really understand it. Someone writing for children, knowing well that children will shut the book if they are bored or confused, may be forced to think more carefully, to work harder at clarification. The result may well be a distillation of the subject. In addition, the imaginative use of drawings and photographs in children's nonfiction can make a tremendous difference in arousing curiosity and clarifying concepts.

Most of us would enjoy knowing more about a lot of things, especially about science, but we usually have neither time nor inclination to read in depth. Like Pete, we just aren't that interested. Children's books are perfect for satisfying this kind of curiosity. With very little effort and a great deal of pleasure, we can read these books to find accuract information about almost anything. For plate tectonics, see Fodor's book Earth in Motion. For black holes, try The Creation of the Universe by David Fisher, a book which explains not only black holes but all kinds of other fascinating phenomena and with such beguiling clarity that the reader is periodically drawn to put down the book in order to check the night sky. Or, for inspiration as well as information, try Anne Ophelia Dowden's Wild Green Things in the City: a Book of Weeds. Anyone who has pored over the outstanding botanical illustrations in this book will never again walk unseeing through a vacant lot. A new world has opened up.

Anyone who can read will enjoy any of these books, adults most definitely included, but some so-called children's books are not for children at all. They are, in fact, adult books. Take this example:

The centripetal force felt by the moon is $F = \frac{mv^2}{r}$ where m is the moon's mass, r the radius of its orbit, and v the speed around the orbit. According to Newton's Second Law this force must produce an acceleration toward the earth, and the value of this acceleration is, since $F = ma : a_c = \frac{v^2}{r}$. We can calculate this value very easily... [6]

This explanation of gravity is in a book intended for children. Perhaps there is an exceptional child who could "calculate this value very easily," but how many of us know one?

There are so many children's books like this--way over the heads of children--that teachers have been known to say: "If these books are for children, all of my kids must be stupid." In some cases, the books are not necessarily too advanced; they are just too long, with print entirely too small. Peggy Thomson's lively portraits of Museum People: Collectors and Keepers at the Smithsonian, for instance, would captivate the right child, but the right child would have to be willing to plow through 302 pages of solid print. Since there are all too few children willing to do this, a superb adult book takes root on a shelf in the children's room.

Linda Grant De Pauw has also written a book well beyond children. Founding Mothers: Women of America in the Revolutionary Era, although packed with so much fascinating detail that it is difficult to put down, seldom leaves the shelves. The logical reader of this engrossing study would be an adult, and what adult would ever think of looking for the book in the children's room?

So it is that a great many nonfiction books are out of place or unappreciated in the children's room. Unfortunately, the same is true of fiction.

"Good reads" on the shelf

If readers like Mrs. Mackenzie realized it, they could all be assured of finding a "good read" on the shelves in the children's room. Book after book has: 1) a real plot; 2) an ending that leaves the reader with hope that the world is not going to hell in a bucket, at least not before next week; 3) language only mildly offensive; 4) characters that go places and do things, but seldom violently; and 5) humor, gentle and without an edge to it. But, above all, readers like Mrs. Mackenzie would find superb writing. The editors of children's books have become a discerning bunch. They have been backing winners for years.

Take Peter Dickinson who has written one spell-binding book, among many others, called Tulku. There is simply no way to stop reading about Mrs. Jones, from the time she first starts shooting bandits in Tibet until she is finally enshrined as a kind of Buddhist Madonna.

The Social Prerogative 331

Or K. M. Peyton who has yet to write a poor book. A recent one, called Marion's Angels, although intended for younger readers, is delightful for any age. It portrays a sensitive girl in East Anglia who prays for a rich American to save the ancient and crumbling church she loves. As she rises from her knees, she hears a voice behind her: "Hi, kid ..." Even she is astounded by God's efficiency.

Or Ursula LeGuin. Her fantasy A Wizard of Earthsea holds the interest of a child at one level while probing important adult questions at a much deeper level. It is a work of haunting beauty and significance.

Or Katherine Paterson. Jess and Leslie in Bridge to Terabithia will leave the reader weeping uncontrollably, but they--and the book--will not be forgotten. It is for children, for adults, for anybody.

Or Natalie Babbitt. Her Tuck Everlasting, a simple story about death and immortality, has the resonance of a parable.

One could go on. Fine books by fine writers crowd the children's shelves: Nina Bawden, Hester Burton, Jane Gardam, Lois Lowry, William Mayne, Susan Cooper, Leon Garfield, Paula Fox, Alan Garner, Elaine Konigsburg, Helen Cresswell, Eleanor Cameron--the list is extensive.

All these books are what Geoffrey Trease has called "onions." In each book, the reader peels down to whatever layer is digestible. C. S. Lewis, then was quite right. Good children's books, like the best of any kind of literature, should leave room for what Katherine Paterson has called "the creative reader." And creative readers come in all ages.

Strong stuff

But some children's fiction, like some nonfiction, misses the child completely. In some cases, the problem is the subject. Cran of Coalgate by Winifred Cawley is an appealing evocation of family life in a Northumberland mining town in the 1920s. Quite apart from the dialect, which is thick enough to congeal the plot, the book is more about childhood than for children. Nostalgia, although in this case not the least sentimental, enhances the story for adults but bores children utterly.

Sometimes the problem is violence, to say nothing of sex. An example:

... The triumphant look in his eyes alerted her to his action. She barely had time to aim and shoot as he sprang.
The roar was stupefying and she fell backward from the

gun's kick, coughed through the rolling smoke, grasped the gun firmly and swung it back like a club. No need. Ray Beard sat on the floor looking with wild concern at the gaping hole in his crotch. His hands frantically tried to hold slithering innards in place. Failed. He grabbed and tucked, grabbed again, looked up at her in horror. The swift slippery blood made his task harder.... Ray Beard's hands suddenly relaxed in his lap and were immediately full, all his work gone for naught.[7]

This is pretty strong stuff, but not so strong as the violence in After the First Death by Robert Cormier. Here masterful writing delivers important ideas in a hair-raising account of the hijacking of some young children in a bus. When one child dies of a drug overdose and another is shot in cold blood--when, in fact, everybody at the end of the book is either dead or deranged--the stomach almost rebels.

Isn't it logical to ask whether such violence is appropriate for children? Not that we need to play censor. Kids can handle this violence, even the graphic rape that precedes the death of Ray Beard, even the fatalism that permeates After the First Death, but why should they? The strength of the writing in both these books deserves to be appreciated by readers who have enough background to understand the point of the violence in terms of the ideas in the books. Children do not have this background.

Some "children's" fiction, then, is too nostalgic for children, some too violent. Still other books may be too subtle, too adult in perspective, or too complex. As an example, one work of fiction deserves to be discussed in detail. The book is Unleaving by Jill Patton Walsh. In this story, the author has placed her young heroine Madge in a summer house in Cornwall where she is joined by a study group from Oxford. She overhears dialogue between students and professor, much of it on level with this excerpt read by the professor:

> Love and hatred are not attributes of the intellect, but of the person who has it, in so far as he does. Hence when this person perishes he neither remembers nor loves, for these things never attached to the intellect, but to the whole which has perished; whereas the intellect is no doubt something more divine, and something more impassive.[8]

The professor continues, after a passing reference to Wittgenstein. "The interesting point is that for Aristotle there remained a division that had to be made between reality which could be attributed to material things, and realities which could not, and that, for him, that division lay not between living and non-living, nor between conscious and not-conscious, but between the intellectual and everything else."[9]

As the professor is propounding these ideas, his mongoloid

The Social Prerogative 333

daughter appears. She is stumbling in front of a normal child who is mimicking her: "[The child] is dribbling, letting spittle run down her chin, and has fingers in the corners of her eyes, pulling them upward and outward, dragging her face into a hideous likeness of Molly's."[10]

This scene comes close to the heart of the book. We are witnessing the conflict between ideas and feeling, between the activity of the intellect and dark undercurrents of emotion. Madge is caught between. She is seduced by the brilliance of the intellectual play of ideas, experiencing for the first time the exhilaration of intellectual awakening, yet she is also caught in emotional turmoil centering around Molly. The real pull is Patrick, Molly's brother and self-proclaimed champion of Molly's soul. It is Patrick on one side, pounding Tchaikovsky on the piano, and the professor on the other, unemotionally listening to Bach. The climax is like a storm breaking. For such a short book, the ideas are incredibly complex. In Unleaving, it is not just a lighthouse that Walsh shares with Virginia Woolf.

Is this a children's book? Of course not. There might conceivably be an extraordinarily precocious ninth-grader who would catch a glimmer of its underlying truth, but even that is doubtful. Walsh deserves to be read--far more than she is--but her readers must first be capable of understanding her. They must be those discerning adults who fretfully stalk the fiction shelves looking for a book as challenging as To A Lighthouse. Those readers are hardly likely to stalk into the children's room.

So we find that children's collections are not exclusively children's collections after all, that the current "adulteration" in children's literature has created--for a combination of interconnected reasons--far too many books that are virtually readerless.

Organizational, attitudinal changes

What is to be done? The answer--if there is one--is bound to be complicated, since the causes of "adulteration" are complicated. Since the problem may be as much the result of publishers' marketing as librarians' classification, the causes may be too convoluted to untangle at all.

In general, however, perhaps it would help to decide that children are children only through elementary school, roughly age 12. Books for young people, in grades 7 and up, would then be classified either "adult" or "young adult." This reclassification would automatically shift more complex and sophisticated material--as well as books that are excessively violent or sexually explicit--into adult or young adult collections. (This is where teenagers, even young teenagers, are inclined to go anyway.) Then perhaps Mrs. MacKenzie might discover All Together Now, Mrs. Herman might study Cathedral, Pete might actually enjoy Disease Detectives, and Pete's ten-year-old sister might stop having nightmares about After the First Death.

In lieu of such a change in library organization, which isn't likely to happen, perhaps a change in attitude might make a substantial difference. Since children's librarians usually read adult books as well as those in their own field, why shouldn't librarians in the adult field become better informed about children's books? They obviously have no idea of what they are missing; and because they have no idea, their adult patrons also have no idea. The result is a short circuit in the vital connection between reader and book.

Above all, we need to be aware of the basic contradictions stemming from the new sophistication in children's literature. As books for children become more adult in content and tone, they continue to be virtually segregated from adult readers. Classification is necessary, but it does form a wall, and a formidable one. Furthermore, this wall--paradoxically--does not actually serve the purpose a wall might be expected to serve. No longer does it protect young children from explicit sex and violence. Perhaps this is not important. Perhaps we don't need to protect children from anything. If a wall is there, however, it should be there for a reason. The reason for the wall in this case becomes less and less clear; the problem with the wall becomes more and more troubling.

We end with more questions than answers:

On what basis do publishers decide whether a book is to be juvenile or adult? For instance, why was Unleaving published as a children's book rather than an adult book?

What is the relationship between marketing at the publishing house and classification at the library?

Is it possible for publishers to put "borderline" titles on both the juvenile list and the adult list? (Was this the case with Watership Down?) Does the marketing procedure automatically exclude one group of readers while targeting another? Is it also possible for librarians to put borderline books in both the children's and adult sections as well?

Has interfiling of juvenile and adult nonfiction been found to be successful when it has been tried?

Is access improved if juvenile titles are cataloged along with adult titles?

Do librarians in the adult field realized that the reading level of many adults is almost as low as that of children in upper elementary school? Are reference librarians, in particular, sensitive to this? Are there effective ways of giving these patrons easy access to the children's collection?

The Social Prerogative

Do adult book selectors ever attend juvenile selection meetings, and vice versa? Do they read reviews of children's books?

Does the location of the children's collection make a difference in access?

Are editors--both for adult and children's books--aware of the problems arising from the current sophistication in books being published for children? Are librarians also aware?

To be aware of the problems, then, would seem to be essential. Only by recognizing the existence of a wall--a wall so substantial that it segregates many books for adults among those for children--only by facing that wall can we hope to scale it. And only then will we be able to offer all readers, young and old, those books that give them an inexhaustible source of pleasure.

References
1. Trease, Geoffrey. "Old Writer and Young Readers," Bookbird, XII:#1, 1974, p. 17.
2. Lewis, C. S. "On Three Ways of Writing for Children," in Virginia Haviland, Children and Literature: Views and Reviews, Scott, Foresman, 1973, p. 233.
3. Egoff, Sheila. "Beyond the Garden Wall: Some Observations on Current Trends in Children's Literature," Top of the News, Spring 1979, p. 270.
4. Townsend, John Rowe. A Sense of Story: Essays on Contemporary Writers for Children. Lippincott, 1971, p. 10.
5. Ibid.
6. Beiser, Germaine. The Story of Gravity. Dutton, 1968, p. 72.
7. Cummings, Betty Sue. Hew against the Grain. Atheneum, 1977, p. 152-53.
8. Walsh, Jill Paton. Unleaving. Avon, 1976, p. 102.
9. Ibid., p. 103
10. Ibid.

SCHOOL BOOK CLUB EXPURGATION PRACTICES*

Gayle Keresey

The Intellectual Freedom Committee (IFC) of the Young Adult Services Division (YASD) recently completed research on school book clubs and discovered that expurgating books is a practice of the three major school book clubs. Expurgation is defined by the American Library Association as "any deletion, excision, alteration, or obliteration of any part(s) of books ..."[1] and " ... such action stands in violation of Articles 1, 2, and 3 of the Library Bill of Rights."[2] YASD IFC was charged with this project by the YASD Board of Directors at the 1982 Midwinter Meeting and spent a year interviewing representatives of the three book clubs, informally surveying authors, comparing texts of hardback versus book club editions, as well as consulting with YASD's Publishers' Liaison Committee and Best Books for Young Adults Committee.

Since the practices among the school book clubs differ, each publisher will be discussed individually. Scholastic has four clubs: Seesaw, for grades K-1; Lucky, for grades 2-3; Arrow, for grades 4-6; and TAB, for grades 7-10, as well as two trade divisions-- Apple, for ages 8-11, and Vagabond, for young adults. In an interview conducted between YASD IFC and representatives from Scholastic, the editors stated that Scholastic makes changes in the text from previously published books, although only 2 percent of their books are altered.[3] The editors identify words and paragraphs that might cause problems in the book club market. The staff discusses the changes with the hardcover publisher, who consults with the author. The changes are negotiated prior to purchase of the book by Scholastic. If all paperback rights to a book are bought by Scholastic, only one edition for both trade and book club distribution is published. Books with textual changes are published without any notation on them that they have been edited. This change also is not indicated in advertisements, trade catalogs, or book club brochures. Scholastic's explanation for this omission is that they used to use the term book club edition on their edited Campus Book Club titles, a club now part of the TAB Book Club, but the notation was dropped because students

---

*Reprinted by permission of the author and publisher from Top of The News, 40 (Winter 1984) 131-138. Copyright © 1984 by the American Library Association.

The Social Prerogative 337

objected to the connotation that the book had been edited. Scholastic says that they make changes because they are marketing to the classroom and have to be responsive to parents and to educators' needs for noncontroversial, supplementary reading materials. Offering edited books allows Scholastic to provide books to the largest number of students, according to the editors. Scholastic's representatives offered several examples of complaints they have received from parents and teachers that have caused them to be banned from selling in some school systems.[4]

These representatives mentioned specifically that changes had been made in two YASD Best Books, Halfway Down Paddy Lane and The Legend of Tarik, as well as in Gimme an H. Gimme an E, Gimme an L, Gimme a P, so these titles in paperback were compared with their hardback originals by the YASD IFC. The results were more comprehensive than Scholastic's editors had indicated to us. An obvious change in Halfway Down Paddy Lane is the title, which Scholastic renamed Out of Time, into Love to better clarify to potential customers what the book was about, according to its editors. In all, sixteen words and/or passages were changed from the hardback to the Scholastic Vagabond edition. These included changing "Jesus and Mary"[5] as an exclamation to "no"[6] in one instance and "Jesus Christ and Mary"[7] to "Mary, Mother of God."[8] Another single word change was the substitution of "creeps"[9] for "bastards"[10] in two exclamations. The other changes were more extensive and involved the removal of some objectionable passages and sometimes the substitution of more innocuous passages. A section referring to Patrick's crotch[11] was completely edited out of the Scholastic Vagabond edition.[12] Another part included in the Scholastic edition involved Patrick admitting he wanted Kate, but the final part of the sentence, "... and I was sure it was the worst sin in the world, being we were brother and sister,"[13] was eliminated in the Scholastic edition.[14] The final change in text was the most extensive. Two passages that mentioned Kate's breasts[15] were removed from the paperback.[16] The tone of the end of the chapter in the Vagabond book was changed so that Kate showed more modesty and Patrick displayed anguish and sadness.[17] The hardback included a natural display of their emotions and softness[18] rather than sadness.

The second book examined was The Legend of Tarik, also a 1981 YASD Best Book for Young Adults. There were only six changes in this title, mostly to remove gore. Three changes involved three single words. God was capitalized in the Scholastic edition,[19] while it was not capitalized in the hardback version.[20] One puzzling change substituted "the"[21] for "his."[22] Bill Backer, marketing director for Scholastic, explained that the substitution was to make the sentence more readable.[23] Another strange editing decision omitted the word "now"[24] in the sentence "Blood now ran down the length of his arm."[25] Still another puzzling change omitted the words,[26] "the twirling shawls went into the faces of the soldiers," [27] from the Vagabond edition. The final two changes in the Vagabond edition were complete sentences eliminated[28] to remove violence, because the paperback was offered in the Arrow Book Club,[29] which serves grades 4-6. The sentences were "The slime from the socket rolled like hot lava down his arm, and then the eye, with a great popping sound, came loose in Tarik's hand"[30] and "On the ground, the hand, still clutching the ax, twitched in the afternoon dust."[31]

The final book examined by the committee was Gimme an H, Gimme an E, Gimme an L, Gimme a P. While it was not a YASD Best Book for Young Adults, Bonham's titles are popular with teenagers. In this title, one word was misspelled in the Vagabond edition, "lesque"[32] instead of "burlesque."[33] Also five pages were rewritten to remove references to breasts and to make the chapter more readable. In the hardback edition, Katie's bikini top comes off in the swimming pool. Dana thinks she has unhooked it on purpose and "ran a hand up to her breast."[34] In the paperback edition, Dana says of a friend of his, "until he was fifteen he thought girls were just soft boys."[35] Katie tells Dana in the paperback edition to feel her biceps. As he squeezes her arm, he pulls her toward him and starts to kiss her. All references to the bikini top and Katie's breasts were removed from the Vagabond edition. One other trade Vagabond title that was not examined by the YASD IFC that Scholastic's editors admitted had been edited was Blackbriar by William Sleator. The editors indicated that five words had been changed in the last ten pages.[36]

Scholastic's expurgation practices concerned the YASD IFC the most because of the three book clubs, Scholastic expurgates more titles. In addition, it is the only book club that has a trade market and sells titles excised for its book clubs to the trade market. Because Scholastic does not indicate that a title has been edited, the purchasers of the book, including librarians, often buy the paperback title without realizing it is an edited version. In addition, Scholastic has marketed the edited trade editions of The Legend of Tarik[37] and Out of Time, into Love[38] as "an ALA Best Book for Young Adults."

In an interview conducted with William Reed, product manager, he stated that Xerox Educational Publications markets young adult titles through the Read Book Club. Xerox does not purchase trade paperback rights for books previously published in hardcover. They market their original paperback titles only through their book clubs. Many of their titles are purchased from paperback reprint houses, such as Dell and Bantam, without any changes being made. Xerox produces some titles for their book clubs with a different cover and format to make the book more inexpensive. Text changes are not frequent, and titles are rarely changed. When a change is made, the promotional material and the book clearly indicate that it is an "abridged" and/or "edited school book club edition," according to Reed. The only abridged title cited by Reed was Poltergeist, in which some explicit language was removed. This title was a joint project by Xerox and Scholastic. The textual changes were negotiated through Warner's educational specialist, who discussed them with Steven

The Social Prerogative

Spielberg, the owner of Poltergeist. Reed stated that Xerox respects books that have been honored by ALA and indicated that they probably would not change them. If changes were made, the book would not be marketed in the book club as a YASD Best Book, according to Reed.[39]

The final book club, Troll Associates, is the smallest of the three school book clubs. In an interview with Vic Cavallaro, vice-president of Troll Associates, he stated that Troll purchases books from paperback reprint houses and produces original titles. Troll does not purchase trade rights of books and does not market their original titles in the trade market. If the book would present a problem, usually Troll does not purchase the title. According to Cavallaro, Troll does not initiate requests for changes in texts of reprints. Occasionally, less than once a year, a publisher approaches Troll about buying a title, usually a movie tie-in. In this case, Troll can request changes because the publisher plans to produce a book club edition. These changes are negotiated between the publisher and the author. The last title that Troll requested text changes in was Grease II. The copyright page of the edited books indicated "book club edition," according to Cavallaro. Some annotations in book club brochures, particularly in the grades 4-6 book club, say "for mature readers." Troll says the changes are made because they receive letters of complaint and requests from teachers for screening of books.[40]

As part of the research into book club expurgation practices, the YASD Intellectual Freedom Committee informally surveyed twenty-seven young adult authors. Of those surveyed, fifteen authors had sold titles to Scholastic book clubs, twelve to Xerox clubs, and five to Troll book clubs. Of the authors responding, nine reported that the book club personnel had requested that changes in the text and/or title be made before the book club would agree to publish the book. Usually the changes requested were to eliminate offensive language and references to sex or human anatomy. Other changes requested were to remove violence and a reference to the devil. While the authors reported that they were allowed to rewrite the passages in question, some were upset that their words were being changed. Others felt pressed to make the changes, so they would not lose the potentially large readership and money offered by a sale to the book clubs. Several reported losing sales to book clubs because they refused to allow changes. Others reported they had never been approached by book clubs because their titles were too controversial. According to the authors' responses, titles were changed in four books without the authors' knowledge or consent. Three authors expressed concern that hardcover publishers were asking for changes as part of the editorial process prior to publication because "librarians will have a fit"; "book clubs would not like a scene"; "it just doesn't seem to work"; and "it won't sell." Deletions requested by hardcover publishers that the authors regarded as precensorship included a mother opening a bottle of champagne; a character saying, "Oh, God"; profanity; and sexual references.[41]

The results of the YASD Intellectual Freedom Committee's investigation into book club practices were reported to the YASD Board of Directors at the 1983 Midwinter Meeting. Several concerns were expressed regarding the expurgation of titles by book clubs, in addition to the concern that the practice is a violation of the Library Bill of Rights. The existence of two versions of a book may put the librarian in a defensive position if both editions are available in a library and a parent questions why the original edition is needed when a "cleaner" edition exists. Not indicating that a book has been edited is deceptive to booksellers, students, teachers, parents, and librarians. In fact, the innocent purchase of these books sometimes violates a library's materials selection policy that states abridged editions will not be purchased. Ultimately, the expurgation practices shortchange young adults who purchase from book clubs. The students are forced to select from a narrow, rather than a diversified, selection of titles so that the criteria of the most conservative school systems in the country are satisfied. In response to the report, the YASD board instructed its president to send letters to Scholastic, Troll, and Xerox stating that YASD does not want them using YASD Best Books designation on books whose title or content differ from the original book. The letters also outlined other concerns regarding the expurgation practices. The YASD president also was instructed to send similar letters of concern to the Children's Book Council and the Authors' Guild.

The Children's Book Council included a passage in its minutes that YASD was concerned that expurgated titles were being presented as Best Books for Young Adults and that the edited paperbacks should indicate that texts had been altered.[42] As of September 1983, YASD has not received any formal response from the book clubs. However, Jean Feiwel, who was an editor of the Camelot and Flare imprints at Avon and is now editorial director and division vice-president at Scholastic, addressed the issue prior to joining Scholastic. Feiwel stated:

> I think that the problem has been that what Scholastic does has remained a mystery to the library market and there are reasons maybe for doing what they do. I think the fact is that when a book is changed, it should say so on the cover. If the edition is in any way altered, I think it should say so, and I think those kinds of considerations are going to be discussed over the next few months. I also think that it is incumbent upon us at Scholastic to let people know what goes into the decision making process when we acquire books and why books that are done in the book clubs and in the trade division sometimes have two separate philosophies.[43]

Mr. Crinsley, executive vice-president of Scholastic, added:

> It has just come to my attention that Scholastic and other book clubs were changing, to a very minimal degree, changing texts to satisfy the needs of the school community. When that is done, I have directed my colleagues to note

this on the books and on all books that we're doing on the copyright page, an edited edition or we're drawing up the language now. This information came to my desk just two weeks ago and I took steps to correct it.[44]

Feiwel concluded the discussion with:

> I think that it's important to know that I feel this is a serious question and I think Scholastic will deal with it seriously and sincerely and that the policy of no comment that has gone on for some time is over and I welcome your comments and suggestions and I hope to hear from you about them.[45]

Alice Bregman, editor of Apple and Vagabond trade titles for Scholastic, has also addressed the issue in stating:

> We are working on the wording to put a line on the copyright page that will let people know the book has been changed from its hard-cover format. The new policy probably won't begin before November, since the books that will be distributed in September have already gone to press.[46]

The education community is most affected by book club expurgation practices. The American Federation of Teachers passed a resolution at its July 1983 convention entitled "First Amendment Rights of Students and Teachers" that stated:

> ... RESOLVED that the American Federation of Teachers goes on record as opposing the practices of expurgation without permission or notice, and RESOLVED, that the AFT members who use the book clubs be urged to write letters stating their objection to the practice of expurgation of young adult and children's books.[47]

The AFT's newspaper, American Teacher, will also print a letter to the editor from media specialist Jean W. Scheu, which urges teachers to send a letter instead of an order to the book clubs noting "that expurgating children's and young adult books without a notice to that effect clearly stated on the book is a violation of the intellectual freedom of the readers."[48] Hopefully, the research of the YASD Intellectual Freedom Committee into book club expurgation practices will cause librarians and educators to discuss and voice their concerns about the editorial process more frequently with publishers.

References

1. Expurgation of Library Materials: An Interpretation of the Library Bill of Rights (Chicago: American Library Assn., 1981).
2. Ibid.
3. Interview with Bill Backer, marketing director; Phyllis Braun, Arrow Book Club editor; Alice Bregman, Apple and Vagabond editor; and Betsy Ryan, TAB editor, Scholastic, held during a meeting of the YASD IFC, Philadelphia, Pa., July 11, 1982.

4. Ibid.
5. Jean Marzollo, Halfway Down Paddy Lane (New York: Dial, 1981), p. 92.
6. Jean Marzollo, Out of Time, into Love (New York: Scholastic, 1981), p. 85.
7. Marzollo, Halfway Down Paddy Lane, p. 78.
8. Marzollo, Out of Time, into Love, p. 71.
9. Ibid., p. 102.
10. Marzollo, Halfway Down Paddy Lane, p. 110.
11. Ibid., p. 53.
12. Marzollo, Out of Time, into Love, p. 48.
13. Marzollo, Halfway Down Paddy Lane, p. 119.
14. Marzollo, Out of Time, into Love, p. 111.
15. Marzollo, Halfway Down Paddy Lane, p. 141-42.
16. Marzollo, Out of Time, into Love, p. 132.
17. Ibid., p. 132-33.
18. Marzollo, Halfway Down Paddy Lane, p. 142-43.
19. Walter Dean Myers, The Legend of Tarik (New York: Scholastic, 1981), p. 79.
20. Walter Dean Myers, The Legend of Tarik (New York: Viking, 1981), p. 85.
21. Myers, The Legend of Tarik (Scholastic), p. 128.
22. Myers, The Legend of Tarik (Viking), p. 122.
23. Interview with Bill Backer, marketing director, Scholastic, during ALA Midwinter Meeting, San Antonio, Tex., Jan. 8, 1983.
24. Myers, The Legend of Tarik (Scholastic), p. 153.
25. Myers, The Legend of Tarik (Viking), p. 159.
26. Myers, The Legend of Tarik (Scholastic), p. 140.
27. Myers, The Legend of Tarik (Viking), p. 145.
28. Myers, The Legend of Tarik (Scholastic), p. 62, 98.
29. Interview with Bill Backer and others, July 11, 1982.
30. Myers, The Legend of Tarik (Viking), p. 68.
31. Ibid., p. 104.
32. Frank Bonham, Gimme an H, Gimme an E, Gimme an L, Gimme a P (New York: Scholastic, 1980), p. 47.
33. Frank Bonham, Gimme an H, Gimme an E, Gimme an L, Gimme a P (New York: Scribner, 1980), p. 50.
34. Ibid., p. 184.
35. Bonham, Gimme an H, Gimme an E, Gimme an L, Gimme a P (Scholastic), p. 172.
36. Interview with Backer and others, July 11, 1982.
37. Myers, The Legend of Tarik (Scholastic), back cover.; also "Scholastic's Fall/Winter 1983 Readers' Choice Program" catalog, p. 29.
38. Scholastic advertisement. Voice of Youth Advocates 5:10 (Oct. 1982).
39. Interview with William Reed, product manager, Xerox Educational Corporation, Middletown, Conn., December 22, 1982.
40. Interview with Vic Cavallaro, vice-president, Troll Associates, Mahwah, N.J., Dec. 29, 1982.
41. Author survey conducted Dec. 1982.
42. Letter from John Donovan, executive director, Children's Book Council, New York, N.Y., to Barbara Newmark-Kruger, YASD president, Elmsford, N.Y., May 27, 1983.

43. "The Publishing Process: Who Decides and How, Part 2," American Library Association program, Los Angeles, Calif., June 27, 1983. Cassette tapes by Eastern Audio Association, side 2.
44. Ibid.
45. Ibid.
46. Edwin McDowell, "Publishing: 'Expurgating' Books for Young Adults," New York Times, July 8, 1983, p. 19.
47. Letter from Sara Lutton, advertising sales manager, American Teacher/American Educator, Washington, D.C., to Evelyn Shaevel, executive director, YASD, Chicago, Ill., Aug. 25, 1983.
48. Letter from Jean W. Scheu, media specialist, Plymouth, Minn., to editor, American Educator, Washington, D.C., Aug. 3, 1983.

Sources Consulted

Author survey conducted December 1982.
Bonham, Frank. Gimme an H, Gimme an E, Gimme an L, Gimme a P. New York: Scholastic, 1980.
_____. Gimme an H, Gimme an E, Gimme an L, Gimme a P. New York: Scribner, 1980.
Expurgation of Library Materials: An Interpretation of the Library Bill of Rights. Chicago: American Library Assn., 1981.
Hartzell, Richard. "Eye on Publishing," Wilson Library Bulletin 58:44-45 (Sept. 1983).
Interview with Bill Backer, marketing director, Phyllis Braun, Arrow Book Club editor; Alice Bregman, Apple and Vagabond editor; and Betsy Ryan, TAB editor, Scholastic, held during a meeting of the YASD IFC, Philadelphia, Pa., July 11, 1982.
Interview with Bill Backer, marketing director, Scholastic, during ALA Midwinter Meeting, San Antonio, Tex., Jan. 8, 1983.
Interview with Vic Cavallaro, vice-president, Troll Associates, Mahwah, N.J., December 29, 1982.
Interview with William Reed, product manager, Xerox Educational Corporation, Middletown, Conn., Dec. 22, 1982.
Klein, Norma. "Some Thoughts on Censorship: An Author Symposium," Top of the News 39:137-53 (Winter 1983).
Konigsburg, E. L. "Excerpts from my Bouboulina File," Library Quarterly 51, no. 1:68-79 (1981).
Letter from Vic Cavallaro, vice-president, Troll Associates, Mahwah, N.J., to Judith G. Flum, chairperson, YASD IFC, Oakland Calif., Nov. 12, 1982.
Letter from John Donovan, executive director, Children's Book Council, New York, N.Y., to Barbara Newmark-Kruger, YASD president, Elmsford, N.Y., May 27, 1983.
Letter from Sara Lutton, advertising sales manager, American Teacher/American Educator, Washington, D.C., to Evelyn Shaevel, executive director, YASD, Chicago, Ill., Aug. 25, 1983.
Letter from Jean W. Scheu, media specialist, Plymouth, Minn. to editor, American Educator, Washington, D.C., Aug. 3, 1983.
Marzollo, Jean. Halfway Down Paddy Lane, New York: Dial, 1981.

_____. Out of Time, into Love. New York: Scholastic, 1981.
McDowell, Edwin. "Publishing: 'Expurgating' Books for Young Adults," New York Times, July 8, 1983, p. 19.
Myers, Walter Dean. The Legend of Tarik. New York: Scholastic, 1981.
_____. The Legend of Tarik. New York: Viking, 1981.
"The Publishing Process: Who Decides and How, Part 2," American Library Association program, Los Angeles, Calif., June 27, 1983. Cassette tapes by Eastern Audio Association.
Scholastic advertisement. Voice of Youth Advocates 5:10 (Oct. 1982).
"Scholastic Paperbacks: Annotated Catalog 1982-83: Special Trade Edition."
"Scholastic's Fall/Winter 1983 Readers' Choice Program" catalog.
Strasser, Todd. "Behind the Scenes Censorship," Voice of Youth Advocates 5:22 (Aug. 1982).

NOTES ON CONTRIBUTORS

LESTER ASHEIM is on the faculty of the School of Library Science, University of North Carolina.

PAUL BARNETT is a free-lance journalist in Exeter, United Kingdom.

MARY BIGGS is a member of the faculty at the Graduate Library School, University of Chicago, and editor of Library Quarterly.

JO CARR is an instructor at the University of Virginia.

AUDREY EAGLEN is Head of the Order Department at the Cuyahoga County Public Library in Cleveland.

MAURICE J. FREEDMAN is Director of the Westchester Library System in Elmsford, NY.

FREDERICK ISAAC is Head of Circulation at the University of Santa Clara Library, CA.

E. J. JOSEY is the President of the American Library Association.

GAYLE KERESEY is the media coordinator at East Arcadia School, Riegelwood, NC.

MICHAEL E. D. KOENIG is an Associate Professor at the School of Library Service, Columbia University.

DONNARAE MACCANN is a columnist for the Wilson Library Bulletin.

FRANCIS MIKSA is on the faculty of the Graduate School of Library and Information Science, University of Texas at Austin.

WILLIAM A. MOFFETT is Director of Libraries, Oberlin College, OH.

ERIC MOON, among other things, is a past President of the American Library Association.

JOE MOREHEAD is on the faculty of the School of Library and Information Science, SUNY at Albany, NY.

ELAINE MOSS is a book reviewer for The Good Book Guide, Braithwaite & Taylor, Ltd., London.

DOUGLAS NOBLE is an expert in computers and has worked with them for years.

VIRGINIA C. PURDY is on the staff of the National Archives and Records Service.

GRESHAM RILEY is President of Colorado College, Colorado Springs.

RICHARD RUBIN is a doctoral student at the University of Illinois, Urbana/Champaign.

HERBERT D. SAFFORD is Director of Libraries, Muskingum College, New Concord, OH.

RICHARD SCHMIDT is a Washington, DC civil liberties attorney.

PATRICIA GLASS SCHUMAN is President of Neal-Schuman Publishers, NY.

CECILE SHURE is a consultant with B-K Dynamics.

TED SOLOTAROFF is affiliated with Harper & Row, NY.

DAVID H. STAM is Andrew W. Mellon Director of the Research Libraries of the New York Public Library.

MARGARET F. STEIG is on the faculty of the Graduate School of Library Service, University of Alabama.

THOMAS T. SURPRENANT is Associate Professor at the Graduate School of Library and Information Studies, Queens College, Flushing, NY.

JOHN C. SWAN is reference librarian at Wabash College, IN.

SUSAN I. SWANTON is Director of the Gates Public Library, Rochester, NY.

JAMES C. THOMPSON is Associate University Librarian at the Fondren Library, Rice University.

FREDERICK WOODARD is Associate Dean of Faculties at the University of Iowa.

DONALD WRAY is Assistant Managing Director of British Telecom.

JANE ZANDE is a graduate of the Graduate School of Library and Information Studies, University of Rhode Island.